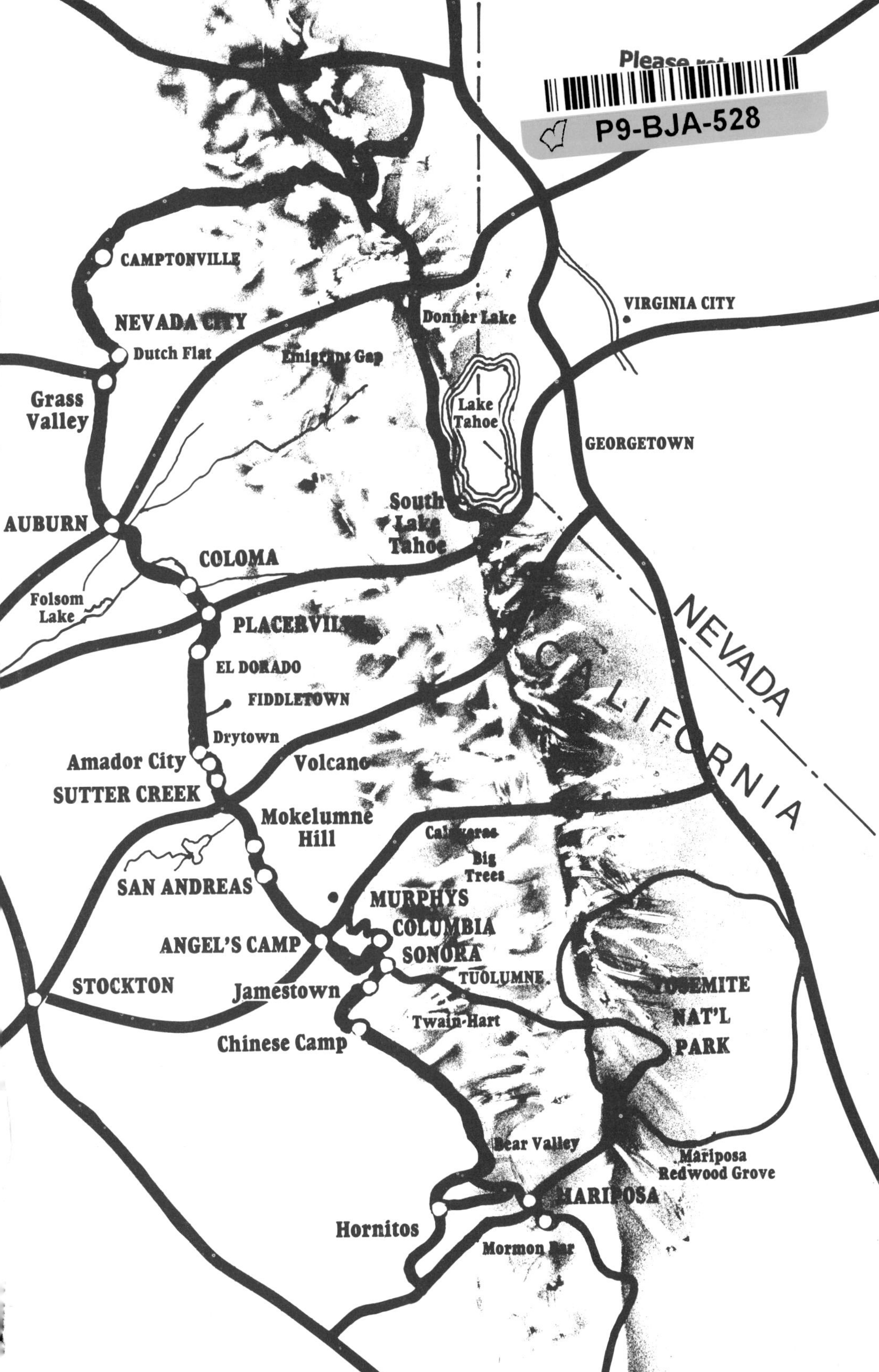
CAMPTONVILLE
NEVADA CITY
Dutch Flat
Grass Valley
Emigrant Gap
Donner Lake
VIRGINIA CITY
Lake Tahoe
GEORGETOWN
AUBURN
South Lake Tahoe
COLOMA
Folsom Lake
PLACERVILLE
NEVADA
CALIFORNIA
EL DORADO
FIDDLETOWN
Drytown
Amador City
Volcano
SUTTER CREEK
Mokelumne Hill
Calaveras Big Trees
SAN ANDREAS
MURPHYS
COLUMBIA
SONORA
ANGEL'S CAMP
TUOLUMNE
STOCKTON
Jamestown
YOSEMITE NAT'L PARK
Twain-Hart
Chinese Camp
Bear Valley
Mariposa Redwood Grove
MARIPOSA
Hornitos
Mormon Bar

THE GOLD CHAIN

To Bob & Donna
Best wishes
Regina Phalen

Hadley and Greenleaf in 1893

THE GOLD CHAIN

A California Family Saga

by
Regina V. Phelan

Los Angeles, California 1987

LIBRARY OF CONGRESS CATALOG CARD NUMBER 87-070994
ISBN 0-87062-178-5

Produced under the direction of
THE ARTHUR H. CLARK COMPANY
P.O. Box 230
Glendale, CA 91209
Publishers and booksellers since 1902

The photograph on the title page
is of Edna Phelan wearing
the gold chain of this story.

This book is dedicated to
MICHELLE HALLIDAY, MEGHAN MATTOX
and BRYAN, JASON and KARINA PRICE,
with the hope they will be inspired by the events
of the past and revel in the knowledge
that their ancestors were a part
of that great scene.

ILLUSTRATIONS

The chapter head drawings and endpaper maps
are from the pen of Alfred G. Champy

ACKNOWLEDGEMENTS

It was Viola Speth who encouraged me to write this book — a book about our family who came to California in the "early days." Our father was a masterful storyteller, relating all the happenings on the ranch and of the people they had known down through the years. Our mother, too, loved to talk about her family. She and her sister, Emma, would talk by the hour. Years later, I wrote many of the stories down. It was my niece, Maryanne Price, who suggested the title, "The Gold Chain."

Harris Newmark, in his book *Sixty Years in Southern California,* describes many of the people our family knew. Dressler's *Pioneer Circus* includes many references to Henry Charles Lee, as does C.M. MacMinn in his *Theatre of the Golden Era.* Chang Reynold, author, provided several valuable references.

The Last Adventure of San Francisco in 1851, translated from the original journal of Albert de Russailh by Clarkson Crane, depicted San Francisco the year Henry Charles Lee arrived. Stephen Massett's autobiography, *Drifting About,* contains excellent descriptive material. The article written by Catherine Phelan was also helpful.

The war record of Andrew Weinshank was found at the Archives in Washington, D.C. Two unpublished manuscripts on the Mounted Rifles were made available by John Slonaker at Carlisle Barracks in Pennsylvania. From the United States Military Academy at West Point, the manuscript of Benjamin Roberts, Captain of the Mounted Rifles, who raised the American flag over the Halls of Montezuma, was typed by Joanne Pidala.

The Circus Museum and Library at Baraboo, Wisconsin, Robert Parkinson, John Draper and Don Francis shared information they had compiled on the Lee family. They also sent books on the early English circuses.

Betty King, librarian at the San Antonio Public Library, sent information from the Hertzberg collection under the Sturtevant file. She also sent a post card of Polly Lee from an old circus poster, which is being used on the cover.

With the help of John Draper, I was given reading privileges at the Huntington Library in San Marino. They have the original Colville Papers describing many benefits performed by the Lees. They also have the Circus advertisement that Henry Lee placed in the *La Estralia* in Los Angeles.

From the State library of New South Wales, the Mitchell Library, I received information about the George Street Orphanage. The Historical Society sent information, as did the Department of Vital Statistics.

The New York City Public Library sent the entire script of John Glenroy.

The Los Angeles Public Library had a wealth of material readily available and their research department is outstanding.

Louis Rasmussen's San Francisco Ship Passenger List, vol. II, gave me the exact date the Lees arrived in San Francisco.

The State Library in Sacramento contained many references of the Lee Family. Mavis Guthrie later sent a picture of the pavilion Lee and Marshall built in Sacramento in 1856.

At the Sonora Public Library an article on Frenchy Rochette was useful. Carlos M. De Ferrari, a few doors down the street, came up with newspaper ads of the Lee circus from the Sonora newspaper and the *Columbia Gazette.*

James Lenhoff of Oroville sent a brick from their courthouse. Up to that time it was the oldest standing courthouse in the state of California. Lee and Marshall gave a benefit for the construction of that building.

James Johnstone, the San Joaquin County Recorder, assisted in locating deeds of the Lee and Marshall Ranch in Stockton. The Stockton Library provided valuable vital statistics.

Wilbur Leed researched the *Daily Alta* newspaper of San Francisco for advertisements, which were very helpful. Other valuable newspaper articles were from the *New York Clipper, White Tops,*

New York Herald, The Los Angeles Star, The Hollywood, La Estralia, The Sacramento Bee, the Daily Alta.

Cindy Birt, Bonnie Weber, Lynette Lowe and Carolyn Rory, research librarians at the Whittier Public Library, were all very helpful in assisting me by sending away for books in the inter-library system, and in obtaining and filling out forms for research work from the Los Angeles Public Library.

Editing was done by Cora Sherzer and Mary Ann Scanlon. Both spent countless hours working on the manuscript. Mary Ann also suggested additions and deletions, going beyond the standard editing work.

Anita Legg with the assistance of her family, her parents Bob and Dorothy, her sister Sandy Palmer typed and put the script on the word processor in its early stages.

The final work on the word processor, as well as some very worthwhile editing, was done by Carole Whitcher. She carried the manuscript to its final stages.

My thanks go to John Halliday for his suggestions on marketing and to Al Champy for his wonderful line drawings used in the book. Rick Elias is the photographer who shot the family portrait used on the dust jacket.

To all these people, I give my heartfelt thanks.

THE GOLD CHAIN

The Battle of Cerro Gordo

Plaza at Mexico City

Chapter 1

The year of 1846 began with a crisis. The United States was faced with the possibility of two wars. When President Polk took office, Congress offered Texas a place as a state in the Union. If Texas accepted statehood, it could mean war with Mexico. The dispute over the Oregon Territory could mean war with Great Britain. President Polk set his plan into motion,— his doctrine of "Manifest Destiny."

"Read all about the war," Andrew heard the newsboy call as he hurried down Basson Street, remembering he had seen an enlistment office there. Congress had made provisions for the establishment of a regiment of "Mounted Rifles" for the invasion of Mexico at Vera Cruz. One hundred sixty acres of land were being offered to any young man willing to go to war, and for Andrew Weinshank, this was a chance he wasn't going to miss.

"How about it, sir? Want to buy the *Daily Piscayne?* Learn all about the war?"

"Ya," said Andrew, handing the boy the money. He opened the paper and on the front page was an article dated January 14, 1847, calling for volunteers:

"Young men of good families especially suited for the service, here's your chance to join the 'Mounted Rifles.' Serve in Mexico for a year, and one hundred sixty acres of land will be awarded to you on your return."

There it was in print, one hundred sixty acres.

Andrew was ready to enlist, but fearful he wouldn't make it, for the article mentioned that only young men of good families who were especially suited for the service would be selected.

He looked up from the paper, and directly across the street was a sign in front of a makeshift building, "Mounted Rifle Recruitment Office."

He paused once more. Should he or shouldn't he? He crossed the busy street, looked at the sign on the door, then turned the knob and walked in. It was just a bare room, with the exception of a makeshift desk for the recruiting officer and a row of chairs. Several others were waiting, so he took a seat. Finally it was his turn. He walked over to the desk and waited for the officer to recognize him.

"So you want to go to Mexico and take part in the invasion of Vera Cruz?" asked the recruiting officer.

"Ya, I do," said Andrew.

"And you want to join the 'Mounted Rifles?' A good choice, I might add. I'm Captain Ruff." He stood up and extended his hand in a friendly manner, looking trim in his uniform. "We're looking for good men. You look healthy. Can you ride?"

"Oh, ya. I can ride. I ride very well."

"Yes, I'm sure you can; you're a fine looking young man. Are you naturalized?"

"Ya. I have papers. I've been in this country seven years."

"Glad to hear it. And you work?"

"Ya, at a lumber yard in Mobile. I make barrels. I'm a cooper, sir. My father made sure I learned a trade; never been indentured."

"Why do you want to join up? I see that newspaper under your arm."

"I'm interested in the part about land, one hundred and sixty acres of it. Where I came from in Neidstatt. . . "

"Neidstatt, where's that?" asked the captain.

"Germany. I was raised in a small village. Our little farm wasn't large enough to support our family, so our father sent us to this country one and two at a time."

"You know this will be for five years or until the end of the war, don't you?" asked the captain.

"This paper says a year," said Andrew, fumbling with it.

"I know, that's why I mentioned it. We're finding we spend a lot of time and effort training men, and before they can be of service, they leave for home."

"I'll go ahead and sign anyway," said Andrew.

"I'll need some more information. How tall are you?"

"I'm five feet, seven inches."

"Let's see," looking up at Andrew. "You're fair-complected, brown hair, brown eyes, and how old are you?"

"Twenty-five, sir," watching the captain as he wrote it down.

"Now if you'll sign here."

"Ya, on this line?"

"Ya. Excuse me, I mean yes. I'm assigning you to Company E under Captain Crittenden."

"Thank you, sir."

"All right, Andrew Weinshank. You're in the 'Mounted Rifles'." And he stood up to shake his hand. As Andrew turned to leave, the captain said, "Next."

They arrived at the Island of Lobos on March 2 and at the anchorage at Antonio Lizardo three days later. The army was in position for the invasion of Vera Cruz by March 6th. On the 7th, a norther came up and the landing was canceled. The men stayed below, sat around, some talking, some playing cards, all trying to take their minds off the invasion.

On the 8th of March, the weather improved and the "Rifles" were ordered to report on deck. All around them anchored in the bay were boats of all types of shapes and sizes from the light schooner to the mighty man-of-war a magnificent sight to see.

"With this calm sea, seems as though we might land. You'd think they would let us in on the plans," Cal, one of the recruits, said as a small vessel came toward them anchoring in a small space allotted to her, all without the slightest disorder or confusion.

Before them stood the castle of San Juan de Ulloa, by far the most celebrated of all the American fortresses, with its walls sixty feet high on the gulf side. As the afternoon sun began to sink behind the great Mt. Orizaba, they heard the signal gun being fired from the flagship. The surfboats cast off from their ships and moved forward into position.

Andrew saw Colonel Smith, the top ranking officer for the "Mounted Rifles," talking to another officer. Smith was a fine looking man, with dark, curly hair, clean shaven and a kind expression on his face. Standing nearby, Captain Crittenden towered above most of the men and watched their admiring glances. He then spoke up. "He served under Taylor, fighting in the northern part of Mexico, and was reassigned to General Scott." The men gave their nod of understanding and the captain continued on.

"Gather around men, we're ready to disembark. Does everyone have his haversack filled with bread and cooked meat for two days, a canteen of water, plus his arms and ammunition?"

"What are we doing all the way down here, anyway?" asked a soldier.

"This is where we have to be if we're going to win the war. Taylor can't win it in northern Mexico. The plan calls for us going all the way to Mexico City. This is all General Scott's idea, and the President agrees with him."

"Why do we need California in the first place?" asked another.

"What right do we have to it? Aren't we invading a foreign land?" asked one young fellow, not quite dry behind the ears.

"That's true, but Senator Thomas Hart Benton from Missouri argues that if British designs succeed, California will go to a foreign power, when logic shows it should belong to the United States. That being the case, it would also mean isolation from our settlement in Oregon."

Then one of the soldiers spoke up. "We don't have long to wait now. I wonder how many of us will make it?"

"We'll soon know, soldier," said the captain. "Those surfboats coming our way were designed by the general himself. They're made in a nest of three, one fitting inside the other, taking up less space, and they hold fifty or more soldiers each, so we'll all fit into one."

"Here comes ours!" shouted a "Rifle."

"Well, let's get ready to disembark. We're next!"

Just as the "Rifles" were lining up, another boat came alongside. A soldier yelled across to them, "Taylor won the battle at Buena Vista, but we came close to losing it. The regulars are mad because the credit for the victory goes mostly to the volunteers."

"Where's Buena Vista?" asked a soldier.

"To the north of us," answered the captain. "I just learned the Mexican General Santa Anna decided to crush Taylor there before returning to Vera Cruz. Santa Anna's supposed to be back here before a landing can be staged, but I don't think he'll make it."

"What about our horses?" yelled back one of the "Rifles."

"Oh! Haven't you heard? Most of them were lost at sea, in that big storm we had. The only two companies with horses now are Captain Robert's and Captain Kearny's. Kearny's rich, so he furnished horses for his entire company, dapple greys, beautiful animals."

Andrew looked at Cal and shook his head. A terrible blow, he thought.

Andrew and Cal stood in line watching, quietly waiting for their turn, waiting for the boat to come alongside. As it pulled up, Andrew quickly got into the boat. Without the slightest hesitation, the boatsman squared away in "line abreast" and with every oarsman straining, they headed for the beach. As the bow of their boat hit the sand dunes, Andrew tumbled out holding his musket high; along with the rest of his comrades, he made his way up the bank with his bayonet affixed. Crouching, he advanced to the crest, but the enemy was not in sight.

The guns of Vera Cruz began their "awful activity" once the Americans were in place; guns far heavier in caliber and greater in number than those of the American forces.

The guns of the American warships began their mighty bombardment. Continuing night and day, without cease they fired an unrelenting, terrifying barrage of gunfire upon the fully-inhabited city. The din was deafening. It seemed as though the very earth was being torn apart. The devastation dealt upon that city was felt in the heart of every man.

Vera Cruz was besieged for three weeks, then surrendered on the 27th of March. Worth's division marched through the lines into the city while the band played on and the other two divisions returned to their stations.

The "Mounted Rifles" were moving out. Their division leader, white haired, white bearded, bull-necked General Twiggs, rode at the head of the column. His six foot tall frame and broad shoulders made him look like a snow-clad volcano mounted on "Old Davy."

Andrew and Cal each had forty pounds of ammunition and four days' rations strapped on their backs. As they fell into line, the order was given to go ahead, with "Old Davy" setting the pace. They headed out in the direction of Jalapa on the 8th of April, without wheeled or animal support.

The first few leagues were nothing but sand as they marched along at a lively clip, trying to keep up, but the combination of bad footing, blistering feet, blazing heat, camp diarrhea and the rate of march of "Old Davy" was too much even for the veterans of the long marches in the northern part of Mexico. When they reached higher ground, Andrew looked back at a command scattered out for miles along the road, giving it the appearance of a great serpent crawling along the surface of the country.

20

By noon Andrew and Cal gave out entirely. All around them the roadside was strewn with equipment and clothing that had been discarded. They lay down under the scanty shade of the palmetto bushes to rest. By late afternoon they continued on.

They camped that night by a small stream, shared a pot of hot coffee with some of the other fellows in their company and ate biscuits and saltpork from their haversacks. Then they found a nice cool spot under a tree and rested by the roadside.

They marched along on the second day at a more reasonable pace with more frequent halts. They were marching on the great highway, graded, paved and guttered, which the Spaniards had built three centuries before. Though the roads were now in ruins, they were still better than those in the United States. They marched along through natural gardens, past adobes with thatched roofs. They passed Santa Anna's magnificent home "Mango de Clavo."

On the third day the column paused at the magnificent stone arch National Bridge across the Antigua, a bridge described as "worthy of the best days of Rome."

One more day they marched. At noon on the 11th of April they reached another lesser stone-arch bridge. It was across the Rio del Plan near the village of Plan del Rio where they set up camp. On the morning of the 12th the Mexicans opened fire and the Americans knew they were in danger. The Mexicans were well-entrenched in the natural bluffs, the gorge of Rio del Plan, the bluffs of Cerro Gordo and up on the hill of Atalaya. The men rested while General Twiggs sized up the situation.

Atalaya was so steep that the Mexican General, Santa Anna, didn't bother to garrison it, so steep that not even a jackrabbit could climb it. Also, the Mexican position prevented them access to water in the stream at the base of the canyon.

An attack had been ordered by General Twiggs for four o'clock the following morning. That evening Generals Pillow and Shields came marching in. Word was spread throughout the division that the battle had been postponed until Generals Scott and Worth could join them.

While this was going on, the soldiers made out the best they could. "This is taking a long time, Captain. Why don't we get at it?" asked Cal.

"I don't know about you fellows, but I'm glad that attack was postponed. I had my doubts about it all along. Seems as though General Patterson outranks General Twiggs and he got out of a sick bed to cancel it, but it's getting late, so let's get some sleep."

Generals Scott and Worth arrived with their troops on the 14th, swelling the ranks considerably, and they spent the next two days in reconnaissance. Captain Crittenden, his solid frame planted firmly on a gun emplacement platform, again called his men together. "Thought you fellows might be interested. The Major was telling me Captains Lee and Grant called the cliff on one side 'unscalable' and the ravine on the other side 'impassable.' So General Scott sent Captain Lee out to take a better look. He worked his way beyond the enemy line. He saw some Mexicans heading down to the stream for water, so he hid behind a log which was screened by thick undergrowth. He had to lie there for hours, motionless, barely breathing. Insects bit him, but he didn't dare scratch."

"I couldn't have handled that," said one of the fellows.

"Oh shut up and let the Captain talk!" said another.

"After dark he was able to leave. He made his way back to camp. Later, he retraced his steps, cut out the path for the army, all without alarming the enemy."

"General Scott knows who can get a job done," Andrew said to Cal after the captain had walked away.

General Scott began to move his troops back into position to take the hill. The Americans would now attack with three divisions headed by the Generals Worth, Pillow and Twiggs. All three divisions took up their line of battle. Twiggs' division with Major Sumner in charge of the "Rifle" regiment was led by Captain Lee.

The guns were put down the slope a piece at a time while the men at the ropes kept their ground on top, playing the rope out gradually, while a few at the front directed the course of the piece. The guns were then drawn by hand up the opposite slope in the same manner.

About noon, while they were making their way along the path, they were discovered by the Mexicans from the hill Atalaya.

"Look over there. There's General Santa Anna dressed in civilian clothes. He's the one galloping on the grey horse." Andrew heard Captain Roberts, one of the "Rifle" officers say.

The Mexicans blew a challenge; the American guns and the rocket battery which had been brought up to the summit in rainy darkness, answered them.

Then the "Rifles" let out a "whoop" and swept over and down the slopes of Atalaya, led by Colonel Harney. They dashed across the intervening hollow, up the slopes of Cerro Gordo, firing as they went. Seventy yards short of the crest they halted. Andrew was able to catch his breath, and then he and his fellow "Rifles" followed their gallant colonel to charge the crest. Before them was Colonel Harney's conspicuous red hair, his six foot stalwart frame, his long arms waving, calling them on, his sturdy voice ringing out as he swept over the stone wall at the crest.

The red, white and green flag was pulled from the staff on top of the stone tower, and the red, white and blue was put up in its place. The "Rifles" swung around, captured the enemy's guns and turned them against the fleeing army. Andrew found shelter behind some rocks and used his rifle, by far the longest range and most accurate shoulder arms of either side, against the enemy. The Mexicans were driven down the hill. Two of the "Rifles" lay dead on the field of battle, and five were wounded. Their Major Sumner was carried off the field.

After it was over, Andrew exhausted, but relieved, fell to the ground.

"It grieves me to see women among the dead," Andrew said to Cal, as he buried his head in his hands. Just at that moment, Andrew looked up and saw General Scott riding by, saluting his victorious soldiers with tears of pride running down his cheeks. Andrew jumped to his feet.

After General Scott had galloped on, Ben Vandewaikon rushed up to where Andrew and Cal were standing and said, "We've got them on the run now. They left in a hurry, didn't have time to take their money. General Santa Anna left his carriage, and all his official papers are in it, even his wooden leg."

With General Scott here, at least we had a chance; had Twiggs been allowed to attack with our division alone, we probably wouldn't be here to tell about it," said Cal.

About nine o'clock the next morning, the American army marched into Jalapa, a lovely little town in a great amphitheater of mountains with the snowy peak of Orizaba thirty miles away. As it came into view, no grander sight could be seen than this mountain with its perpetual snow and a little cloud that hovered at its top.

The church bells rang peals of welcome as the men marched in, to the music of their bands. The "Rifles" were dressed in fine Mexican clothing from their find the day before, bayonets fixed and flags flying. The people of Jalapa, neither unfriendly nor afraid, lined the streets, eager to be on good terms with the conquerors.

The army marched through the city and continued out to the northern end of town, and then set up camp in the open fields.

In the early morning hours of August 5th, 1847. The men gave a mighty "Cerro Gordo!" shout, then headed out.

The Americans had won a firm foothold on the great interior plateau of Mexico and were within 120 miles of the capital.

The first thirty-six miles of marching was over dusty roads walled by corn on either side, then came the climb over the mountains, over ten thousand feet above sea level.

They paused to rest at a swift little river whose waters flowed into the Pacific. Here the bitter winds made Andrew shiver in his overcoat.

Back on the mountain road they found it slippery, making trouble for the artillery and the wagons on the steeper grades and on the elbow turns. They marched down roads that wound down the mountain in great loops through oak and tall pine. They looked down upon magnificent views at every turn. Between them and the City of Mexico were many lakes and marshes and miles and miles of lava fields, which were like a raging sea that had instantly turned to stone.

At the bottom of the descent they marched along through immense olive groves and wide market gardens bordering the shallow waters of Lake Chalco. On the fifth day they arrived at Ayolta, and camped along the north shore of Lake Chalco. The next day they headed in the direction of Conteras. Off in the distance on a hill the main body of the Mexican army, an army greatly outnumbering their own, was well entrenched.

They made camp alongside a small stream enclosed by dykes. The rain was falling in torrents. Water collected in the road where they lay.

Word passed through the ranks that they were on the verge of a fierce and bloody battle. Three o'clock in the morning was set for the time when the troops were to move forward to attack, bringing in the element of surprise.

At daybreak Andrew heard the signal and sprang to his feet. Word was passed along the line that the "Rifles" had been cut off completely from any help or reinforcements. This would mean certain death. Countless numbers of troops, heavy artillery, and cavalry were surrounding them. Then General Smith appeared amongst them and someone whispered, "Here he comes," and another one, "Now we'll have at them." Andrew had undying faith in General Smith, but even his fine character and ability did not completely quiet his fears.

The rain was falling. In darkness the "Rifles" moved out.

Andrew, soaked and groggy from his sleepless night, and his buddy Cal kept close to the soldiers in front of them, fearful of going astray. As Andrew marched on, he became nauseated from the smell of other bodies, he began to feel squeamish about hand-to-hand fighting, and felt like vomiting right then and there. But the line opened up, he caught a whiff of fresh air and was able to continue on. The path was narrow, the "Rifles" trudged on through the swollen stream before they reached their destination. They approached their field of battle from the rear.

Then General Smith gave the command, "Men, forward." In an instant, with a wild fierce yell, they sprang and dashed up the hill. The storming party appeared and led the way. The "Rifles" then protected them by throwing in a deadly fire upon the startled enemy, and then gallantly rushed forward to participate in the assault. The battle was deadly, but it had caught the Mexicans entirely by surprise, causing them to surrender, and resulting in far fewer casualties on the part of both armies.

After it was over, Andrew shared his rations and water from his canteen with the wounded Mexicans with the same care he did his own. Then finally he gave out and fell to the ground. Cal rushed over to him, his clothing in tatters, dirty and blood stained, fell to the ground at his side. Their captain, with great emotion joined his men and started to speak. Andrew pulled himself to his feet to listen. With pride in his voice the captain said, "All during the night Captain Robert E. Lee crossed the Petregal. He was ordered to inform the various commanders of operation of the situation and the plans of the others. Because he knew the terrain and hazards better than anyone else, he was able to make his way among the boulders across fissures and chasms, without landmarks to guide him other than an occasional flash of lightning from the storm. All the while he was running the risk of falling in with the enemy. Captain Robert E. Lee had every company in its proper place at the right time, and now a superior force has been defeated."

"I wonder if the people in the States will ever recognize his greatness?" mused Andrew.

After the Captain left, Andrew and Cal again sat down for a few moments' rest. But they had barely enough time to catch their breath before they were ordered to fall in. They left the field of battle and headed in the direction of San Pablo de Churubusco. In less than an hour, they approached the fortified hacienda, surrounded on all sides, by a high thick wall. It was located at the head of the causeway leading to the western gate of the city and had to be passed to get onto the road. Inside was a large stone building with a flat roof which they could see above the walls. The steeple of the church and the convent of San Mateo were crammed with Mexican troops and heavily armed with cannon.

Along the banks of the river the drainage canal was already lined with American infantry.

Just then, Major Sumner rode up. "Look, Andrew! Here comes the major," said Cal.

"Great, he's back in action," answered Andrew. "Haven't seen him since he fell at Cerro Gordo." Then the major took off his cap in answer to their cheers, the mark of the Mexican ball could be plainly seen on the side of his head, just at the edge of his hair. This brought shouting from the men, and patting the wound he shouted back, "We'll pay them for this today." This made the men wild with excitement and more than ready to undertake any deed required of them.

Because they were hampered by the tall corn surrounding the hacienda, they were ordered to make a quick attack. Captain Robert E. Lee came charging up. He sent the men to wade the canal, which was about four feet deep, to seize the highway at Los Portales, and cut the enemy's line of retreat to the city.

It was now noon. Other groups joined them. As they approached the wall, the grape round shot and musketry began sweeping over the ground in such a storm, the cornfields quickly became strewn with the dead and dying. Then General Smith came up, he stationed them in front of the convent, using its wall for protection.

The Mexicans fought as they had never fought before. Andrew could see soldiers going at it hand to hand. The Americans broke, rallied, broke and rallied again.

"We're being fired on by some of our own men!" one of the "Rifles" shouted.

"What does he mean?" asked Andrew of the soldier next to him.

"They've recognized some of the men who fought in the north. They're called the Battalion of Los San Patricios, fighting on the side of Mexico."

"Well, I'll be damned," said the soldier next to Andrew. "Fighting against our own men!"

Still subjected to heavy fire, all around him Americans were storming the rampart with their bayonets fixed. They overran the batteries and turned them around; all the while Andrew fired his long-range gun from behind the protection of the wall.

General Smith was everywhere giving orders, directing the firing. The one "Rifle" company that had mounts under the command of Captain Kearny was in the middle of the fight. Kearny was carrying his pistol in one hand, his saber in the other, his reins in his teeth, and was fighting like a mad man.

"The San Patricios are pulling the white flag down as fast as it is being put up," said a "Rifle."

"They're not allowing their Mexican comrades to surrender," said another.

It was past three o'clock before the attack showed any sign of succeeding, but as the Mexicans' ammunition began to fail, the guns fell silent, and finally the white flag stayed up.

After the battle was over, Andrew fell to the ground, dirty, hungry and exhausted. He hadn't eaten at all that day. Just at that moment the commanding general, General Winfield Scott rode up, and Andrew jumped to his feet. All around him shouts went up that could have delighted the heart of any soldier, no matter what his rank. The General moved forward to speaking distance, and after quiet was restored said, "Brave 'Rifles', veterans, you have been baptized in fire and blood, and have come out steel."

The next day thunder rolled, lightning flashed and again as on the previous night, there was a torrential downpour. The "Rifles" marched on to Piedad where Andrew and Cal feasted on green corn and ripe tomatoes and asked no questions as to ownership, date of payment or price. An armistice was called, giving the men a chance to rest.

After two weeks, General Smith gave the order to march. At the break of day, Andrew fell in line, and they headed out in the direction of the Castle of Chapultepec, the military academy of Mexico, arriving just as the guns were being put in place. The castle, built on a rock, was surrounded by giant cypress all draped in Spanish moss, and at its base was a high wall. It was located at the outskirts of the city directly in line with the causeways of Belen and San Cosme, the routes over which the Americans would travel when they advanced.

The Americans started pouring a storm of shot and shell upon the castle in unrelenting furor. Then the guns were quieted. A five minute lull gave the signal for attack. They turned their fire on the castle once more as the columns advanced. Ladders were quietly planted against the wall. The men carrying crowbars and pick axes, swiftly ascended.

Andrew watched as the first ones up were either killed or wounded, but others quickly took their place, and in spite of the resistance, a foothold was at length obtained. Stormers went swarming up the ladders and over the wall. When the Americans reached the top, they pulled down the red, white and green tricolor and ran up the stars and stripes.

The "Rifles" were next; after making it to the top of the wall, Andrew pressed through the grove of cypress through an incessant storm of musketry coming from behind trees, rocks, and breast works. General Smith was everywhere, encouraging the men, giving orders. The Mexicans were retreating.

At length they reached the ditch and wall of the main work. There they had a chance to rest while the scaling ladders were again brought up. Andrew looked out over the valley below. Dotted here and there were spires and domes of the churches.

Then he heard the order and they entered the castle proper. Inside the magnificent building were young cadets fighting with their comrades, bayonet to bayonet; mere boys with their blue tasseled caps and smart grey uniforms, fighting to the death rather than surrender.

They moved on. The City of Mexico was before them, a great metropolis, one of the most magnificent cities of the western world, built over an elevated causeway, an aqueduct flanked on both sides by ditches. The "Rifles" worked in concert with the "Bayonets" of the South Carolina regiment who were placed in advance, three "Rifles" and three "Bayonets" under each arch. The artillerymen placed two howitzers into action, one on either side: one an eighteen-pounder, the other a twenty-four. There was an opening of some twelve feet for the passage of vehicles between the city and Chapultepec. This was completely swept by the guns of the citadel.

The Mexican sharpshooters from behind the arches of the aqueduct kept up an incessant discharge of grape and canister. It was a matter of life and death to cross the passage from one side to the other. Andrew looked on as one of the "Rifles" started to cross it; instead of going over in double quick time, he crossed leisurely and was shot down. He raised himself several times on his elbows, but could not get up. General Smith ordered a party to bring him in. Several soldiers stepped forward, but were unable to make it.

The order was repeated, but the men stood as if paralyzed. General Smith then stepped up, unbuckled his sword, and without saying a word, ran to the wounded soldier and stooped to raise him up.

Andrew shouted to the others, "Come on! The General needs help." In an instant a dozen men and officers were at his side, dragging the soldier in, all getting back safely. The enemy, fortunately, had held their fire. The man they brought in was dead.

The General spoke to Andrew. "Were you the one who called for help?"

"Ya, I did, sir."

"What is your name, Private?"

"Andrew Weinshank, sir."

"I'd like to see you later. I could use a good man like you if we get through this ordeal alive."

"I'll come see you, General; you can count on that."

The "Rifles" were the first troops on the causeway leading to the city through the Belen gate. The enemy's gunfire again swept the arches of the aqueduct, keeping the "Rifles" in check until the howitzers were able to subdue them. Andrew dodged from arch to arch and was in the group of men who finally rushed the gate. Upon taking the garita, the "Rifles" and South Carolina regiments rushed forward and were within one hundred yards of the citadel. They took the gate at the very edge of the city, but were still pinned down and were being fired upon from the rooftops. It was about dark. Andrew was exhausted. Their losses had been heavy. They were running short of ammunition.

The general had them move forward steadily and firmly, entering the battery along with the storming party where they took several guns and many prisoners. The "Rifles" were again placed in front, their general in the lead. It was their job to prevent the arrival of enemy reinforcements and at the same time cut off the main avenue of retreat toward the city by the Belen gate.

They knew they would have to storm the city filled with street fighters as well as the regular army. Then all of a sudden, a white flag was raised.

A man nearby shouted out, "General Santa Anna left with his army in the direction of Guadalupe Hidalgo and the city is yours." Then the firing ceased. Captain Roberts mounted, his horse white with foam, entered the city and raised the American flag over the Halls of Montezuma.

Jubilantly, Andrew fell in line. Proudly the "Rifles" with the

Carolines behind them marched into the enormous plaza through the Alameda, down the Calle San Francisco, past the Imperial Palace. The Conquistadores long before had built the Spanish colonial town with its broad streets and spacious squares and its low, flat-roofed houses. Facing into the plaza were many handsome two and three-story buildings with shops downstairs and living quarters above. Andrew could see the American flag floating in the breeze over the Halls of Montezuma.

After they were dismissed, Andrew wasted no time in calling on General Smith. "Private Weinshank reporting, sir."

"Yes, Private. It's good to see you again. I'd like you to be my orderly while I'm stationed here. You'll have better quarters and keep, and this will make up in part for what you did for me at the aqueduct."

"Thank you, General. I'd like that very much. I'll get my gear and be right back."

When he reported to his captain, who was sitting on a camp stool, slumped over, working on some papers, Andrew said, "General Smith has asked me to serve as his orderly, Captain. He sent me to ask for permission."

"Very well, Private, but I'll need you back here for the ceremony at the plaza tomorrow. I want every man here, dressed 'spit and polish'."

"Thank you, sir. I'll be here," said Andrew. "Now may I go?"

"Yes, Weinshank, and give my best to General Smith."

"Ya, I will, sir."

Andrew found Cal with some of the other men. "I've been assigned to be General Smith's orderly, Cal, but let's keep in touch."

"You're lucky, Andrew. If you get any time off, come back to visit."

"I will, Cal. Take care of yourself," and the two men shook hands.

In the early morning hours of September 14th, Andrew stood at attention in the ranks of the "Mounted Rifles" when "Old Fuss and Feathers," the commanding general, himself, General Scott, galloped into the Grand Plaza, a plaza so large the entire army could parade in all its splendor with plenty of room to spare. The General, a big man, mounted on his beautiful sorrel horse, all decked out in the glitter and feathers pertaining to his rank and position, looked the ideal conquering hero, wearing his fore and aft hat, full dress uniform and gold sash and sword hanging from his saddle. Standing next to Cal, Andrew's heart swelled with pride as General Scott passed by, for he knew he was seeing one of the great military men of all time. His own General Smith parading alongside him was wearing the uniform Andrew had taken such pains to make presentable for this great occasion, his boots so highly polished he was able to see his own reflection.

Close by General Scott was Captain Robert E. Lee. After they passed, Cal gave Andrew a nudge and said, "Captain Lee was so exhausted he passed out at the very gates of Mexico City. He's one of the great ones, all right. If we ever go to war again, he'll be a general for sure."

After the ceremony, Andrew again said good-bye to Cal. He was eager to return home, but knew the "Rifles" would be staying put, until their general was relieved from his assignment, for General Smith was assigned to act as military governor and was given orders to secure the city.

One day while Andrew was in the stable, grooming the General's horse, the General walked in with another officer. He overheard them talking. "Your 'Rifles' did a very commendable job, Persifer. You have a lot to be proud of."

"Yes, I'm very proud of my men, but it was General Scott who deserves all your praise; he put it all together. He was half-equipped, half-supplied, and still won the war."

"Yes, I couldn't agree more. But your men put up a great effort."

"You never know what to expect from these fellows though, or how they might embarrass you, I might add. While General Scott was riding along the line at the Plaza, very near the main entrance to the palace, and was moving away from the front of my regiment, he came face to face with some of my men. They had a basket full of the reddest tomatoes I ever saw. The General stopped, ordered the men to return them to the marketplace and then continued on. You can imagine how I felt."

Andrew was proud to remain as the general's orderly and felt fortunate to have his own quarters off the stable. Each morning in the cookhouse along with the other hired help, he was served a big bowl of refried beans and warm tortilla cakes over which he spread plenty of nice fresh butter.

He would wait for the General to start working in the sala, then go to his bedroom to check on his uniforms, make the necessary repairs and make sure that everything was in order.

Then Andrew would go out to the stable, groom the horses and remain on duty, waiting for further instructions. If the General was to be gone for any length of time, he'd say to Andrew, "I won't be needing you for a few hours."

"Thank you, sir. I'll be here when you get back."

"I know I can count on you, Andrew."

On one such day Andrew returned to camp and caught Cal off duty, so the two men went to the city.

"Where's Bob and Ben? I didn't see them at camp." inquired Andrew.

"I don't know. I haven't seen them for several days," replied Cal.

When they got into the city Andrew got an American newspaper. In it Andrew read an article on the first page. "Listen to this, Cal. Daniel Webster got up in the halls of Congress and thundered, 'California isn't worth a single dollar'."

"I guess that tells you what he thinks of us down here risking our lives for a piece of wasteland."

Andrew waited outside the courthouse, tending to General Smith's horse while the General attended the trial of those who deserted, those Americans who fought against their own countrymen in Churubusco. Many had been recruited while they had been serving under General Zachary Taylor in the north. The story went around that the church had urged all good Catholics to desert, promising 320 acres of land and Mexican citizenship to those who would fight for Mexico. After the court martial was over, the general returned to where Andrew was standing patiently waiting for him. As Andrew handed him the reins, the general could see the anxious look in his eyes. Then the general spoke up, "It was fair; a number were declared not guilty and released. The Mexican clergy tried to intercede, but General Scott felt the law should be upheld. Follow me, Private, this shouldn't take long," as he walked in the direction of the prisoners. There the men were tied to trees, their backs bare, waiting for their punishment.

One soldier was singled out. The letter "D" was branded on his cheek, fifty lashes were laid hard upon his back while his arms were wrapped around a tree, his head was shaved, his buttons cut from his uniform; he was then drummed out of camp to the tune of the "Rogues March."

Andrew standing nearby overheard some soldiers talking. "That was Sergeant Riley fighting for the Mexicans at Churubusco. He taught artillery at West Point, and was considered to be the best soldier on both sides. He killed more Americans than anyone. He should be hanged!"

Someone else said, "That didn't matter, he deserted before Congress had sent out the edict, so he got off easy."

"He was saved by a technicality."

"Someone should have shot him in the back."

"Oh, he'll probably marry a beautiful señorita and build a grand adobe on his 360 acres of land and live out the rest of his life in luxury."

The general returned for his horse. "We can go now, private."

That night, General Smith was sitting in the sala when Andrew walked in. "Oh! I'm sorry. I didn't see you. I'm here to check your uniform to get it ready for tomorrow."

"That's all right, Andrew. You didn't interrupt anything. I was just sitting here thinking about today. It was a dreadful experience. I was close enough to Riley to feel him wince."

"What happens tomorrow, sir?" asked Andrew, pleased to be called by his name.

"The hangings. The men needed this afternoon to dig their graves, forty-nine of them."

"Desertion is a bad business. Good night, General. I'll have your uniform ready for tomorrow."

"Oh! Yes, for the hanging. Good night, Andrew."

Early the next morning Andrew held the reins and waited for the general to mount.

"Let's get started, private. There's no need to keep those poor devils waiting, nothing will be done 'till I get there." They rode along in silence. As they pulled up to the camp ground, the wagons were lined up, forty-nine of them, each man was in a separate wagon, a noose was around his neck. Colonel Harney was in charge. He was everywhere, his long arms waving, rushing around, trying to keep the teams in line. Then as soon as General Smith took his place in the line of observers, Harney gave the signal and the wagons pulled out. Andrew, sitting in his saddle at a discrete distance looked on. Rather than look at the men dangling, he threw his head back and looked up. Looming majestically in front of him was the American flag floating over the Castle of Chapultepec.

One day General Smith walked over to where Private Weinshank was working on his saddle and said, "Andrew, we'll be leaving Mexico in a few days and you're to report back to your company commander. I want to thank you for being a fine orderly. I'll never forget the support you gave me at the Belen Gate."

"It was my duty, sir," said Andrew. "I was glad to serve."

"I'm being sent to California as military governor, and would like you to work for me there."

"I would be honored General, and I'd like to go there."

"By the way, Andrew, I'll bet you'd like my nursemaid. She's a sweet little German girl. When you get back home, come to New Orleans. I should then know more about my plans for California and you can meet Regina."

"I'd like that very much, General, and thank you for all your help. I'll get my gear and be on my way."

Back at camp, Andrew packed his few possessions and got ready for the long march back to Vera Cruz.

It was good for Andrew to see the men again, Cal especially. "Say, what about Ben Vandewaikon and Bob Woodridge? Did they ever come back?"

Someone spoke up and said, "They deserted."

"What?" asked Andrew. "Where?"

"Right here in the city, haven't seen them for days."

"I suppose they didn't want to leave their ladies," said Cal. "Can't blame them. Many of these señoritas are a sight for sore eyes."

"They probably got tired waiting to go back home. I was luckier than most, working for the general."

Company E was going home. They marched out on June 6, 1848. Those same big fellows who climbed the hill at Cerro Gordo, made the seventeen minute dash at Contreras, fought at Churubusco, Chapultepec, and charged the Belen Gate, bawled like babies when they marched away from their señoritas whom they had known for such a short time.

They arrived at Perote June 14th, and marched in view of the castle, where years earlier the American prisoners had been kept, Texans who on Christmas Day of 1842 entered the town of Mier and crossed the border into Mexico to retaliate for the Alamo and Golidad. The Texans were forced to surrender, and one out of every ten was shot. The others were driven to the old castle sitting on the hill in front of them, built in the eighteenth century of stone. There they lived and died within its damp walls. Earlier the building had been used as a storehouse for the gold that was shipped from Vera Cruz to Spain. They left Camp Perote June 19th. At Vera Cruz they embarked on the ship "Tyron" on July 6th and headed for New Orleans. As they pulled out of the harbor, Andrew and Cal stood on deck looking back at the city. They stood there watching the sun as it began to sink behind the great Mt. Orizaba, casting a shadow on the Castle of San Juan de Ulloa.

As they pulled up to the wharf in the busy harbor at New Orleans, a crowd was waiting on the dock. It was an exciting moment for Andrew as he stood on deck, looking below at the anxious upturned faces. It was over, he was home. Standing in the crowd was a little curly-haired lass holding the hand of a small boy. Their eyes met. He knew she had noticed him, making his heart beat faster. He stood watching her as the little boy whose hand she was holding struggled to get free. She put her arm around the boy and gave him a squeeze. He then looked up at her as if she were the grandest lady in the whole world. Then she looked back at Andrew. Andrew wondered if she was the one the General had told him about. Then he saw General Smith wave to her and Andrew's heart skipped a beat.

"See that young lady down there, Cal?" asked Andrew.

"You mean the one with the little boy? Yes, I see her, what about her?"

"I'm going to marry her," said Andrew.

"You're what!" then Cal gave him a tug and they fell in line to disembark.

On the wharf the soldiers formed a line of march. Proudly, by company, heads up, sabers glimmering in the setting sun, the men marched along the wharf. The crowd gathered around them, gave them cheer after cheer for their safety and success. Andrew held his back straight and his eyes forward. As he passed the lovely young lady with jet black hair and big dark eyes with her arm around the little boy, he couldn't resist turning his head in her direction. Their eyes met. The child looked at her, then at Andrew, not knowing what to think, but Andrew did. He knew it was love at first sight, thought she was the loveliest young lady he had ever seen. Right then and there he knew he would be calling on the General as soon as he got back from Jefferson Barracks.

Andrew's company boarded the "Aleck Scott," a majestic steamboat plying the Mississippi River with its fancy saloons and private rooms. As Andrew walked up the gangplank he looked back once more at the young lady on the wharf. He was now traveling the last lap of his journey in luxury to his final destination of Jefferson Barracks along the banks of the Missouri River to be mustered out of the service. The date was August 19, 1848. Some of the men were doing poorly because of their wounds.

A man all decked out in fancy clothes walked up to Andrew, shoved a piece of paper in his face. "What's that for?" asked Andrew.

"To buy your land scrip. I'll pay in cash. You can sign your property over when you get to the fort."

"Sorry, sir, I'm not interested." The man gave Andrew a scowl and quickly turned away.

Andrew had a chance to relax, sit on deck, eat good American food for the first time in many months, and enjoy the newspaper, the *New York Herald.* He spotted a small article that took his notice. Gold discovered in California.

"What do you think of this? Gold has been discovered in California!" exclaimed Andrew.

"I've had enough of that country," said Cal. "I'm only interested in getting home, and anyway, no one else seems to be talking about it. It can't be a very big strike, and besides, what would you do with it if you did find it?"

Andrew replied with, "All the gold in the world won't keep me from going back to New Orleans."

The steamboat did well in the slow-moving Mississippi, but when it reached the mouth of the Missouri the river was throwing water and mud into the main stream, and they seemed to be standing still. The boat edged closer to the northern bank, and with a burst of steam they were able to enter the main channel and again into calmer water.

It was a bright morning on the eighth day of their passage when they approached St. Louis, a beautiful city along the riverbank. At noon they were gliding beneath the broad ensign floating from the flagstaff of Jefferson Barracks, the largest army post in the country. The quadrangle of the barracks enclosed the parade ground, and was backed by the broad summit of a noble bluff swelling up from the water. Its white-washed cottages, crumbling with the years, and the grey walls of the arsenal stood out in the rear of the esplanade. Anxiously waiting to land, they stood on deck looking at the lofty spire and dusky walls of St. Louis Cathedral, and on rounding the bend they saw the gilded crucifix gleaming in the sunlight from its lofty summit and the glittering cupolas and church domes. Their eyes fell on bright foliage of the forest of trees which was the setting for the private homes nearby.

At the barracks Andrew and Cal enjoyed the good food, got plenty of rest, received the praises of the officers, and did the necessary paperwork. They were given their land scrip, and then as quickly as it had begun, on the 28th of August in 1848, they were out of the service and heading for home. It had been almost nineteen months since that cold rainy day Andrew entered the enlistment office in New Orleans with the newspaper, the *Daily Piscayne,* under his arm, offering one hundred sixty acres to any young man, from a good family, especially suited for the service to fight for his country in Mexico.

It was time for the two men to say good-bye. For Cal it was back to family and friends. For Andrew it meant back to the land of cotton, Mobile and its wide streets lined with shade trees located along the banks of the Mobile River. He harbored sweet dreams of going to California. To him this meant "heaven on earth," but for now it would have to wait. The trip took an eternity, for his thoughts were on the girl on the dock, and it was there where he really wanted to be.

When Andrew returned to Mobile, family and friends were there to greet him. It was a day of rejoicing, with the bells ringing, the flag flying and a march through the city streets, followed by a grand dinner. The people at home knew only of the battles they had fought, the losses they had endured and the victories they had won. There was a tumultuous joy on their return and a great deal of sorrow for those who hadn't come home.

Most of the men were home to stay, to live out their lives, but for Andrew it was back to the lumber yard only long enough to build up his stake so he could go back to New Orleans to renew his acquaintance with his general and to pay a visit to the young lady he saw on the wharf.

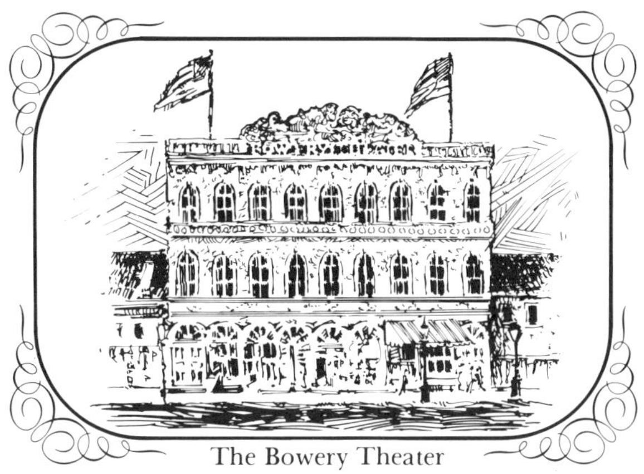
The Bowery Theater

Chapter 2

From the deck, Henry Charles Lee stood looking out at the bustling City of New York on a cool November day in 1848. The Lee brothers —Lavater, Henry, and Hercules—, a family of acrobats dating as far back as the lineage had been traced, were all celebrated artists of high caliber.

They retired to their cabin for the night. The next morning after a short inspection, with great anticipation, curiosity and hope, they walked down the gangplank and onto American soil.

Many changes had taken place since 1836 when they first came to the United States, traveling in one of the early wagon shows.

Henry was now thirty-four, a handsome man of average height, thin, blue eyes, dark curly hair, a trim mustache, wearing clothes of the latest fashion, and his manner was rather aloof. Henry performed with his two little boys, Francis and Eugene; his wife Margaret, an acrobat herself but now unable to perform for she was heavy with child. She was fair of skin with soft, curly blond hair, and blue eyes. They set out looking for a hotel. The choice was somewhat limited, either the Astor House, unrivaled as to extent and splendor, or the Howard Hotel, the one they chose, which was quite comfortable and more modest in its charges.

After making arrangements for their rooms, the three brothers went in search of a theatre. They took a hackney to the Bowery, a magnificent building very much like those of Europe. The door was open, so they walked in. The stage was large enough for a good sized tanbark ring. It had ample seating capacity, several tiers, private boxes, and a pit and gallery.

"What a splendid theatre," said Lavater the eldest of the three brothers, as he looked around. "Let's talk to the manager."

"What can I do for you?" asked one of the two well dressed men approaching them.

"We're the 'Lee Brothers Circus.' We're interested in an engagement."

"This is the man you want to talk to. His name is Rufus Welch. His circus has taken over the theatre for an engagement."

The men shook hands.

"What's your background?" Rufus, the heavy set one, asked.

It was Lavater who spoke up. "We've performed in several London theaters, in the Cirque in Paris, in the Royal Theatre in Dublin. We were managed by Mr. Batty, you've probably heard of him."

"Yes, I have. What does your act consist of?" his eyes fixed on Lavater.

"On my benefit night I balanced a plank forty feet long, vaulted over fourteen horses, threw a half-dozen weights of a hundred pounds each over my head, bent backward over a chair, and in that position lifted a bar weighing one hundred pounds. I threw a back somersault on a horse going at full speed, and turned twenty-one forward somersaults with the aid of a springboard."

"You did all that in one performance?"

"Yes, I did."

"And you?" motioning to Hercules.

"I'm the cannon ball expert. I perform the feats of strength. Henry here is the bareback rider."

Then Henry spoke up, "It's my specialty to hold my boys in various poses while riding bareback around the ring."

"Well, men," said the manager, "sounds wonderful, you're hired and I'll be looking forward to your performance."

"Thank you, sir," said Lavater. "As long as we can please the crowd, I trust you'll keep us on the bill."

"You do your part," said Welch, "and I'll do mine."

"Thank you," said Lavater.

"Good day, gentlemen."

On opening night the Lees found the audience to be far different from what they had experienced in the past. They had always been accustomed to the controlled, passive, restrained but appreciative audiences of the big cities such as London, Dublin or Paris.

But at the Bowery, as elaborate and handsome as the building was, the crowds were different. The rowdies picked fights, the old men took naps, the mothers nursed their babies, lovers held hands, and the prostitutes strutted around the place soliciting business. The theatre served as a social club, a picnic ground, a meeting place and a watering hole.

But the spectacular always caught their fancy and the audience cheered wildly and demanded encore after encore.

It was on December 5th 1848, while the Lees were performing at the Bowery that the news hit like a bolt of lightning. . . "GOLD DISCOVERED IN CALIFORNIA."

As soon as Colonel Mason's courier, Lt. Beale, reached Washington, President Polk confirmed the discovery to Congress. After the announcement, the startling news from California had been accepted at face value, and the entire world was gripped with mining fever. Thousands were clamoring to leave for California, for everyone thought that gold was to be had for picking it up off the ground. One week later throngs of people were on the wharf at New Orleans waiting for passage to the Isthmus on the "Falcon." The ship was being held up waiting for General Persifer Smith and his family to board. The General was taking command of the forces on the Pacific.

With the Rio Grande as the international boundary and California ceded to the United States following the hostilities with Mexico, it opened the way for westward expansion, and the discovery of gold in California in '48 produced a wild rush to "El Dorado."

The war with Mexico had opened up the territorial expansion westward, making the nation transcontinental. Many veterans just released from the service were ripe for new adventures. The revolutions that swept Europe in '48 and the depressions that followed added to the restlessness of the times. Many who immigrated to America were heading on to the gold country.

By January of '49 "everyone" was off to the mines. The gold fever swept the Atlantic seaboard, jarred staid New England, coursed through the Ohio Valley, and up and down the Mississippi. News spread to Canada, across the Atlantic to England, from the European continent to France and Germany, the Baltic and the Mediterranean. Not everyone joined the rush to California; some were too old, some too young, some too rich and others too poor to make the move.

They used three main routes—by sea, around Cape Horn; by a combination sea and land making the journey crossing at Panama; and by overland trails across the continent.

They came from all directions, some from over the Gila route, crossing the great desert lying west of the Colorado. This whole region was scorching and sterile with its burning salt plains and shifting hills of sand. They came in droves, many afraid of making the trip, but on they came.

All during the spring of '49 they gathered along the banks of the Mississippi, waiting for the grass to grow tall enough to feed their livestock for the trip to California.

On the route from Independence to Fort Laramie, the line of wagons, horsemen, herds of cattle and men on foot extended in an unbroken succession across the plains.

In California the towns became virtually depopulated. Monterey was left unoccupied except by the old and infirm, a few women, a gang of prisoners and some soldiers. The fever spread southward to Santa Barbara and on to Los Angeles. Gold fever talk was prevalent, and it seemed as though everyone was clamoring to leave for the gold country. Along the way as they paused for rest, they asked southbound travelers where to dig for gold. By the time they reached the gold fields, they knew all about Yankee Hill, Rich Gulch, Fry Town and others. On the way many stripped the orchards bare of fruit. The mission fathers had to protect their holdings from the invaders. The gamblers, cutthroats and thieves followed the gold, stopping at Los Angeles, staying over at the Calle de los Negroes before moving on to Sidney Town in San Francisco. Gamblers had their disheveled women and their friendly pimps.

They came down from Oregon. They came through Vera Cruz to San Blas, and underwent terrible suffering on the march up Baja California.

Mounted soldier-postmen carrying the mail down El Camino Real spread the word that gold had been discovered at Coloma. It wasn't long before businessmen started hiring help to do their digging for them.

People from Los Angeles went by carretas, sailors jumped ship, soldiers abandoned their regiments. Another group of soldiers, three hundred of them, from General Zachary Taylor's campaign of the Rio Grande, were stationed in Los Angeles, and many just up and took their leave and headed for the gold fields. Even a jailor took his prisoners who were waiting trial to go to work in the mines. Those coming from the eastern cities eagerly booked passage for the journey around the Horn, favoring the perilous passage through the Magellan Strait. They came by boat from all countries of the world.

Day after day vessels arrived in San Francisco—on of the greatest migration of man with a single purpose in mind.

Andrew Weinshank returned to New Orleans. He knocked on General Smith's door and was admitted into the parlor. When the General and his wife appeared in the room, they were accompanied by the petite, dark curly-haired, German girl Andrew had seen at the dock in New Orleans. He couldn't take his eyes off her. Then the General spoke up. "I don't think you've met my wife, and this young lady is Regina, our nursemaid," he said, hoping Andrew was impressed.

It was the General's wife who spoke up, a very attractive woman of slight build. "It's good to meet you Andrew, but you caught us at a rather bad time. Word just reached us that gold has been discovered in California. One huge piece has already arrived in Washington, and the General has been assigned there. We're in the midst of packing. Perhaps you can chat with Regina while we carry on. She's going with us, you know."

"Glad to, Mrs. Smith," said Andrew happy for the chance to be alone with Regina, yet still unsure of himself.

It was awkward at first for Andrew, for he didn't know what to say, but when Regina started speaking in her native tongue, Andrew began to feel more at ease. They found they had a lot to talk about. Andrew talked about fighting in Mexico, about coming to this country as a lad from Neidstatt, of his home town in Germany, and Regina talked about what it was like in her town of Baden-Baden.

"I was the only girl of six children, my brothers were all tall, all over six feet, so they had to serve in the army. My father was a cobbler and made all their boots, but he felt the burden of clothing so many sons in uniform, so when I was fourteen he sent me to the south of France to live with my grandparents."

"That's why we were sent to this country: our parents couldn't support us. Only one or two came at a time," said Andrew.

"Yes, but you were the lucky ones. My brothers couldn't leave."

"That's true. What did your grandparents do?" asked Andrew.

"They made fine wine for the gambling houses in Monte Carlo. They also owned a restaurant, and one day while I was waiting on tables Colonel Smith and his wife came in. Colonel Smith offered me a position as nursemaid for their little boy and asked me to come back to Alabama with them. I took the position because I could read and write in German as well as speak French, and being able to speak two languages, I was certain I could learn English as well."

"He was a colonel when we were at Vera Cruz, but he later became a general and very deserving, one of the best," said Andrew. "He's very fortunate to be assigned to California. That's where I'd like to settle down. They say it's like 'heaven on earth,' where the weather is mild and seldom extreme."

"It does sound wonderful, Andrew."

"Ya, I'd best be running along, though, Regina. I'm sure you have a lot to do."

Andrew stood up and took Regina's hand. Their eyes met, again making Andrew tongue-tied. Not knowing what to say, he just squeezed her hand and without a word walked out the front door, fearing all the while the Smiths would take her to California with them.

This fear prompted Andrew to return to the General's house the following day. Because the house was to be closed, Andrew knew he would either have to ask Regina to stay and be his wife or stand the risk of losing her forever. He hadn't much time.

He stood outside the house, marshalling his courage. He'd spent the better part of the night before deciding what to do, what to say, and how to go about it. Taking a deep breath, squaring his shoulders, he marched up to the door, knocked and was again admitted to the parlor, this time asking only for Regina.

When he saw her, his eyes fell. Now that the time had come, his well-planned thoughts and words escaped him. Then he had the wild thought that maybe, just maybe, she was as attracted to him as he was to her, so with renewed courage and the feeling of hope, he blurted it out. "While I was the General's orderly in Mexico, he told me about you, and when the General's wife said you were going to California, I was afraid I'd never see you again. Regina, I don't want you to go. I want you to marry me. I must return to Alabama and help my brothers in the lumber mill, but we could go to California as soon as I've made enough money, but that could take some time."

"Calm down, Andrew. I'll marry you. You don't have to make any promises. I'd much rather be with you. The General has already made the decision for us. He's very fond of you. I was so afraid when you left yesterday you wouldn't be coming back. I didn't sleep a wink last night."

"And so it's settled."

"Yes, Andrew. I know you talked to the General earlier, but I want to hear it from him. I want him to say he approves. You'd best go now."

When Regina found the General, he was again busy checking getting everything in readiness for the trip. As she walked up, he said, "I'm not too sure we'll make it on schedule. We've had such short notice. Regina, are you ready?"

"No, that's what I want to talk to you about. Andrew was just here, and wants me to marry him. He feels we should return to Mobile to help support his family by working at the lumber mill."

"That's what I like, a man who can make up his mind, Regina. It's obvious the two of you have already had a meeting of the minds. You're very fortunate to find such a nice young man. He'll always be a good provider."

"I think you were the one who found him, General," said Regina.

"Yes, I could have had a bit to do with it," he answered. "And if you do come to California, because I'm sure Andrew has it in the back of his mind, look us up. We'll be stationed in San Francisco."

"I will," said Regina. "I must get back to work, but I do want to thank you for your blessing. I'm sure Andrew wants to live in California, but for the time being, it will have to wait."

When word of the discovery of gold reached New York, the Lees were still performing at the Bowery, in an array of spectacular events. On the same bill was Sam Lathrop, the famous clown. Welch provided seventy-five horses and hired fifty men. Their season closed March 17th, 1849, almost five months in duration. Though men were leaving in droves for California, the Lees felt no need to join them for they were performing before full houses and pleasing the crowd.

On October 23, 1849, Henry Lee and his family performed for Welch at the Walnut Street Theatre in Philadelphia. Rufus Welch, a leader in the circus world, had converted the theatre into a magnificent amphitheatre. The chandelier, as lovely as any the Lees had ever seen, was made up of many gas lights which illuminated the stage, arena, and all parts of the theatre. The drop scene, founded on the memorable description of Lord Byron's dream, was painted by John Wisor. A full orchestra had been hired to play the favorite airs of the most admired French, German and Italian operas.

In January of 1850 the Lees opened at Barnum's American Museum. By April 5th, they were on the bill at the Olympic Theatre. Lavater, Henry and the two boys, Masters Eugene and Francis, and Lavater's little La Petite Sesqui, were all called upon to give a variety of feats of strength and agility. The following evening Lavater's little girl Virginia, only five years old, performed with her father on the revolving globe.

The Lees continued to be very popular among the theater-goers in the East. By August of that year, in Brooklyn, the Lees were featured with Dan Rice, the world famous clown. On October 16th they were featured at the new Broadway Circus at the Alhambra near Spring Street. They were the hit of the show and held over for a second engagement.

After their final performance, Rufus Welch had supper served in the dressing room. Colonel Mann, his manager made all the arrangements. Welch got up to speak, "I'd like to thank all the participants and congratulate the performers on a job well done, but please keep this in mind, no matter how highly skilled you are: we must levy fines for those who fail to show up for performances. This is a standard procedure and we adhere to it. One other item of business: we're always trying new acts to improve our show—do any of you have any ideas we might use?" Henry asked permission to speak. "Yes, Henry. You have a suggestion?"

"Yes, in England while we were performing at Astleys, the famous Ducrow family performed with us. Ducrow straddled two horses while trotting around the ring. It was quite a spectacle. I haven't seen anyone doing it here and thought this type of act might improve the show."

"That would be spectacular! I'd like to see someone work on that."

Henry continued to explain, "Ducrow would sit as a patron in the audience. From the ring they would call for someone to come up and ride one of their fine steeds. He would volunteer, mount a horse, start shedding his clothes layer by layer until finally he would be in complete ring costume and continue performing with such skill and daring he held the audience spellbound."

Rufus replied with, "Yes, this is the sort of act I'm interested in."

"Thank you, sir," replied Henry.

"I also want to add this, we're the largest circus of its kind in the United States. No other circus is well enough off to hire roustabouts for the rough work of pitching the tent, making the ring, spreading the sawdust. We're the first circus to have a street parade and mount our band members on horseback. We're also the first to use elephants to precede us through the streets; all this makes us unique, I'm proud of our accomplishments and intend to present the finest in circus entertainment possible. Thank you all for your contributions."

After the supper Welch, the owner, went over to Lavater. "We're taking the show on tour along the Spanish Main. I'd like to include the Lees."

"I'll talk to the others, but I've already made other commitments. I'll be performing at the New Manhattan Circus with the Rivers' family."

"Think it over and let me know."

"I will."

That night at the hotel, the three brothers met. "What do you think?" asked Lavater. "I've already told Rufus I plan to stay because of a prior engagement."

"I'm interested in going," said Henry, then both looked at Hercules.

He thought it over a minute then said, "I prefer to stay. Personally, I think this is where the interest is, but there's no reason why you shouldn't go, Henry. I'm sure you'll get a lot out of the trip and no telling what horizons it might open up."

Henry and his family left on tour with Welch's Troup, traveling toward the Spanish Main.

As Henry and his family traveled from port to port, the little boys became more and more part of the act, their father balancing them in first one position, then another as they performed.

The circus was now under the management of "Old Man Burr." His orders were to make first landfall at Surinam Bay in the Guianas.

They laid anchor, waiting all day before the health officers boarded to give them a clear bill of health before they could sail up the river to the city. The horses and baggage were lowered into the shark-infested water to swim ashore, for want of a wharf, which gave them a few anxious moments.

On shore the performers watched the Negroes and Indians as they walked around, wearing only the skimpy breech cloth to protect them from the elements.

From Berlice they went on to Demerara where they showed for three weeks, then continued on. They entered the pass leading to the Island of Grenada. On board ship, Henry and Charles Thorne stood at the rail, looking at the lush foliage along the banks, talking about their past experiences.

"Well, Henry, I'm glad I wasn't with them when they made this trip back in '42. John Glenroy was telling me about it. Colonel Mann was in charge that time. Instead of taking this pass, he ordered the captain to take one of the smaller ones. The captain was against it, because he was afraid of losing wind, but the Colonel insisted—as it happened, the wind died down and it was only by a miracle they were able to make it. It upset the Colonel so much, knowing he would have been the cause of losing so many lives, no one ever again talked about it in his presence."

After Grenada, it was on to Tobago, then on to Barbados for a week.

They performed before good crowds at St. Vincent for four days, then on to St. Lucia, then Antigua for a week, and on to St. Thomas, where they showed at the Queen's Wharf. They approached the shore and a beach of powdery white sand. All around were sugar and cotton plantations, thriving in the deep, rich soil. Everything was growing in abundance: tobacco, avocados, pineapples, oranges and bananas and sleek, glossy horses grazed nearby. After a week of that garden paradise, they went on to St. Croix.

They approached the island, surrounded by the beautiful blue sea with its benign climate, soft scenery; well endowed by nature, sheltered, almost tideless, with spectacular lush vegetation, lofty palms swaying in the gentle breezes; they were in awe of the beauty producing a fairyland effect.

It appeared to Margaret that Henry was preoccupied, quiet. "What's troubling you, Henry?" she asked as they were pulling away from shore, waving to those who had come to bid them farewell.

"Margaret, everyone I've talked to lately is either thinking about going to California or are already making plans to go—I think we should go, too."

"We're doing well. We've made good money these last several months."

"I think we could do even better."

"But, is there anything there?"

"From what I've heard, San Francisco is growing by leaps and bounds. There are three theaters there already."

"I thought everyone was off digging for gold."

"Yes, but Charles tells me he talked to one of the men who just came from there. The miners are starved for entertainment. They're going in droves to Joseph Rowe's amphitheatre to see him perform on his horse 'Adonis' and the miners throw gold nuggets at his feet."

"Then you'll be talking to the 'old man'?"

"Yes, when the time is right, Margaret."

From St. Croix they went on to Trinidad. They followed the northern-most coast of South America, the "Spanish Main," traveling westward moving closer to California with each stop along the way.

Their first stop was at Margarita, then on to Barcelona, La Guaya, and Caracas; then back to the coastal towns of Puerto Cabello, Caro, Santa Marta, Barranquilla and on to Cartagena. When they arrived at Cartagena, Henry sought out "Old Man Burr," as he was affectionately called, and told him of his plans.

"We won't be going back to New York, Mr. Burr. I'm taking my family on to California."

"So, you caught the 'gold fever' too, Henry. Can't say that I blame you, but I'm too old for that. I understand Charles Thorne is headed there too. Are you going together?"

"No, he plans to go by way of Nicaragua. We're going by Panama. I booked passage this morning."

"Do you plan to perform in the gold country, Henry? I understand that's located in the foothills of the Sierra."

"We'll try the towns first—San Francisco, Stockton and Sacramento. The boys and I will do gymnastics. Then I plan to buy some horses and work up a show."

"I wish you well, Henry. For myself I'll be glad to get back to New York. This has been a hard trip."

The next morning, Henry and his family, with gear in hand, went on their way—to another town, another place— and this time it was San Francisco.

Henry Charles Lee

The Constitution

Chapter 3

Henry and his family made the crossing at the Isthmus of Panama, traveled through the disease-infested tropical jungle, and waited at Panama City until Henry could book passage on the steamer the "Constitution," cabin class, heading north. That was on the 2nd of October, 1851.

They walked up the gangplank of a majestic sidewheeler and headed for their cabin. While Margaret got settled, putting everything in order for the trip north, Henry talked to another passenger from one of the nearby cabins.

"I think we're quite lucky to get such comfortable accommodations," said Henry.

"Yes, we are, but we did have to pay a pretty stiff price. What line of work are you in?"

"I'm a circus man. Henry Charles Lee is my name."

"I'm Horace McGowan," said the distinguished looking man, with a slight Scottish brogue. "Seems as though everyone I've talked to lately is going to California."

"Yes, I'm sure you're right, and from what I've heard, they're coming from all over the world."

"Can't say that I blame them. That's why I'm here. I've heard some of the diggers have become rich overnight. I don't know what it's bringing now, but gold was worth as much as twelve dollars an ounce, and some miners averaged five ounces for every hour they worked. One man scooped up two and a half pounds in fifteen minutes. Another man started digging and found one piece that weighed fourteen pounds, one that weighed seventeen, and several weighing anywhere from one to four pounds."

"Was it that easy to find?" asked Henry.

"Well, at first it was. It was actually picked up off the ground, and some was picked out of the crevices of the rocks with ordinary knives. Some miners merged into companies and hired Indians to work for them. For a six week work period, seven men divided 275 pounds amongst themselves."

"I understand there's still plenty of gold."

"That's what I've heard—unlimited, in fact. Well, I guess the ladies have had a chance to settle in. Perhaps we'd better join them."

"Hope we can talk again," said Henry.

"Same here," said Horace, and the two men parted company.

As Henry was still standing at the rail looking at the sunset, a man walked up to him, a stocky man with brown curly hair, big round eyes, and bushy mustache. "Going to be digging for gold?" the man asked.

"Oh no! I'm a circus man. I'm going to stick to my own profession. I think it's better when a man labors at the trade he knows. Let the others dig for gold. I'm just hoping they'll have the time to come see my show. By the way, I'm Henry Charles Lee. And you?"

"I'm John Marshall," and the two men shook hands. "You mean you'll go up into the gold country where the men are digging to perform? I understand they're the foothills of the Sierra."

"I'll go if I can get a wagon up there," he replied.

"I've been watching you work out with your boys. Would you be interested in a partner? I don't have much experience, but I've always wanted to perform. I'm fairly witty and I can play the banjo. I first became stage struck when I was a kid growing up. Will you give it a little thought?"

"Yes, I will. I'll need all the help I can get. I think we might work something out." And the two men parted company.

Henry thought it over for a day or two, and the two men entered into a partnership. John was several years younger than Henry, born in Limerick, Ireland. As a lad he learned the trade of silversmith.

As they were making plans for their first show, the men around them were mending their clothes, making chests for their gold, sharpening their knives and shovels and packing and repacking their belongings. Most were young, all anxious to get to the gold fields. They were either fighting, gambling or complaining about the food. They speculated on how much gold they would get and how long it would take them to get it.

But the Lees had other plans. They practiced their gymnastic events and perfected their act. Henry worked on deck during the day with his little boys, Francis and Eugene. Margaret had a new baby to care for, named Theodore after one of Henry's brothers, hoping he would follow in the footsteps of his uncle and become a great performer. They continued on, traveling along the coast. On October 9th, John Newton, a seaman, a native of Scotland, died of consumption. On the 11th, both Andrew Smith and Abraham Baker died of Panama Fever. They called at the port of Acapulco, Mexico, and departed from there October 14th. On the 19th Robert Fyfe, an Irishman, died of dysentery. He was sick when he left, and his wife and child had to witness the dreadful act of his burial at sea.

Henry remained on deck leaning against the rail, wondering what lay ahead of him when Captain Welsh, a short, stocky man walked up to him. It was Henry who spoke up first.

"Burials at sea are very depressing. I'm sure that's one of your duties you don't care to perform."

"No, I don't. I try to do it as quickly as possible. Sometimes it gives people the feeling I don't care, but that's not so. It's bad enough. Why try to drag it out?"

"Yes. What a pity for those poor men who traveled such a distance in search of riches, to die before they could pass through the Golden Gate."

"Yes, poor devils. But if they came to dig for gold, maybe they'd strike it rich, maybe they wouldn't."

"I'm sure you're right."

"Well, Mr. Lee, it won't be long now. What are your plans? Are you going to build your own arena?"

"I really don't know yet. First we must go through customs, then go on from there."

"You can find the Customs House, a big three-story affair in the middle of town. Can't miss it. You can see the American flag on the roof floating in the breeze."

"Thank you, I'm sure I'll find it. What do you think our chances are for success?" asked Henry.

"I can't rightly say, but before 1848 there was hardly anything in the way of entertainment here in California except fandangoes, bullfights and horse races. In fact, before gold was discovered, there wasn't a lodging place anywhere here except Brown's in San Francisco, and the only transportation was by carreta, but these last two and a half years have brought about a lot of changes."

"Blossomed overnight," remarked Henry.

"It certainly did. Well, I must be going. We'll be heading for the harbor tomorrow. I just wanted to wish you luck. Not too often do I get celebrities such as yourselves traveling with me."

"Thank you, Captain Welsh. It's good to be appreciated for your work. Good night, sir."

Early the next day, on October 27, 1851, the Lees and John went up on deck as the huge sidewheeler entered the harbor at San Francisco. They passed through the narrow passageway into a rim of low, barren hills. In the distance they could see the city itself, surrounded by the most beautiful picturesque mountains.

As they passed the Golden Gate, the entrance to the magnificent harbor, they saw a huge, solitary rock, standing like a sentinel guarding the gateway. Passing it, they entered a great expanse of water.

In the background the coastal range was covered with wild oats. Colorful clippers glided by on their outward voyage to other parts of the world. Everywhere were ships of many countries, row upon row of masts all sizes and shapes, hulks of deserted ships resting on the mud flats. All the shipping of the world seemed to be gathered in that one place.

The town itself came closer into view, situated on the inner slope of the coastal heights. The long wharf looked like a watery village, carelessly planked with crowded shops and stalls. Hackney carriages were being driven at full tilt. All San Francisco was linked to the Bay, and it was all there to see.

A man of medium height, obviously of wealth and culture, stepped up beside Henry. "Looks pretty dry out there, doesn't it?"

"Yes, it does," said Henry. "I wonder what it would be like if a fire got started. I've heard there have been a couple of humdingers

"Yes, I understand on Christmas Eve of '49 a fire broke out at the Plaza, and the El Dorado, the Parker House and the United States

Coffee House all went up in flames, but in three days the rubbish was cleared away and new buildings were built on the same spots," said the stranger.

"At least they didn't waste any time," said Henry.

"Then the following year on May 4th another fire broke out and swept away three entire blocks of shops and warehouses. On June 14th still another fire wiped out the district bounded by Clay and California Streets, Kearny Street and the waterfront."

"I can see some brick buildings off in the distance. If some more brick buildings are built, it'll cut the risk of fire," said Henry.

"Yes, they've made a lot of progress in the time I've been here. I went back East to see my family; now I see a lot of brick buildings are going up. The city is bound to grow, for the supply of gold seems to know no end."

"Yes, from all I've heard, you're probably right. It won't be long before we dock. I'd better get organized. Nice talking to you," said Henry.

As they pulled up to the long wharf, they watched the sailors rushing around unloading while the passengers waited impatiently to disembark. They were ready to be on their way to hunt for living quarters, to taste shore cooking, to inquire for mail from home, and to start making plans to go to the gold fields.

Then finally the gangplank was dropped; the passengers pushed and shoved till Henry, Margaret, the boys and John found themselves to be some of the last to leave the boat. They went to where their many boxes and trunks were stacked on the wharf ready to be claimed. It was too late for Henry to find help carrying their bags, so he and John and the boys picked them up, and they were on their way.

All San Francisco was drawn to the wharf. Enthusiasm ran wild. It was the most wide-awake town imaginable, and Henry sensed immediately it would be a great place for the circus.

Wares of all kinds, sizes and shapes were displayed outside the many shops that lined the wharf. There were markets for vegetables, poultry, fish and candy. There were saloons and gambling houses along the narrow and crowded wharf. There were packing cases in their way. They had to be careful as they walked along for fear of stepping into the rotten cabbages strewn all over, the smell of the stinking fish turned their stomachs, and holes had to be avoided that could cause them to lose their footing. There was the possibility of bumping into a drunken sailor or being trampled by a runaway horse. On either side of them were ships of many sizes and shapes, discharging their cargoes in good order.

Then they found a carriage for hire and so were able to continue on along the long wharf in style, passing crowded shops and stalls.

As they rode along, all San Francisco was alive around them. Cargoes of tea, silks and shawls were being unloaded. Ships that had been beached and embedded along the shore were now turned into shops and houses. Everything was hustle and bustle up and down the streets. The wind was blowing constantly, carrying clouds of sand, dust was everywhere. They saw storekeepers sweeping their doorways so people could enter their stores. There were houses everywhere, some frame, some just tents.

They passed by shops displaying miner's implements stacked inside. "Look at that!" Henry pointed out the jeweler's windows gleaming with chunks of gold. They turned into Portsmouth Square, and the whole blazing life of San Francisco lay before them.

They entered the large plaza area that was enclosed by a corral. All around it were the gambling houses, "El Dorado," the theaters, the "Third Jenny Lind," the "Bella Union," the "Verandah" and the "Parker House." All the garbage of San Francisco was in its streets: the boys held their noses as they passed the big piles of egg shells, cabbage leaves, potato parings and onion tops. It was everywhere and especially heavy at the crossings.

Their eyes opened with wonder as they watched men dashing about on horseback, wild with excitement and people as they were moving to and fro with so much to do and so little time in which to do it.

Their carriage turned on to Commercial Street, a regular market place where the wagons were in unending lines, taking provisions for the mines to steamers going to Sacramento and bringing back cargo from ships that had come in from all parts of the world. Everywhere flags were floating in the breeze, looking as if an eternal fire were going on.

Their main concern was to find lodging, but first they had to report to the customs house which was located on the corner of Montgomery and California Streets. It was a large three-story affair, built of half brick and half wood. It stood above all other houses in the city, built like a chalet with an outside stairway, and as the captain had said, the American flag was floating from the roof, a symbol it was a public building.

The Lees and John went in. Inside they were greeted by a clerk who questioned them about the things they had brought with them.

"What is this, sir?" asked the customs clerk of Henry.

"These are some of the trappings we need in our work," he said.

"What do you do?" asked the clerk.

"We're acrobats. We'll be performing as soon as we can work up our act."

That didn't seem to impress the clerk, but he could see these were things the Lees couldn't do without. "I think a hundred dollars would be a fair duty, don't you?"

"Isn't that rather high?" asked Henry.

"If you don't pay, you'll have to come back and fill out papers of appeal," said the clerk.

"In that case, I'll go ahead and pay."

When they left, Henry said to John, "I'll bet he pockets some of that money," and John replied with, "I'll bet he's the richest man in town."

Back in the streets the Lees found there was no paving nor planking as in the eastern states, so boxes of plug tobacco were placed in the road for stepping stones. Back in their hackney, they drove on. Margaret pointed to some men helping the ladies cross the street. They put a board down for them to step on. They passed many frame buildings, a few of brick, some tents and shacks here and there of every size and shape, and shanties built of every usable material.

As they drove along they watched the people go by, people of all nationalities, young Americans galloping through the streets decked out in bright serapes, glittering spurs and brilliantly decorated saddles as in the days of old, mounted on horses adorned with saddles of pure silver, playing the role of the native Californians in their days of splendor.

People from every nationality of the world had congregated there. They saw the brightly painted carriages lined with rich silks, drawn by pairs of fine horses; red-shirted miners on foot flinging their pistols with an air of grandeur; the boys laughed as they pointed at the Chinamen with pigtails and loosely fitted outer garments; they saw gamblers in their snowy white shirts with large diamond studs or massive gold breastpins. There were men everywhere, predominantly young, with only a sprinkling of women. All around them was evidence that business was flourishing, bankers were heaping up profits from bold speculation, workers were laboring to support their families, the arts were flourishing as were the lowest of the low vices.

"This might be a place where thieves can go undetected, the gambler can ply his trade and the murderer can flee from justice," said Henry.

"Do you suppose they have any law and order at all here?" wondered Margaret.

"We'll soon see," was Henry's reply.

They pulled up to a hotel where they found lodging. After settling in, they went to one of the local restaurants, and paid outrageous prices for food and services. Henry talked to one man while waiting in line to be served.

"We're all having to share the one room in a hotel down the street. Do you know of any place that would accommodate six people?"

"Not much around here," replied the portly man. "You ought to consider going father out—Sacramento or Stockton."

"I heard it rains so much at both of those places," said Henry.

"It rains here, too. During the winter of '49 so much rain fell the dirt streets were churned into quagmires. They dumped loads of brushwood into them. The mud was so deep horses' legs got entangled in the brush and weren't able to get out. Someone put up a sign, 'This street is impassable.' Another smart one came along and wrote beneath it, 'Not even jackassable'," his stomach shaking as he laughed.

"The streets are in bad shape," said Henry chuckling to himself.

"Kearny Street between Adams Express Office and the store of Simmons Hutchinson and Company a couple years back was paved with bags of coffee beans, sacks of fine Chilean flour and boxes of Virginia tobacco. The people threw everything into the street, cooking stoves, and in one place a piano because there was no other material available. It rained so much one winter rich pockets of gold were exposed by the wash from the rains in the foothills of the Sierra," he added.

"Nice talking to you, sir, perhaps we'll meet again," and the two men shook hands.

Henry and John made the rounds of the theaters and started out looking for more permanent quarters.

The high price of San Francisco caused Henry to inquire of a more suitable place to locate his family to make preparations for a full-size show. From all the people he talked to, he learned that Stockton would make the best location for the circus.

Stockton

Chapter 4

Henry booked passage on a schooner that would take them south to Stockton, a fast-growing community which was much closer to the mines and where land could be had for less money.

As they walked up the gangplank, Henry wished his brothers, Lavater and Hercules, were with him. He wondered what he was doing in this God-forsaken country, beautiful as it was; it was a great risk at best. What did these people know of talent? He had performed in the great theatres of the world; the "Cirque" in Paris, "Astley's" in London, the "Royal Theatre" in Dublin, and the "Bowery" in New York, and now he would be performing before miners and a few townspeople who had never seen a man stand up on the back of a horse as he galloped around the ring, let alone balance two small boys at the same time. He still hoped he had made the right decision, and perhaps later the others would join him.

As the sun was setting, Henry stood on the deck which was crowded with men of every nationality, looking at the rolling hills, tawny and flecked with trees, surrounding the bays of San Francisco, Suisun and San Pablo. The earth was a sea of wild oats suggesting a land of gold.

In the background were the Sierra Nevada with their golden tinted crowns of snow. The river up to the junction of the Sacramento and San Joaquin was broad, swelling out in noble vistas. He watched the large boats as they cut the water moving in the direction of Sacramento through the inland waterway. As their steamer traveled up the river, they passed another going back to San Francisco. Benicia was an impressive sight with many frame houses. Along the wharf many government ships and other small vessels were anchored, a continuation of San Francisco Bay, surely one of the most noble in all the world.

Opposite Benicia was the quaint little town of Martinez, where herds of cattle roamed the hills. They stopped and took on freight.

After entering the river, on his right was the range of Bear Mountains; a part of the coastal range on his left. The land was low, hilly country.

Along the banks large herds of antelope were grazing. The moon and stars were in all their splendor, and the mountains seemed to be a natural adjunct to the loveliness of the heavens which held a wild and graceful beauty. While standing at the rail looking out over the countryside, a man came up, obviously more cultured than the run of the mill, "You a stranger around here?" he asked.

"You might say that," Henry replied. "We hope to settle in Stockton. How about you?"

"I've been in these parts for over a year now. Part of the time I'm in San Francisco, then back to Stockton," he said.

"What is Stockton like?" asked Henry. "I've been told it's a trading center for the miners."

"Yes, the miners come down during the rainy season to get away and stay in more comfortable quarters where the steamships come and go. You'll also see many trains of mules and ox teams bringing people to town from the mines."

"How are the miners doing now?" asked Henry.

"It varies. One man may sink a hole and without much trouble take out one, two, three or four ounces of gold dust daily. A man right next to him may come up with little or no dust at all."

"All a matter of luck," said Henry, as his eyes followed the shoreline. "It's beautiful country here."

"Yes, indeed it is. On the trip I took last spring this entire area was flooded, and a few weeks later the countryside was a sea of flowers. I've been all over, but I've never seen a more handsome assortment of spring flowers than I've seen right here in California. There is no brighter sun, no milder climate, no scene more picturesque than we have right here."

"You could be right," said Henry, and he excused himself saying, "I'd better go look after my family," and went to join the others. "I don't know about spring, but right now it is hotter than blazes," he thought to himself.

He found John scurrying around, looking for shelter. "Aren't these mosquitoes awful?" he asked. "One of the miners was telling me that they're so bad in this area that if your hat blows off, it stays in mid-air buoyed up by the mosquitoes!"

"I can believe it," said Henry. "I packed some blankets in a box over there. Let's bring them out, at least they'll give us some protection."

By the time they reached the mouth of the San Joaquin through the tules and marshlands, the boat had to be worked around the bends, and the sails became useless for the want of wind. The river was narrow and very deep. It was a sluggish stream winding through the marshy grounds of the Tulare Plains. The heat was intolerable, but the blankets Henry brought out made it preferable to letting the mosquitoes "eat them alive." In spite of the protection a few got to them, causing Henry to say to himself, "That man certainly didn't mention the mosquitoes when he was bragging about the state."

After a tedious, painful voyage taking the better part of three days for the want of wind, they arrived at Stockton, a village of tents located a few hundred yards from the river on the plain. There the land was level in all directions with the same hustle and bustle of San Francisco.

As they pulled up to the wharf, another steamer was slowly pulling away on its homeward trip to San Francisco.

They walked across the gangplank, picked up their gear and started walking into town. They caught the feeling of the excitement and the closeness to the mines.

Here they saw the real live miners, men who had actually dug out the shining metal, who had huge buckskin pouches in the pockets of their pantaloons. Men who would know about the chunks of gold weighing one, five or ten pounds, of the pockets in the land where a quarter of a bushel of gold dust had been washed out. Men who dressed in red shirts, Mexican hats, their huge uncombed beards covering half their faces. Colt revolvers attached in the back of their belt, their cuchillo stuck in the leg of their boots, these men were awful objects of curiosity. All the town lay out in front of them. They walked past the El Dorado, a large gambling house on the corner of Levee and Center. They continued on and paused in front of the "Corinthian Theatre."

"It looks nice enough from the outside, Henry," remarked Margaret.

"Let's get settled, and John and I will come back to talk to the manager; maybe we can get a booking."

They paused at the principal section of town, bounded by Weber, Hunter, Main and Center Streets. Merchant's Row was on Weber Street. The buildings on the south side of Main between El Dorado and Hunter were called "Piety Rowe."

Along those streets oak trees had been planted. Everywhere were houses being assembled from sections that had been shipped in. The frames were covered with cloth, tules and lumber, any handy material. Most of the houses were two stories in height. There were also many adobes, but mostly buildings were still tents, and all the business was transacted in those flammable shells. Looking inside one store they saw shelves containing groceries on one side of the room and on the other a tailor mending coarse clothing of a miner or merchant. Another tent was a saloon. Inside one they could see a barrel that served as a counter.

They stopped in front of a hotel. Then Henry said, "Well, looks as though this is where we'll stay until we can build our own house. It may not look too good, but it does have an impressive name—'The New York Hotel'."

"It isn't exactly like the one we stayed in in New York, though," commented Margaret.

After getting settled Henry and John headed back to the Corinthian Theatre to try to get a billing on the show. Henry saw the man he talked to on the boat on the way to Stockton standing on the stage talking to another man. As Henry and John walked down the aisle they looked around. They could see it was a very charming but small playhouse. It had cushioned seats, pinwale boxes, and damask curtains.

When the men were finished with their business, Henry and John walked up onto the stage. "I'm Henry Charles Lee, and this is my partner, John Marshall."

"Well, hello, again. I'm Dr. Thompson. I'm the manager here. Good to see you, again."

"Likewise. If it meets with your approval, we'd like to perform at your theatre."

"Talent's kind of scarce around here. What sort of act do you do?" asked the doctor.

"Tumbling and acrobatic work with my two boys, and John sings and plays the banjo."

"Well, that sounds like something the people around here might enjoy. I'll give you a try. Can you start right away?"

"We can start tonight," said Henry.

"Fine with me," said the doctor. And Henry and John went back to the hotel to tell the others the good news.

It wasn't long before Henry and the two boys were the featured performers and became favorites of the patrons.

When they started they had neither horses nor canvas. They were willing to give entertainment in halls or theatres wherever they could get a booking, and the "Corinthian," though small by their standards, was better than expected in that newly formed town so far from San Francisco. While performing, Henry displayed remarkable skill posturing his two small boys. They could perform athletic feats and gymnastic exercises so skillful, so artistic in design, so graceful in deliverance, they became the hit of the show. This was due in part to their selection of content and the care they took in their presentation, which required much more than just ordinary zeal.

They performed before the miners who came down from the gold fields, tired and many half sick from working long hours in rivers and streams with crude implements panning gold. Those men were thankful for a place to go to relax and enjoy a good show. In appreciation, they threw gold nuggets onto the stage. After the performance was over, Henry collected them and put them away for safekeeping.

The Lees were prospering, so they purchased two lots in town, east of Center Street, facing Market. On one they assembled their house of canvas and used the other for a place to train horses for the show.

While they were performing nightly at the Corinthian, they worked during the day to get up a circus tent, break horses and make wardrobe. Henry and John purchased canvas for the tent, and the men sewed it themselves.

The family continued to practice and perfect their act. The Lees all respected their bodies as bankers guarded their gold. Their bodies were their livelihood, which they bravely gambled on every performance. They practiced long and hard, for new skills had to be developed for new acts and accomplishments. More than once Henry had to get out the whip, cracking it in such a way it kept the boy's attention on their work. Margaret winced, but was fully aware of the necessity. As they improved their act, the need for the whip decreased and the boys began to enjoy the appreciation expressed by the audience and began playing up to it, which in turn improved their skill.

The children wearied, but their father was an unrelenting taskmaster. He knew their very lives depended upon his skill and training. At first Henry balanced the boys as he performed, but in order to follow in their father's footsteps they knew they too had to master the intricate feat of somersaulting on horseback, a feat few people were able to execute. The horse, while trotting, moved slightly up and down as well as forward. The rider had to return to the horse when the animal was in a downward motion, requiring split-second timing. The small size of the ring made it necessary for the rider to twist his body in a curving motion while yet in the air; he had to execute the figure perfectly in order to land in an upright position. When the skill was finally perfected and had become second nature, they were ready to move on to other things.

Henry and his partner John together gathered equipment and personnel for a full-sized show. They set about looking for greater opportunities to increase their patronage, and in so doing looked in the direction of San Francisco. They liked living in Stockton because of its climate and its location, as it had the best access to the southern mines. Their plans called for taking the steamer back to San Francisco, having an engagement there, continuing on to Sacramento, traveling through the northern mines, then through the southern mines, then back to Stockton. Henry and John talked to the doctor at the Corinthian about Sacramento and the opportunity for taking the circus there.

"What sort of theatres do they have in Sacramento?" asked Henry.

"They have the 'Eagle Theatre.' It was the first one to be built in California. They had a rough time of it, though, because the Eagle wasn't much of a building and it was built too close to the river."

"When it rains, doesn't the river overflow its bank?"

"It certainly does. As the miners were watching a show one night, the water was already six inches above the flood level and the men had to stand on benches. One night some of the men got up on the railing around the orchestra. A couple of miners were sitting on the rail. One man threw out his arms and knocked a couple of the others into the water. One of the men took it all right, but the other wanted to fight, so while the show was going on, they went at it."

"When was it built?" asked John.

"It opened in 1849, but it was only open a short time."

"How come it closed?"

"The season began in mid-January. It ended seven days later because the treasurer of the company lost the week's receipts in a game of Monte the night before payday."

"Any others?"

"They have other theatres there—'Lee's Exchange,' the 'National Arena', which was built by Sam Brannan for Joseph Rowe, the circus man."

"Is he still in the area?" asked Henry.

"No, he left, went to Australia."

"How early did he come?"

"Forty-nine; came in on the Tarso in the middle of October. He called his circus the 'Olympic Circus,' performed over on Kearny between California and Sacramento Streets."

"What sort of a show did he have?"

"Bareback riding, lots of acrobatics. He rode his famous horse 'Adonis,' striking classical poses, a beautiful animal all right."

"I'm familiar with the the horse. He is famous," said Henry.

"There's also the 'New Hall,' the 'Pacific' and they did have the 'Tehama,' but I heard it burned down this last summer."

"Perhaps the 'National Arena' will be available," said Henry. "I'll look into that."

The Lee's troupe was growing. George Peoples, a perfectly bald man, a versatile performer, joined the group. He could play the parts of clown, equestrian, tumbler, vaulter, Greek warrior and Indian, all with equal ability.

Then along came a miner by the name of Frenchy Rochette, a wiry fellow with dark hair and eyes. He came down from one of the mining towns, Sonora, saw the show and looked up Henry.

"What about hiring me on? I do almost anything. I ride, lift weights." He handed Henry a newspaper clipping which read: "Rochette was bubbling, possessed a sparkling personality as a wit. The bards from Shakespeare down were on his tongue, and his powers of appropriation and assimilation were immense. The people love Rochette, the wit of the age."

Henry read it and handed it back, saying, "If you're willing to work, stick around. I'm willing to work with you. Why did you give up mining?"

"Too many problems and I didn't do well. I'll be glad to get back to what I know."

"You're welcome here. Let's get to work. When the weather permits, we'll pitch our tent at the head of the Stockton Channel on El Dorado Street. We're featuring trick riding and clowning by George Peoples. I'll be tumbling with my boys, Francis and Eugene, and we'll add you to the bill."

Henry planned to have a show ready to perform in San Francisco by December, presenting "The Wild Horse of Tartary," starring George Peoples. Henry was able to purchase a very fine horse and began the arduous task of training him.

The story they were enacting was one written by Lord Byron. It was about a young Polish page in the retinue of a count who loved his master's wife unwisely and much too well, and was punished by being tied to an untrained horse and sent off across the steppes. Pursued by wolves, wild horses and vultures, the horse raced on until it fell exhausted. Mazeppa was rescued by a Cossack and was greeted on awakening by the Cossack's beautiful daughter. While Mazeppa lay unconscious, Abder, Khan of Tartary, arrived and recognized him as his long lost son. Mazeppa was then crowned King of Tartary, went into Poland with the cavalry, conquered the Count and married the lady. And that was the end of the story.

Henry started training his newly acquired horse. This was the ultimate of all the circus productions involving a horse and rider, and had been a classic at "Astley's" in London. Henry spent hours working on the revolving steps that would give the audience the impression the horse was going uphill, and it would appear and re-appear in the distance until finally the horse and rider were lost to view. The skill which Henry used while working was sheer art, for few men could ever achieve such a high degree of performance. With patience, love and determination, he was able to get his horse to walk up the steps of the wheel with the bodily motions of dire struggle. And what a stroke of luck. Charles Thorne, a good-looking man, though a bit high-strung, a world famous performer formerly engaged by the celebrated Batty as a cannon ball performer, was available. He had performed at London, at Hyde Park, Birmingham, Liverpool and Manchester. Henry hadn't seen him since he left Welch's company for California. Henry thought that with Thorne in the leading role, they would be able to present the famous story and give the people of San Francisco something they would never forget.

Thorne was to be strapped on his horse's back for fifteen agonizing minutes during each performance. One strap was to be placed around his waist, one around each ankle, each wrist and upper arms. In front of the steps they planned to place scenery to give the audience the impression the horse was going up the steep steppes of Russia.

After a lot of work and practice, the show was ready. Now that all the equipment had been constructed, the horses trained, the actors well versed in their parts and the costumes made, Lee made ready to return to San Francisco by early December, when they concluded their engagement at the "Corinthian."

On their closing night, Henry talked to the proprietor, "Where do you plan to go from here?" asked Dr. Thompson.

"We're going to San Francisco, put on 'Mazeppa and the Wild Horse of Tartary,' then on to Sacramento."

"I'm leaving the 'Corinthian' to take a position as Manager of the 'American Theatre'. It hasn't been completed, but will be soon. Why don't you look me up? Perhaps we can work out something. It will be by far and above the best theatre in town."

"We'll surely do that," said Henry.

"I wish you luck and hope our paths will cross again," said the doctor.

"In San Francisco, no doubt," and with that they took their leave.

Henry was anxious to get back to San Francisco.

Wild Horse of Tartary

Chapter 5

Henry drove through the downtown streets of San Francisco, the ring horses called upon to pull the wagon laden with heavy props. As they moved along at a slow pace, they could hear the noises of the gambling establishments, the shouts, the laughter and the sounds of the fiddle and flute.

They passed the theatre, the third "Jenny Lind," then came upon the "American Theatre" on the corner of Halleck and Sansome Streets, a very pretentious structure of wood and brick. They paused only long enough to take a look and again continued on.

They found a hotel where they could stay. Just one room was all they could get, and they shared the bath with the other boarders. While Margaret freshened up with her "spit bath," Henry and Frenchy went down to the local "shaving saloon" to get their bath as well as a shave and shampoo. While they were getting the works, they sat in velvet chairs and admired the marble top washstand with its fancy gilt work.

Back at the hotel they found their food was better than that in Stockton, for they had the choice of bear, elk, deer, turtle, duck or fish, and though not good by their standards their quarters were acceptable.

They went back to the "American Theatre," walked through the entrance that had to be effected by a footpath on wooden horses because there was evidence that at high tide the water had been rising up several inches along the entire length of the passageway.

Henry and John were happy to renew their acquaintance with their friend, Dr. Thompson, and anxious to make arrangements for an opening.

Just inside the door was a bar. Dr. Thompson, standing near it, greeted them.

"This is all very beautiful. I'm very much impressed! Is this the usual?" asked Henry pointing out the bar.

"It is here," said the doctor. "We all have them, even the 'Adelphi,' and they really cater to a sophisticated crowd."

"Interesting," said Henry.

"Let me show you around," he said as they walked up on to the stage. "It has two balconies and a gallery, a dress circle, orchestra seats and several stage boxes and a seating capacity of two thousand."

"Very lovely," said Henry.

"Did you see the problem we have out front?"

"Yes, we did."

"I hate to say this, but the builders weren't too sharp. They built on an insecure foundation of sand and mud so, on opening night this entire building sank an inch or two. Just think only two years ago all San Francisco was nothing but a tent city and everything here was made of canvas and all of this had to be shipped in."

The interior of the theatre was painted in white and gold and decorated with paintings and laden with gilt work. The boxes had red velvet curtains, and the seat cushions and backs were upholstered in red plush. Handsome lamps adorned the interior, and the carpets were thick and soft. From the dome was suspended a beautifully ornamented ceiling with a brilliant revolving sun as its centerpiece. The gilded dome shed its rays over painted clouds and transmitted a radiance to the scene below. At the sides of the proscenium near the top were two spreadeagles with chandeliers hanging from their beaks. The drop curtain and scenery were magnificent to behold.

After making arrangements for their first performance, Henry and John went to the local slaughterhouse to obtain tanbark for the ring. Here they found a good quantity of ground oak hemlock and chestnut all ground up in a huge pile just for the taking. They loaded their wagon with the moist pulp and headed back to the "American."

When they arrived, they spread a tarpaulin over the stage, spread the tanbark, filled a couple of pails with water and sprinkled in some straw. At the front of the stage they placed an octagonal frame of boards facing the audience. As they were doing this, Dr. Thompson walked back in.

"What are you doing that for?" he asked.

"We build that just in case one of the horses kicks some of the tanbark into the open flame of the footlights. It has happened from time to time."

"You seem to know what you're doing, all right," he said. "It sure smells, though."

"I've been doing it a good many years," said Henry. "Say, John, open those windows in the back to air the place out."

"It'll be better by show time," said Henry, and he and John hurried out to join the others.

That night the people stumbled into the theatre by the glimmer of lanterns, walking in from the muddy streets. Most of the audience was made up of men sitting shivering, as they waited for the performance to begin.

As great as the performers were, it might be said the horses were the principal actors. On a huge stage and backed by mechanically-adjusted platforms that rose one above the other, companies of horses fought, 'died', plunged into cataracts, leaped battlements and scaled mountains. They were made ready for their parts in 'dressing rooms' under the orchestra, where a rank stable smell rose up to contaminate the pit. The props were put in place; then all was ready.

As the men in the audience sat there watching the show, they were very much on edge. Whenever they heard the sound of the fire bell, they jumped up, and ran out into the street to see what was going on. But, as quickly as they left, they returned to their seats and again watched the performance until they heard another bell, which sometimes was only a matter of minutes.

The reviewer for the *Herald* was well-satisfied with the show. He declared that, "The horse and rider did their rather arduous part to great perfection," in referring to the production of the "Wild Horse of Tartary."

One night after the show, Henry, John, Frenchy and George walked over to the to the "El Dorado," the town's leading gambling establishment, to see what was going on. Inside it was very crowded. Many of its mostly male patrons, gave the appearance of celebrating a vast and noisy masquerade ball, all decked out in exotic costumes.

For those who went to the saloon, it was a place to get out of the rain and away from the dust. It was open around the clock, including Sundays. The saloon had thick rugs on the floor, oil paintings on the wall, a mahogany bar, free lunch counter, dining room, wine cellar and brass band.

Henry remarked, "For every man who makes a fortune here, there are many more who won't."

"The same goes for the digging of gold as well," added Frenchy.

Many of the gamblers were Mexican. They sat there buried in thought. Some were playing monte, some vingtetun and some langsquenet. Not one lifted his head when the men walked in. They never spoke without a tremor, and were as cold and impassive as stone.

"I'm sure many a man has returned home empty-handed, saying he had been humbugged about the gold when in reality he bum-rigged himself about the work," remarked Henry.

On the other side of the room the other gamblers, the Americans, were just the opposite. They were bawling or cursing at the faro or roulette games, carrying their revolvers with one hand poised ready to use them.

There was lots of drinking going on, but some men were just sitting at the bar reading the newspaper. Then all of a sudden amidst the din and turmoil of the crowd and the noisy music, a pistol went off, gamblers flew in all directions. Some got behind a post, some under the tables. Henry and the others were not in the crossfire, so they merely looked on. Then a couple of men walked over, picked up the wounded man and carried him out. The others went on gambling. The owner, meticulously dressed, a diamond stud in his cravat, just watched, said nothing. He walked over by one of the gaming tables.

John observing him said, "He may be on the small side, but he looks tough enough to handle the job."

"These gamblers are a special breed, able to speculate and willing to take advantage of men's passions," replied Henry.

Then he came over to where they were sitting. It was Henry who spoke up. "I'm Henry Charles Lee. This is Frenchy Rochette and George Peoples, and my partner, John Marshall. We're putting on the performance at the 'American' down the street of 'The Wild Horse of Tartary'."

"I've heard of it," said the owner. "People coming in here have been very much impressed. Belle and I'll try to catch it one of these nights."

"Please do, and be my guest. I'm sorry, I didn't catch your name."

"I'm Charles Cora."

"I'll leave your name at the box office."

"Thank you very much."

"Quite a place you have here," said Henry.

"Yes, it is now. Up until May we were housed in a tent. We wanted to tear the old tent down, but we were doing such a rip roaring business we would have lost too much money if we closed down just to build another place. Of course the fire on May 3rd decided that for us."

"I heard about that fire," said Henry. "I understand most of San Francisco went up in that."

"Yes. It happened at eleven o'clock the evening of October 27th."

"The one last month you mean," added John.

"That's right. The warning shout was heard in Portsmouth Square and was immediately repeated all over town. People ran out of doors and ran toward the danger point."

"Did you find out how it started?"

"I understand the fire began in a paint shop on Clay Street here at the Plaza. The flames spread rapidly through the oil and other flammable materials, gained the upper floor and caught the adjoining houses. A heavy mass of smoke rolled toward the bay, then we knew the city was in trouble. The wind was unusually high that night, and the flames spread in a broad sheet over the town. Even the brick buildings crumbled in the heat, many lives were lost and the damage of the property destroyed was unbelievable."

"Do they know who started it?" asked George.

"The Sidney Ducks were given credit because they were the ones who had something to gain. They were seen everywhere looting everything in sight. The merchants were the hardest hit. Some of them lost their entire capital that was tied up in inventory, and their warehouses were wiped out. After that the Vigilante Committee got going."

"Are they the leaders of the community?" asked Henry.

"I'd guess you'd say so. Sam Brannan is president, Johnathan

Stevenson, Colonel of the First New York Volunteers is on it: a couple of the members are ship captains, a couple of auctioneers, one is a clerk, another a bookkeeper and one man is a lumber dealer."

"Did the committee do anything?" asked George.

"After it was over and all the debris was cleaned up, they dangled a couple of Ducks at the end of a rope."

"By the time we'd arrived the committee had already renounced its power," said Henry.

"They're only sleeping, and can be awakened at the sound of the fire bell," said Cora.

"I'm sure you're right," said Henry. "Who are these Hounds I keep hearing about?" asked Henry.

"They're some of the men that came to California under Johnathan Stevenson. They were the first to head for the hills. They came out West to do guard duty while the territory was being occupied. Many of the men were fine upstanding members of their community back home, but they had a bunch of 'bad apples' in that barrel. They called themselves the 'Hounds,' and the vigilantes kept an eye on them because they were a public nuisance."

"They sound bad, all right," said Henry.

"They paraded up and down the streets in motley uniforms and helped themselves to whatever took their fancy. They bullied the merchants by day and shot up and looted the foreign settlements at night. Some had come from the streets of New York, city thugs, bullies, street fighters. 'Either sign up or go to jail,' they were told, so they signed up."

"Not much of a choice," added John.

"While they were in the hills some caused trouble, some were chased out of camp, and often escorted out, and many drifted back to San Francisco because the work of digging for gold was too much for them."

"I know that kind. In Sonora we escorted a few out of town ourselves," said Frenchy.

"They set up their headquarters at Commercial and Kearny streets naming it Tammany Hall. Their leader was a man by the name of Roberts. One night they converged on Telegraph Hill, a miserable place, filthy and strewn with garbage, known as 'Little Chile' after the Chileans and Peruvians, the ones who caused so much trouble on the steamer 'California' coming north. That night in the middle of the summer of '49 these Hounds went up there and burned tents, beat some of the men to a pulp, tore the clothes off the women, ran them down the street shooting at their feet. They outraged one woman and her daughter, they killed the woman, but the daughter got a Bowie knife away from one of the Hounds and was able to escape. But this time they had gone too far."

"I would think so," said John.

"This was too much for Sam Brannan. He mounted a barrel on the corner of Montgomery and Clay and began haranguing the people passing by. His eyes were flashing, he was half-choked by emotion. Then someone yelled, 'Let's go to the Plaza,' so with Sam in the lead, they headed here. He climbed up on top of the alcalde's box using its roof as a pulpit. Baring his thick chest, Sam's booming voice was heard above the noisy crowd, 'Kill me you Hounds, fire on me if you dare!' and as you can imagine, all San Francisco rallied 'round him."

"Quite a man," said Henry.

"They rounded up as many Hounds as they could, put them in the hold of that old abandoned ship they used as a prison, the 'Euphemia.' Later they put them all on trial."

"Did they hang any of them?"

"No. Nothing really came of it. Some wanted them hanged, others wanted them chased out of town and others preferred they get a big swift kick in the behind, but even though nothing was done, they kept relatively quiet after that."

"Something good came of it then," said Frenchy.

"It's good to know these things," said Henry. "A bunch of them could come into the theatre some night and stir up a bit of trouble. We'll keep our eyes and ears open. It was good to meet you, Mr. Cora, but I think we'd better head back to the hotel."

As they walked out the door, George said to Henry, "He's quite a man. I like him."

One afternoon after the matinee, as they were walking back to the hotel they passed some women on the street, and Henry said, "It isn't hard to tell the upstanding ladies from the other kind by the paint on their faces, or the lack of it."

Then Frenchy, the worldly one, had to put in his two cents worth. "Most of the women here are prostitutes and of all nationalities. The Chinese have their slaves who operate from the cribs, they're considered the lowest ones in town. The French have their 'soiled doves.' Many are Mexican, their 'Mal Vidas' coming from Sonora in Mexico."

"But from what I've heard, when they have the money, they all buy their clothes from the same French shop on Commercial Street," said Margaret.

"I can believe it," said Henry. "They make enough money."

"The very sight of a woman walking down the street here causes quite a stir," added Frenchy. "The men empty the saloons in order to take a better look."

As they walked along, Margaret took her husband's arm; men stopped to stare at her. "Don't let all this attention turn your head," said Henry. "Remember, here even an old battle-axe will bring the men out."

Then one man put a plank down to let Margaret cross the street, another offered to carry her, but Henry declined and picked her up himself.

"Why, Henry? Why now? I can manage by myself. I'm an equestrienne, remember? Why don't you let me cross the street?"

"I'm not concerned whether or not you can manage, but I don't want this expensive dress to get soiled. Maybe it came from that French shop on Commercial."

"You certainly want me to dress as well as the prostitutes, don't you?"

"Yes, but I don't want you to be mistaken for one."

"Oh, Henry!"

Farther on down the street they walked past a Concord Coach that was parked nearby. Henry and Frenchy went over to take a good look at it. "Oh, this is a work of art! Look at that iron, and the body is solid oak. Oh, this is beautiful. The men who work on these are craftsmen, all right."

"How fast will it go, Henry?" asked Frenchy.

"Oh, ten, twelve, maybe even fifteen miles an hour. There're a lot in the East, but I never dreamed I would ever see one out here. When we can afford ours, this is what I'll have my eye on."

The announcement in the *Star* late in 1851 that "Mazeppa of the Wild Horse of Tartary" was being presented at the American Theatre aroused the liveliest anticipation. The newspaper account stated that "The grand ascension on the flying steed created a stunning sensation," and it was said of the horse, ". . . which for a few superlative exciting moments very prominently and actively occupied the center of the stage was under the training of the expert hand of Mr. Henry Charles Lee, a much esteemed circus man."

Elisa Biscaccianti, the opera star had already been booked for the "American," so Lee and Marshall closed their show on schedule. . . for they were ready to move on to another town, another place.

CIRCO NACIONAL DE LEE

Y HIPPODROME.

Sabado

Y

DOMINGO,

ENERO 29 y 30.

Tendran lugar en las dias SABADO y DOMINGO por la noche, Fechas 29 y 30 de Enero,

ALGUNAS GRANDES EXHIBICIONES DE EQUITACION.

EL DOMINGO

EN LA NOCHE,

ENERO 30,

La Funcion sera dada por

Beneficio

BENEFICIO de la Sra. LEE.

BENEFICIO de la *Sra. LEE*

de la Sra. LEE

En cuya ocasion, aparacera en una manera graciosa y admirables ACTOS DE EQUITACION.

LA SENORA H. C. LEE aparacera tambien en la CUERDA, y representara una gran variedad de nuevas y sorprendentes suertes.

Miss ANNEREAU aparacera en su celebre acto de "EL MENAGE."

DON JORGE RYLAND aparacera por la primera vez en California, representando un acto nuevo, de equitacion, titulado.

Don Juan Montado a Caballo,

Tomado del celebre poema por Lord Byron.

Para la primera vez representara la GIMNASTICA en el columpio.

GRAN DEMOSTRACION DE ABILIDAD por toda la Compania, a lo cual asistiran los Senores MANSO.

Primera Noche de TRES SIMPLETONS, o TRES TONTOS, representada por toda la Compania.

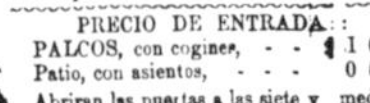

PRECIO DE ENTRADA:

PALCOS, con cogines, - - -	$1 00
Patio, con asientos, - - -	0 50

Abriran las puertas a las siete y media, y empezaran la funcion a las ocho de la noche.

Imprenta de la Estrella.

Circo Poster
Courtesy, Huntington Library

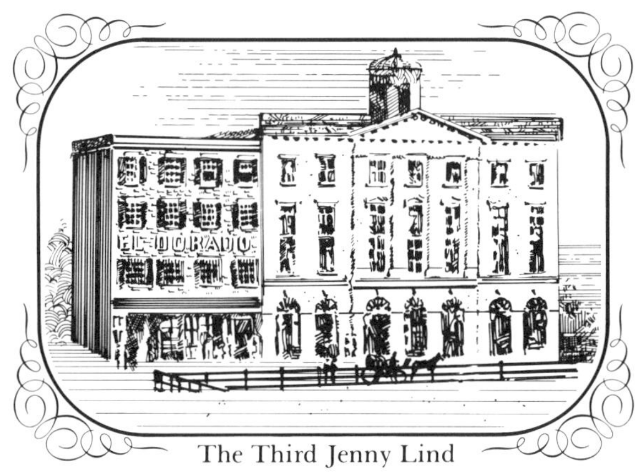

The Third Jenny Lind

Chapter 6

The circus left the foggy bay of San Francisco for Los Angeles in January of 1852, amid the cheering of passengers and the good wishes of those they left behind.

Their steamer stopped at the small coastal town of Monterey with its whitewashed buildings and red tiled roofs scattered over the countryside. Monterey had been a focal point of intrigue and government in Mexican-Californian history. They exchanged mail and dispatched passengers.

After a short stopover the circus continued on down the coast. As they approached Los Angeles, their sidewheeler's paddles churned the water into a frothing foam as it moved slowly into the harbor. On board they heard the roar of the signal-gun making the announcement to travelers and friends alike that the voyage had been a safe one.

They unloaded their gear, wagons and animals on shore and headed for town, traveling over twenty-seven miles of flat open country, creating quite a spectacle as they passed the lone Dominguez adobe along the way. As they entered town, they passed rows of adobes, saloons and gambling houses very much like the mining camps in the north. Moving slowly along, they heard loud strains of harp and guitar emanating from the vicinity of Calle de Los Negroes. The townspeople gathered in the muddy streets agog at all there was to see, for they had never seen a circus in their town before.

The wagons pulled up to a saloon. Henry got down and walked into a gambling hall to inquire about the location of the newspaper office. Inside, both men and women were looking after the tables, dealing monte or faro, as well as operating other contrivances. Those in charge of banks wore pistols and knives, ready to settle disputes on the spot. It was as tough a neighborhood as Henry had ever seen.

After getting directions, Henry got back up on the lead wagon, and they continued on, looking for a place to set up the tent. Henry had problems enough without the possibility of a shooting or a stabbing, so he decided to put up his tent as far from town as possible, without going too far out.

After Henry got the work started at the lot, he went to put an ad in the newspaper *La Estrella de Los Angeles* located in the lower room of a small wooden frame house on Los Angeles Street, behind the Bella Union Hotel.

"Good day," said Henry. "I'm interested in putting an ad in your paper."

The clerk, a small man with thinning hair, responded, "Before I can quote you a price, I need to know if it will be in English or Spanish."

"Let's do it in Spanish. Looks like most of the people here speak it."

"Yes. There are over three thousand people living here now, most of them are Spanish, some Mexicans, and a few Indians. If it's all right with you, I'll set it up and you can come back and we'll talk about the price." "Very well. I'll do that," said Henry, as he went out the door.

On January 29th, in a small tent within easy walking distance of the Plaza, the Lee Circus and Hippodrome made all the necessary preparations for their first show. Over the entrance of the tent, the men tacked up their banner with their title, "Circo National de Lee y Hippodrome." They charged one dollar for a cushioned seat in the circle and fifty cents for those sitting in the pit. A grand change of program was planned to present for Saturday and Sunday nights with brilliant equestrian scenes and gymnastics. Included in the show was a grand cotillion, with Mascaroni playing the role of the Italian banditti.

The next day, while Henry and John Marshall were walking back to the circus grounds, after having had a bite to eat at the Bella Union, they stopped to watch a group of proud caballeros riding into town, their spurs jingling and their silver ornaments flashing in the sunlight. The beautifully groomed horses bobbing their heads and prancing, were as aware as their riders they held center stage. The entire scene was enough to cause the bystanders to applaud as they passed by.

A man standing next to them said, "These Californians are the best riders in the world."

Henry turned to John, "If those men plan to attend our show tonight, we'll certainly have to be on our toes." John nodded his head in agreement, as they continued on to the circus lot.

Their program began with a grand entry, composed of trumpeters, a band, beautifully costumed performers, both mounted and marching with various typed wheeled vehicles. In the audience were some of the same riders Henry had seen on the street that day, and he was most anxious to please them.

As Henry stood, balancing on the horse circling the ring he was aware of feeling a special sense of satisfaction, as he charged full speed around the ring, knowing the Caballeros of the afternoon were in the audience. They would have an understanding born of their own experience about the skill and daring he was able to display.

After the performance Henry walked out of the tent with pride, knowing the supremacy of the riding skill of the Caballeros had been challenged and met with the same high quality of style and great performing feats.

The circus returned to San Francisco. Henry and John went in search of a booking. They went to the third "Jenny Lind" located in the Plaza, over a saloon and gambling house.

They met the owner as was their custom, a man by the name of Tom Maguire. He was a quiet man, who wore his hat tilted to one side and smoked a long cigar at the opposite angle. He had penetrating eyes, a ruddy complexion, a heavy mustache, and a full head of black hair. He was faultlessly attired, adorned with a big diamond in his cravat and a large solitaire on his finger. Across his front he wore a massive gold watch chain and charm.

"I have a show I'd like to present," said Henry.

"What is it?" asked Maguire.

" 'The Wild Horse of Tartary,' based on a story written by Lord Byron. We have an excellent equestrian taking the lead role."

"Who is he?"

"His name is Thorne, Charles Thorne. Ever heard of him?"

"Yes, I've heard of him. The show's that good, huh? Is that the one that was written up in the paper?"

"Yes, it was," said Henry.

"I hope it stands up to its rave notices. I may not be able to read or write, but I can make or break you show people, and don't you forget it. If you perform in my theatre, you'd better be here and do all you say you can do or you won't perform in any other theatre in this town."

"You can depend on us," said Henry.

"Then when can you start?"

"As soon as the theatre's available."

"I'll think about it and let you know the date as soon as possible."

"We'll be ready to perform," said Henry. "We will be here, and the show will make you proud. Good-bye, sir." The men shook hands and parted.

On the way back to the hotel Henry asked John, "What did you think of the theatre?"

"It's lavish all right but it lacks the warmth of the 'American.'"

"That bar out front was a thing of beauty though," added Henry. Maguire did hire them on, and they were lucky to get that booking because San Francisco was teeming with entertainers. They had come from all over, from the showboats of the Mississippi, from the small theatres of Mobile, New Orleans, Galveston, Nashville, Cincinnati, from New York City. Actors, opera singers, musicians and circus performers—they were all there. They had come from all parts of the world—from Australia, China, Germany, England and France. They came in by steamer, overland, just any way they could; it was a melting pot and exciting place to be, and the Lees had no intention of leaving.

The National Circus, as they were now called, finished their engagement at the "Jenny Lind," and started making plans to move on to Sacramento. They did not remain confined to the indoor stage. Sometimes their show would last but a few days and they would move on. Along with George and Frenchy, they kept on improving the company and expanding their scope. They engaged Alonzo Hubbell who handled three cannon balls so capably he was hailed "the strongest man in the world." Brewer and Moore were their bar performers.

They set up their canvas tent Thursday evening, March 25th for four nights on Pine, between Montgomery and Sansome Streets.

Their tent was held up by boards made simply so it could be set up and taken down quickly. It had one ring with pit and tiers of boxes around the outside.

They featured a troup of equestrians as well as putting their trained horses and ponies through their paces. Again the Lee family were the gymnasts.

The circus possessed an enormous pull for the miner, even in his wildest days, and whenever he went down to San Francisco, he saw the shows.

The circus was doing well. Henry wanted to expand, so he and John went in search of a ranch for their winter quarters, one that was was large enough to raise feed for the animals and a training area. They went to see Charles Weber, the founder of Stockton, to inquire about land to buy.

"I have a ranch about five miles out of town on the Mariposa Road," he said. "It has a house on it and some animals."

"That sounds good to me," said Henry. "When can we take a look?"

"Anytime you say." So they agreed to meet at the appointed time. John and Henry liked the ranch and bought it. On August 16th, Henry and John took possession of their newly acquired land, containing one hundred sixty acres. Besides the house and household furniture and outhouse, it had a cow, a calf, and twenty-seven fowl.

At Stockton, Henry's every waking moment from dawn to dark was spent in acquiring, keeping, training and breeding the best stock money could buy, and he was masterful in the selection of horses. His "leisure" time was spent making arrangements for the arena.

Henry and John now had Frenchy Rochette, George Peoples and the Annereaus working for them. Alonzo Hubbell, Brewer and Moore had been hired on for only the one engagement on Pine Street in San Francisco and Charles Thorne had left to join another group. George Ryland returned East.

At the ranch, an arena was constructed and everyone was scheduled for workouts. Henry worked with the boys on the revolving globe and on their tumbling act. Margaret, Mrs. Annerreau and her daughter were busy working on their equestrian act. Mrs. Annereau, the star of the show, was a very striking woman with beautiful long black hair. Her petite daughter,

Jeanette, possessed the skill and agility of a ballerina.

After all the costumes had been made, the acts ready, Henry and John made plans to move out.

August 20th they were again back in San Francisco. This time they pitched their tent at Montgomery and Jackson Streets. They featured "St. George and the Dragon" with Henry, Margaret, and their sons Eugene and Francis. George Peoples was the rider. Their little one, Theodore, only two years old, dressed in his pink tights, was held by his father as he rode bareback around the ring.

It was a very weary circus troop that traveled over the rugged country and poorly kept dirt roads to Contra Costa. But hungry, stiff and miserable as they were, they made an impressive entrance. As was their custom, they paused outside of town, watered the horses, shook the dust off their clothing, rested a bit, then continued on into the small town of Oakland, made up of a few wooden houses, many tents and a hotel. Their gaily colored wagons were spotlessly clean, their many caparisoned horses were performing at their very best. Henry wanted those who saw them to see them as a vision of beauty and grace.

They pulled up to the door of Colonel Burrel's hotel. Henry jumped down off the wagon, entered the hotel lobby and walked up to the desk. It was Colonel Burrel, a small man, who greeted him with, "I want to welcome you personally. You're the very first ones to take rooms in our hotel." And he walked over to shake Henry's hand.

The Colonel's son and daughter were peering out from behind a door, watching the distinguished-looking guest, talking to their father.

"That's quite an honor," the man said. "I'm Henry Charles Lee. I'll need several rooms and meals as well. The ladies are tired, so would you mind showing them to their rooms?"

"Glad to oblige."

Three ladies waited just inside the door. Then Margaret, holding the hand of a small boy and Jeannette Annereau, walked up the stairs with a fairy-like grace, followed by her mother. Olive, the Colonel's daughter, followed them and peeked in to watch them as they unpacked their costumes. It was Jeannette who invited her in.

"What is your name?"

"Olive," she said. "I'm Jeannette. This is Mrs. Lee, and this is my mother. Would you like to stay a while?"

"Oh, yes, I would. It's very kind of you to invite me in." The ladies were sitting on the edge of the bed, taking turns rubbing each other with liniment. After getting up courage to speak, Olive asked, "What's that for?"

"That's to take the stiffness out," said Jeannette, all watching Mrs. Annereau as she rubbed and massaged Margaret.

"We must go now so Mrs. Lee can get some rest. Are you coming to see the performance, Olive?"

"I don't know. I don't think my father will let me. He says the boys can go, but it isn't ladylike for girls to attend."

"Oh, dear!" said Jeannette. "I'm so sorry you'll miss it."

"Are you going to perform?"

"Yes," said Jeannette motioning to the others, "we're all equestriennes."

Outside on the adjoining lot there was work to be done, and Olive's brother was there taking everything in. The clown, the most woebegone specimen of mankind alive, was sitting around moping. The rubber man, a perfectly bald man, went around kidding everyone, making trouble.

With just the help of two men, Henry and John did the work of twenty. They were everywhere. They put in the posts, attached the canvas on the outside and put the seats in place. On the outside of the ring they put up stands with candles on bars. They set up the quadrilateral framework which held a great many candles. And all this time the Colonel's son stayed around the tent taking everything in. Handbills had been distributed in the outlying towns of San Pablo, Hayward, San Antonio, Alameda, San Leandro and Martinez, so Henry and John were confident of a full house no matter how small the town. Outside the tent they put up the posters, which were just a little short of being marvelous. Henry and John then fed the horses, got a bite to eat themselves and finally got some rest.

After dark Olive quietly left her room, walked next door to the circus tent and found a small tear in the canvas to peek through. Inside were her father and brother. Olive watched the people as they filled the arena. The band began to play, and as if by a miracle, all the players began to revive. They were all smiles and litheness, ready and waiting to take their turn to perform.

The candles in the frame were lit, and the frame was hoisted to the top of the tent. Olive watched that operation as if it were some kind of magic. The candles around the ring were lit in turn. Outside the torches were burning brightly.

The band struck up the fanfare, and the glittering cavalcade came prancing into the ring. The cheap finery became cloth of gold, and the tarnished spangles were gleaming gems of purest ray, reflecting back to the twinkling candlelights, making it a fairy spectacle.

The beautiful bareback riders jumped through hoops and over banners. The Little Equestrienne was especially graceful and absolutely fearless riding bareback around the ring. The drunken sailor and the countryman crept over the railings to ride the balky horse. The rubberman writhed and twisted himself into a doughnut. The whole audience was held in awe and breathless fear by the wonderful feats they performed.

Great was Olive's adoration for the one small acrobat, the little boy who had held his mother's hand in the lobby. She thought him a cross between the Angel Gabriel and a picture of a beautiful little cupid with his pink tights and spangled trunks, the pure gold band around his head, and golden sandals on his feet. He was being held in various positions by his handsome father as he rode around the ring.

Then, suddenly, it was over. Olive watched as the people left that great arena where wonderful feats had been performed. Outside, guided by the torches, the people got back into their wagons and headed for home.

The Embarcadero

Chapter 7

John Marshall left for the East to purchase material for costumes and equipment. Henry booked passage on a steamer for Sacramento, a majestic riverboat of ornate design. The cabins had plate glass mirrors, marble top tables, red plush upholstery and gleaming brass lamps. The captain plied the Sacramento River and jockied for position on the graceful bends past drooping willows amid shouts of laughter. They listened to the lively music, ate good food, and slept on beds with clean linen. The decks were crowded with men, and a sprinkling of women, all in good spirits with a feeling of excitement and adventure. It was dusk when they neared Sacramento City. They were welcomed by flares and torches along the bank.

As the boat moved along the levee, they saw ships of all sizes and shapes tied to the wharf at the Embarcadero.

"What's this for?" asked Francis referring to the levee.

"This was built to hold the flood waters back during the spring. If they didn't have it, the town would flood."

A surly sort of man standing nearby said, "It does help, but sometimes it rains so much part of it gives way and the town floods anyway."

"Well at any rate, Francis, I'm sure it helps a lot."

The man pointed out Sutter's Fort, now falling into decay and all but abandoned; the gates were gone and the roof was caving in. It was all there to see as they moved toward the city.

As the circus performers walked down the gangplank, before them all Sacramento was decked out with its gaily painted houses, its wide streets and trees giving the town a cheerful appearance. The American flag was in evidence everywhere, as were signboards of every size and description advertising various wares—hay and grain, butter or other products for sale. Every other house was a boarding house or hotel.

All around traffic was heavy, teams of wagons stirring the dirt into a red powder, the wind making the town very dusty.

"I'll bet the streets are very muddy during the winter," said Margaret.

"I'm sure you're right," replied Henry. "I want to locate as near the river as possible to load and unload easily to return to San Francisco. Let's find a hotel because we need to organize this gear and make preparations for our first performance."

Henry, Margaret and the boys went in search of lodging while the other men went in search of a lot to set up the tent. They were able to find rooms at a French hotel, the "Orleans" between J and K Streets on Front. At the desk, Henry remarked to the clerk, "Nice place you have here."

"We think so. We brought this building all the way from New Orleans, around the Horn, all pre-cut and ready to be put together." Henry, sensing the man could talk for hours, tipped his hat, picked up his bag, and they went up to their rooms.

The next morning after breakfast Henry and Frenchy set out, "This town is laid out well," said Henry. "The streets running along the levee are the letters of the alphabet, and when you go back from the water toward the higher land they're numbered 1, 2, 3 on up."

They walked down to the wharf past the hotel on Front Street. There the coaches were lined up and crowded together, drawn up three abreast on a narrow street, some only with an awning for a covering.

Henry saluted one of the drivers, a big man with a heavy head of hair, "Quite a business you have here."

"Yes it is, sometimes these roads are crowded with stages coming back to town from the mountains. Some carry anywhere from twenty-five to a hundred thousand dollars' worth of gold," the big, husky-voiced man answered.

"What are the roads like up in the Gold Country?" asked Henry.

"Mainly trails, very narrow; you have to have pretty good weather to make it."

"I heard it gets pretty bad here in town, too."

"That's when the real problem comes. When it rains the roads are bad; boats have to be used to go through the main streets, even some small steamboats. I heard one time a man returned home and found a cow in his drawing room. He tied her to a banister, and the flood took her upstairs during the night."

"At least she could take care of herself. That's something," replied Henry. "But we best be going. Good day to you, sir."

Henry and Frenchy continued on, stopping only long enough to admire the beautifully painted Concord coaches, handsome in design. Alongside them were other coaches crowded together. The animals were pawing and snorting, men were trying to quiet them down, drivers calling out the names of the towns they were bound for. "This way, sir, Auburn. This stage goes to Sonora."

They paused to look at Lewis Keseberg's restaurant on K Street. "Oh, I've heard of this place," said Frenchy. "This man Keseberg was the last one to survive lakeside where the Donners themselves had suffered. He claimed he had never murdered any human being, but he did boast of eating meat from every corpse he could get his hands on."

"I suppose some people like to go in just to take a look at him; I guess that's human nature," added Henry.

On the way to the circus grounds, Henry remarked, "Say, Frenchy, I think we need some rope. Before we start working, why don't we go back to that hardware store on the corner of 3rd and K Streets and get some?"

"That's a good idea."

When they got to the store, they walked in. The clerk behind the counter was a big man. "Are you fellows miners?" he asked.

"Oh, no," said Henry. "We're circusmen. Were putting up our tent on the vacant lot on down the street."

"Well, you're smart," said the proprietor. "My name is Collis Huntington. I worked out there in the gold fields about a half a day and said to myself, 'That's enough for me.' I prefer to make my money by supplying the miners and letting them do the work. This is my partner, Mark Hopkins, a man without any vices. He doesn't smoke, curse, drink, gamble or spend money. He's what I call an ideal partner."

Hopkins, a tall, frail looking man, walked over to Henry and Frenchy. "I just heard what you said, Collis. I don't even own a horse or carriage myself because I plan to live close enough to walk to the store. But if I did ride to work, it would be in one of those Concord Coaches I keep seeing on the streets. Do you plan to take your circus to the gold fields?" he asked Henry.

"Yes, we're thinking about it. We are wondering which wagons will make it. I understand it's pretty rugged out there."

"You'll need sturdy wagons all right. Your first stop will be Hangtown; I'm from Hangtown myself. It's the stopping-off spot for both the northern and southern mines. Its fairly flat ground until you get there, but rugged further on, especially in the northern gold country. You'll have to wait till the spring snow melts. You don't want to get caught out there like the Donners did."

"A lot has been said about them, but I can't understand why they couldn't make it on their own," said Henry.

"Their wagons were too big. One of the families in the party, the Reeds, had an ungainly ark, a double-decked affair outfitted with bunks and a stove, so don't make that mistake. Keep to the smaller wagons."

"You fellows can sit here and chew the fat," said Collis, "while I measure out that rope." While he was doing that, Henry asked, "Any banks in town?"

"No, but I have a safe here in the store."

"Would I be able to use it?" asked Henry.

"Feel free to do so any time. Just mark your sack and it'll be here anytime you want it."

"Thank you, I'll do that," said Henry as he and Frenchy left the store.

As they walked to the circus grounds red dust was blowing everywhere. They made some of the necessary repairs on the tent. Then Henry remarked, "I wonder if there is a sawmill around here. We could use some wood shavings to spread around to settle this dust."

"Water may help," said George.

"I'm afraid it might just make it worse. Let's see what we can find."

"What'll we do about these rats? I've never seen so many. I've seen a half dozen here already."

"I imagine they come from those dismantled hulks tied up at the wharf; they're usually the breeding places for them," said Henry.

"They'll be overrunning the town in no time at all, ruining the merchandise, and frightening the poor womenfolk half out of their wits."

"They'll make themselves scarce when the people come. But let's do try to get those wood shavings."

Even in the third and fourth years the Gold Rush showed no signs of slacking.

By the time the circus was ready to leave for the mines that year, the mining population was already nearing, if not surpassing, one hundred thousand. Some were making it big, but that number was few, and if a claim paid more than an ounce a day, it was considered worth holding on to. Many a miner had already given up and gone home.

Making the circuit of the mining camps was even more of a test than performing in town. Traveling by horse and wagon, staying at primitive hotels, living on rough fare and performing under the tent meant the performers had to rise above circumstances. In fact, to take the circus through the gold fields during the year of '52 was almost unthinkable. Very few had risked the dangers and ordeals of traveling over roads no more than dirt paths through mountainous territory so steep a man on foot could hardly traverse it, let alone horse and wagon.

They packed up their little tattered canvas tent, the one they made when they first arrived at Stockton, all the dingy tinsel they could scrape together and their few scant properties and wardrobe.

They assembled their gear in front of the hotel on Front Street alongside the stage coaches. While the men were working with their own wagons, Margaret watched drivers hitching up their teams next to them. As the last strap of the harness was buckled, the drivers got up on their seats, shouted to their teams, and they were off at a run at full tilt through the city and out over the great level plains.

Henry decided they too might just as well move out, for he was anxious to get on the road. The Lees in the first wagon, George, Frenchy, and the Annereaus following, he gave the signal, and their wagons pulled out.

The sun was beginning to peep out as they traveled along with high spirits over roads that were no more than paths worn down by the wagons carrying supplies to the miners.

As they rode along they watched the enterprising and excitable young men clad in their red shirts carrying pistols on their hips, wearing their slouch hats, men who had settled upon a sandy level, about as large as a poor widow's potato patch.

It was spring time, all was activity. Miners were out digging for the precious gold. The circus traveled on with high hopes, for they were ready to undertake the most difficult task of piloting their two small wagons through the foothills of the Sierra to perform every night before the miners, not knowing what their fare would be.

They headed in the direction of Hangtown, the hub of activity. Just outside of town they stopped to rest a bit before making their entrance into town.

While they were freshening up, Margaret said to Henry, "These poor men out digging for gold. A miner's life must be the hardest in the world."

"Yes, maybe we can help give them a little entertainment at least," replied Henry.

"I hope so. These poor men must put up with a lot, working in icy cold water, putting up with their own poor cooking, catching all sorts of ailments, and being so far from their families."

"I'm beginning to wonder if it's wise for you to come with us, Margaret. You'd probably be better off back in Sacramento. I'm afraid this is going to be too rugged for you."

"I'll be all right, I want to be with you, and the boys can help me with the baby."

They passed many clapboard houses, paraded down Main Street muddied by the spring rains.

Henry got down from the wagon and went to the newspaper office, just a bare room with a counter and some large boxes on the floor. Henry put an ad in the paper. He checked to see if there was a Masonic lodge in order to make arrangements for a benefit, for he was told that many of the mining towns had them, located somewhere in the business section of town. But Hangtown didn't have one. He did find a hotel, the Cary House, which gave them a chance to get a good meal, bath, and a night's lodging.

Henry arranged for a lot nearby where the tent was set up for the night's performance. Handbills were passed out. The men set to work getting everything in readiness. They placed their candles in the wooden chandelier in the form of a stepped pyramid, eight or ten feet square at the bottom, ready to hoist onto the center pole at the proper time.

The torches were lit, and at dusk the miners came down from the hills to watch the show. Just before the cavalcade was to begin, the candles were lit then hoisted up the center pole illuminating the tent.

As the enthusiastic young men walked in, they emptied their pockets of dust onto the scales and the fare was dropped into a small box on the ground. During the performance when something caught their fancy, they tossed small bags of gold nuggets into the ring.

Masters Eugene and Francis received tumultuous applause for their incredible skill. Their father put on his great act of the "Sports of Atlas" and the boys "The Revolving Globes." They played their parts in "St. George and the Dragon" and the "Seven Champions of Christendom," the first time it had been presented in any circus. Frenchy kept three cannon balls in the air, George did the clowning. Mrs. Annereau and Jeannette were visions of beauty as they rode bareback around the ring. After the show was over, the miners found their way out by the lighted torches. The men took down the tent, and loaded the wagons. Henry gathered up the little sacks of gold nuggets and put them away for safekeeping.

The next day Henry and George went to the assayer's office. Henry talked to a fellow by the name of Alexander Todd who carried the mail to the miners at the diggings as well as working for Wells Fargo and Company.

"I'd like to send some dust back to Sacramento," remarked Henry, looking around the cluttered office.

"I'll take it back for you," replied the enthusiastic young man. "I do it all the time, or better still, why don't you get one of these large iron boxes to hold your gold dust in? Then you can carry it yourself. I'll sell you this one," pointing to a big sturdy box nearby.

"Good. I'll take it, but I want you to take the proceeds from our show back to Sacramento and leave it at the hardware store. They'll keep it until I return. We did well here. Can we expect as much in the other towns?"

"You should. This was real good digging country from the start."

"We can't complain, either," said Henry. "We just wanted to know what to expect. How did the town come by its name?"

"This used to be 'Dry Diggins.' Five men were caught while

trying to rob a local gambler. They were tried and given thirty-nine lashes apiece. Then more charges were brought against the same five men for a robbery and murder the year before on the Stanislaus River. The men were too weak to attend the trial, due to mountain fever. A man by the name of Buffum was here; he tried, he got up on a stump and protested the hearing, and they threatened to hang him if he didn't quiet down. Well, that shut him up. The men were found guilty, and as soon as they got out of their sick bed, they were placed on a wagon bed, nooses tied around their necks, the ropes tied to a limb of a tree, and the wagon was driven away. That's how Old Dry Diggins became Hangtown."

Henry just shook his head. He had nothing to say to that, so after working out a satisfactory arrangement for both men, he left the gold dust. Henry and Frenchy carried out the box, and they continued on their way.

From Hangtown they headed north to Coloma. The day was lovely, with a clear blue sky. Above them were the high peaks of the Sierra, laden with snow.

The rivers ran through wild canyons from one to three thousand feet in depth. The faces of these canyons were so abrupt, and steep that in a few places only the sure-footed pack mules could zig-zag their way up and down their dizzy heights, and any upset could send their little party hundreds of feet below. It wasn't long before they came to a sharp decline, and for quite a distance they were traveling along the side of the mountain. Holding the team back was done with great difficulty and all the while living in fear of the wagons plunging into the deep ravine below. From this descent the land leveled out, and it became comparatively easy for some distance.

The canyon through which the river flowed widened out on both sides leaving a space of level ground on which the town of Coloma was built. On their way into town they passed a wagon pulled by ten horses.

They passed the stores, saloons and hotels, all constructed of wood on either side of the main street. A lumber mill built along the river bank was now in ruins.

"This is where it all began," said Henry, as he pulled the wagon to a stop. The others stayed in their wagons while Henry went to the *Golden Era* newspaper office to put an ad in the paper. Talking to the clerk Henry said, "Quite a town you have here."

"This is a boom town, all right. Pick and shovels sell here for fifty dollars; food is out of reason."

"We'll keep our eyes on ours," Henry responded as he plunked his money on the counter and hurriedly left the office.

Back on the main street men on horseback passed them at a full gallop, going like the wind through town, picking up knives from the ground and then suddenly rearing up their horses, whirling them up on their hind legs. Then without stopping they dashed off in the opposite direction. They were blocking the roadway, so Henry was held up.

One man standing by him said, "Those men were Doniphan's riders in the Mexican War. They were part of the Army of the West, the Missouri Volunteers. They covered 3,500 miles, contending with dust, sand, summer heat, scorpions and snakes. They fought in a couple of battles, escorted a trading party, the Magoffins, to Satillo; went on to the battlefield of Buena Vista where that Mexican General, Santa Anna, got the whipping of his life. After that they went on to Reynosa on the gulf; back to New Orleans, then home to Independence, Missouri.

"Yes, spectacular riding, obviously they've spent a lot of time in the saddle."

"Now they're back in the thick of it here, and they can equal the skill of the caballeros in their feats of horsemanship."

Henry answered with, "I hope they can come to see our show tonight; you too, perhaps we can give them a treat."

"What do you mean?" he asked.

"Come and see."

Henry quickly got back up on the wagon and they headed on. They pulled up to Little's Hotel, the largest frame building on the right bank of the river. It served as a post office, store and tavern. While the others were looking over the menu posted on the door, Henry joined them. They stood in front of the closed door anxiously awaiting the second signal to be admitted.

Finally the door opened, the crowd gathered around rushed into the dining room. They sat in regular chairs, the tables were set with silver plated forks and spoons and real china. They enjoyed a wonderful meal of boiled salmon, corned beef, rice pudding, green peas and peach pie.

All around them were the unwashed, half-famished sunburnt crowd of bearded men. Many stared at Margaret, her soft blond hair falling to her shoulders. Her gentle blue eyes and rosy cheeks caused the men to gaze with a hungry look in their eyes.

"Never have I seen a crowd of rougher looking men. They're staring at me as if they had never seen a woman before. I feel strange among them. Look at the way they dress. There isn't a single coat in the whole crowd, few vests, no neckties, no collars."

"Some of the French men are wearing fancy shirts, though," commented Frenchy.

"That's true," said Margaret.

"Hope they come see us perform tonight," added Mrs. Annereau.

Henry replied, "I do too. I'm sure many of those men were upstanding in their towns back home. Some are probably lawyers and doctors and are now tending bar, being waiters, some even teamsters."

That night while riding around the ring, Henry spotted some of the men who had been in Doniphan's regiment, those he had seen on the street earlier in the day, so he nodded and saluted them as he passed by, causing them to let out a howl in return.

After performing before a large crowd, they packed up their gear; Henry walked around picking up the small sacks of gold from the ground. Frenchy lifted the money box up on the front wagon and they pulled out, and continued on, toward another town, another place.

After leaving Georgetown, they traveled down the craggy mountains. The road was so narrow that only at certain known points could two vehicles pass, so often they had to pull to the side of the road and wait.

Following them was a stage loaded with passengers. The driver had one foot, two arms, both shoulders and all fingers working. After the stage had passed them, it was Margaret who spoke up. "You wouldn't think anyone could drive a stage at such a breakneck speed and stay with it very long."

"Those men certainly know how to handle the ribbons," said Henry.

"Doesn't that take a lot of training?" asked Margaret.

"Once a man has learned to hold the whip, handle the multiple lines, maneuver the brakes, sitting behind four or even six horses pattering along before him, it becomes old stuff. Watching each horse, knowing his separate capacities, calling each one by name, telling them what to do, signaling at the most precise moment, urging them on—that's what it's all about."

Over rough and narrow trails they went; then finally the little circus took the ferry across the American River.

The first thing Henry did when they arrived in a new town was to go to the newspaper office. This time it was to the Auburn *Herald* to put in an ad. Auburn was the center of extensive staging and freighting operations. From there the supplies were delivered to the various mining camps which had sprung up by pack mule in all directions. Even the saloons were on a grander scale and had more class, and the citizens were more genteel.

"I'll be much obliged if you'll put this in right away," said Henry.

"I'll certainly do that, sir."

Back on the street, Henry got back up on the wagon. They passed an elegant saloon, a beautiful "round corner" building with three doors; then on to set up their tent amid confusion with great anticipation of a good and generous house.

That night the audience was more polite, though no less enthusiastic, more generous in their praise in that quiet, prosperous, law-abiding town, and the gold dust was more plentiful. They charged one dollar for box seats, fifty cents for the pit.

After a good performance, Henry gathered up the little sacks of gold and tucked them away. With the gold dust in the money box, the performers went back to the hotel.

Rochette pulled the last stake at daybreak; the wagons had been loaded the night before. George finished hitching up the team; they were ready to start.

As they pulled out, the sun began to rise in the distance, and the whole valley was spread before them. Live oaks dotted the countryside, and here and there were small patches of snow on the ground.

They traveled north, stopping each day and performing at small mining camps, stopping at the small towns along the way. They stopped at Todd's Valley which lay a dozen miles out of Auburn. Their Jenny Lind mine produced two thousand dollars worth of gold a day. As they drove along on the way to Michigan Bluff, they clung to a steep slope above the yawning gorges of the American River. They could hear the bells of the church, as sweet a tone as anyone would want to hear. They saw many cabins on the hillside.

They paraded down Main Street, setting up their tent well before the sun went down. The boys were full of energy. Their mother relaxed and watched their little one, Theodore, as he played nearby. Henry, George and Frenchy all bustled around and got ready for the performance. The miners flocked in, emptied gold dust from their pockets and took up seats in the tent. The candles were lit and the show began.

From Michigan Bluff, they climbed another steep and meandering path up the opposite canyon wall over roads that had been graded by private turnpike companies, resulting in a toll charge. They wound their way up the deep gorge of the north fork, over roads clinging to the side of the mountains far above the stream. Carved out of the rocky and declivitious canyon wall, they had been built only through Herculean effort.

The next town was Dutch Flat. They stopped at the hotel to secure lodging for the night. The company performed before a full house that night.

The next morning they pulled out of town moving at a leisurely pace, Henry taking the lead wagon, calmly watching his horses with a knowledge of their separate capacities, calling each by name. His horses were the best that money could buy. He knew his horseflesh; he loved and respected them and asked no more than they were able to produce. These same horses were called upon to perform in the ring with the grace and dexterity few horses would ever be called upon to do.

But in the mountains these same horses were subject to the same stresses as other teams. They were easily spooked, nervous, temperamental, and yet they had to pull their load. Henry would hold them in or give them the rein, which better suited his purpose, telling them each what to do, signaling at the precise movement through the individual or multiple lines, urging them on or holding them back.

Along the dirt road, live oaks dotted the countryside, the elder were in bloom, wild roses and blackberry vines were in abundance, ruddy larks sprang from the early, pearly white convolulus opened their spreading wheels.

"This is beautiful country, Henry," said Margaret. "I'm glad I didn't have to stay back in Sacramento; here I can have all this beauty before me."

"I know I should have, but I could never leave you back there, Margaret," said Henry as he pulled her closer to him. "I'd miss you too much."

Over this trail poured a continuous stream of wagons and pack animals into the mining camps, passing a number of stations and road houses along the way. It was along this stretch of the trail that Henry was most fearful of bandits, and if the truth be known, they were probably carrying as much gold as the stage coaches, tucked away in their money box. Henry was alert as he drove along for fear if the horses were spooked it could cause him to lose control, and the wagons could go careening down the side of the mountain to the canyon below. It was at such a time Henry trusted the ribbons to no one save himself.

He traveled along at a slow pace. Margaret sitting next to him, drowsy from the sun beating down, closed her eyes, put her head on Henry's shoulder and dropped off to sleep. Henry looking over at her, relaxed, the sunlight catching her beautiful blond hair, her gentle face, her eyes closed. Then they hit a bump and she awakened.

"I wish you would rest in the wagon, Margaret. There's room."

"I'll be all right, Henry. We'll be there soon."

They passed miners out washing gold in the streams, passed camps where the miners pitched their tents or constructed crude log cabins and at last they came to Grass Valley.

After their one night stand they continued on. They passed peddlers walking along with heavy packs on their backs. The more prosperous ones had mules to carry their heavy burdens. They traveled over the high winding roads with rifts of copper pink in the hills beyond deep valleys, purple and lavender, and to the north of them lay the rousing camp of Rough and Ready.

After the performance, Henry, George and Frenchy walked into a refreshment tent where the gold poured in from the rich gulches and was gambled away. They noticed the women dressed in their low shouldered silk dresses with long rippling full skirts, dancing to the tune of whistling bullets riddling the ceiling. After a few drinks they went back to the hotel for a good night's rest.

The next day they went on to Chinese Camp. They pulled up in front of Rosenbloom's Store and hitched up to the rail along with several packed animals. The miners were coming and going, getting supplies for the surrounding diggings. While Henry was inside purchasing a few necessary items, Margaret and the others waited near the wagons, looking at the strange building with a sod roof. "These are very common in Ireland boys, in fact, most of the homes have sod roofs. Soon they'll sprout, turn green and will be beautiful. This kind of roof will keep the building warm in the winter and cool in the summer. I didn't expect to see anything like it here."

Henry was slow in getting back so they went into one of the stores. Part of it was used for merchandise; the other, a jewelry store. The jeweler had all sorts of jewelry around him made from gold. "Yes, a lot of this will be sent back to members of their families back East," the jeweler said to Margaret.

"Here comes Daddy," said Francis, and they hurriedly left the store.

When they got back in the wagon, Eugene asked his father "Have you ever been in Ireland, Daddy?"

"Oh! Yes, we performed there many times, Dublin mostly."

From Chinese Camp they traveled through the sequoias and high sugar pines, and over rough mountain roads until they came to Calaveras. Later on in the day they pulled their wagons onto the ferry at Knight's Crossing. When they reached the farther bank, a crack of the whip, and they were on their way.

As they rode along to Columbia, there was noisy confusion everywhere. Shouting, cursing and laughter mingled with the silvery tunes of the mule bells on impatient pack animals. They saw miners hurrying along, men on horseback and passed wagons bogged down along the rutty roads. They were heading in the direction of one of the largest camps in the mountains. It had grown up overnight, situated in a secluded spot surrounded by the rolling hills.

The town had a great number of establishments, lots of hotels, several butcher shops, drug stores and bath houses. The town rang with the clamor of hectic activity amid shouts and curses of the miners, gamblers, merchants, dance hall girls, and camp followers. The fandango houses rocked with the beating of drums and the blasting of trombones.

They pulled to the side of the road as a stage coach came rattling into town. The road was crowded with freight wagons bringing in provisions and goods.

Henry put an ad in the *Columbia Gazette* and made arrangements to put on a benefit for the town and one for themselves. While the editor was looking it over, Henry said, "We saw a lot of Chinamen on the way into town."

"Yes, we do, we have a lot of Chinese out washing the tailings around the camp. We have three joss houses and a slave market where female servants are bought, sold and sometimes even exchanged."

"A strange way to live," said Henry, "I hate to see slavery. Where can a person get a bite to eat?"

"A man by the name of Antone built a brewery at the head of Matelot Gulch, which is very popular. He encourages picnics, parties and has several tables near his beer cellar for his customers. You might want to go there."

"Thank you for the suggestion," said Henry. "You certainly have a prospering town."

"Yes, we had our problems at first without water, but a lot of flumes have been built so the water now comes from Five Mile Creek. Thousands of miners gathered here for the eventful occasion, watched it as it came rushing through. Columbia is again booming."

"I can see it's a lively town all right," said Henry.

"The first miners came through were armed with pick, pan and shovel. As the pickin's grew slimmer, the miner with the pan was on his way out, although there are a lot still working that way. Now it's the long Tom, the cradle and the sluice."

"Progress," said Henry, "but I must be going, good day to you sir."

"Good day."

After the performance was over, the last thing Henry did was to gather up the little sacks of gold from the arena, and they retired for the night. They couldn't find accommodations at the hotel, so they set up their hammocks in amongst the trees the weather was getting warmer, the nights more comfortable. Henry and Margaret were lying there, their little Theodore between them, looking up at the starlit sky.

"It's beautiful out here tonight, Henry," remarked Margaret.

"Yes, it's so bright we could read or write without a light."

"Henry, why do you pick up those little sacks of gold? They have so little in them; the others won't even bother with them."

"Some day I will have enough to do something worthwhile with them, and when I do, I think I will have them melted down and made into something for you."

"Oh Henry! I will cherish it always."

The next morning they headed out from Columbia, traveling over a winding dirt road, passing fields of wild lilac, through the countryside of pines and scrub oaks. The grade was steep in places, with long intervals of fairly flat land. California was a paradise in beauty and scenery and heavenly climate. In the clear mountain air, as they traveled past blue meadows of mountain iris, the journey took on the aspect of a holiday.

Up the narrow trail they wound their way to Sonora. Finally they came upon a wagon drawn by eight yoke of oxen bogged down, unable to budge, blocking the way. The men jumped off the wagons, all put their shoulders to the wheel and pushed it free. They continued on, passing wagonload after wagonload of provisions for the mines.

"We're going to need the blocks from the back," said Henry. "You'll have to take over for awhile, Margaret."

Traveling up hill was slow. Margaret pulled ahead and Henry placed the block under the back wheel so the wagon would not slide back, then she pulled ahead again. Just before entering town, Henry put the blocks back into the wagon, shook off the reddish dirt from his shoes and took over the reins as they entered town. They pulled up to Holden's Hotel.

Sonora was a wild town. Washington Street was lined with buildings made of adobe hewn planks, sail cloth and tin. They could see evidences of where horse races, bull and bear fights had been held, and on the streets were lots of painted ladies. On Stewart Street there was IOOF building, and the town had a City Hall lying within the sloping outline of low rolling hills. The town had a plaza; the rising street had a pleasant turn, a few houses of handsome style with spacious yards. Hawthorne was in abundance as were pomegranates, crepe myrtle, and bay with hedges of box.

"I'll never forget this place," Frenchy said as he walked up to them, as Henry was getting down off the wagon. "In May of '49 there were seventeen of us who came here from Mokelumne Hill and started prospecting. We were the first to arrive. It was called Yorktown when we were here. After working a short time, we met and elected town officials. That was when I was elected sheriff."

"Quite an honor," said Henry.

"Yes, it was, but I felt the only way to be a halfway decent sheriff was to have a jail. Even if the materials were available, the miners wouldn't take the time to build one strong enough to hold even the puniest of prisoners, and who would take the time to watch them?"

"They just weren't civic minded, were they?" asked Henry.

"Well, anyway, it was easier for all us miners to call a mass meeting and decide the punishment, and what we always wanted anyway was a hanging. We didn't even take time to give the poor devil a chance to explain. But I wasn't suited for it, so I let a man by the name of Alexander have it."

"Then you went back to mining?" asked Henry.

"Yes, but mining was hard work, and I didn't do too well. I thought there must be an easier way to make a living; that's why I went back to Stockton and joined up with you."

"I hope you haven't regretted it."

"No, this is where I belong."

They performed that night with their highly-trained horses and fancy ponies. Their money box was getting heavier, harder to load on the wagon, and of course it was Frenchy who got that job, being the "Hercules" of the show.

The next and last town for the season was Jamestown, surrounded by lofty mountains. There were beautiful trees along the narrow and canopied sidewalks of the main street. A river ran through town, dividing it into two parts.

Hundreds of flags were flying from the roof tops of the taverns and gambling houses, and with the miners going in and out, the scene was very much like San Francisco.

They passed by the edge of the stream where the miners were knee-deep in water, as cold as the melted snow could make it. Some were washing gold with tin pans, some were using the common cradle rockers. All the while the sun was beating down on them.

They went on the Mariposa, stopped at the "14 Mile House" for food and rest, then on home to Stockton.

Their next engagement was at the American in San Francisco with the production of "Tom Cringle" followed by a circus performance. George Peoples took the part of Uncas, the Wild Son of the Forest, and Frenchy Rochette was the Hercules in his grand antagonistical cannon ball act.

At one performance they started with "William Tell." George took the part of the Greek warrior in "Timour the Tartar." He also appeared as the Wild Indian, introduced "The Great Coon Dog Boxer," and concluded in his best comic vein with "Pike County Visit to the Circus." While they were performing in San Francisco on a windy night on November 4th, a fire broke out in Sacramento. Most of the city was burned in a single night, leaving people homeless and most of the town's buildings in ashes.

National Theater of Sacramento
Built by Henry Charles Lee and John Marshall
Courtesy, California State Library

Sierra Nevada Road

Chapter 8

In the fall of '52 the circus returned to Sacramento. Back in Sacramento, rebuilding was well underway, and this time more attention was being paid to the materials, for many buildings were being built of brick. Henry made arrangements for a benefit so they returned to the gold country for a short engagement. As they descended into the valley, heading toward Coloma, George was following closely behind Henry. Both drivers were keeping a vigilant eye for fear of the highwaymen stalking alongside the trail, ready to take any proceeds they might have aboard. They were watching also for boulders being loosened by the mining operations for fear they might come crashing down across the trail.

They continued on farther and farther into the valley below, keeping to their strenuous schedule. Margaret, holding little Theodore on her lap, became drowsy and dropped off to sleep. Henry's team was startled and became increasingly difficult to hold back on the steep descent. Suddenly there was a loud cracking sound. Margaret awoke with a start. The baby jerked. A tree crashed across the trail in front of them, and the team reared, then bolted. With Herculean effort, Henry headed the wagon into the uphill side of the trail, avoiding plummeting into the canyon below.

As the wagon overturned, Margaret and the baby were thrown clear. But, the money box, too, came flying out, pinning them beneath it. George was there in an instant, grabbed and uncoupled the spooked team and led them away to calm down. Henry rushed over to his wife and frantically pulled the money box from her limp body. He lifted Theodore from his mother's arms. His baby was dead, killed instantly, his skull crushed by the weight of the money box.

Stunned, Henry held his baby to him while the men carried Margaret to the other wagon where Jeannette and her mother made a bed for her. Without saying a word, Mrs. Annereau gently took the baby from Henry. She carefully cleaned him and dressed him in his pink tights and his golden slippers, and they buried him there where he died, beneath an oak tree.

The men all pitched in, Eugene and Francis too, to right the wagon. They turned it around and headed it in the opposite direction. Henry got up behind the reins, and they drove off. In back Mrs. Annereau kept a moist cloth on Margaret's forehead as she moaned, crying for her baby.

Margaret's fever rose very high. A bone had punctured her skin. They traveled over torturous, rutted roads, their wheels rattling, the great gusts of dust billowed out behind them as they wound their way through the mountainside. Then gradually, the rock-strewn ridges gave way to smoother landscape, fields dotted here and there and finally they made it back to Stockton and to the ranch.

The doctor was called in and gave Henry little hope. "Well, her leg's badly infected, but that's not the worst. I suspect she's all broken up inside —I'm afraid there's nothing more I can do." Margaret continued to lose strength, and on the 4th of December, 1852, she quietly slipped away.

"Oh, my God, she's gone, and she was so young!" said Henry. "She's been through so much, and just as we were getting our feet on the ground. I had so hoped I could build a fine brick home for her."

"She's at peace," soothed Mrs. Annereau.

"She was too delicate to take to the mountain towns, but she wanted to be with us, and I selfishly allowed her to come," Henry berated himself.

"Don't blame yourself, Henry."

"She was such a graceful performer, never complaining, no matter how weary she was," he cried.

"She looked angelic standing balancing bareback, rhythmically matching her movements to the horse's," agreed Mrs. Annereau.

"I can see her now," said Henry his head bowed speaking in a whisper, "when the door of the arena was opened, her lovely blond hair in ringlets around her face, her flashing blue eyes sparkling, so slim in her soft flowing gown and tights. Oh! She was so loving, and I'll miss her so."

The wagon carrying the coffin was draped in black, the horses beautifully groomed and harnessed. It was followed by the family solemnly taking their places, the two boys beside their father, Mrs. Annereau, and Jeannette with the other performers behind. They headed for the Citizen's Cemetery in Stockton. The men carried her coffin to the graveside along the river's edge, and there they said their last farewell. As sorrowful as Henry felt, he knew he had to go on. He learned that Sonora had been reduced to ashes and was very much in need of a benefit performance. He wrote to their Masons that very day saying they would perform there on the 27th.

It was a two-day journey back to Sonora. The circus went over roads no better than paths, they slowly climbed the foothills; travel was slow, but though their hearts were heavy, they were needed to help the town.

When they arrived in Sonora, they were horrified to see the damage and learn that the fire had swept through the flimsy structures with the speed of a whirlwind. Washington Street had been widened from thirty to sixty feet to prevent another fire from jumping across the street. With heavy hearts they set up the tent, and after performing before large crowds, they returned home by Mariposa, stopped at the "14 Mile House" for food and rest, then on home to Stockton.

By February of 1853, the circus was back in San Francisco. They again opened at the American Theatre on Sansome and Halleck Streets. They featured Thomas Neville, the great equestrian and somersault rider who performed in the grand scenes of the circus arena.

Following that engagement they returned to Stockton in March. Whenever the weather permitted, the South American Circus, as they were now called, put up their tent on the property called 'Weber Hole' at the plaza at the head of the Stockton Channel on El Dorado Street. Along with their other performers, they added trick riding by Virginia Lioni, clowning by Devere and Dawner, and Henry and his two boys did their tumbling act.

They also worked at the ranch making preparations for a new

show and perfecting their acts. John Marshall returned from the East with new gear for the show. By the end of April they were on their way to Sacramento. There they found the Orleans where they had stayed the year before was now a brick building. They entered the hotel, and Henry stepped up to the desk.

The clerk asked, "How many?" and Henry replied "Ten," then went on to ask, "Did the other Orleans go up in flames in that February fire?"

The clerk answered "Yep, it sure did, but this time we added a reading room, a billiard room and a saloon. Upstairs there's a parlor, family rooms and chambers. I'm sure you'll be quite comfortable."

"I'm sure we will" said Henry.

"I didn't see your wife in the group this year. Did she stay back at the ranch?"

"No, I wish that were the case," Henry answered, stiffly. "She died. She was thrown from the wagon in the gold country."

"Sorry to hear it," murmured the clerk, at a loss to know what else to say.

After they settled in, they were anxious to get out and see the sights, for there was lots of activity on the streets. Miners were milling around, coming and going, there were now good restaurants to choose from, interesting shops to visit, boats coming and going, the gambling houses going around the clock, and the gold dust was pouring in.

Their show was well attended, and the citizens were beginning to recognize them as they walked around town. But they were anxious as always to head out to the mining towns.

As they headed out for Hangtown, Mrs. Annereau and her daughter Jeannette rode in the lead wagon with Henry. John, Frenchy, George and Henry's two boys followed in the other wagon. As they rode along, they passed long lines of wagons drawn by innumerable oxen plodding along; they covered their faces to protect themselves from the dust blowing in their direction. They passed miners on their way to town, men who looked like they could use a bath, a shave and a good suit of clothes.

Outside of town they rested an hour to make their entry with the look of fatigue smoothed away and to enter with an air of pleasure and high spirits.

Hangtown was now the main supply center for the mining camps and a stopping place for miners on their way north or south.

They passed by many small stores, Studebaker's Wheelbarrow Shop on Main Street, and Phillip Armour's butcher shop on down the street and continued on to the outskirts of town where they set up their tent.

At the newspaper office, Henry made arrangements for his ad. "I'd appreciate it if you'd put this in right away. We'll only be here a night or two."

"The people will read it tonight," the clerk said, thankful for the business.

"How's the digging these days?" asked Henry.

"Good, I'd say."

A man standing nearby spoke up. "Gold digging is not an easy job, though. Buffum's my name. It's made up of canal digging, ditching, laying stone walls, being exposed to the burning rays of the sun and all the while you're living on poor provisions."

"Then I guess I'll stick to what I'm doing," said Henry.

"What's that?" asked Buffum.

"The circus business. I'm a circus man."

"I guess I made digging sound pretty bad, but there's the good side, too. I started in the dry diggings at Weaver Creek. The very first day out I got down into an excavation and found a crevice, along a rock which was filled with a hard bluish clay and gravel. I took out my knife. There on the bottom along the whole length of the rock was the bright yellow gold in little pieces about the size of barley. My heart began to beat wildly. I sat there looking at it for several minutes, then I scooped it out with the point of my knife and an iron spoon."

"That must have been something," said Henry. "That much gold can last you the rest of your life. Well, I must be going."

Henry left the office and joined the others at the lot. That night the men came down from the hills willing to part with some of their gold dust for the chance to enjoy the beautiful horses, the performance of Henry and his boys, and the Annereaus, mother and daughter in the grand equestrian feats. They laughed at George in his comic acts taking the part of clown, and marveled at the sight of Frenchy lifting his cannonballs. Henry picked up the little sacks of gold thrown into the arena more from habit than anything else, but his heart was heavy, having lost his reason for collecting them, now that his Margaret was gone. When they pulled out of Hangtown that year, their money box contained a goodly sum of gold dust.

The next day they headed on. They left the moist temperate regions of the foothills and headed into the dry, cold, bracing air of the Sierra. They reached the ridge of the mountains and the gold country stretched away for miles before them. They saw the white peaks of the Sierra Nevada in the distance. It was along this stretch of land where the accident had occurred. Henry kept his eyes glued to the road. He had nothing to say. Along the steep red hills miners were at work, below them, many waist-deep in water, toiling to construct a race to turn the course of the river.

At Coloma they rode along Main Street. After a short stay, they continued on to Georgetown, the pride of the mountains, high up in the pines where there was more snow on the ground.

When they arrived in Georgetown that year, they found the town to be quite different from the year before. Main Street was now one hundred feet wide. They passed a beautiful two-story frame house with a veranda and balcony, both with railings circling the house.

They secured their lodging, and while the men were setting up the tent, Jeannette and her mother and the two boys went looking through the stores.

In one shop they talked to a clerk. "That was a beautiful home we just passed coming into town," said Mrs. Annereau.

"Yes, that is the Shannon Knox House," said the clerk. "That lumber came all the way from around the Horn."

"It's the most beautiful home we've seen so far," said Jeannette.

"This is a wonderful setting for a mining camp!" said Mrs. Annereau.

"I like it. It was started by a bunch of sailors, and they did a lot of gambling as well as digging."

"Let's go back, Jeannette," said Eugene. "I want to help set up my gear. Dad says I'm old enough to look after my own act."

No matter how early the circus got on to the trail, they would see the miners getting their breakfast by campfire, or already out working their claims or the high booted men in the old north bend, squatters standing, gently rocking their cradle-like gold washers on the river's edge. After traveling some distance through the pine trees, they occasionally caught a glimpse of the American Fork River. Flowers were blooming everywhere in rich profusion, especially the yellow poppy. Some of the miners were working deep pits, hacking at the rocky soil with pick and shovel, prying boulders loose, with only their heads showing. Others were carrying buckets of dirt from their claims to the rockers at the river's edge.

By noonday most of the miners were seen resting along the mountainside. They continued on; then by afternoon they watched the miners as they again resumed their tasks with renewed energy.

In the mining town of Auburn, they saw many Chinamen on the streets. As they rode along the main street looking around, Mrs. Annereau said, "The Chinese have a knack for knowing what communities are going to be permanent."

"I think you're right," said Henry. "I'm going to get down and go to the newspaper office. Will you please ask John and the others to set the tent up?"

That night they were justly rewarded, for their money box was getting heavier each time it was loaded on to the wagon and the evening's proceeds were their best so far.

Above Todd's Valley was Forrest Hill, a roaring and successful camp with its several hotels, stores, banks and a newspaper office where the rich drift mine poured out enormous amounts of the yellow metal. They heard the chimes of the church bells. "I've been told those are the sweetest-toned bells ever brought to the mines," said Mrs. Annereau.

"A wonderful sound all right," replied Henry.

They were heading in the direction of Michigan Bluff, clinging to a steep slope above the yawning gorges of the American River. Many cabins could be seen in the background. Ditches were dug all around, some several miles long. There they saw the greatest network of flumes and ditches anywhere in the mines where giant nozzles were being used in hydraulic mining to wash away entire mountainsides. As they rode along, they could see great circles cut deeply into the mountainside.

"It is sad to see this happen to the countryside," said Mrs. Annereau. "All this beautiful country. I wonder if it will ever be put right again."

"I doubt it," said Henry. "A man has a way of taking everything he wants from the earth and neither worries nor cares about the destruction he has caused."

In town Henry pulled his team to a stop, got down and walked into one of the local stores. Inside a dark-haired man of medium stature was standing behind the counter, surrounded by all sorts of merchandise. Henry picked up a few items.

"Sometimes we have problems at the evening performance. In case we need to get something, do you live in town?"

"Oh, I have a house nearby. I'm Leland Stanford, I own this place. Most of the time I sleep right here on the counter. I don't even bother to go home. You can catch me here any time, day or night."

"I'll remember that," said Henry as he departed to join the others at the tent.

From there, they continued on north, stopping each day and performing at small mining camps. At sunset as they approached a camp, the shacks along the way seemed deserted. There were no fires to give the sign of activity in or around the place.

"The miners don't seem to stay around in the evening, do they?" asked Jeannette.

"Oh, no, they hightail it to town. Stay around in these hovels or huts? No. They would rather be in the saloons where the lights are bright, where there's lots of noise around, the excitement of gambling, trying to make a fast buck. They follow the gamblers with their fancy ladies, who pitch their tents and start collecting the gold as fast as the miners take it out of the ground. It's a story as old as Eve. Men want to be where the women are, and really don't seem to care so much if they are the 'other' kind."

"What are the 'other' kind?" asked Jeannette.

"Never mind," said her mother.

"Sorry," said Henry. "I forgot about her age. She seems older than she really is. I'll put it this way. The men out here have no home ties or social checks. As you know, it's wild in these mining camps."

Before them were the high Sierra. After a few hours, the road began to ascend, grow steeper past miners out washing gold in small streams. It looked as though gold lay everywhere within their grasp in the sifted earth; the miners trooped by them on foot, some on horseback with expressions of hope and fulfillment.

They could see activity everywhere. All around them gorges were being spanned, tunnels dug, shafts sunk. Water was being lifted from the deep canyons over ridges and foothills. Wooden flumes were being built to great lengths. There was no doubt about it, these young miners of the world were an inventive bunch, and they weren't afraid of work.

They rode along over hills and valleys covered with tall grass interspersed with flowers of every variety. A delightful fragrance filled the air. The elder were in bloom, the wild roses and blackberry vines were in abundance. Ruddy larks sprang from the earth. Along the hillside, the miners stopped long enough to watch the circus pass by, then continued on with their work.

"Do you think we'll do well tonight?" asked Jeannette.

"Oh! These men are so starved for entertainment, the accumulation of gold will simply have to wait," replied Henry. "I'm sure some of the dust that was dug out today will pay their way tonight."

"How do they find it?" asked Jeannette.

"They follow the crevices in the rocks, and when they spot the yellow stuff, they call it 'pay dirt'."

They passed merchants carrying their packs on their backs, carrying all sorts of items: velvet, silk, calico, coats, laces, sealing wax. One peddler even had a copy of Dickens strapped on his back. The more prosperous ones had mules to carry their heavy burdens.

They drove their wagons through Grass Valley, past stores with wooden awnings, looking down the side streets. At the corner of Mill and Walsh Streets, someone pointed out, "That's where Lola Montez, the famous dancer, lives with her pet bear. She even keeps it in her house."

They continued on to the town called Nevada, just a short distance away, and the setting for the town was even more delightful. It was built along the banks of a river, perched along a canyon with a creek at its base, and the whole hill was rich with gold with the backdrop of beautiful pine-clad hills. In town they passed a building built of stone. The assay office was another attractive building on the corner, adding charm to the hillside town.

Over the high winding roads they rode through country with rifts of copper pink. In the hills beyond them were deep valleys of purple and lavender. A short distance away lay the rousing camp of Rough and Ready. They stopped only long enough to give a performance, and then headed on. From there they headed south, anxious to get to the southern mines where the larger towns were and the gold dust was more plentiful.

They were unable to find hotel accommodations, so they set up their hammocks among the trees. Jeannette's mother slept in one of the wagons, but Jeannette wanted to sleep outside. Lying there looking up at the stars, breathing in the pure air and in no time at all she was fast asleep. Henry wasn't ready to retire, so he walked around checking things over, looking after the horses. As he walked past Jeannette's hammock, he looked down at the sleeping young lady and thought to himself, such tenderness, such kindness, the joy of the group. He wanted to touch her hair, but held back, then went to check on other things.

It was after dusk the following night when they reached Chinese Camp, an oasis amid grass and tarweed fields. As they approached the town, the campfires along the trail were so numerous they needed no other light to mark their route other than the embers of those who had gone before them.

It was dark before they got their tent up, but there was a crowd of Chinamen standing around, patiently waiting to see the show. Though the performers were bone-weary from the long day's travel, they shrugged off that feeling of fatigue and performed to their usual standard.

The next day on the way out of town, they stopped at the post office. While Frenchy went in to check to see if they had any mail, they saw a couple of Chinamen in their loose dress with their heads shaved and hair drawn back arguing with each other on the street, both talking in a dreadful uproar at once, nose to nose with arms extended, but finally they tired and each went his separate way.

When they left, John said, "Those poor devils, they have it tougher than anyone else. As soon as they get to this country, they're met at the boat, supplied with mining equipment and sent off to the mines, only to pay a tax on everything they find."

Then Henry added, "One thing about them though, they don't just drink it all away."

"That's something," said Mrs. Annereau.

"Here comes Frenchy. Giddyup, horse, we don't have all day to sit around," said Henry.

They were backtracking to Columbia, following the established trail. There the road was a narrow dirt path. Travel was slow. They crossed the Stanislaus River on Knight's Ferry. Here they had to pay a toll. On the way across, John started talking to the owner of the ferry.

"Doing pretty well?" he asked.

"Yes, we go as high as five hundred dollars a day. We have some repair work, but most of it is profit. My name is John Dent. My brother Lewis and I took over when William Knight was shot in a gunfight last year."

"Poor man," said John. "But killings are so common up here."

"Yes, they are."

"We're heading for Columbia," remarked John, "have a show to put on tonight."

"Circus, eh?"

"Yes."

"Oh, you'll make it easy. Just up the road a spell."

"I know," he said. "We came here last year. I thought I'd have a chance to talk to Knight, but that isn't possible now."

When they reached the far bank, the wagons were unloaded, and with a crack of the whip they were on their way. They rode along the countryside and into the hills, covered with wild oats and gashed by mines. The country was a hunter's paradise, for they could see deer and antelope along the way.

Their wagons stirred a cloud of dust as they traveled along the rutty roads. In town Henry put an ad in the *Columbia Gazette*. Columbia had enormously rich deposits; and now with plenty of water it was again a booming town.

After they pulled out of Columbia, they traveled up the mud-rutted streets of one of the wildest camps, Mokelumne Hill, where one killing a week was the average, and in one week they had five. For seventeen weeks on end there was at least one killing every Saturday night.

All along the road were gambling houses and places where they could get a meal. Many two-story buildings intermingled with canvas shanties. They stopped along the road for a bite to eat, siting down to a good meal of beefsteak, boiled potatoes, stewed beans and dried apples. After eating, they again hit the trail.

At Sonora they pulled up to Holden's Hotel. On either side of the street were large gambling houses built of flimsy material, very flammable. After they had settled in, the men decided to have a drink. They walked into a gambling house with its glittering chandeliers throwing brilliant light on the piles of gold stacked on each monte table. They walked over to the bar.

In the saloon there was lots of squabbling going on. Noticing Henry was taking everything in, Frenchy said, "The miners from the East distrust and dislike the Mexicans whom they call 'greasers.' They don't like us French, but we're respected, and the Chinese are the lowest of the low. The best they can do is to crawl into camp after everyone had deserted it and find a claim and try once again to gather a little dust. Everyone's hands are against them, even the greasers hate them."

"Too bad people can't get along. There's plenty of gold out there for all," said Henry.

Then Frenchy added, "I'm not too sure people of different races will ever learn to get along."

"Time will tell. Well, Frenchy, you're home! Glad to be back?" asked Henry.

"Am I ever! I'll get some good French cooking and maybe a chance to see some of my old friends. I think after we put up the tent I'll head out and see if any of the fellows are still digging."

Back out on the street Henry walked past miners walking along, bag in hand, coming into town for supplies.

After the tent was up, Frenchy disappeared, and the others made plans to go back to the hotel. Frenchy had selected a French restaurant for the others to eat at because the French men were such good bakers and they served the best wine. In their places there was always singing, gaiety and good humor as well as good food, quite a contrast to the other saloons where there was a lot of drunkenness.

Wherever the circus performers went, the people turned and looked. The men all smartly dressed stood waiting in the lobby for the ladies to come down. They went into the dining room, to enjoy the good French cooking. During supper, Jeannette chatted about the show. Henry took it all in, catching her enthusiasm and began to feel good again. Jeannette was showing promise as an equestrienne but her mother still demanded top billing, which kept her out of the spot light.

After the main course, Henry said, "The pastry will have to wait," catching Jeannette's eye as he rose from his chair. "There's a job to be done, a performance to give, so I must get ready for the show."

When the performance was over, Henry picked up the little gold nuggets, tucked the money box away, then went back to the hotel for a good night's rest. In the saloon downstairs the sweet sounds of the flute and violin serenaded him the whole night through.

They stayed at Sonora on May 13th, 14th and 15th, then on to Jamestown for a one-night stand, then started their two-day journey back to Stockton and to the ranch. On the way they descended hill after hill. The road to Stockton was bumpy, the day was warm , but the last part of the journey was easier for Henry, for his mind was filled with a sense of peace which he could only attribute to pleasant thoughts of Jeannette.

Sawmill at Coloma

Chapter 9

The circus went back to the ranch, to Stockton the trading center, where many of the miners went during the rainy season to get away from the hills and stay in more comfortable quarters. The daily trains of mule and ox teams traveled along the Mariposa Road, passing by the Lee and Marshall Ranch.

At the ranch they set up winter quarters for the company. Here they broke stock, made costumes, and perfected their acts for the following season. Henry was spending more time with Jeannette, helping her work out, giving her special attention. Jeannette was working on the tight rope, Henry making an occasional suggestion. Then, out of the blue one day, Mrs. Annereau said, "Don't make any plans for us Henry; we're moving on. Jeannette and I will be joining another group."

"I wish you'd change your mind."

"No, Henry, we'll be leaving in the morning."

Shortly after that, the circus returned to San Francisco for an engagement on October 30, 1853. This time they set up their tent on Stockton and Vallejo Streets. Of the five theatres that were open for business—the American, the Adelphi, the Union, the San Francisco Hall and the Olympic—only the American and the Olympic could accommodate a circus, and often they were booked. They were able to secure an engagement at the American.

They featured "Jack and the Giant Killer." Henry re-engaged Virginia Lioni as a replacement for Jeannette and gave her the title the "Fairy Queen of the Circus." As Henry watched her perform, talented as she was, he felt there was something missing. She lacked the warmth and sparkle of his little equestrienne.

In early 1854 the circus was back in Sacramento for a short engagement. Henry had a chance to take in some of the Masonic meetings at A.A. Bennett's spacious building on J Street between Front and 2nd. He was an active Mason, working his way up the chairs.

He attended the meetings when in town and worked with his fellow Masons putting on benefits throughout all his travels. Of course it was good for business. This meant the most influential, prestigious people in town would attend his show and spread the word, giving him better attendance.

One night when he was at a meeting, everyone seemed to be excited about the new capitol building now under construction. That was the night Sam Brannan's name came up for membership. Sam was there. He was a handsome man, meticulously dressed, an Irishman with endless energy and enthusiasm. His hair was deep brown, his eyes dark and flashing. It was easy to pick him out of a crowd because of his booming voice. Sam Brannan was the Mormon leader who had been sent to Washington by Brigham Young to solicit aid for the Mormon exodus to the West. Sam had a couple of stores he stocked with the tithes of his fellow Mormons and never refused credit to any of Sutter's employees, preferring to let their debts accumulate for later reckoning. This way Sam was able to get most of Sutter's land in Sacramento, putting poor Sutter to bed with the chills. It was Sam Brannan who spread the word about gold being discovered at Coloma. Sam dressed more like a gambler than a Latter Day Saint, with samples of gold in his pocket. He went to San Francisco, whipped out a bottle of gold dust, from inside his long coat and went down the streets shouting, "Gold, gold, gold from the American River!" Those who could, gathered up a pick and shovel, and a few provisions, and followed Sam up to the hills in the direction of the sawmill.

The men talked it over whether or not Sam should be considered. The consensus of opinion was that Sam wasn't doing right by his fellow Mormons and that his drinking was a problem.

Henry had nothing to say. Sam had built Joseph Rowe an amphitheatre a few blocks away, and Henry didn't want it to sound as though he would vote against Sam because of sour grapes.

But Henry did have strong feelings about Sam. He had done a lot for charity, but when Sam Brannan did anything, it was all for show. Sam had purchased a fire engine for the city of San Francisco, costing him $10,000. It had taken the company three years to build and had been transported around the Horn. When it arrived, the ornate machine was put on display for everyone to gape at and marvel over. Then Sam staged a parade, complete with band and military escort to show it off.

One day while the firemen were fighting a fire, the brakes on the fire wagon gave way. It went reeling down one of the steep San Francisco hills and landed in a heap at the bottom. Then Sam had to put more money into it to put the broken fire wagon back together again. While Henry was thinking about this, Sam was voted down, and the matter was settled.

It was time for the circus to move on. The mining town of Hangtown was now called Placerville, which was a more respectable name. The hangings that plagued them earlier had ended.

By early 1854, Placerville was a serious contender with San Francisco in wealth and population, a depot for supplies. Charles Bennett and Jacob Wittner, the teamsters who hauled goods to Coloma before the news of gold had leaked out, were working there with their meager equipment, a wagon and draft animals assembled by Sutter and a few of his neighbors.

The circus traveled down Main Street, muddied by the spring rains, passed many narrow lanes and crooked side streets which led up the ravines and hillsides covered by clapboard houses.

After a well-received performance, they headed for Coloma, about eight miles north of Placerville, cradled among steep hills. In Coloma they passed many stores, saloons, and hotels on either side of Main Street.

One couldn't go to Coloma without hearing about James Marshall, the man who had discovered gold in the first place, who back in '48 was overseeing the construction of a sawmill with some Mormon brethren, three other white men and some Indians when he discovered gold. At first the ditch was not deep enough to carry off the water sufficiently, and it backed up on the wheel. In order to carry out the river water after it had turned the wheel and to dump the waste downstream, they built a long trail race.

Each morning James Marshall checked to see what had washed through the night before. On the morning of the twenty-fourth of January, he decided to go down to the bottom, there he saw some bright yellow speckles. Now he was down in the mouth for not getting the 640 acres he felt he was entitled to. He had made nothing from his discovery, and now all the land surrounding his mill, which was his by right of settlement, was taken from him without "leave or license." He had nothing left but fame, which, as he said himself, "bought neither victuals nor clothes for anyone."

After performing in Coloma, the circus followed the trails of the year before. While performing in Georgetown, John was the nightly supervisor of the performances and let nothing escape his vigilant eye. The whole performance operated like clockwork. After Georgetown it was Auburn, then on to Dutch Flat which they found to be colorful among the pine-clad mountains. Its one street was lined with poplar and locust trees. Many Chinamen with their long pigtails hanging down their backs were walking up and down the street.

As they pulled up to the hotel, Henry said, "This seems strange. I remember this as a single story building. Now it has two stories. Certainly makes it look different. And this bridge across the street wasn't here. Even the name has changed. Now it's Dutch Flat Hotel Annex, and that National Hotel across the street is new," he said as he pointed out the bridge connecting the Dutch Flat Hotel to the National which was gaily decorated with bunting and banners of evergreens and flowers.

They passed McClure's Bank with its graceful southern colonial porch, the pride of the community. While the men were putting up the tent, Henry went back to the bank and walked in. Inside was a huge stone and brick vault where the miners kept their gold dust. The Masons held their meetings upstairs. Henry went up to see if anyone was there, hoping to meet with some of the leading citizens of the community to work out plans for a benefit for the town.

While he was doing this, Virginia, Francis and Eugene went into the emporium nearby and looked around at their wares, from brandy to buttons. Stores held a fascination for Virginia, for she was anxious to see the pretty things to buy, and Henry insisted the boys go with her to keep a watchful eye on her. They went back to the Wells Fargo and Company office which was alongside the bank and waited for Henry.

That year they performed at Chinese Camp. As they entered town, they passed the new post office, an attractive brick structure, and drove through town.

"Wherever the Chinese are you will always see these, they're called 'The Tree of Heaven'." said Henry.

"They're beautiful," said Virginia.

The next day as they approached the Stanislaus River, Henry fully expected to pay the ferry charge. It was a pleasant surprise to find a bridge had been built across it. They continued on, performing at Columbia on May 13th and 14th, and at Springfield on the 15th, drawing large crowds wherever they went. Gold was not as plentiful as it once was, so the miners were spending more time in town, many gambling away their hard-earned money. Some were becoming more civic minded; the towns were getting larger.

On July 1st they performed at Sonora, on the 2nd in Springfield and on the 3rd and 4th of July they were again back at Columbia performing at the Olympic Theatre, one of the most complete of its time in the mountains. On the same program some of the town's leaders were making orations about the importance of the day. John became restless because the speeches were taking so long. "Some people just don't know when to quit."

"This is their big day," said Henry. "We'll have to make up time when we do get on the road."

When the program was over, everyone pitched in, got all the gear in the wagons and on they went. This time it was San Andreas, where the Mexican miners had been chased out of town by the overbearing Yankees. The Chinese had been allowed to stay because they were willing to be subservient. They also ran some of the stores and practically all the laundries.

From there they went to Mokelumne Hill. Henry and John went into a local saloon to have a drink. While standing at the counter, they struck up a conversation with one of the local inhabitants. He started talking, "One day a Negro came wandering in. He inquired how could he get some of that gold dust that everybody had. One miner spoke up and said, 'You dig for it.'

"'You mean it comes out of the ground?' he asked.

"'You bet,' they said. 'Try it and see.'

"He was sent to a spot where the men knew there was no gold, up on a barren hilltop. They didn't hear from the man for a few days. At the end of the week he came in, his pockets loaded with nuggets and dust. The miners didn't wait for a word of thanks; they just headed out for that same spot."

They performed at Sutter's Creek, a town changed from a settlement of tents. Because there were so many fires, it was built of brick and stone. It was a prosperous town, situated on an incline along the more traveled road, and they played to a good house.

They went on down the road to Volcano. It was here Sutter had a brief fling after gold, but wasn't lucky, so he left. Sutter always seemed to get the short end of the stick. In Sacramento, Sutter had vast tracts of land: his Russian tract, centering around Fort Ross, his new Helvetia where his fort was located and his Sobrante grant of 87,000 acres; but none on the American River where the sawmill was located and gold was discovered. Later, when others went into the Volcano district, they found gold quite plentiful. One miner got as much as five hundred dollars from a single pan of gravel.

Hornitos was their next town, a village like "Old Mexico." It was the wildest of all the southern mines with their lynchings and wild fandangos, and nothing but saloons and gambling houses facing the Plaza. Everywhere they saw the cloth and paper houses with a sprinkling of log cabins. There was a Wells Fargo building and a store where a man by the name of Ghirardelli went into business, selling chocolate. They continued on to Chinese Camp.

Following an engagement there, they headed back to Sonora. In town they stopped at the Plaza to give the horses a chance to rest. Virginia and the boys looked around town, walked past the charming frame houses with their lovely gardens, where the crepe myrtle were beginning to leaf out. They set up their tent close to town.

In July they were again in San Francisco where Lee and Marshall presented an afternoon performance free to the children of the public schools, and the adult admissions went to the school libraries. On that same evening the adult admissions went to the Fireman's charitable fund. They also had a benefit for the Masonic fraternity which was well attended on August 30th. They presented "William Tell," followed by "The Wild Indian," "The Great Coon Dog Boxer," and "Pike County's Visit to the Circus," in which George Peoples was the star.

The rains came early that year so they went back to the ranch at Stockton, known as "Slough City" because of its heavy rain during the winter. If the sloughs overflowed, the entire area was flooded. When they arrived home that year, it had been raining for about two weeks. The roads were in poor condition, and the only way to get into town from the lowlands was by boat. Several bridges had been swept away, many buildings were carried off by the floodwaters. Most of the wharf was underwater, and it was rising every hour. Ferries had to be built to cross the main street. One store moved and ended up in the street. Water on the ground floor was four to five feet deep.

But at the ranch in spite of the muddy conditions, the work went on as usual with horses to train and animals to feed. All the performers had to practice, there were costumes to make, new acts to prepare, for every season they had to have a completely new show ready. There was no time to sit around.

By the spring of 1855, the circus headed back to the mining towns. On April 14th they performed at Columbia.

Up and down the foothills of the Sierra they went, stopping for a one-night-stand at each town along the way, then back to Stockton. The hillsides were emerald now, the madrones brilliant with orange berries. Occasionally it had rained during the early part of the season, but they had many days with the clear blue sky above them.

Henry promised another engagement for Columbia, so they returned to the Olympic Theatre from the 9th to the 11th of June. Their program included Madame Austin and Frenchy, Henry and the boys.

Then back to Coloma they went. This was the year Coloma had a double hanging. Henry put an ad in the paper. "Lee and Marshall's National Circus & Hippodrome will Exhibit in Coloma on Wednesday 27th June 1855. Box seats $2.00, Pit $1.00. Door opens at 7½ o'clock. Performance to commence at 8:00."

In the large box tucked behind the driver's seat was the money box full of gold dust, for the season was very successful, and they were drawing large crowds.

Back and forth between the towns they went. On July 4th they again went back to Columbia, participating in a celebration and oration in the pavilion. On Saturday, July 16th, they had a crowded tent; one thousand people were in attendance, and the money came flowing in. The following Monday the Masons sponsored a benefit for the circus. On July 20th the National Circus and Hippodrome again performed there, and on the 21st they moved on to Sonora.

They went to Todd's Valley, about a half mile from Spring Garden, a lively camp. It had several merchandise stores, a fandango house, and was noted for the string band called "Old

Shave's Band." The circus included Miss Sinclare. The Lees were the trapeze performers, George Peoples climbed the pole and Frenchy made fun of the Chinamen.

Then, it was back to San Francisco. During their stay in August, Madame Austin's performance was very spectacular. She made arrangements with Henry to set up a tightrope on the ground of the vacant lot opposite the International Hotel to be fastened to the top of the hotel. At eight o'clock one morning, Madame Austin made an ascension and descension over a busy street in the heart of San Francisco, which was a breathtaking event.

Henry was approached for a benefit for the orphanage. He and John talked it over. "I'm sure there are other benefits that would help us more."

Henry replied with, "If the city's riches and pleasures are ours, its poverty and suffering must be ours, too. I think we should put on this benefit. A lot of the orphans are out there on the streets."

"I don't look at it that way. It's true, many of their parents have died in cholera epidemics or were washed overboard at sea, but those kids prefer to be out there on the streets. They're always hanging around, and I'm always chasing them away," said John.

"All the more reason why we should give them a benefit."

"One city official was telling me the City Treasury is deeply in debt. No matter how much gold is exchanging hands, the people are adverse to paying taxes, so they look in our direction for support. Why are you so soft hearted about orphanages, Henry?"

"I would hope that if I ever had to call on their help for any of my children, their door would be opened."

So, in spite of John's objection, they presented an afternoon performance free for the children, and the evening proceeds were presented to the Catholic Orphan Asylum. Their program included a "Zoological Exhibition" and dioramic dissolving views of the war in Crimea.

That season they had performed many benefits, and Lee and Marshall in return received commendations for their liberal, generous and unsolicited bestowal of benefits on churches, schools and fire companies throughout the State to a sum of $30,000. Then they returned to Stockton for more work and rest. Henry learned that the Annereaus were in need of a situation and so wrote a letter to their ranch in Sacramento, offering them a position. Then they went back to San Francisco.

They set up their tent on the corner of Jackson and Montgomery. The Annereaus attended the show. After the performance while they were talking, Mrs. Annereau spoke up. "We got your letter, Henry. Is the offer still good?"

"Yes, it is. We're leaving on the 5th for the Sandwich Islands, and you're welcome to join us. I'll give you star billing," he answered, trying not to show his interest in Jeannette, knowing her beautiful dark eyes were sparkling as she looked up at him.

"We'll be ready," she remarked, and they left.

They played the three dates - the 3rd, 4th and 5th of October using the same acts as on their August engagement.

On the night of the 5th they pulled down their tent, packed up their gear and headed for the wharf. After boarding their equipment they led their horses up the gangplank.

Just as the wagons arrived at the wharf ready to load, Mrs. Annereau with her daughter appeared, gear in hand, ready to board the ship.

The last line fell from the dock, and the noble steamer with its mighty throb and a deep sigh bid adieu to San Francisco. They steamed out of the bay and soon lost sight of the city.

Henry stood at the rail, looking out watching the waves as the boat plowed through the water. He looked up, and close by was his little equestrienne, Jeannette, tiny, fairy-like, gentle in her manner, leaning over the rail, now blossomed into a beautiful young lady. The moon was out, the light reflecting on her perfectly formed body. Henry walked over to her and gently touched her hair.

"Isn't it too chilly for you to be out here without a wrap?" asked Henry.

"No, Mr. Lee, I'm fine." Looking up at him, her eyes telling him she adored him, he put his hands on her shoulders and gently drew her to him, kissed her on the forehead. Then she pulled away and was gone in a twinkling of an eye, but Henry knew in his heart his little equestrienne had eyes only for him.

Days passed, yet Henry did not see her, keeping his nightly vigil on the deck.

In due time Diamond Head came into view, and a few hours later they dropped anchor at Honolulu. Waiting to greet them was King Kamehameha, all decked out in his finery. They were greeted warmly and were invited to set up their tent nearby, which was just outside of Honolulu, a thriving city with its many handsome brick buildings on the beautiful tropical island, with its lush growth and flowers in great profusion. They were entertained at the royal court by the native dancers and marveled at the sight of the skill in which the native men were able to throw their flaming torches. Henry caught Jeannette's eye one evening as they were watching the dancers perform, but when he looked around after the show, she was gone.

The next night, for the royal performance, they had everything in readiness. King Kamehameha and his court arrived in full costume and took their places.

The performers entered the arena and rode around the ring, the horses prancing to the music in the lead, the riders balancing, somersaulting, clowning. That night, Jeannette performed to perfection on the high wire, Henry anxiously watched from below. The king and his family enjoyed the show immensely and showered them with flowers.

They went to the other islands, always finding appreciative audiences, so it was with sadness they left that beautiful tropical paradise and headed back to San Francisco. On the trip back Henry spent much of his time up on deck, but his little equestrienne was elsewhere, and he again began to have his doubts.

Panama Crossing

Chapter 10

It was fall, 1855. Andrew Weinshank selected the Isthmus of Panama for their trip to California. Andrew sold the 160 acres of land he received for fighting in Mexico to a man in Georgetown, Washington. With that money he was able to book passage for their trip. What was left, plus some money he had saved from working at the lumber yard, they were able to buy furniture. The Weinshanks traveled from Mobile to New Orleans, their port of debarkation, to book passage on a steamship to Panama. When they headed out their children were small, Carrie six and Frank two. Carrie was managing quite nicely on her own, a pretty little girl, with light brown hair, deep brown eyes; Frank was at an age when he had to be constantly watched, for he was getting into everything. It would have been easier had he been a babe in arms. Andrew was holding Frank's hand, Regina had Carrie at her side, they went into the ticket office. "I'd like to book passage for the four of us," Andrew informed the clerk.

"Here's one. This one started out in Boston, picked up some passengers in New York, then on to Norfolk and Charleston, and now it's here in the harbor. There are some spaces on it. Cabin or steerage?" he asked.

"Cabin," said Andrew. "We also have some furniture to be put aboard."

Regina kept some things she would need along the way. Holding on to Frank's hand and Carrie alongside, she walked up the gangplank while Andrew stayed on deck looking after the furniture. She felt sorry for the poor unlucky souls who got the task of carrying it aboard. She could hear them curse and swear, for it was heavy, all made of black walnut. The heaviest was the dresser, followed by the bed. They carried the sofa aboard, a beautiful piece stuffed with horsehair and covered with shiny black silk. Regina relaxed when she saw it safely on deck. Then came the chair that went with it. The last piece to be carried up the gangplank was the marble-top table. The top, a beautiful piece, started to slip off, but they steadied it, and finally the furniture was all placed safely aboard. The family had all their worldly goods with them, for California was to be their new home—there would be no turning back.

With the usual delays, the scurrying around, they found their quarters and settled in. After a long wait the captain gave the order to pull in the line, and finally under a full steam ahead, they got underway.

They followed the Gulf of Mexico with stops in Havana and Kingston. As they approached the shore, the Weinshanks went on deck. Standing at the rail, they watched the sturdy Negresses filing up and down the gangplank balancing sixty-pound tubs of coal on their heads to store aboard ship.

"What heavy work for women to be expected to do," said Regina.

"I'm sure they're used to it," replied Andrew.

"What will we do, if for some reason we can't work for the general, Andrew?"

"I'll go back to making barrels."

"Why don't we go into business for ourselves? You can make barrels. I'll fill them with foodstuffs from the recipes from the restaurant."

"Well, let's wait and see, but it's certainly something to fall back on."

"Let's go inside, children. We need to get ready for dinner."

As they continued on, they passed through the channel between Cuba and San Domingo. Cuba was in sight all day. It had been a lovely day. There was a fine breeze from the coast, a trade wind. The east end of the island was very rough, high mountains rising from the interior. Finally, they came in sight of Jamaica. They entered the harbor of San Juan and took on more coal. From then on they were in constant sight of land which was quite mountainous.

They arrived at Chagres and dropped anchor two miles or so from town. It had taken about ten days to make the trip. They had been told they would have twenty-seven miles of river, mountain climbing, only to drop almost straight down into the broad plain before reaching Panama. In the background high on a projecting rock was an ancient building, the Fort of Chagres. They stayed on board that night. The next morning by rope ladder and sling, they landed along with the freight. Each passenger dug out his own baggage from the pile which had been dumped on the beach by the lighters. The furniture stayed aboard. The steamer would continue on, following the coastline of South America, around the Horn and on to California. They would pick up their furniture in a warehouse near the wharf in San Francisco.

The town stood on the right bank of the Chagres River, made up of many single room, grass and bamboo huts with roofs thatched with palmetto leaves. Dogs and pigs were in abundance running around. The dogs were barking, the pigs were squealing. Carrie stared at the naked children and pointed at them, to the embarrassment of her mother. They watched the barefooted men in soiled white trousers and the cigar-smoking women walking around.

It was the most filthy place imaginable, and Regina wanted them to be on their way for the sake of the children. On the left bank were white frame houses used as hotels. Above them on the bluff was the abandoned castle of San Lorenzo.

Andrew was one of the spokesmen who talked to a boatman, a 'padrone' as he called himself, dressed in his muslin shirt, dirty white pants and large Panama hat, smoking a large cigar in his still larger mouth. They agreed on a price and made preparations to board his boat, which was a large hollowed-out log.

As they got into the bango, all was excitement. Some had misplaced their baggage among the others on the landing, but after getting everything straightened out, they were all of good cheer. With a sense of adventure were ready to head up the river. There were no seats, so everyone had to sit on his own luggage. Regina spread out her feather tick, a large sack filled with goose down which she brought along for the family, thinking they might have use for it.

The padrone took his own jolly good time to get under way. But finally, off came his Panama hat, his shirt, his pants, leaving only his loin cloth as his sole protection against the sun and the rain. Carrie's eyes grew as big as saucers, for she had never seen a man like this before. "Look, mama," but before she could get any more out, Regina planted her hand over her daughter's mouth to quiet her down and prayed he hadn't noticed. With the unrobing ceremony completed, they knew they soon were to be on their way.

They were glad to leave the town behind them with its stench from the filth and offal. "It's good to breathe this clean, pure air again," said Regina, as she kept turning her head looking at both side of the banks, lined with vegetation. Her eyes never wearied of the thick tangle of luxuriant foliage of tropical growth where trees flourished wherever they could get a foothold.

The padrone kept the boat close to shore, cradling his long pole against his bare shoulders so he could propel the boat. Sometimes he would tow the boat from the riverbank, and on occasion, by jumping into the water, he seized the gunwales and dragged it ahead. When they arrived at the most dangerous part of the rapids, the boatman exerted all his skill and dexterity to keep his boat from dashing against the rocks. All along the banks were remnants of the broken boats that hadn't made it.

"I wonder if lives have been lost here," said Regina, trying to remain as calm as possible.

"By the looks of the wreckage, you'd certainly think so," Andrew replied.

The padrone started yelling and cursing, for this part of the rapids gave him trouble. The boat slapped the water with such force the passengers were drenched. Little Frank cried while his father protected him the best he could with his own body. Regina and Carrie clung together. Then all of a sudden it was over. When everybody had regained their composure, the ladies fussed with their hair, smoothed out their dresses, all were grateful for their safety. When they got to calmer water the padrone spent time resting wherever a patch of shade presented itself.

They came upon the plain. Along the banks were sugar plantations, rice paddies, fields of corn and grazing cattle. As their journey lengthened, the bango became uncomfortable, the heat oppressive. Sweat ran down their faces, their hair fell in disarray, the ladies furiously waved their fans, and the rattling of the awning became a distraction of no value, for it was no protection against the sun.

From time to time, when it got too hot, the padrone would slow down the bango, take off his loin cloth and dive into the water for a swim, taking no heed nor having concern for those sitting in the boat trying to keep as cool as possible. After he was refreshed, he pulled himself back into the boat. Each time this happened, Regina took Carrie's hand and gently turned her daughter's head while the padrone put on his loin cloth. They continued on.

The half-caste boatman poled slowly, the air was heavy and the odor intense, the heat was unbearably oppressive. Monkeys chattered in the trees, parrots and water fowl darted along the water's edge dipping and shrieking. Alligators slid off the mud banks, disappearing into the water with hardly a ripple. This frightened the children, but their father held them tightly.

Every living thing clung and intertwined itself into the various trees along the way. Along both banks was the rich bright green of the parasitic plants covered with flowers of every hue of the spectrum as well as large patches of water lilies.

They spent the night at the water's edge. Some brave souls preferred to sleep in the huts along the way, but Regina preferred to lay out their feather tick in the boat and make out the best they could. The children slept between them. Either Regina or Andrew had to keep one eye open for fear their little Frank would try to move around and fall overboard.

The next morning the boatman got everything in readiness, and they continued on their way. It was another day on the river and another night before they arrived at Gorgona. Regina passed out dried jerky, apples, apricots and molasses to the family from her own store of food, simple but life-sustaining, to get them by until they could buy fresh meat and vegetables. Then the padrone decided he wouldn't continue on without further payment. "Maybe this will change your mind," as one of the passengers whipped out his gun, pointing it at the padrone. Though the women and children were frightened, all was dead silence. Andrew was able to intercede, and in his simple Spanish said to the padrone, "Finish the trip and I'll see what I can do." When they again got underway, the man holding the gun said, "This is the only thing he understands."

"That may be true," said Andrew. "But he pulled us through the rapids and feels he's entitled to more money. I'm not too sure I don't agree with him.

The next town after Gorgona was Cruces, a little hamlet of thatched palm huts. Men and women moved about while the little children played naked as jaybirds. "They don't wear any clothes, mama. Why do we?"

"We're not as hardy as they, Carrie. Your skin is delicate."

"I hope that satisfied her," said Andrew.

"It will till she sees some more," replied Regina.

At Cruces, Andrew passed the hat. The padrone was given a piece of change and left with a smile on his face. Here Andrew hired a donkey for their journey on to Panama. He threw the tick over the beast, helped Regina on, handed her little Frank, lifted Carrie up behind. "Now keep your arms around your mother at all times," he said as he started off on foot guiding them. At first, the critter wouldn't budge. Andrew pulling, then pushing him. Regina leaned over, patted him on his neck, and he started out.

The road was in poor condition with deep ruts in many places, and along the way they saw many dead animals being devoured by the vultures. They spent the night alongside the road.

The next day they had a high mountain to climb. They made their way steadily up, crossing streams, stumbling over fallen trees that blocked their path. They kept on going through the tropical forest with its lightning, thunder and incessant rain. The children were frightened by the noise. They traveled over a cobblestone path so narrow they had to stop and move off to the side to allow an approaching mule train to pass. After reaching the top of the mountain, Regina looked over. It looked as though it was straight down.

"Andrew, I can't make it. I'm frightened."

"You will, Regina. Try not to look down. This donkey is a sure-footed animal. Stubborn yes! But if we can get him going we'll be all right. You're as safe on his back as you would be if you walked, and it will be easier on you. Give it a try at least."

"I'll try Andrew, but hold on tight."

"You can count on that, Regina."

The descent was more arduous than the climb. Step by step they made their way down the path constructed of rocks placed in steps by the early Spaniards, the same road over which they took precious gems from Mexico to Spain.

They passed native men carrying produce strapped to their heads on their way to Chagres. As they descended into the valley, one of the men became ill. He wanted to turn back but was unable to; Andrew helped one of the other men strap him on one of the donkeys, and they continued on. Finally the mountains gave way to the table lands, and in the distance was the welcome sight of Panama.

At length they reached the coastal plains and looked upon the tiled roofs, bell towers and the blue waters of the Pacific. As they approached Panama, the country was flat, and they had no protection from the sun. The city before them appeared to be a lively place, a vista of enormous signboards, and the American flag was in evidence everywhere. It was a very imposing city, situated on a rocky promontory jutting out into the placid bay, with its massive fortifications and most of its buildings two stories or more in height. Many of them were in ruins, others abandoned. Many had been built of stone, adobe and some of wood.

"Oh, what a relief," said Regina. "I do hope that poor, sick man will make it."

"I'm afraid he doesn't have a chance, not if it's Panama Fever," said Andrew.

They tramped endlessly across the cobblestones, looking for a room and supplies to replace the things they had lost, broken or consumed along the way.

As they traveled along, they saw women in their long full calico skirts, nearly bare to the waist covered only by a thin gauze jacket showing their plump breasts. Their long black braided hair was elaborately decorated with flowers. They passed many saloons and gambling establishments. On a vacant lot they saw a priest taking bets on a cockfight.

"Andrew, look at that—disgusting isn't it?"

"No different than it was in Mexico, Regina, but I wonder what my brother would say if he saw him."

"You mean the one who entered the priesthood?"

"Yes. Then again, maybe it wouldn't bother him."

When they passed the ticket office, they found many people waiting to arrange passage for San Francisco. Many looked sickly to Regina, which prompted her to say, "Let's stay by ourselves and prepare our own meals."

"I agree," said Andrew. "Food is your department. I'll find a spot in the country, and we'll camp out."

"Why don't we go get settled," suggested Regina.

"Yes. I'll come back here tomorrow," added Andrew.

They set up camp in a campground on the outskirts of town. There was a nice market nearby where they were able to purchase some fresh fruit, the first in several days. The next day Andrew went to the ticket office and stood in line most of the day trying to arrange passage for the trip up the coast.

They knew they would have to wait for their ship, so they decided to see the sights. They visited the Catholic Cathedral, a large stone structure, the old gloomy style of architecture with its four towers and several bells, most of which were cracked, for they had been hammered on by the servants twenty-four hours a day throughout the years.

When the day came for them to depart, they assembled on the beach below the sea wall. One by one they climbed onto the bare shoulders of the native porters who carried them through the breakers to a boat waiting to take them to the ship.

On ship, even though they were crowded together, the gentle breezes of the Pacific were a pleasant contrast to the hot, humid climate of Panama. They departed that ancient city and followed the coastline of Central America. Once they had crossed the mouth of the Gulf of California, they had more wind and a rougher sea. The mountains of Mexico were in view. The balmy weather made the trip very enjoyable. The Volcano Colima was in sight all the next day, a good 140 miles away, a massive cone-like peak rising into the clear blue sky with clouds curling above its summit. Regina and Andrew sat on deck, Regina holding Frank and watching Carrie play close by.

"This is the most beautiful sunset I have ever seen, more beautiful than Baden, or in the south of France, even more beautiful than on shipboard on the Gulf. The rosy pink light that illuminates those snowy peaks in the distance is more pronounced here than anywhere else I've been."

"All of Mexico is beautiful, Regina, but wait 'till you see California."

Aboard ship it was noisy and dirty, and the people were quarrelsome. They saw men sitting around spitting tobacco juice, picking their teeth with their knives.

They called at Acapulco. The harbor was a beautiful site, hemmed in by hills, but hot. The ship anchored in the bay, for there were no wharfs. They were taking on sacks of coal and cattle as well as other provisions, including an ample supply of food. The Weinshanks went ashore to spend the night. In town the plaza was filled with natives selling fruit, shells and liquor. Some were gambling.

They walked through a spacious park, purchased more delicious fruits and nuts and checked into a hotel for a good night's rest. The town had many adobe buildings and a beautiful fort built of white sandstone appearing to be capable of destroying any force that would enter the harbor. They hated to leave that beautiful spot, but the next day they returned to their ship, for it was scheduled to continue on.

The trip north was a succession of warm days with fair winds, sparkling seas and occasional showers. Spray and waves would sometimes sweep the deck. Their meals consisted of coffee, hard bread and molasses for breakfast, salt pork or corned beef and beans for dinner and hard bread and sugar for supper. For the next few days the shoreline looked desolate with its barren shores.

They became very excited when they sailed through the Golden Gate, the narrow strait between two rocks and into the bay itself. Andrew looking out over the placid bay remarked, "Such a large harbor, all the ships of the world can anchor here and have room to spare."

Finally they saw in the distance a cluster of buildings silhouetted against the dark hillside. As they sailed through the narrow entrance to the bay, before them were the dusty California hills, the large brick buildings, the gray tents and dusty shacks on the edge of the town blended into the chaparral and dirt of the hills.

Their ship pulled amid the forest of masts of steamers, lumber barges, whalers, and China clippers. Along the shoreline were rows of long narrow wharves extending into the bay on pilings, such a beautiful place with the town built on the gentle slope. Andrew could tell by her eyes that Regina was falling in love with San Francisco.

Regina Weinshank

Andrew Weinshank

Hanging of Cora & Casey

Chapter 11

When the Weinshanks arrived in San Francisco, Andrew looked up his old commander, General Smith, thinking perhaps he could suggest a place for them to stay, and again offer him employment. But when Andrew went to look him up, he learned the General had left California and returned to finish out his military career in the East. Nor did he have a chance to chat with his aide, William Tecumseh Sherman, for he was away on business.

By the time the Weinshanks arrived in San Francisco, gambling had been outlawed, so gamblers had become very unpopular. The gambler, Charlie Cora, had the biggest and fanciest and the most popular saloon in town, the El Dorado, and so was the most hated. Many a gambler had spent an hour relaxing in the lobby of his saloon, the only place in town where a man could get in out of the rain, have a bite to eat at the free lunch counter and transact a little "business" on the side.

Cora was a little man, less than medium height, slim with dark complection and large eyes. He wore a black mustache down over his mouth. He dressed immaculately and always wore a diamond pin in his cravat. Cora's woman, Belle, was slight of build, above medium height, with skin delicately tinted as the pink blossoms of a peach, possessed a form that was beautifully seductive. They had never married.

They attended the American Theatre on the evening of November 15th, 1855. Belle was the best dressed woman in the house and felt perfectly at home sitting in the red plush seats in the first balcony, watching the performance of "Nicodemus."

Sitting a few rows in front of them was Mrs. Richardson, the wife of the United States Marshal for that district. It was her opinion that the likes of Belle should either sit in the seats behind the balcony or in the proscenium boxes.

It was Mrs. Richardson who was the first to complain. She told her husband, "If you don't get 'those people' out of here, I'm going home." Her husband walked back to Cora and Belle and ordered them to leave. They refused. He then went back to his seat, spoke to his wife, and they left.

The next afternoon the Marshal was in the Blue Wing Saloon, and while talking to the bartender, he said, "I'm going to slap Cora's face." Just about that time Cora walked in. The two men were introduced, they had a drink together and both walked out and started down the street. Suddenly, there was a shot. Richardson fell dead on the street, and Cora was hustled off to jail.

All of a sudden, there was an epidemic of civic virtue. A vigilante committee was formed to do something about Charlie Cora, the gambler, who had shot Marshal Richardson. Some folks thought had it been the other way around, there would have been some way to exonerate him.

The Lees set up their tent on the corner of Jackson and Montgomery Streets. They were now performing before the sophisticated city folk, for the raucous and rowdy miner was scarcely seen any longer. On the program was a French Troupe, Madame Austin, the tightrope dancer, Monsieur Austin, while Cordona and Frenchy were the clowns.

One day Henry and John Marshall walked into the Bank Exchange, a very prestigious saloon, which took up the entire ground floor of the Brannan building. Everything in it had come by ship around the Horn. They walked up to the enormous solid mahogany lunch table to get a bite to eat, got a drink from the elaborate bar and sat down at a damask covered table to enjoy it.

"This place isn't lacking anything," said John. "Every bit as nice as any place back East."

Henry wasn't listening. He picked up the newspaper, looking for news about the theatre. "Listen to this, John. 'The Forrest Theatre is being built in Sacramento." Then he put the paper down. "I had hopes of building a theatre there ourselves, and that would mean competition for us, wouldn't it?"

"I'm sure Sacramento can handle two nice theatres," said John, his mind obviously on other matters.

"I guess we were smart to leave San Francisco when we did," said Henry. "According to this paper, there has been a lot of cholera here."

"People die like flies from that dread disease! Maybe some day they'll have a cure. Here's something, John, Charlie Cora is in jail for shooting Marshal Richardson."

"Times have changed, a few years back nothing would have been done about it." Being close to show time, they headed back to the tent.

They moved on to Sacramento. There Lee and Marshall went in search of a piece of property to build their own pavilion. All the buildings on the north side of K Street from 3rd to 17th had been razed in the recent fire. They found a suitable piece of property between 4th and 5th Streets and bought it. It was on high ground above the flood level, overlooking the stores below.

Merchants nearer the levee at the river's edge were making plans to bring in dirt to raise the level of the streets. Either their buildings had to be raised up on stilts, which most of them preferred, or they had to turn their first stories into basements, with the second story then becoming the ground level. At any rate, the streets had to be raised.

The pavilion Henry and John were planning was to be an ornament to the city, a building that could be used for opera and other theatrical events as well as for the circus. Being concerned about the constant threat of fire, they built with brick.

The Lees were now in their heyday, at the top of their profession. Everyone the country over was caught up with the glamour of the circus, and they were reveling in the popularity and praise had been bestowed upon them. Henry hired Frank Rivers to act as General Agent. Rivers was in the eastern states making preparations for an elaborate show—new wagons, better equipment and costumes.

"As I live and breathe," declared Henry one day, as a familiar face entered the tent. Henry strode over and welcomed the newcomer with open arms. "Sam Latrop! I never thought I'd see you here! The last time I saw you was at the Bowery Theater in New York, when I first came to this country."

"That's right, I heard you were here and doing well in California. Thought I might look you up."

"I'd like to include you on the bill," said Henry. "One thing about clowns—you can always use more than one. George Peoples and Frenchy Rochette have both been clowning for me for almost as long as I've been here, but I'm always looking for new talent. We keep on perfecting our show. In fact, I'll feature you from time to time."

"Sounds great," said Sam. "This is an exciting place to be."

"I said that myself when I first came here, but it's not quite as exciting as it used to be."

From Sacramento, they went to Columbia for a special performance on April 5th, giving a benefit for the school. Sam Latrop was the hit of the show. That night the editor of the newspaper attended and gave it a good review.

By May 5th, the circus was back in San Francisco at Jackson near Kearny Street, on the lot next to the International Hotel. The Weinshanks attended, enthralled at all there was to see. Little Carrie was agog watching the ceiling walking by Lenton, and they all laughed till their sides ached at America's greatest clown, Sam Latrop.

Also on the bill were Mr. Peoples, La Petite Lizzi, and Madame Annereau the Queen of the Arena, who enjoyed the double title Sprite of the Circle and Ariel of the Tightrope. Henry had an array of talent unequalled anywhere on the coast.

While in town Henry and John decided to build a hippodrome, so they went to see a man who specialized in canvas work. "We want our tent to be eighty by one hundred sixty feet long."

"That's a pretty tall order. Never heard of a tent that big, but I guess it can be done."

"Yes, it will be large," said Henry. "I want one like the one P. T. Barnum has in New York."

"It will cost you a bundle," the tent maker answered. "In the neighborhood of forty thousand dollars."

"I'm sure it will, but I'm willing and able to pay it. You let me know when you can start. I'll want to supervise and will want to be here from time to time."

"It'll take some doing to get that much canvas. But I'll let you know when I'm ready to start. Well, I've got to get back to my work. Thank you for your order, sir."

The Weinshanks loved living there in the hustle of the young and thriving town. Andrew was working at a lumber yard. Regina was spending her time keeping house and caring for the children.

The gambler Cora was still sitting in jail, awaiting a second trial, for the first one had resulted in a hung jury. Then, another fellow by the name of Casey shot James King of William. Casey, a young man of 28, a political power, an expert ballot box stuffer, a desperate fighting man, was the editor of a small newspaper. For reasons unknown to others, he had decided to lay low for James King of William, the editor of the *Bulletin,* and caught him as he was walking down the street. He shot him, only wounding him. Casey was arrested and put in jail along with Cora.

One day while Andrew was in the business section of town, on an errand for his boss, he noticed an angry mob, milling around in the street, outside the jail, waiting for justice to be served. He passed the circus tent, looked inside and noticed the crowd was sparse and concluded the people had a more interesting show to watch in the vicinity of the jail house.

The crowd kept calling for both prisoners, but when word came that James King of William was doing better, the tension lessened, and the crowd went home.

When word was received that James King of William had died, the angry mob again assembled.

The streets were empty on Sundays, so the Committee of Vigilance chose that day to move. They struck from all directions.

The committeemen rode up on horseback, their bayonets fixed, glittering in the sun, heading in the direction of the city jail. They had a brass six-pounder, which they mounted in front of it.

The Commander of the Vigilantes knocked on the door of the jailhouse and demanded that Casey and Cora be handed over to him. This accomplished, they took the two men to Fort Gunnysack in carriages and tried them on the court house steps before a small crowd. Both men pleaded self-defense. Both were found guilty as charged.

The funeral for King was on May 22nd. Throngs of people crowded the streets in all the available spots along the route—in windows, on balconies, on the hilltops, along Stockton, Montgomery and Bush Streets, thinking the funeral of King to be the main event of the day. The Weinshanks, Andrew, Regina and the children were there.

Henry Lee in the circus tent nearby, had a matinee to perform no matter how sparse the crowd. He felt a funeral under those circumstances would only stir up the crowd, and he wanted no part of that. The other members of the troupe wanted to watch the funeral, but Henry stuck to his guns, so they too had to remain inside. Then too, Henry felt Charlie hadn't been given a fair trial.

Henry pulled into the ring at the head of the grand cavalcade as usual, while outside the crowd moved in the direction of Fort Gunnysack, where a platform was being erected. A man running past the Weinshanks turned and yelled, "You'd better hurry—they'll be hanging Cora and Casey before you get there!"

As they walked along, being hurried by the crowd, Andrew said, "They may deserve it, but this isn't any way to go about it."

On down the street they could see the vigilantes pushing both men onto a platform high above the crowd. A white cloth covered both their heads and tied down around their necks, their arms tied down to their sides and their feet were bound. In his hand Cora held a handkerchief.

Cora remained silent, but Casey wanted to speak his piece, so a man stepped up and removed his cover. While he was talking, the Weinshanks were being pushed along with the crowd and were within the sound of his voice. "Why is he being strung up?" asked Andrew of the man alongside him. "Some say he had it in for James King of William, because King exposed him for being an ex-convict."

Then Regina spoke up, "Andrew, I don't want the children to see this. Let's go home."

"A wise decision, Regina, let's. Let us by folks," and the people graciously opened up a space for them to leave.

As they were walking away, Cora's head was uncovered, the platform was pulled out from under them and they were left swinging in mid-air. The handkerchief Cora was holding went fluttering to the ground.

Then Andrew got an order to make barrels for the miners of the territory. It meant the family would have to move to Los Angeles. The plan called for Andrew to make the barrels and Regina to prepare the foodstuffs to fill them, using the family recipes, used in the restaurant at Monte Carlo in the south of France. Their contract called for catsup, pickled turnips and sauerkraut. They considered themselves fortunate, for they already had a market for their products.

As soon as their contract was signed, sealed and delivered, they made their plans to move to the Pueblo of Los Angeles. Andrew made arrangements to have their furniture shipped to Los Angeles, and it was stored in a warehouse near the bay.

There was great hubbub on the wharf as the Weinshanks were getting ready to head on down the coast. Boats of all sizes and shapes were anchored nearby. The children were excited, taking in everything as they walked up the gangplank of the long, sleek, majestic sidewheeler. She was two decks high and topped by a lofty black stack. With her white paint glowing and her flag fluttering lazily overhead, stirred by a mild breeze, she created quite a picture. They stayed on deck as they left the harbor, watched the paddles churn the water into a frothing foam out of proportion to the speed they were making.

After a short but pleasant voyage, they stopped at Monterey. As they rounded the point, the town burst into view. Above it loomed the rolling mesa, mantled in emerald green with its pine-covered hills beyond. Immediately before them stood the Presidio buildings, a large quadrangle with an imposing chapel dome towered above the walled-in enclosure. To their right, lay the anchorage. From the deck they could see a few houses with white walls and red roofs scattered over the grassy plains.

It was here on July 7, 1846 that Commodore Sloat planted the American flag taking possession of California. On July 16th, only nine days later, an English ship entered the harbor. Because it was now occupied, its Commander, Admiral Seymour, pulled anchor and sailed away.

The "Ohio" continued on down the coast. The following day, they dropped anchor in the bay of Santa Barbara.

The Weinshanks watched from the deck as they entered the harbor looking at a scattering of white washed adobes with red tile roofs clustered inside the crumbling walls. On the beach men were riding horseback, and their families were following, lumbering along in their carretas.

There was no wharf, so the passengers and freight had to be taken ashore in small boats, a time-consuming job. Andrew and Regina, holding onto their children, watched anxiously waiting to see if the passengers would make it without serious mishap. One boat capsized and emptied its passengers into the water to the amusement of those on board.

As the boats approached shallow water, the people and their baggage were carried to dry land by the sailors. After the people had been delivered to the shore, the sailors returned to the ship and they continued on toward Los Angeles.

Pueblo de Los Angeles

Chapter 12

The passengers were startled by the sound of the signal gun, letting those on shore know that the voyage had been a safe one, as the sidewheeler "Ohio" approached the harbor of Los Angeles on a beautiful June day.

One passenger who made that trip frequently was quite disgruntled. He gave the other passengers a full account.

"You wouldn't believe it, but this boat has a name change every few months. Today it's the 'Ohio,' a few months back it was the 'Goliath,' the 'Sea Bird' or the 'Southerner,' but always the same old boat. Oh, she looks good, all right but it's like makeup on a whore, it covers up the hard use, but the core is old just the same. If they didn't give such miserable service and if she were more seaworthy, maybe they wouldn't have to change her name so often. The only thing that remains constant is the captain. His name is Captain Haley, Salisbury Haley."

"This is common practice," said Andrew to Regina. "Circus people do it all the time, too. Each year they take a new name, and people think they're seeing a new show."

"I'm sure that just comes under the heading of good business, doesn't it?" asked Regina, not waiting for a reply, for they were ready to disembark.

As the "Ohio" pulled into the harbor at Pueblo de Los Angeles, Regina asked Andrew, "Where's the town?"

"It's twenty-seven miles inland. We'll take a stage here into town."

The crew readied the small craft for the passengers to go ashore. The ladies and children were first, followed by the men. When they reached the shallow water, they were carried ashore by the sailors.

On shore there were no buildings, just flat, open space. They were met by a big, powerful man, coatless, vestless, who wore neither necktie nor collar; his pantaloons were at least six inches too short, his socks had large holes and his shoes were crude. His bright-colored suspenders added to the picturesque effect of his costume.

"Welcome to Los Angeles," he said as he directed them to his stage which was waiting to take them to the pueblo, the common Western variety, six broncos with primitive harness. The stage had four rows of seats. Each row held four people. The front row included the driver, a big burly man with piercing eyes and scraggly beard. "My name's Sam, Sam Jones. You can call me 'Jonesy' if you like. Everybody does." Regina sat by him, then the children squeezed in and Andrew on the outside. Andrew gave Jonesy five dollars for the fare. As soon as the seats were filled, not a minute was lost. He cracked his whip, called out to his team and they sped away at breakneck speed.

With the trip well started, Jonesy relaxed and became talkative. "That man that greeted you when you came on shore was Banning," he yelled over to Andrew, "I've been driving for him for some time now and I can say this about him—he can drive a six-horse stage faster, over rougher roads, than anybody who ever cracked the whip or pulled the ribbons."

"Sounds like quite a man."

"He's quite a fellow, all right. Just last year Banning and some other fellows bought fifteen wagons and one hundred fifty mules and transported goods from the harbor to the Mormon settlement at Salt Lake in the Utah territory over the Old Spanish Trail. They stopped at San Bernardino, left there in May and returned in September."

"That must be quite a distance."

"Sure is, and over a lot of hot, dry desert land. Now we're going through Rancho San Pedro. After Don Juan Dominguez died, his nephew, Manuel Gutierrez took over. He sat out there on his horse and watched his cattle graze over the countryside. We'll be stopping there."

"They do have a beautiful view of the ocean," remarked Regina.

"You bet it is. Then Don Francisco Sepulveda settled on some of the Dominguez land. He wanted to file on his own name, so he went to Monterey to ask the governor for a grant. On the way back to Los Angeles he stopped at Mission La Purisima. Some unfriendly Indians attacked the mission that day, and he was struck by an arrow and died. When the governor heard about it, he sent word to Los Angeles that Don Francisco's children were to be given part of the Dominguez Rancho, calling it Rancho San Vicente."

"What about the dry seasons?" asked Andrew.

"We've had some terrible droughts—cattle die by the thousands, and you can hardly stand the smell, both in town and in the country."

"What do they use that for?" asked Regina, pointing to the strings of hide hung on the fences drying in the sunshine.

"That's rawhide. They use it to make slits for the latch strings and the hinges, for laces for their shoes, they let their bucket down the well with it; they use it to weave their chair seats, twist it to use for lariats, stretch it over the bedstead to hold their mattresses, for mats for the floor, as glue and nails, they use it as rope on the wooden plough or on the ox carts. They use it for everything."

"It's amazing," said Andrew.

"One large rancho supports lots of people. The Lord and master, his big family, his poor relations, harness makers, wool combers, tanners and carpenters, and they have many Indian vaqueros and servants, so they need a lot of everything."

"And large adobes to house them," added Regina.

"I'll say, and mostly bedrooms, for their cooking is done outside. Their beds are made of cowhide, fastened to a frame which has four legs and they're alive with fleas. They also have them in all the cracks of the walls in their adobes and in the hides that are strewn around. They call them little 'malditos'."

"And the work?" asked Andrew.

"All with Indian help. They make adobe bricks, plant the corn, crush the grapes, grind the flour, bake the bread, cradle the babies and haul the hides to the ships."

The driver pulled to a halt at the halfway house. "This was the Dominguez adobe at one time," said Jonesy. It was here the driver changed horses, and they had a chance to get a bit to eat before continuing on. While the driver was leading the fresh horses into position, Andrew offered to help.

"Did you see that Indian taking his squaw down to the beach?" asked Jonesy.

"The ones we just passed?"

"That's so the squaw can be used by the sailors. Ain't that somethin'? When she gets done, they divide the money. Sometimes they get caught and are whipped and have to carry mud and adobe bricks for the new buildings going up in town."

"Here, too!" remarked Andrew.

"You bet, here too! Well, I guess we're ready to pull out. If you men will help the ladies and children in, we'll be on our way."

Back in the wagon and again on the roadway, Jonesy again started talking, "It hasn't been too many years since Stockton and his men came through here and took over Los Angeles."

Then Andrew added, "That happened about ten years ago, didn't it? I signed up for the war in Mexico about that time."

"Oh? Where in Mexico?" asked Jonesy.

"All the way to Mexico City."

"There were several battles here in California, at San Pasqual, San Gabriel, the Mesa and the last one was at Cahuenga."

"I had enough fighting in Mexico to last me all my days."

"Is there a church in town?" asked Regina, trying to change the subject, as she did whenever Andrew began to talk about the war.

"Yes, Our Lady Queen of the Angels, and then the old Mission San Gabriel is just a short distance away."

"We're Catholics and are looking forward to attending mass there."

"Just because we have a beautiful church doesn't mean our sleepy little Mexican village is law-abiding and all that. The place is alive with 'Mala Vidas,' you know what they are don't you?" Not one to blush at realities, Regina nodded her head in the affirmative. "And we have lots of saloons and gambling houses."

"Is this the only road leading into town?" asked Andrew. Now he was trying to change the subject.

"The only one from the harbor, but there are others. There are several coming in from the ranchos. They also lead out in all directions like the spokes of a lopsided wheel through the vineyards and cornfields to the ocean or to the mountain country."

"Then there's more out there than just ranchos?" asked Andrew.

"Oh, sure!" One road leads to the Mission San Gabriel, one to the tar pits, one to the Mission San Fernando, one to the cemetery, Campo Santo on Eternity Street. One road leads to San Pedro, another to Redondo where salt can be obtained, one to Santa

Barbara. If the Yorba family comes to the pueblo in a carreta, or if a priest is coming to the mission from San Diego, they come by the King's Highway, El Camino Real, the most important highway of all.

"Why do they leave the peace and quiet of their ranchos for town?" asked Regina.

"They like it in town. They come to make cattle deals or to buy liquor or saddles, sometimes to see a horse race or watch the bear or bull fights or play a little monte or call on a priest to arrange a baptism, a wedding, or a funeral, or maybe pay a visit to the 'Mala Vidas'," said Jonesy, catching Andrew's eye, then continued talking, "The pack train caravans come in from Santa Fe, New Mexico, with goods to trade for horses and mules, so the people in town are able to get about anything they want or need."

"By the way, are there any nice hotels in town?"

"The Bella Union. It's the one and only, the best hotel this side of San Francisco."

After traveling the twenty-seven miles over the mesa, they approached the town, continuing on until they reached San Pedro Street, a narrow lane no wider than needed to pass another stage or wagon. The roadway was lined with willows, and off to one side were many rows of grapevines. Carrie covered her ears to cut out the shouts and yells as their driver was hailed by every inhabitant and dog along the way. At last they arrived at the Bella Union Hotel, a single story adobe on Main and Commercial Streets.

Andrew helped Regina and the children down, and they all entered the hotel where they were greeted by the manager, Dr. Hammel. The doctor, a small energetic man, ushered them out the back door of the hotel to one of the small rooms where they would stay until they could find a place of their own. The room was small, scarcely six feet by nine, with a low ceiling and earthen floor. There was hardly room for a bed and their baggage. Regina looked about her ruefully, "At least it's clean," she thought.

What do you think of our town?" asked the doctor.

"I saw many a town like this in Mexico during the war," Andrew replied. "In fact, many of the cities in Mexico are far more advanced than anything we have in the United States. There the buildings are larger, better built, and their streets are paved. Their houses are made of white sandstone, and they have red tiled roofs."

"We do have a long way to go, I'll admit, but we have a map of Los Angeles with all the lots drawn up. A fellow by the name of

Ord did it in '49. So, you were in the war. Several others who fought in Mexico have settled here: Billy Getman, Gabe Allen, Dr. Reed."

"Billy Getman, I knew him. I'll look him up. Maybe we can exchange a few yarns."

"Come on back to the dining room and we'll scrape you up something to eat, then I'll take you to the plaza and you can make up your own minds about our town."

"That's very kind of you," said Regina.

If Regina had misgivings about the town Andrew had selected for them, she kept them to herself. Though it was a far cry from San Francisco, it possessed a certain charm which appealed to her, and she sensed it was steeped in history. This was the case, for it was in this valley protected by the San Gabriel mountains where Felipe de Neve was granted permission by the Viceroy of Mexico, Bucarelli, to establish a pueblo on the plain, near the mission San Gabriel Archangel, ordained by royal decree.

The Spanish grant of Felipe de Neve and his party covered four square leagues, extending "one league to each wind" from the Plaza, and they named their settlement, El Pueblo de Nuestra Señora Las Reina de Los Angeles.

Eleven men, eleven women and twenty-two children brought from Sonora lived and prospered on their land, and their crops flourished, but all the while the pueblo remained a squat Mexican village, teeming with goats, chickens and children.

After the Weinshanks had a bite to eat, they started out with Dr. Hammel to walk around the town. They found the Plaza to be the center of life in the little hamlet, and a dumping ground for refuse.

"Is there a tin shop nearby?" Andrew inquired. "I'll need some bands for my barrels."

"Yes, Ozro Childs has one on Commercial Street."

"Seems like a busy place you have here," remarked Andrew, trying not to notice the garbage in the street.

"Yes. From early dawn to evening everything is on the move, jingling spurs, cavorting steeds, and whizzing reatas."

Though the town was small, it was rip-roaring with its bordellos, saloons and gambling houses galore. All around them were impressive adobes. Toward the north they could see a distant adobe with a single pepper tree providing the only shade, and nearby there was a stone reservoir. They looked at the other buildings facing the Plaza. Then they stopped and listened to the sweet chimes of the church bells penetrating the peace and quiet of the sleepy village. The church of Our Lady, Queen of the Angels, faced the large corral-like Plaza, surrounded by a fence with a loop at each corner.

"Isn't this a beautiful church, Andrew?"

"Ya, it is."

"I'm anxious to see it inside. It gives me comfort to know we have such a gracious place in which to worship."

They walked past Don Ygnacio Del Valle's adobe on the east side of the square between Calle de los Negroes and Vine Street. The doctor pointed it out to them. "Del Valle has been the Alcalde for several years. That's where Don Ygnacio Colonel lives," pointing his adobe out. "He's a young man of culture and refinement. He has the only public school in town. The city pays him fifteen dollars a month to hold classes at his home. He served as Captain under General Flores when they fought against Fremont at Cahuenga."

They stopped in front of the home of Don Vicente Lugo. "Don Vicente was killed not far from here in the battle of San Gabriel. Over there is Ygnacio de Valle's adobe. It's Valle's job to record the brands and grants and other property transactions. Across from him, on the other side of the street, lives Don Augustin Olvera. And in that brown house is where Francisco O'Campo lives."

As they walked along, they passed Indians sitting around in groups on the ground, the sun beating down on them.

"Don't stare at them, children, it's impolite."

"Are there any other towns nearby?" asked Andrew.

"The Mormons have started their own settlement—San Bernardino—up at the base of that range of mountains. Between here and San Bernardino is the small town of El Monte, and close by is the Mission San Gabriel. The rest is all open cattle range."

Carrie pointed to a sign pointing in the direction of the ravine north of town. Noticing her point, their host said, "That's where the bull and bear fights are held."

"Are there a lot of ranchos here?" asked Andrew.

"Oh, yes, twenty or so. Some cover thousands of acres."

"Are they close by?" asked Andrew.

"One is just outside of town, Rancho La Ballona. It's just south of the pueblo. It belongs to Don Machado. Jose Sepulveda, too, has one close by. He has a beautiful adobe on his land northwest of Sonora town."

"Looks like all these adobes were built to last," said Regina.

"That's Cristobal Aguilar's adobe facing us, and this one over here is owned by Antonio Carrillo. He was in the battle of San Gabriel. Those are real tiles on his roof.

"After the Americans took over Los Angeles, Stockton put Gillespie in charge of the men stationed here. His headquarters were in a small adobe where the Bella Union now stands. After the battle, the adobe, was torn down and the Bella Union was built in'49. Ever since I took over I've wanted to put a second story on it and hope to one of these days."

"On the way to town the driver was telling us several battles had been fought here in California. Did all of the dons take part?"

"Quite a few. I know Don Sanchez from Rancho Merced and Don Ramirez from Rancho Santa Gertrudes, both fought in it, and so did Don Luis Vignes and Don Francisco Reyes. Don Francisco Reyes was killed in the battle on the mesa."

"Were any of them sympathizers to the American cause?" asked Andrew.

"Oh, yes! B. D. Wilson was. He came to California with the Workman-Rowland party, married one of Bernardo Yorba's daughters. He influenced his father-in-law in the direction of California being a protectorate. Forster was another one that was in favor of the United States."

They paused at the Avila adobe on Vine Street.

"Commodore Stockton made his headquarters here. Stockton, you know, rescued Kearny's men at San Pasqual and they came from San Diego to retake Los Angeles. The next morning after the battle of San Gabriel, the Americans crossed the mesa at a leisurely pace. The Californios opened their artillery from a long distance, then started the charge. The Americans were forced back by heavy fire, then the Americans opened up their guns. They knocked many Californios from their saddles and after a round of grape the Californios scattered. The Californios stripped the dead horses on the field without dismounting and carried off most of their saddles and bridles and wounded men to the hills. The Americans came up this very street with Stockton, Kearny and Kit Carson at the head of what was left of the Army of the West. They stopped here at Avila's adobe. Avila's widow was afraid, so she fled to her daughter's home farther out in the country. The widow left a little boy to guard the house. He wasn't to open either doors or windows, but when he heard the music of General Kearny's band, he couldn't resist the temptation and went out to listen, leaving the door open. Some of Stockton's men saw what it was like inside, saw the beautiful furniture, told Stockton about it, so he decided to make his headquarters here."

Then, on January 14th, Fremont and his four hundred men and six guns rode into town in pouring down rain, with the Treaty of Cahuenga tucked away, the treaty which ended the war in California.

"That was the day I signed up with the 'Mounted rifles'."

"Yes, you did that on an historic day, all right."

Then he pointed to the two-story adobe belonging to Vicente Sanchez, a beautiful adobe. While they were looking at it, he talked of others.

"Don Pio Pico's house is over there, closer to Calle de Negroes.

Little Frank kept tugging at his mother's skirt as they passed women dressed in beautiful silk gowns, their long black braided hair hung halfway down their backs.

Dr. Hammel was enjoying his role as guide. "When the señoritas first came into town to shop, they wanted sidewalks so their sweeping skirts wouldn't get dirty. So those were put in so they didn't have to walk in the mud in the winter and dust in the summer. But you know women. They're never satisfied."

"Yes, but what would you do without us?" remarked Regina.

"That's true, I'm afraid women are more in charge than we want to give them credit for.

"They not only fussed about the sidewalks, but they didn't like the idea of tar dripping on them from the rooftops, so they got a law passed so the shop owners wouldn't let it drip. The next thing they worked on was getting hitching posts put up to keep the rancheros from taking their lead ropes into the stores."

Milling through the crowd was an elderly man, beautifully dressed. "That's Antonio Maria Lugo. He's the judge of the plains."

"A handsome man," remarked Regina.

Coming toward them were caballeros, riding ten abreast, jingling as they approached, making Carrie and Frank jump up and down and clap their hands. The men were mounted on gaily caparisoned horses, with saddles so highly adorned with silver it seemed unlikely anyone could possess such wealth. The men were wearing short, tight-fitted jackets of brightly-colored material of blue or green or yellow, trimmed in gold or silver lace of fringe with matching pantaloons. On their feet they wore fancy, high-heeled boots looking so small they would hurt their feet, and on their heads they wore the fine Panama hats.

After the horsemen passed, Frank stood there watching as if he had been put under a spell. Andrew took his hand as they continued on.

"Circus, Mama!"

"Yes, Frank," replied his mother. "Children, aren't they amazing? He'll never forget that performance we saw in San Francisco."

"You mean the National Circus? They were here too. Put on a magnificent show a while back." added Dr. Hammel.

"Do the merchants buy up hides to re-sell?" asked Andrew.

"Hides, oh, yes, a lot of hides come into town. Quite a few of the men deal in them. They have quite a trade. They store them here, then when they accumulate a goodly number, they take them by carreta to the ships waiting in the harbor. I'd say it's the biggest business we have in town."

"It seems as though everyone in Los Angeles is rich," mused Regina.

"As a matter of fact, many are."

"Do they do all their trading at the ships?" asked Andrew.

"Yes, after anchoring in the shallow waters of San Pedro, they ride into town to inform the people that the ship has laid anchor and is in readiness to trade."

Hammel and the Weinshanks were enjoying seeing the town as they walked along at a leisurely pace, the only distraction being the creaking of wheels of the carretas stirring up the dust, those lumbering carts mounted above two solid wheels of sawed-off logs drawn by oxen. They sauntered along Main Street looking at the sights, watching the people pass by.

"The men are so handsome, no matter what their age. Such style, such grace," remarked Regina.

"John Goller, a German fellow, another immigrant who came by way of the Salt Lake, has a wagon shop nearby on Los Angeles Street. You can find his place easily because all his stuff blocks the road."

"That's good to know," said Regina. "The stage driver told us about the San Gabriel Mission and I'd like to go there some day. Can we rent a wagon from Mr. Goller?"

"He'll have something for you. He's an accommodating fellow."

The children became restless, and so Dr. Hammel and the Weinshanks went back to the hotel.

Blessing on Leaving Ireland

Chapter 13

In the little village of Clonmel, in the county of Tipperary, in Ireland, there lived a family by the name of Phelan. Daniel, the father, was an honest man who worked hard and knew the value of money. He was a devout Catholic and possessed a keen appreciation of the benefits to be gained through education; he encouraged his seven children to drink up all the knowledge they could. Daniel's wife, Winifred, was a gentle woman, always bowing to the better judgment of her husband.

Their oldest child, Mary, was living in San Francisco where she worked hard and saved every penny to help her family come to America. She was the family favorite, now so far away from home. For the fifth child, Tom, one day stood out from all the rest: the day the letter arrived from America. On a beautiful day in June, 1856, Daniel was called in from the field, and all the family gathered around the kitchen table. "Dear sweet family of mine, I have enclosed money, steerage fare for two of my brothers to come to America."

Their father read on, but Tom did not hear. He knew he was one of those to go. His sister, Mary, had sent them passage money just as she had promised. After Mary, it was Billy, now a grown man, a big fellow with black hair and blue eyes. He was in line to inherit the land, but since life was hard in Ireland he was willing to go to America. The next two boys, Patrick and John, had begged their father not to send them away, for they both wanted to stay in their little village of Clonmel with their family and friends.

Tom, a fine, strapping lad of thirteen, a boy with curly black hair, blue eyes and a ruddy complexion, spoke up, "I'm wanting to go to America," though in his heart he was sorrowful to leave his family.

He could hear his father saying, "The only thing left for us is to send our children away, and we thank God that Mary could scrape up the money, so they can go to America. The other day I heard Father O'Malley say they're pouring out of the country by the hundreds of thousands."

"How can they all make a living there?" asked his wife.

"It's a big country, Winifred."

"I will never get used to seeing my laddies go, no matter how many times it may happen. Many a night I've lain awake weeping, knowing they'll be going, never to look upon them again," she sobbed, the tears streaming down her face.

As Tom sat there, his only thoughts were on going to America. But even so, their lot was better than some, for they had their own small farm. He heard his father say, "But when the famine comes, as it has this year, no potatoes can be grown in our fields, and we suffer, along with all our neighbors, so to stay in Ireland would surely mean starvation, for when the food gives out, I've seen houses where whole families are huddled together, all still and moaning with no more than skin stretched over their bones. We have the little ones to think of. We cannot feed them all. Thank God, we have Mary to send us money," he concluded, trying to comfort his weeping wife.

As it was in Ireland every five or six years, the scourge of famine and disease was felt in every corner of the country, and so it was in the County of Tipperary in the little hamlet of Clonmel, a quaint little village nestled in a valley among the hills.

From the time the family first announced their intention of sending their own dear ones away to their final departure date, their friends and neighbors gathered around them in a most affectionate manner. There always ensued a scene of tears and lamentations, for they were two among many making that great exodus to a land far across the sea.

The night before they were to embark on their journey, the family met in the best room. They were joined by the priest, who led the family and a small gathering of friends in prayer. It was harder on their mother to see her laddies go. She, too, knew there was nothing there for them in Ireland, and she wanted them to have more than just to eke out a bare living. They gathered to mourn them as they would the dead, for once they left Ireland, they left forever.

At daybreak the next morning the boys sat down to their last meal prepared by their weeping mother, then gathered up their knapsacks.

"Now, Billy, you look after Tom and don't you boys let me down. I want to hear from you, and it will be for you I will be praying. Oh, God, be praised. I'll never see the likes of you again."

"Now don't you fret," said Billy "I can write my letters and see that Tom does the same."

The boys gathered around their dear sweet mother and gave her that last embrace and tried to hold back the tears, then their pa, then their brothers. Tom grabbed up his little sister, Ellen, his favorite—a little red-headed, blue- eyed lass of five, and gave her a big hug. Tom took one last look at the baby in the cradle and turned away. Without another word they walked out of their humble cottage, not daring to look back for fear of being unable to continue on.

Anxious to be on their way, they passed along the road toward Cork. They came upon more emigrants, the girls looking most picturesque in their gay plaid shawls and straw bonnets. They were the country's youth, anywhere from ten to thirty years of age. They too knew that for them to stay in Ireland would mean starvation. It had been the priests at the parish who had the task of making all the arrangements for the tickets for their passage and providing them a place of lodging while they waited for their departure from the country. Scarcely a month went by that the church didn't have to send some of their best young Irish folk away to America, and it was a sorrowful time for them as well as for the families who had to let their dear ones go. Their little hamlet was being deprived of its fine able-bodied young men and women, and only the old and infirm and the very young were left.

Arriving at the quay in Cork after a long journey of nearly sixty miles, all on foot, they stretched out among the boxes and straw to seek a few moments rest. At the emigration office they were pounced upon by man-catchers, crimps, and touters. They were taken advantage of because of their abject poverty. A man walked up to them.

"I can accommodate all of you for a night. What about it? Food and lodging. Better act quickly or others will take it."

"I'm thinking we'd better do as he says or we might be out in the cold," said Billy, as he walked up and gave the man the money for himself and Tom. They were then thrust into an overcrowded room with only straw on the floor.

Tom showed his displeasure, "This isn't fit for beasts to stay the night in."

His brother Billy said, "It will only be for a night or two."

"But the smell is fierce," said Tom.

"We'll make do," said Billy. "Put your knapsack down and rest a bit."

They sat down at a table of meager rations. The food was rancid. The overcrowded conditions added to their misery. The filth and offal of the place were enough to endanger their health. They spent the night crowded into that one small room, sitting on all their worldly goods, wondering if this was an omen of what was to come.

The following day they were crowded to near suffocation in a steamer packet to Dublin, plying them across the Irish Sea to Liverpool, the great port of debarkation.

"At home we were led to believe we would embark from an Irish port," said Billy to a fellow emigrant.

"Ah, the booking agents can't be trusted. They tell you what you want to hear, anything, just to turn a penny, and fill the boats."

When finally they arrived in Liverpool, they walked up the gangplank of the great ship, and their spirits soared; they had more cause for hope now that nothing was ahead but opportunity, while behind them was the remembrance of misery.

Billy and Tom descended the steps of the steerage cabin only to find all the berths had been taken. As they looked around, some of the passengers were sitting around talking; others were sleeping, some were sorting out their goods. The women talked, the children cried. Some were shouting, some singing, but they could see no evidence of sorrow for leaving their country or friends. If their hearts were heavy, they couldn't tell it.

They watched the dancing of the jig and reel to the strains of the fiddle and flute in the various sections of the steerage section which was overladen with passengers.

"It's a wonder so many people can be packed into this one small space," observed Billy.

They returned to the deck as the captain gave the order to pull the anchor. The sails caught the wind and they were underway.

The beginning of the voyage was very pleasant: Billy and Tom watched the fresh sea breeze as it filled the sheets, making them feel quite jaunty. But as the land passed from their view, the wind increased, and the vessel began to toss and roll from the action of the open sea. They remained on deck until the distance obliterated their view of the shore. "It will be forever more a memory, a part of our past, for there is no place for us in Ireland," said Tom, for he entertained no thought or hope of ever returning home.

"If only the others could have come along. But money was too scarce for that. The plan was for just one or two of us to leave at a time," said Billy.

At the first sign of darkness, they scurried below deck, there only to listen to the crying of the children. They could faintly hear the swearing of the sailors in the shrouds. They cringed at the sound of the women scolding their children, all adding to their discomfort. All this was heightened by the darkness of the night, the rolling of the ship, making it a continuous nightmare. Just a few short hours before all was gaiety and hope. A nice family made room for them, "Put down your knapsacks, boys, and get a night's rest." As they were doing this, the hatch was shut down above them. As they were spreading out their blankets, a fellow emigrant called to Billy, "It's guard duty for you tonight, so come along with me."

Tom lay there alone listening to the waves break upon the deck and the wind as it tore through the rigging, the ship as it creaked and groaned as if it were going to break. In the pitch black of midnight all hands had been called on deck. He could hear the captain as he shouted his orders through his trumpet and was answered by the wails and chants of the sailors in the shrouds. He lay there in silence and darkness, for no lights were allowed belowdeck. The tramping above and the confusion all around frightened Tom immensely, as he was left to suffer out the rest of the night alone. With each roll of the ship he was hurled from side to side, and the water on the floor stood ankle deep. People everywhere were seasick, vomiting, causing a stench that was beyond belief. At first Tom was able to hold his breath. Finally he succumbed. He was unable to hit the slop bucket. His mess was added to all the others and without means of cleaning it up. For once he was glad for the darkness of the night.

The next morning the women set about cleaning up. Billy joined Tom, and they went on deck to wash their clothes. By the time they returned to the steerage section, the beds had been rolled up, and the place was fairly tidy.

That same big burly man came up to them. "Both you lads are big and strong. Get to work and slop the floor."

He handed them a foul-smelling liquid which they added to the water. They tossed it over the floor. "It smells so bad it's a question as to which is worse, the vomit or this," said Tom. While they were doing this, some of the men got busy throwing the refuse overboard.

With the morning's work done, Tom and Billy watched as the women cooked their breakfast on deck over an open fire contained in a large case, lined with bricks with iron bars in front, large enough to hold kettles of all sizes and shapes. They listened to the angry women, as they threw insults at each other because their baked cakes got encased in burnt crusts, quarreling endlessly about whose turn it was to cook. So Tom and Billy walked away. That evening when they went past the ladies cooking their suppers, they were still bickering, right up until seven o'clock that night when the fire was doused by water. Then the women snatched up their pots and pans, half blinded by the steam, and descended into the hole with their half-cooked suppers. "We'll eat what little fare we have without the aid of cooking, for I'm not able to cope with the women in order to get a turn," said Billy.

On the voyage babies were born, and many passengers died. Billy and Tom watched, along with the others, as the captain committed those dear sweet ones—in most cases Irish souls—to the deep, and dreadful was the sound of the splash of the bodies as they were thrown overboard. When it was all over, Billy said, "The captain recited the burial ceremony with such lack of compassion about those poor dear souls, it gives me a feeling of despair. Never have I seen such a clear distinction of such consideration and attention to the wants of the cabin class, while we in steerage are left to fend for ourselves."

This miserable situation lasted many weeks. The boat tossing and rolling, passed through storms with an occasional pleasant day. "We were told this passage was going to take exactly three weeks," said Tom.

"Yes, and our skimpy supply of food is running low. I'm going to have to dig deep to buy a little food from the captain's store, only enough to keep up our strength. Our only hope is that our journey will soon be over."

Then, finally, one day after many weeks they sighted land, and hope returned to their bosoms. They had crossed the stormy Atlantic, and they could see the city of New York in the distance.

As they approached the harbor, the captain gave the order "cast anchor" and awaited the arrival of the health officer. A boat came alongside with vendors peddling fresh meat, vegetables, fruit, butter and eggs. Billy took his last few pennies and bought some fruit. He and Tom ate so fast, hardly a bite was tasted on its way down.

Finally the gangplank was lowered, and they stepped onto American soil for the first time, and their feeling again returned to a high pitch. "Those past weeks aboard that filthy disease-ridden ship are behind us, and now we're in the land of plenty."

They headed out for Illinois, sometimes on foot, sometimes catching a ride on a wagon of some farmer going a short distance. Often they would have to stop for a day or two, get work doing odd jobs to earn enough money to get by, but finally they made it to where other relatives lived in Waverly. They entered the small country town, no bigger than a wide spot in the road, built around a public square. As they entered, joggling along on the back of a wagon, the driver tied his horses up to the hitching post and said, "Well, boys, this is the town you're looking for. Waverly, Illinois. Nice town. It has two schools, a brick seminary, and a boarding house and other small stores. Also here in the town is a wool carding factory, a flour mill and a blacksmith shop. Hope you like our town."

"Looks mighty fine to us, sir. And much obliged for giving us a lift."

"Glad to do it. Any time."

When they arrived at the house of their relatives, they were greeted by the family and taken into their home. All their aunts and uncles and their children gathered around them, and thanked God for their safe journey to the new land. "Let's get down on our knees and pray for those we've left behind," said one of the Halligans. Then they sat down to a piping hot meal of good fresh meat and potatoes. In the evening they sat around and talked about the farm and their families in Ireland, and of the great prospects of striking it rich in America.

"Of course you'll need a stake; then you're all set. A few years back people went to California for gold, but that's not as plentiful now. Land is what you want today, good land with plenty of water," was the advice of one family member.

Tom sat there and took it all in. He too wanted to go to California and stay with his sister Mary, but that would have to wait.

First Tom got a job on a farm outside of town, kept up with his studies and worked his way through district school.

Carreta

Chapter 14

It was unusually warm on the day late in July, '56, when the Weinshanks moved into their own adobe at 744 Fort Street, situated on a narrow, dirt lane of a few scattered one-story adobes. In front of the house was a veranda supported by posts, and the roof was flat. It showed signs where the mud had washed away.

Andrew tried the hand-hewn door for Regina and the children to enter; it was open. It could have been locked with a key, if only they had one. They walked into the barren room. Inside the thick white-washed walls, the windows swung on hinges, opening inward, and could have been locked in the center, but why bother. In the corner of the sala sitting on the earthen floor, was a brasero, a pan used to hold hot coals for heating. Off that room were two small bedrooms which gave Regina some concern, but trying to be optimistic she said, "I think we can get our bedroom furniture in here Andrew."

"A close fit, but we'll make do. We'll get furniture for the children's bedroom from Temple's store. I've already looked everything over, Regina. Just three rooms, the cooking will have to be done outside, but its the only house available in town and it beats the Bella Union."

"I'm so glad to be in a home of my own, I'll not complain."

Soon after they moved in, they got word their furniture had arrived from San Francisco.

Andrew found Captain Salisbury Haley of the "Ohio" at the Bella Union, his favorite haunt, playing cards in the dining room.

"What do you say, Captain? When can I get my furniture?"

"Meet me here first thing in the morning, and we'll see to it."

The next morning the Captain and Andrew went back to the side-wheeler anchored off shore. The furniture had already been carried up from the hold and was on deck when they arrived. The sailors then let it down piece by piece by rope to the waiting flat boat, then to shore to the waiting carreta to be taken into town. The driver and Andrew got in. Andrew made himself as comfortable as possible among all their possessions. The twenty-seven mile trip back to Los Angeles was slow and bumpy, and Andrew and the sturdy furniture got a good jostling around.

As they were carrying it in, a rickety wagon drawn by two broken-down horses with several large barrels pulled up and stopped at their door. The driver, a tall American about thirty years old with red hair, a bushy mustache, wearing long rubber boots, gave them a helping hand in carrying in the furniture, and then got right down to business. "My name's Bill, I'm the water man. I charge fifty cents to deliver all the water you can drink and deliver once a week, but not on Sundays."

"That sounds fair enough," said Andrew. "If you'd like, you can start right away."

Bill placed a jug on the veranda, an urn-shaped vessel made of burnt clay. "This will keep the water cool, and I'm leaving you this gourd dipper. It'll hold up for some time if you're careful."

"We'll take good care of it," said Andrew.

"I get my water from the river which, I'm sorry to say, is none too clean, being the favorite bathing place for the children and all. The ladies do their washing there, which doesn't help, and everyone throws their garbage in it. The town council prohibits it, but no one pays any heed to them. I don't like it, but what can one body do?"

"Yes, I know. But if we have an illness one of these days, maybe the people will take notice and follow the rules," said Andrew.

After he left, the furniture was set in place. Andrew and Regina unpacked their kettles and barrels and got down to business, for a great deal of work had to be done before they were ready to send their foodstuffs off to the mines. Regina gathered together her spices and arranged them on the table. Andrew left the house in search of cabbage, tomatoes and cucumbers. When he got back home, he along with their two new Indian helpers, Jesse and Arturo, all set about their work of getting the day's supply of foodstuffs ready to sell.

For Regina, making tomato catsup meant lots of boiling, lots of stirring. Regina worked and sliced a peck of ripe red tomatoes, always looking for the good ripe red ones. Then she immersed them in the boiling water she had on the fire, until the skins were ready to come off, then boiled them. She sliced two good sized onions and cooked them until they were soft. Then she put both the tomatoes and onions through her sieve to pulp and put it back on the stove. She then added some cayenne pepper, and boiled it down. She then poured two cups of vinegar into a pan, made a spice bag out of an old clean cloth and in it put a broken up stick of cinnamon, one tablespoon of whole cloves and three finely chopped cloves of garlic. She put that in the vinegar and cooked it slowly. When her tomato pulp was reduced by one half, she removed the spice bag from the vinegar, measured one and a fourth cups, added a cup of sugar, two and a half teaspoons of salt and a tablespoon of paprika, put it in the tomatoes and onions then let it boil some more. After the first batches had been cooked and made ready for market, Andrew loaded his hired wagon with a barrel each of catsup and pickled turnips and headed out on his rounds. He planned to go up one street and down another making contacts along the way.

Andrew made his first stop at the "Montgomery," a well-known gambling house near Stearn's "El Palacio." One of his old war buddies, Billy Getman, ran it. The Montgomery was a long building, fronted with a veranda, facing Calle Principal. As he pulled up to the saloon, coming toward him down the street were Indians chained together like animals, picking up rubbish. Andrew quickly got down off the wagon and walked inside the saloon. Billy Getman was at one of the tables.

"Well, I'll be switched—Andrew Weinshank, good to see you, what are you doing here?"

"I brought my family here to live, Billy. We're selling foodstuffs. I came by early last week, but one of your dealers said you were away.

"In San Francisco, Andrew, buying some new equipment."

"Are you in the market for foodstuffs?" asked Andrew. "Well now, maybe I'll buy some. Have to patronize my old war buddy. We were in the thick of it at Cerro Gordo, weren't we? I didn't know whether or not I would make it that day, but here I am."

"I was lucky, too," said Andrew. "We lost two of our men that day, closest I ever came to losing my own life. I don't even want to think about it."

"What happened to you after that?"

"All the way to Mexico City, every battle. We ran into trouble at

Belen Gate just outside the city, but it was the 'Rifles' who raised the flag over the Halls of Montezuma."

"Where did you settle after the war?"

"When I got back to New Orleans, I met a girl, we got married, went back to Mobile where my family was, worked in a lumber yard making barrels. Our two children were born there, but I always wanted to come to California, so out we came. While we were living in San Francisco I got an order to make barrels and sell foodstuffs for the miners so we came down here."

"That's great, I hope you do well, Andrew."

"We're anxious to get started. I make the barrels, and my wife and our Indians, fill them. We've been real busy lately, settling in and getting everything ready. It'll take a while to train Jesse and Arturo. Wait till my wife sees those Indians in chains. She'll set up a howl, you can count on that."

"Good for her, I treat my dog better than that. Andrew, where's your stuff?"

"Out in the wagon. I have some catsup and pickled turnips. We'll have sauerkraut later. It takes longer to set, and only have a barrel each for now."

"Bring them in, Andrew. I'm glad you came. I'll pay in cash, cash on the barrel head."

From the Montgomery, Andrew went to the heart of the business section between Main and Spring Streets, to John G. Downey's drug store. As he crossed the road, a wagonload of ice passed him going in the direction of Sonora Town. As he walked along the plank sidewalk under the veranda, he could feel the vibrations of some local urchins running foot races over his head.

He passed a man pushing a wheelbarrow, stopping whenever a customer appeared. Andrew stopped and looked his produce over, "Quite a cart you have here."

"It'll do," he said.

"My name is Andrew Weinshank. I guess we're in the same business."

"Free country. Suit yourself. I'm Andy Briswalter, I grow everything here in my backyard."

"Maybe we can buy from you; we'll need tomatoes, cucumbers and turnips."

"Yes, I grow those. Let me know what you need, and we'll try to work something out."

"I'll do that."

Coming toward him was a Mexican woman peddling huevos in a pan. Andrew's last stop was the Bella Union, hoping to get an order from them, then on home.

The Weinshanks and their new friends, the Childs, rode out into the country on a pleasant spring day, by way of Aliso Street, which narrowed down to a picturesque little lane. Ozro had light brown, wavy hair and blue eyes. His wife, Emmalina, was a small woman. Both were the "salt of the earth." The children rode in the back taking in all there was to see. It was a relaxing drive, all talking and laughing on their way to the Mission San Gabriel Archangel. They crossed a stream and headed for the open country. The children were excited as they rode along because they would surely be getting treats and a chance to play in the rooms where the branding irons were kept. They might also have a chance to look down into the pits where the tallow had been rendered in the old days.

There were sycamore and oak trees here and there and willows in evidence along the riverbanks and country lanes. On the hills and meadows wild mustard grew in great profusion. Bees were swarming around the wildflowers.

They drove through lands covered with vineyards in all directions, until at last, they came to where they could see Mission San Gabriel ahead of them. As they drove on, they could hear the mission bells.

As they approached the grounds, they saw the ruins of the surrounding adobes where once had been a good sized town. Immense labor had once been wrought upon this lovely valley making it into a veritable paradise, but all was now desolate. Only a few tall date palms still stood.

They found it was largely overgrown. The church itself was very much in decay, and the outer buildings showed little evidence of their former walls. They hitched their buggy to the hitching post.

At the mission door they were warmly greeted by a priest. An Indian helper took the children off to the cook house for treats while the grown-ups talked and looked around. "It's good to have you here. Not too many people come around, except to mass, and I hope you make it often."

"It's such an enjoyable ride and in a wonderful setting," said Emmalina.

"Oh, yes, we'll make it just as often as we can," said Ozro.

Taking their time, the padre showed them round the church, telling them about the mission, pointing everything out.

"When the mission was first built in 1771, life was somewhat primitive, though comfortable. It was built in this lovely setting with the clear blue sky above, an occasional cloud hovering overhead, with the blue Pacific Ocean in the distance. It was here where the first huts of willow branches gave way to log buildings, and they in turn gave way to adobe structures. The storage bins were filled, many acres of land were put under cultivation, cattle were put out to graze on the surrounding hills.

"They built dams, erected an aqueduct and winery. From their cuttings they planted orchards. Their crops flourished, their fruit and vegetables ripened, their vineyards thrived, making good wine and brandy, of which the padres were very proud. The padres taught the Indians how to make their own oxcarts and plows as well as their agricultural instruments.

"Later the Yankee trading ships came from Boston and the hides and cowhide bags of tallow were carried to the water's edge and floated out to the ships beyond the surf to exchange for tools and textiles, furniture, gunpowder, books and musical instruments.

"In 1810 Mexico revolted against Spain because her mother country had become weak from fighting the Napoleonic Wars. Spain was forced to cut off funds for the military in California, and much of that which was produced on Mission lands went to support the idle soldiery.

"The government of Mexico ceased to support the padres, and the Indian wards found themselves suffering great privation.

"Each Indian was to be given his own little plot of land to work and profit by it. The padres thought they could help them to the point that they would be able to care for themselves, but even with all their help, the Indians were unable to fend for themselves. When they were released from bondage, they could not make it on their own. Some returned to the mission, some found work on the ranchos, some went to Los Angeles or Santa Barbara where they lived in squalor, some returned to the primitive ways of their people, some ran off to the mountains, and some were herded to the mission at San Juan Capistrano. And all the while the mission was deteriorating, plaster began peeling off its walls, weeds took over the vegetable gardens, irrigation aqueducts began to crumble.

"In 1833, the young Mexican republic desecularized the missions. Then a pall descended over the mission San Gabriel Archangel. William Hartnell, the Englishman who spoke fluent Spanish, was given the task of hearing complaints. One disgruntled man told him the padres were making the mission into a brothel.

"And so the mission period ended as quickly as it began, 'for history is but a passing wind, it brings and it takes away'."

The Weinshanks and Childs were enjoying their afternoon. They walked into the courtyard where the graveyard was. "In some places we have as many as fourteen Indians in a single grave. The Indians caught the white man's diseases, and they were buried by the score."

"That is indeed sad," said Regina. "But what a pleasant place to while away the time, being here in these lovely surroundings. We're enjoying your warm hospitality and imagining what it was like when the mission was flourishing."

"It was a fair sized town, and we did a lot of trading here. One of the traders was an Scotsman, who came on a sailing vessel in 1832, a man by the name of Hugo Reid. He liked our little Mexican village and decided to stay a while."

"One day, he saw our lovely Victoria, the daughter of the chief of the Yang Na. Of all our Indians, she took to our teachings far and above all others. She was anxious to learn and a joy to teach. He spent many pleasant hours here, talking to the priests, telling them about his native country and all the wonderful places he had been, but his mind was on the lovely Victoria.

"He stayed on at the mission, then asked permission to ask Victoria for her hand in marriage. She consented, making the early padres very happy. They gave her, as a wedding present, a large rancho within easy riding distance of the mission and the pueblo."

They walked to the garden where orange trees were heavily laden with fruit, propped up to keep from breaking under the load.

"I'd like to be able to grow trees like these," said Andrew.

"Perhaps we should look for a place in the country where you can, Andrew."

"We have so much to be thankful for here," Emmalina said to the padre. "The climate is heavenly, so soft and the air is so pure. We have the most magnificent sunsets, with our mountains in the background, and sometimes the sky is gorgeously painted with every hue of the spectrum."

"Yes, this is beautiful country," said Regina. "The scenery far surpasses anything where I came from, and I think anywhere in Europe where I've been."

"In this land of abundance you wouldn't think we'd have a care in the world, but without our Indian help, we can no longer tend to our orchards and fields. Most of the land has been taken from us, our vines are dying, and we have no money to pay for help."

"That is very sad indeed," said Emmalina, as they continued their stroll about the grounds.

They went into one of the shops. "This is where we used to tan our hides; out over there is where we melted the tallow," the Padre said pointing in that direction. "We once had a bakery, and over there was where we kept our brands."

When they got to that shop, Andrew said, "Yes, this is interesting," picking up a brand.

"Every brand is different. We decided to take the first and last letters of the word temblores for our cattle brand, from the river, Rio de San Miguel de los Temblores, named so because there was an earthquake the day the party of Franciscans came from San Diego to establish a mission."

"That's very interesting. Who were the first Americans to come to the mission, padre?" asked Andrew.

"Jedediah Smith and his party in November, 1826. The padres gave them food, wine and clothing and a place to rest. They brought news of the outside world and learned that sea otter could be had for the taking, then headed on."

"Was any gold found in the hills around here?" asked Andrew.

"Yes, the Indians found some. They didn't know what it was, or for what purpose it could be used. It disturbed the padres for they felt if the word got around, the rancheros would go in search of it and take our Indians from us."

"Why were the missions founded here in California?" asked Regina.

"To keep the Russians out, but that's quite a long story. I'll tell it to you the next time you come."

"It is getting late," said Regina. "Don't you think we'd better head for home, Andrew? I'll go round up the children."

Regina found them in the cook house, gathered them up and they sauntered back to their wagon. The children slept, all bundled up in the back and were still sound asleep when they got back to town.

Andrew was in the market for bands for his barrels. Regina too had some things to get from the store. So they gathered up the children and went in the direction of Ozro's tin shop on Commercial Street. Regina broached the subject as soon as she walked in, "I'd like to go back to the mission one of these days soon, Ozro, to hear the story about how close we came to losing California to the Russians. Would you be able to go with us?

"Whenever you have the time," he said. "I'll just close the shop, and we'll make a day of it. We can make arrangements with John Goller for a wagon. But first I need to stop at the post office. Let's go over now. Then we'll go on down to Goller's," he said, as he quickly locked his door.

Inside the post office the children looked around, just one small cubby hole, nothing more. The postmaster was sorting out the mail.

"Howdy, William," greeted Ozro.

"Likewise," he replied.

"How's business coming along, Andrew?"

"Can't complain."

"How come you came to California in the first place?"

"Served in the Mexican War," answered Andrew, "in '47. Whole regiments vowed they'd come here, but not many did. Both Regina and I worked for General Smith, and you might say we followed him out."

"I came here with Stevenson's Regiment in '46. Looks like I got you beat."

"You sure have, I can't argue that."

"I'm not always here, so if you would like, you can help yourself to your own mail. If it's not sorted, it'll be on that soap box over there."

While Regina and the children went on, Ozro and Andrew walked over to a group of men on the veranda of the Montgomery House, sitting around a box playing cards. Sam Foy was in the group.

The men didn't seem to notice them come up, so Ozro spoke up. "This is Andrew Weinshank. He's new in town."

"Where do you hail from?" asked one of the men.

"Came from Mobile, Alabama. I fought in the war and heard so much about your climate, decided to make my home here."

"Welcome. I'm John Reed, came in with the Army of the West. Now that you're here, how do you like it?"

"I do."

"Where do you live?"

"We're living on Fort Street now. We stayed at the Bella Union until we found a place of our own."

Another man spoke up. "When I first came here in '54, I stayed at the Bella Union. We had a heavy rain and the ceiling caved in on me so I had to find another place. By the way, I'm Cameron Thom."

"Well, I'm glad we got located before that happened to us."

Another man looked up at Andrew after playing his card. "I'm Sam Foy. I have a wagon shop on Main Street Between Commercial and Requena. Like some of the others around here, I came out here to prospect for gold, came down here in '54."

"We actually came out in '55," said Andrew. "We were in San Francisco a while before coming down. I'm not in a position to buy a wagon now; we're just getting started, but I'll be over one of these days and take a look."

"Hope you do!" said Sam.

"Maybe we ought to hire a wagon from Sam," suggested Ozro. "How about it, Sam? Do you have a wagon for hire? We're planning to ride over to the mission one of these days."

"Sure do," said Sam. "Come on over. I'll fix you up."

"I'd best be getting along," said Andrew. "The folks are in the store, and they'll be anxious to get home."

The Weinshanks by now had settled into that little Mexican village of mud walls and dirt streets surrounded by vast lands covered with vineyards.

A few days later, Andrew said, "Children, do you want to go back to the mission?" The children jumped for joy, so he said to them, "Let's get ready."

Regina packed a few of her good products for the padres to enjoy. Andrew put them in the wagon, helped Regina and the children in, and they were on their way. In town, they stopped at the tin shop and picked up Ozro, Emmalina and their little girl, Emma, now Carrie's friend and then headed for the mission. As they bounced along the country road, Frank with all the eagerness he could muster up, said "Sister, I'll bet I see the mission first!"

"I bet I'll see it first, Frank!" But the children became distracted, and it was Andrew who spoke up.

"Well, children, you both lost. Your mother and I saw it before either of you. Better luck next time!" As they pulled up to the big church door, the children were taken away by the Indian helper to the cook house. Andrew unloaded the wagon, and they went inside.

"Remember, Padre, you said you'd tell us another story the next time we came. You haven't forgotten, have you?"

"No, Mrs. Weinshank. Let's go out in the patio; we can sit down under a tree, and I'll tell it to you. I don't want you to go back to town and tell the good people I broke my promise."

"Good, Padre. I've been looking forward to hearing it."

"This is a true story," the padre said as they sat down. "Baron Nicolai Petrovich de Rezanov was the first Russian ambassador to Japan. He had been sent by the Tsar to New Archangel where he spent the winter and learned firsthand of the privations and suffering of his company during the long arctic months, when the storms were incessant and when there was little or no food to eat, so he went in search of warmer climate. He learned of California and decided to come here. He bought a barque, 'The Juno,' from a Yankee skipper, and its cargo of merchandise.

"When he sailed through the Golden Gate, in the month of April, 1806, he was forty-two years of age. He looked upon that great protected harbor and thought it would be a wonderful port to hold the Russian navy. He could visualize the surrounding hills with beautiful palaces, the churches with their slender crosses, the lofty towers of their Tartar Domes, the California sun beating down on their marble walls and golden roofs.

"Resanov was a handsome man, towering above the Californians, wearing a superb uniform of his rank. A ball was held in his honor the evening of his arrival. He was received by Luis Arguello, the commandant of Yerba Buena, but Resanov's eyes were only for the commandant's lovely sister, Concha, a beautiful girl of sixteen. She had fine, dense black hair and flashing black eyes. Her skin was white, and her cheeks were as pink as Castillian roses. She attracted the handsome Russian by her dignity and vivacious intelligence as well as by her exceptional beauty. He became her constant companion during the following weeks.

"He asked for Concha's hand in marriage, but the fact that he was Russian disturbed her brother greatly. In order to quiet Arguello's fears, Resanov said he was willing to go to Rome for a dispensation, to Madrid to get the King's permission as well as to his own sovereign to get his blessing. With such willingness on the Ambassador's part, Arguello's resistance was broken, and so the formal betrothal took place.

"Rezanov not only allowed himself to fall in love, but he also had plans for an alliance between Russia and New Spain. Upon his return, he planned to live in California and welcome more colonists from his own frozen land. His people would propagate in the hospitable climate until they outnumbered the Spanish. This failing, he would encourage hordes more to descend from the north and snatch the province from New Spain. Nor was it California alone that he desired, but as far inland as he could reach from San Diego north, he would find worthwhile to penetrate.

"In late May Rezanov sailed out of the Golden Gate with a real vision of happiness, knowing he had a magnificent gift for his country, a vast territory over which he as viceroy would rule with a power as absolute as that of the Tsar of Russia.

"However, his own Concha was unaware of what he had planned for her people, for the last time the lovely Concha saw her loved one was the day he sailed out the Golden Gate. Resanov died before he could return. Concha, distraught, entered the church to become a nun, never knowing of his plans to grasp the shores of California for his native country of Russia."

"A beautiful but tragic story, " said Emmalina.

"Perhaps, but it would have been more tragic had he returned," added Andrew.

"Yes, it does give you food for thought," said Ozro.

"When our children are older, I'll tell the story to them, but it will be a while before they understand the significance of it."

"I want to thank you good people for all the delicious things you brought. We'll enjoy them very much."

"We're glad to, Padre. We look forward to our visits here," said Regina.

"Andrew, you and Ozro pick some of those oranges. The branches are so heavily laden they need to be picked."

"Much obliged, Father. We'll do that while the ladies gather up the children."

Tumbling Act

Chapter 15

It was August of 1856, and Henry Charles Lee was still at the top of his profession. He married his little equestrienne, Jeannette, and theirs was a happy union.

Henry had spent most of his time that summer at the property on K Street, overseeing the construction of their new pavilion and making plans for opening night. Every time Henry had need of John Marshall's advice, he was told John was in the shack working on the books. When Henry went in search of him, he was nowhere to be found.

Their pavilion, the National Theatre, opened August 11th, and was reported in the newspaper to be one of the largest and finest buildings of its kind. Henry would know, because he had been in the great ones of the world. The building had a 60-foot frontage, 160-foot depth and a 35-foot ceiling. The stage was 57 feet wide, 45 feet deep; large enough for a 42-foot tanbark ring. The theatre seated 1200 people and cost fifty thousand dollars. There were five private boxes on the left side of the parquet and one on each side of the proscenium. Mr. William Sefton, the interior designer, painted a scene on the front curtain of a spirited equestrian race—Nero driving a chariot in a contest for a prize, the steeds of the Emperor and his competitors apparently about to plunge into the ring.

The rear of the proscenium had ample arrangements to give both equestrian and dramatic entertainment on the same evening.

The stage was so designed that at the fall of the curtain they could change from circus to opera to comedy to farce in only eight minutes.

The arena was on stage. The horses were housed below, and when the door was opened to take them to the stage, an aroma that was peculiar to that species was noticed by the audience.

They opened at the pavilion for a stay of about a month. They had the finest talent money could buy. The show gave top billing to Madame Annereau, the Queen of the Arena. Henry's two boys, Francis and Eugene, the Olympic Apollos, were received with great enthusiasm. George Peoples put on his usual great performance because of his incredible skill. All in all, they included about forty performers in their troupe, many of whom were stars in their own right. The wardrobe was professionally sewn by Miss Florence Needham of New York. The most influential leaders of the community attended opening night, their wives strutting around in their best finery.

Inside, the decor of the pavilion was magnificent. The interior, unique in its character, was both pleasing to the eye and surpassing all others of its kind of accommodations for comfort and convenience on the Pacific Coast. As the people entered the theatre, below them at the water's edge were lighted torches, making it a spectacle to behold.

They gave many benefits, providing funds for the immigrants' relief, hospital construction and for the public schools. In return, they received much recognition. The writer for Coleville papers was especially complimentary about their performance, ". . . so skillful in design, so graceful in their deliverance, they rapidly won their way to the goal of public favor." The article went on to say, "The judicious selection of their entertainments, the case bestowed upon their presentation before the public, the punctilious and liberal manner in which they discharged all their pecuniary obligations, their rapid exodus from town and considering the extent of their cortege, it required a great deal more than ordinary zeal and attention. Their most liberal, generous and unsolicited bestowal of benefits on churches, schools, fire companies, their bestowal of $30,000 or more over the years. . . "

Yes, Henry understood the whole rational of equestration. Little did the people know that his training and background were in the workshops of the finest theatres of Europe.

They were doing so well financially, Henry decided to make a trip to Stockton to increase the size of the ranch to bring it up to a full eight hundred acres.

Others had done spectacular acts, and Eugene and Jeannette felt they, too, were ready to perform something more daring and thrilling than all the others for they now had a lot of experience behind them. Young Master Eugene made plans to trundle a wheelbarrow up a rope to the top roof of his father's pavilion with Jeannette preceding him. The wheel on the barrow was made in a concave shape, to hug the rope. Two years earlier, Madame Masconi had walked the tightrope from the stage to dome over the heads of the audience, an act that caused great commotion and fanfare all over the City of San Francisco. But this event, if successful, would be more daring and spectacular.

The day finally came when they were ready for the ascent. With anxious eyes, the people from below watched the scene unfold, with deathlike stillness, broken only by the soft tones of the musicians. Jeannette started up the rope, arms extended. Eugene followed, both taking each step slowly, not daring to look down, Eugene pushing the wheelbarrow, using it as a balance pole, occasionally would falter, the people below catching their breath as he made the correction.

Henry watched, hardly daring to breathe for fear of distracting them, never letting his eyes wander. Frenchy, George, Francis and Jeannette's mother, all stood by in stone silence, all watching from below, wondering if they had made the right decision. But it was too late to turn back. Then finally, they reached the top for a few moment's rest. The crowd below shouted and yelled, but stayed glued to their spots, waiting for the descent, which was even more difficult. To add to their fear was the possibility of the wind coming up.

As Eugene and Jeannette appeared ready, the crowd again quieted down. Eyes turned upward, watching Jeannette, as she started down the tightrope slowly, that first step or two giving her trouble. Then Eugene appeared, placing the wheelbarrow again carefully on the tightrope. Jeannette paused because it caused a disturbance under her feet, the tightrope vibrating beneath her. Then Eugene started down. The band struck up again softly, only loud enough to soothe the audience, and step by step with arms extended Jeannette continued on. Jeannette faltered, causing Eugene to falter, and the crowd below held their breath while he made the adjustment and they were able to continue on down the rope. Jeannette made it down to safety, and Eugene followed her. Then Eugene tossed his wheelbarrow on ahead and jumped down on his own power. Jeannette grabbed him and gave him a hug.

"I knew we would make it, Eugene. I have lots of trust in you."

"I feel the same way. A bit shaky on that rope, but we made it, didn't we?"

The audience was thrilled by the event they had just witnessed. They cheered wildly, pushing and shoving to get near Jeannette and Eugene to congratulate them. Henry made his way through the crowd, gathered up Jeannette, and whispered softly in her ear, "Cherish this, my love, for I'll never let you take this chance again. I died a thousand deaths while you were up there."

Soon after that spectacular event they made plans to move on to the gold fields. Henry and John leased the building to Mr. James Dowling for eight weeks. His first performance was to be the "Three Guardsmen."

They were now traveling in style. Their magnificent carriages and baggage vans were manufactured by Abbott of Concord, New Hampshire, the makers of the Wells Fargo wagons, eight of them in all. Their gorgeous band and advertising wagons were built at the Premium Manufacturing Company, the Fielding Brothers of New York. The harnesses worn by Mr. Lee's superb horses were embellished by "minarets of bells of pure silver," which were made by Kelsh and sons of Philadelphia.

They made a short trip to the mining towns performing at Columbia on August 30th and 31st. Then they went on to Oroville.

As they neared town, they stopped and rested for an hour, time for the band members to get out their instruments for the performers to put on their costumes and to make their entry into town with the look of fatigue smoothed away.

With an air of high spirits, they started out. As the band struck up, they entered town with all the fanfare they could muster, the horses prancing, the wagons shining and the performers with expressions of confidence. When they got to the main street, the spectacle was in all its glory, and they headed in the direction of vacant land to put up their circus tent.

Henry's first stop was the newspaper office, then over to the Masonic Lodge to see if a community project was in progress. When he knocked on the door, it was answered by a man, broom in hand. "Well, what can I do for you?"

"I'm Henry Charles Lee. I've just brought my circus to town and am looking for someone to discuss the possibility of a benefit for the town."

"You're looking at him. I'm the one you want to see. So, you want to do something for the town, do you? I thought you entertainers only worked for yourselves."

"No, it's good business to put on benefits. We give you a benefit, you encourage people to attend one for us. We have better crowds this way, you profit by it, and so do we."

"Well, I'll tell you this, we've been thinking about a courthouse around here for some time. Maybe we can work something out. I'll bring the Masons here for a meeting this afternoon, and you can present your ideas."

"That sounds good to me," said Henry. "Set the time, and I'll come back."

"It'll take about an hour to gather them up."

"I'll be here. Glad to have made your acquaintance."

"Same here. A circus man, you say. I hope we can work out something. Good day, sir."

While the arrangements were being made for the benefit, no time was wasted. The men set to work, hurrying about, setting up the tent. Post holes were dug and the posts put into place, the big canvas was stretched on the outside and a small pathway left for the people to pass through. Scales for weighing the gold dust, the main form of currency in the mining towns, were set on a table at the entrance. The big money box was brought out from one of the wagons and set on the ground by the scales. Torches were placed at various spots, the seats were placed on a wooden platform in tiers, and stacks of cushions were brought out so each lady could be furnished with a nice cushioned seat.

The following night a benefit was held for the town of Oroville. Henry no longer went around looking for the little sacks of gold, for the miners were seldom seen at the circus grounds.

After settling up their finances, the man Henry met when he first came to town, said to him, "I'm very pleased you came our way. We're going to get this courthouse underway a lot sooner because of you."

"We were very glad to be a part of it, and I hope all goes well. Hope it serves you for a long time." Henry walked away, well satisfied with the performance and what it had accomplished.

From September 22nd to October 4th, the circus was back in San

Francisco at Montgomery near Washington. Miss Maryanne Whittaker was their equestrienne, George Peoples a four-horse rider, Francis and Jeannette Lee and John Armstrong equestrians, and John was also a double somersault thrower. John Marshall was the ringmaster.

For some obscure reason, the editor of the Sunday *Varieties* had conceived a savage hatred for John Marshall. In the newspaper he wrote that John, ". . . was vulgar, a scurrilous piece of humanity, a low, ribald."

Henry figured it was a personal fight that had been going on, because the editor went on to say that as far as he knew, "Lee was a clever gentleman," so obviously, the attack was not on the circus or Henry, but on John himself.

When Henry confronted him with it, he could tell John had gotten his "dander" up, but John's only reply was, "I don't know what's bothering him. I bounce so many people that come snooping around. Maybe he was one of them."

Henry accepted the answer, but in the back of his mind he felt it went much deeper, so later in the day, he brought the subject up again.

"What about the article in the Sunday *Varieties*?" he asked.

"The newspaper sent this reporter around, and he started asking a lot of questions."

"What do we have to hide?" Henry was seriously trying to pry the answer out now. He had the feeling that John's always being elsewhere had something to to with the situation.

"Well, I guess he got me on a bad night."

"What do you mean, 'on a bad night'? We've been doing so well financially."

"Well, I had just learned that stock I bought before leaving San Francisco for the Sandwich Islands went down. It was the money from the proceeds."

"What? You had no right to spend our money that way—half that money was mine!"

"But, it was such a great opportunity. Had it worked out, we'd never have to work another day in our lives."

"That money was to pay for the pavilion."

"I just gave them a small down payment and bought stock with the rest."

"What do you know about stock? That takes special knowledge, special training. . . " Henry clenched his fist, was ready to swing, then held back, in a rage, he shook his head and stomped away.

Just before the matinee, while Henry was waiting to enter the ring, John walked up to him.

"Henry, I'm leaving. I've been thinking about selling my share of the partnership to Bennett. I think I'll go ahead and do it, and you can buy my half of the ranch."

"That's fine by me," said Henry with fire in his eyes as he pulled into the ring.

Competition would be greater now that Joseph Rowe had returned to circus life. Rowe had dispatched the same Mr. Rivers, the one who had made all the arrangements for Henry's and John's show, to New York to engage a complete company for him and took on a new partner, a Mr. Smith. They named their circus, Rowe's Pioneer Circus.

The roads to the mining towns had been improved; the sturdy wagons they now owned made traveling to the foothills of the Sierra easier and quicker.

They returned to Columbia on December 6th, 1856, and played before a small audience, giving a benefit for the hose and ladder company.

On the 11th of December, Henry and Jeannette sold their two town lots at the corner of American and Market Streets, in Stockton, for Henry knew they would have to start disposing of some of their property. Henry knew full well this would only be temporary relief at best, that the worst was yet to come.

Other problems began to surface. The money had dwindled to nothing; the payments on the ranch and the pavilion could not be met. Henry learned that the performers had not been paid, and they were becoming downhearted. He had let John have too much voice in the business, too much control over the money, and because of it, they were going under.

The performers began to talk amongst themselves. The only ray of hope for Henry seemed to be with his wife, his petite equestrienne, Jeannette. She got her father to help. He and Henry went over the finances, and together they decided that much of the ranch would have to be broken up and sold.

Jeannette's father put up money and took part of the ranch himself, then they sold parts to others. They sold not only their horses, but paid John Marshall far more than he deserved. John had let many, many thousands of dollars slip through his fingers. All the money they had worked so hard to come by, was gone.

Henry again dragged out his little tattered canvas tent, all the scant properties he could scrape together and began again. So from his greatest height to his lowest depths, he was back where he began, but in spite of this, he held his head high. After signing everything over, he walked over to his little equestrienne, took her in his arms, and whispered softly in her ear, "Another town, another place, another fortune to be made, but we cannot give up hope."

Plaza Church

Chapter 16

The Weinshanks and Childs made plans to go down to the river to wash their clothes. Regina wanted to wash her curtains especially to have everything fresh for Christmas. This too was fun, for Carrie now had her friend, Emma, and the two of them, with little Frank tagging along, went off to play. The grown-ups had a chance to visit while they washed and kept an eye on the children.

Regina was careful to place her board on the outer edge of the canal so her dirty water would not mix with the water intended for drinking purposes.

They spread their things out on the rocks to dry and sat down to chat.

"It does make one think a bit. I'm sure people in time will at least try to be more careful where they wash, and hopefully they won't throw their garbage in the river."

"I plan to bury our garbage, Regina," said Andrew. "In Neidstadtt all that is put back into the soil."

"All but the stems will go into the soup, Andrew. Our family has always used every smidgen; nothing is wasted. I plan to keep a kettle on the stove at all times. Did I ever tell you my aunt cooked for the Grand Duke?"

"No, you didn't," replied Andrew. "We never had anyone so important in our family, except my brother who became a priest."

"I'm sure a priest is more important than a cook, even if she did work for the Grand Duke."

"Where there many white families here when you came, Ozro?" asked Regina.

"Not many. We weren't here but a few days when we had met them all."

"Let's see, there was Francis Pliny Temple. He was a young man when he arrived, and went to work in his brother's general store. The good padres had no substitute word for Pliny, so they added Don Francisco, and because he was so small, they called him Templito. He sold his cattle for hides and tallow, owned ranchos outright and was in partnership with others.

"Henry Mellus was here. He came with Henry Dana in 1835 on the brig 'The Pilgrim.' He became Issac Williams' clerk. He came in 1839. He, too, went into the business of trading in hides and tallow. The Lanfranco brothers, Juan and Mateo, opened a grocery store on Main Street. Juan married a daughter of Loreto Sepulveda, and the celebration lasted five days. The Hazards came overland, taking nearly two years to get here. Charles Ducommum and John Downey came in 1853, hired a carreta to transport their belongings to town, but on the way it broke down, so they came in on foot. Then there was Newmark, Alexander, Meyers, Nichols, Brent, Ogier, Hancock, Hansen, Mott, and Beaudry. All these men came in early.

"When we got here, the town was mostly populated by Indians, a few soldiers stationed at the mission, some descendants of the families brought to California by Governor Felipe de Neve, a handful from Stevenson's Regiment of New York volunteers who stayed on after the war, some who came in with the Army of the West, a sprinkling of Chinamen down from the mines, some chased down by the vigilantes from San Francisco and a few who came with the Mormon battalion who stayed on, and that was just about it."

"What do you do for excitement around here, Ozro?"

"It's too bad you didn't get here last year. We had a horse race that was the most exciting event that's ever taken place in this town."

"Tell us about it, Ozro."

"It was quite a horse race, all right." Emma nearby overheard her father begin the story and wanted Carrie and Frank to hear it too, so they sat down at Ozro's feet. "Sarco belonged to Don Pio

Pico and Black Swan to Don Jose Sepulveda. People came from San Francisco and San Diego to watch and place their bets. The distance for the race was nine miles. It started at San Pedro Street and went to a point four and one-half miles away. They were to circle the post and return to town.

"Both Pico and Sepulveda thought their horses would win the twenty-five thousand dollars they put up in gold, five hundred mares, five hundred calves and five hundred sheep put up by the loser. All this had been written up; it was witnessed and made legal.

"Sarco, Don Pio Pico's horse, was well known to be the best and fastest in California. Don Jose Sepulveda had Black Swan brought in from Australia. Don Pio Pico had a local Mexican as his rider, but Don Jose wouldn't say who his rider was."

"He must have had a reason to keep his identity secret."

"You're right. On the day of the race, the streets of Los Angeles were crowded with people mingling in wild confusion. Nothing of that importance had ever happened before."

"With twenty-five thousand dollars at stake, I can see why."

"Members of both the Pico and Sepulveda households passed gold pieces out to their servants to bet on their owner's horse. When the race was about to begin, both horses were led to the starting place. The Mexican mounted Sarco."

"And Black Swan—who was riding him?" asked Regina.

"A Negro boy, dressed in a fancy bright outfit appeared. The crowd noticed he wasn't a boy at all, but a very small man, and the saddle he was using was of the light-weight English type."

"Looks like Sepulveda was trying to put one over on Pico," said Andrew.

"Then the starting signal, and they got off at full speed. They got to the post together, but when they went into the final stretch, Don Jose Sepulveda's horse, Black Swan, pulled out ahead and won the race."

"That must have been exciting," said Andrew. "Don Sepulveda's rider was a professional, no doubt."

"The weight and the experienced rider made the difference all right, because it certainly did that day, for those who bet on Sarco."

"But depressing for Don Pio Pico," added Regina. "Poor man. How did they get their gold? The driver on the way into town said they sold their hides and tallow by barter."

"They did at first, but when gold was discovered at Colma, they drove their cattle to San Francisco. When gold was discovered Hugo Reid went to the gold fields to check it over. While he was up there, he wrote to Don Abel Stearns suggesting the rancheros herd their cattle north. Prices went soaring, and their numbers seemed without limit.

"The price went to thirty dollars a head and better. At one time beef even got up to one dollar a pound. Before that, they brought five dollars a head. So huge herds, sometimes numbering in the thousands were driven hundreds of miles to San Francisco. Sometimes as much as forty thousand dollars' worth of cattle moved out at one time."

"A long way to drive cattle," commented Andrew.

"It took over a month to make the trip. At nightfall the vaqueros would set up camp, cut out a steer, lasso it, butcher and dress it, barbecue what they needed and leave the rest to rot. Now the bones and skulls can be seen along the path from the pueblo to San Francisco. Sometimes they were bothered by the heavy fog, losing some of the stock in the tall fields of mustard. Occasionally they would run into poisonous weeds. When they got near the gold fields, they made arrangements to graze their cattle, giving them a chance to fatten up."

"What else is going on around here for excitement these days?" asked Andrew.

"Not much," said Ozro. "Bullfights are put on in that painted corral just north of the church. They claim the toreadors come from Mexico, but that's not so. They're usually Mexicans from nearby ranchos. Sometimes they have bear fights if they can lasso a couple. Sometimes they have cock fights; those are especially popular on the ranchos, and the men around Sonora Town go for them."

"In other words, not much."

"I'm sure you're used to a lot more."

"No theatre here?" asked Regina.

"No."

"No circus?" she asked.

"One came here in '52."

"When we were in San Francisco, we saw a wonderful show put on by Lee and Marshall."

"That's the one, they came here too, put on quite a show. Once in a while Don Abel and Arcadia Stearns have a fiesta at their El Palacio. Stearns came to Los Angeles in 1829. He was the first white man to come and stay here. He traded hides and tallow to the incoming ships and from the proceeds purchased tens of thousands of acres. His Los Cerritos Rancho alone contains twenty-seven thousand acres, which he purchased from one of the Nietos heirs.

"He became fast friends with Don Juan Bandini, a very important ranchero in San Diego, fell in love with the Don's fourteen-year-old daughter, Arcadia. Her father gave his approval of the marriage, even though Stearns was foreign born and forty-three years old at the time."

"Oh, my! That is quite an age difference."

"Anyway, the Don's parties are grand affairs. Their hospitality cannot be equaled anywhere else in the country. They have only to pass the word, and everyone joins in, and I hope you do, too. We certainly enjoy them. The wealthy Don Pio Pico comes to town from across the mesa from his 'El Ranchito' to attend Don Abel's fandangoes."

"That sounds like lots of fun," remarked Regina.

"Sometimes Don Bandini, Don Coronel and Don Andres Pico all get together and rent a hall. Of course, everyone is asked to buy a ticket, and the money goes to a charity. Solomon Lazard is usually the floor manager at the balls and fandangoes."

"Do you go to the dances?" asked Regina.

"We wouldn't miss them," said Ozro. "Long tables of food are set up, and we all dance to the sweet strains of the guitar and violin. Even if you don't dance, it's great fun to watch the beautiful dancing of the Spaniards with their senoritas on their arms. It's a great affair and the dancing continues far into the night. The only lights here in town that will shine are those from the building where the dance is being held, otherwise, all is total darkness."

"I wouldn't know. We go to bed with the chickens," added Regina.

"I'm afraid we picked a poor day to come here. Those clouds look very threatening," said Emmalina.

Then Andrew felt a drop of rain, then another. "We'd better head for home, folks." It began to rain harder, so they hurriedly gathered their things, put them back in the wagon, and were on their way.

It rained all that night and all during the following day. Their roof began to leak by the end of the day.

Regina went looking for Andrew and found him out in the shed working. "Andrew, we must get this roof tended to. If we don't, it'll cause damage."

"I'll go see Vicente as soon as I finish this barrel," and Regina went back inside. Then the rain began to pour, and it came down in buckets. Andrew decided as soon as it let up a bit he would put up his tools and be on his way. He had been attaching a tree limb to a log to make a chouncer for the sauerkraut, to force the cabbage down in the barrel.

He went by Calle de los Negroes, stopped a man walking by. "Can you tell me where Vicente Salcito lives?"

"Yes, down the road and around the corner. You can't miss his place. He has a lot of barrels of tar in front of his house."

Andrew found him at home and lucky too, for he caught him before he got too busy. The two men decided on the price, and after making their deal Vicente said, "I'll be there as soon as I can with my stuff."

A few days later Andrew heard a racket outdoors. When he went out, he saw Vicente setting up his huge kettle in the middle of the road. He placed it directly in front of their house and started working, set about building a fire under the kettle, and while that was heating up, he went up on the roof and cleaned it off. He went back to his kettle, threw in some pitch, and melted the tar. Then he hauled it up in buckets and spread it over the leaky roof.

That done, the Weinshanks felt better, knowing their roof was fixed. Rain, though it caused a lot of damage, was important to them. If the rain fell, the stock flourished; then everybody thrived, but if it was dry and there was no rain, the cattle and horses died, and everybody's pocketbooks were empty, so rain for them meant the difference between success and failure. So no wonder that every day Andrew and Regina looked to the sky for the overhanging cloud, praying for it to come forth with that much-needed rain.

Regina needed the help of a man with the sauerkraut, so Arturo became her helper. Jesse watched the catsup on the stove, and Regina and Arturo kept busy shredding the cabbage. Andrew had his hands full making the barrels, getting everything ready to take to town.

As Regina placed a two-inch layer of shredded cabbage in the bottom of the barrel, Arturo tamped it down. First she mixed it with her hands; then Arturo tamped it. She added the salt to taste, and again he tamped it down. "Tamp the heck out of it, Arturo. That's what makes it good—to get as much juice out of the cabbage as we possibly can, and the liquid covers it." She then put in more cabbage, more salt, more tamping. She had to get just the right amount of salt in because, too little or too uneven and it would turn the kraut pink and cause the growth of certain types of yeast.

They kept layering the cabbage, salting and tamping it until they reached the top of the barrel, hoping the brine would come to the top but not over it. This done, Regina put a clean cloth over it, and Arturo filled a container with water from the urn on the porch to weight it down, and it was left to ferment for from two to six weeks, depending on the weather.

Out back in the shed Andrew got the barrels of hardwood as smooth as glass, spending hours sanding them on the inside, using brass rim stays from Ozro's to keep them tight. While he worked he listened for the squeaking sound of the carretas, because he knew they would be carrying women and children who would come to buy their barrels of food. The carretas would be followed by howling dogs, and alongside would be a handsome caballero on horseback prodding the wandering oxen, holding them to the road.

This would give them time to get everything in readiness, Jesse and Regina inside, Andrew helping Arturo get their products lined up for the ladies to see. When the carreta pulled up in front of their adobe, its occupants all climbed out.

As the ladies entered the house, they smelled the good aromas, they sniffed the sauerkraut, sipped some of Regina's catsup and tasted her cooked vegetables. She explained to them in her simple Spanish that "The sauerkraut was good for the bowels and would keep well." They smiled at her and bought some and left.

Later that day they went to John Schumacher's store in the area of Spring and First Street. While Regina looked around, Andrew had a drink of beer. John also served a drink he called "Peach and Honey," containing a good mixture of Peach brandy, but the beer was more to Andrew's liking.

"Well, John, how about it? Will you take some of our foodstuffs to sell to the folks here in town?"

"I'll be glad to. I've already heard about Regina's recipes. I've even had a sample at the Bella Union. Bring me a barrel each of catsup and pickled turnips, and say, by the way, the beer is on the house."

"Mighty fine, John. Well, we'd better be on our way."

Out on the street Andrew and Regina were joined by Jesse and the children. They stopped to watch a parade. The people the country over had come to witness the big event. The riders were all dressed in their fancy clothes adorned with silver buttons, mounted on their high strung horses. Their beauty and grace, fearlessness, agility and poise, and the skill by which the caballeros rode was no less than superb. Their dress was costly, and the men were handsome.

As the Weinshanks walked across the street, they looked at the rudely lettered signs on the store fronts on unbleached cloth advertising wares. Mr. Newmark had one over his. It was around noon. Andrew tried the door. It was open, but no Mr. Newmark.

Andrew remarked, "Oh, I'll bet Harris is off playing cards somewhere."

"Why don't these merchants tend to business?" asked Regina. "People expect me to have my food products ready when I say I'll have them."

Then she started looking over his merchandise, to pick up a few trinkets for the children for Christmas, and while she was doing this, Mr. Newmark walked in. "Just talking to some of my neighbors. Can I help you people?"

"We're looking around. I'll let you know what we need."

Then Mr. Newmark turned to Carrie, now six years old. "This might interest you. This Mexican woman came in and picked up a pair of shoes, and put them inside her clothes. I walked up to her and said, 'Dispense me va!' and she gave them back. She smiled at me just as nice as you please, bowed, and walked out of the store."

Regina joined them and said, "I doubt if she ever steals from you again, Mr. Newmark. I hope you don't ever do that, Carrie. I'd like to buy these."

"Thank you, kind lady. Can we just put them in your bag?"

"You certainly may."

Just then the church bells began to chime, and Mr. Newmark stopped to listen.

"Those bells send many a devout to early mass or announce the time of vespers, and I might add, call many a merchant to his day's labor and dismiss him to his home."

"They do have a comforting sound, and they're very helpful for us in our work, too."

"I eat in town and have been enjoying some of your handiwork, Regina."

"It's nice of you to say so. Well, it's time to go home, Carrie."

"I hope you'll come back soon," said Mr. Newmark.

"We will, thank you and good day."

Regina and Carrie then walked over to Mr. Hellman's store. Regina looked up to see a caballero, one she had seen performing in the parade. She noticed he had a reata in his hand. As she walked past, he bowed politely, lowered his reata, she stepped over it and walked into the store. They looked around and on one counter Carrie saw some books.

"Look at these, mama!"

"Carrie, would you like to borrow one?" asked Mr. Hellman, as he walked toward her smiling.

"Yes, I would like to, Mr. Hellman. Maybe one of the Sisters will help me with it." So with her book in hand, she was a happy little girl, and they walked out the door.

Carrie was attending school conducted by the Sisters of Charity. She was one of the seven children that enrolled that year. The Sisters were conducting both the school and an orphanage comfortably situated in one of the first frame buildings in the pueblo on Alameda Street sold to them by Don Benito Wilson. It included ten acres of fine orchard at the corner of Alameda and Macy.

The school was well run from the start, for Sister Superior had ample funds to manage it; however, the public schools didn't fare so well. The only one in Los Angeles was on Bath Street, housed in a two-story brick building and had two rooms. The town council made all the decisions, and some of the men felt the frills were unnecessary. They refused to hire a janitor, for they felt if the public school classroom floor was to be swept, the teacher should appoint a pupil to swing the broom.

The Sisters of Charity had arrived in January of that year. Bishop Amat, a very important man, having been the alcalde at Monterey, was responsible for bringing them to Los Angeles. He called a meeting to make preparations for the Sisters. Don Abel Stearn presided, and John G. Downey took notes. John, an ardent worker, a lifelong Catholic, was the owner of the only drug store between San Francisco and San Diego, and was one of the largest property holders in Los Angeles.

The Sisters held fairs to earn money, scheduling them on "steamer day." Regina made one or two of her favorite dishes, and the family joined in the festivity.

Some of the Sisters didn't speak English. "I can't understand some of them," said Carrie when she got home. "They speak another language."

"Yes, they speak Spanish, and now is the time to learn it. You're young, and if you expect to talk with people here, you'll need to speak their language. Your daddy learned to speak it in Mexico, and Emmalina Childs is teaching me."

Several days before the Christmas festivities took place, Andrew and Ozro went to help other parishioners clean up rubbish from the Plaza that had been thrown out over the year. Later Regina went over too. While Andrew and Ozro were working, Regina sat and talked to one of the padres. "When was the church built, Father Mora?" asked Regina.

"It was begun in 1818. The townsmen subscribed five hundred cattle to the building fund. With the sale of the cattle, the walls were built up to the window arches. Then the funds ran out, and the unfinished church weathered while waiting further donations. Then the padres at the mission gave us seven barrels of brandy."

"What did you do with that, sell it?"

"Oh, yes! The people in town drank willingly for the good of the church."

"I'm sure they did."

"When the church received more contributions, they were able to continue with the work. Appeals were made to various missions to contribute. From San Bernardino came handmade furniture, and San Buenaventura offered help. San Miguel, San Luis Obispo and Santa Barbara also responded."

"That certainly must have been encouraging."

"Two Angelenos were caught smuggling at Malibu, and their fines were contributed to the church. Don Francisco Avila donated the bells."

"Beautiful sound," said Regina.

"Antonio Maria Lugo did as much as anyone. He was the son of Salvador Lugo, a soldier who was assigned guard duty stationed at the mission. The Don grew up to be a fine upstanding member of the pueblo. He became the alcalde and was awarded a large rancho nearby signed by the King of Spain."

"What an honor," remarked Regina.

"He became the Judge of the Plains and the best rider in California and was in charge of the round ups. He held court, either in the saddle or on an open hillside in order to settle disputes. He said the vaqueros could drive their cattle into a corral, segregate them so the steers could be slaughtered for hides and tallow and so the calves could be branded.

"He expected every man to remove his hat and to keep it off until he was out of sight. Poor Pedro Sanchez refused to do so, making Don Antonio very angry, so while he was mounted on his horse, he nearly trampled poor Pedro to death."

"Oh, no! That was inexcusable," said Regina.

"Several rancheros tried to remove him, but he was too powerful. He built a large adobe within walking distance of the Plaza, and let his cattle out to pasture, his herds propagated, his wealth increased tenfold until he became the richest man in town."

"No wonder he got away with so much."

"He certainly did. He married the daughter of Marianna Vallejo, who had a large land grant in the north. It was his father-in-law, Don Vallejo, who was arrested by marauders and taken to Sutter's Fort because some Americans thought he was furnishing arms for Castro in his fight against Don Pio Pico, but the only guns he had were some old antiques. This was when Sonoma was declared a Republic and the Bear Flag was raised."

"Yes, but from what I've heard it was rather short lived."

"That's true, Don Antonio Maria was called north to help fight Hippolyte de Bouchard, the pirate who was plundering the coastal towns of their treasures. It was Don Antonio Lugo who lassoed one of Bouchard's men, a man by the name of Joseph Chapman, and brought him back to Los Angeles as a prisoner. He couldn't put him in jail because there wasn't any. Since Chapman was a master of many trades, Lugo took him to the Mission and put him to work on their water wheel, the one that was used for grinding corn."

"That was wise!"

"The padres then sent Joseph Chapman and some men to the mountains to cut trees. It was Chapman's idea to drag them first on one side, then on another until by the time they reached the Plaza they were smooth. Then they were cut into large beams and lifted into place to support the roof of the church."

"Clever man," said Regina. "I'll take a good look at them the next time I'm in church."

"We have a lot of beautiful artifacts from Spain that you will enjoy."

"I'd appreciate it if you'd point them out to us, but now I'd better find the men. I'm sure they're ready to go home."

"I'll go with you. I want to thank them," said the padre. They found them settled under a lone pepper tree, resting.

"You've done a good job, my friends. Thank you for your help."

"I do hope the people will take heed and let us get our program over before they start making a mess of it again," said Andrew.

"Perhaps when they see the altars going up they'll know we are having our most important event of the year and will be more careful for a while at any rate," added Father Mora.

On Christmas Eve, Regina took Carrie to the church, Our Lady Queen of the Angels, to take part in the program.

The procession started at the church after four o'clock service and proceeded around the Plaza; the children were all robed in white. In the procession the girls were carrying baskets of flowers. The boys were grouped together forming a choir. Twelve men were bearing candles when they left the church. They proceeded slowly, worshiping at each altar and presenting their pastoral plays, portraying the life of Jesus. One little boy took the part of the devil and scared the little children of the hamlet.

After the play was over, the dons in the various adobes invited them in for a treat. They then went from altar to altar which were decorated with silks, satins, laces and costly jewelry. After they had made their final presentation and eaten their bunelo, they returned to the church and concluded the service.

On the way home, Carrie said to her little brother Frank, "Did you like it?"

"Oh! Yes! I liked the bunelo best, and it was so big and good!"

Then they all laughed. "Now we know what he likes, but Andrew let's get these children home and to bed."

"Let's, and yes, it was a wonderful program, wasn't it?"

The Gila Crossing

Chapter 17

In Los Angeles on January 9th, 1857, at half past eight in the morning, the Weinshanks were preparing foodstuffs for the market when the earth began to tremble. The walls of their adobe shook, big kettles out back tipped over, and barrels fell from the shelves. At first the shocks were light, then stronger. Andrew and Regina gathered up the children and ran outside. Jesse and Arturo ran away. Horses were darting in all directions, running at full tilt down Fort Street. Fearful of further shocks, the Weinshanks stayed outside.

After a few minutes it quieted down, and they were able to go back inside. Everything was in shambles. "Andrew, just look at this house! Everything's a mess, and look at my lovely vase, it's in a million pieces. What in the world causes the earth to shake like that? I've never in all my born days felt anything like it."

"Those quakes can certainly scare a person out of his wits, but from what I've heard they don't happen very often."

"I guess we can be grateful for that," replied Regina uncertainly.

After everything calmed down, Jesse and Arturo returned, and everyone went about setting things straight and repairing the damage.

It was a dry season; consequently times became very bad. Even the richest of the rancheros felt the pinch, and many began to part with their lands to secure relief to tide them over.

One day the sheriff, James Barton, a big, burly fellow, with bushy mustache knocked on the Weinshank door. "Hello, folks, I'm here to collect the taxes."

"Pull up a chair, James," said Andrew joining Barton on the veranda. "You're not in that big a hurry, are you? Nothing earth shaking going on out there, is there?"

Barton shook his head, smiling, "No, everything seems fairly quiet for the moment."

Regina brought James and Andrew tall glasses of cool water and the two men sat down and talked.

"I hear you were in the Mexican War, Andrew. Is that right? John Shumaker was telling me about it."

"Yes, I was. We were in some rough battles. How about you?

"I came out with the Army of the West under General Kearny, Andrew, marching all the way leaving Fort Leavenworth for Bent's Fort. We left Fort Leavenworth in the middle of June, '46, protecting the freight caravans to New Mexico. Our guide was Tom Fitzpatrick. Tom had survived some of the bloodiest trapper battles in the early days of the Rockies and was mighty hard to frighten. Of all the mountain men, he was probably the greatest.

"We reached the Arkansas at its great bend. There the country was more rugged, the wind stronger, the sun hotter, there was less water and more dust. The beautiful blue sky above was the only saving grace. At night the air was cold, and we had only the heat from buffalo chips to keep us warm.

"We were stretched out for miles. When we saw Pike's Peak in the distance, we yelled in delight; we knew we had come a long way. We took up the march across the last stretch of parched sand and sagebrush and finally sighted Bent's Fort rising from the plains. Five hundred and thirty miles we had come on the north bank of the Arkansas— before reaching the fort at the Crossroads of the west. Sometime before noon one day late in July we started filing into the fort. Some of the adobes were two stories high, and there were walled corrals beyond. There were all sorts of buildings there, warehouses, a smithy, a wagon shop, and even an ice house.

"In early August we pulled out in the direction of Raton Pass. From Bent's Fort to the summit was the most difficult part of the entire trail. For four days there was almost no grass for the horses and our rations had to be cut. We moved toward the mountains. There we found a cool stream of water, drank our fill, went swimming and washed our clothes. Some supplies caught up with us and we ate freshly butchered meat. When we reached the top of the Pass, all New Mexico spread below us." "A beautiful sight I'm sure."

"General Kearny was in the lead as we entered Santa Fe in the middle of August, our bridles jingling, our sabers clanking, riding down the twisting, dirty streets. We filed into the Plaza and stood at parade rest. We raised our sabers, the bugles blared and our flag went up. We had taken New Mexico without firing a shot.

"We continued toward California. We left the Rio Grande and headed for the Gila, keeping to the established trail.

"We passed through the little town of Rio Abajo where the general haggled for food and horseflesh and met with bands of Apache. We had a chance to rest and relax, sit around and wait for orders. Then we moved out. Just out of Socorro we met the famous mountain man, Kit Carson.

"Kit was hell bent for Washington to report the conquest of California and then on home. He hadn't seen his family in Taos for some time and didn't want to be away any longer. After the general talked to Kit, he assumed the Americans were in full control of California, so he sent Major Sumner and the rest of his men back to Santa Fe, and kept only Captain Benjamin Moore and about a hundred of us to serve as escort. Kit stayed with us and Tom Fitzpatrick went on to Washington with the dispatches.

"We were now seasoned soldiers, a far cry from the greenhorns we were when we started out. At first some of the men put whiskey in their canteens and had to be picked up and put in wagons, or they drank bad water, their bellies swelled, and they had to lie down along the trail."

"Now, you didn't do any of those things, did you James?"

"Oh, fiddlesticks, Andrew! Maybe I was guilty of some of them, but not the whiskey. I don't go for that hard stuff. Fighting was what I enlisted for— not to dig wells, hunt firewood, shine boots, salute fellow townsmen. I wanted to fight."

"And did you?"

"Yes, I sure did, at San Pasqual, at the Mexican village near San Diego. We arrived at Warner's Ranch in early December. There we heard that Andres Pico had a group of about one hundred fifty rancheros at San Pasqual waiting to ambush us. General Kearny learned the details of the revolt, that the conquest of California was now in jeopardy and that we would have to do some fighting.

"At one o'clock in the morning we packed up and moved out. Kearny first ordered us to a trot, then to a gallop. As soon as we knew we had been sighted by the Californios, our bugle sounded the battle cry, and we were face to face with the main body of Californios, armed with lances.

"We attacked, the Californios engaged us in hand-to-hand combat. Captain Moore was killed, and General Kearny was badly wounded, as well as every other officer in the command.

"The fight lasted only a few minutes, but in that time eighteen of our men were killed and fifteen more were wounded.

"We held up at a rocky point and remained there during the night, burying our dead and tending to the wounded. The next morning we continued on in the direction of San Diego. We limped along and about evening, just as we were about to make camp near a watering hole, the Californios again charged us. We retreated behind some rocks. The Californios took their stand behind another hill and again opened fire.

"Our howitzers became ineffective, so the officers decided to send Kit Carson, Lieutenant Beale and his Indian servant to San Diego for help. As soon as it was dark they moved out. They had to pass through the enemy's mounted sentinels who were spaced about twenty yards apart, so we didn't know whether or not they would make it.

"The next morning we moved out. We went limping along, unaware of what lay ahead. We were heading straight into an ambush, so overwhelming that it was altogether probable that not a single man would have lived to tell the tale.

"Just then Stockton's men came riding in at top speed, a mighty welcome sight. The enemy, seeing all those American soldiers approaching, fled. We then continued on under protection to San Diego.

"When our enlistment was up, the government wanted us to settle down to keep the peace. I was glad to have that experience behind me, but it did give me the start I needed."

"I'm sure you did more than your share."

"The most amazing thing of all is that even though we fought to the death, Andres Pico and I now are great friends. Well, Andrew, how about the taxes? Remember now, it's Manuel Coronel who says how much you have to pay. It's just my job to collect them."

"I'm afraid we don't have any money just yet. We're trying to get started. So far we've had to take everything out in trade, but as soon as we get our feet on the ground, you'll be the first to be paid."

"You're not the only ones. Because of the hard times, even Don Julio Verdugo is unable to pay."

"Poor man," said Andrew. "To have had so much and now be unable to pay his taxes."

"I know, times are hard all over. So far I haven't collected a single cent. I may be out of a job myself."

"I hope that doesn't happen."

"What we need now is a good rain." Just then a man rushed up.

"Thank heaven I found you, sheriff!"

"What are you here for, Elmer?"

"Pancho Daniel has broken out of San Quentin and is holding up at San Juan Capistrano. He and his band of more than one hundred men have already killed a German by the name of George Pfeugardt, and he's planning to kill more."

On hearing this Barton jumped to his feet and started giving orders, "Andrew, have Regina take the children and go to Armory Hall on Second and Spring where they'll be safer, and you, Andrew, grab your gun and come along with me."

As the men hurriedly left, Regina gathered up the children, took Jesse and Arturo along for help and they too left.

In town at the jailhouse, Barton sent word to the big, husky Texas fellows from El Monte for help. He wanted them to join the posse. They responded quickly. As soon as they got organized with Barton himself in the lead, they started out to apprehend and punish the culprits. Before leaving town, Don Jose Sepulveda warned Barton he was outnumbered two to one and should take more men, but Barton disregarded Sepulveda's advice and pushed on. The next day he met the marauders in Santiago Canyon. A shoot-out took place, four men from Los Angeles were killed, and Barton was one of them.

Word was spread in Los Angeles the next morning, and nearly one hundred armed men left to track the fugitives. Andrew left in the wagon filled with coffins to bring the bodies of Barton and his comrades back the following day, returning around noon. They drove down Main Street. Business was suspended, and the townfolk turned out in mass for the funeral following the wagons carrying the bodies. They went directly to the cemetery.

Don Abel Stearns and his wife, Arcadia, rode up in their stylish formal carriage, a strong, light, graceful vehicle with a closed top. The gossips in town insisted the old man imported it from Spain to please his young wife. The Gollers drove up in their wagon, some arrived in carretas, and all the others walked.

After the coffins were lowered into the ground, Regina walked over to where Andrew was standing and spoke softly to him, "This is such a sad thing to happen. The sheriff was such a fine man."

"Yes, to march all the way from Fort Leavenworth across the desert, risking his life at San Pasqual, to be shot down by a good-for-nothing bandit who doesn't deserve to live. It makes you wonder where justice is."

"Men like James are our only hope for law and order. He gave his life for that principle. Let's go home, Andrew."

"You go ahead, I have to take this wagon back to Gollers."

As Regina and the children were walking away, Andres Pico mounted his horse. He and some of the other men headed out in direction of Santiago Canyon.

James Thompson took over as Sheriff and quickly captured fifty-two of the culprits. For those who were returned to town there was quick justice. Judge Scott presided outside the courthouse next to the school yard. The judge had once been a prominent lawyer in Missouri, came overland to Los Angeles in 1850 and was now in a law partnership with Benjamin Hayes. The Weinshanks stood in the crowd outside.

One after the other they brought the prisoners up; Judge Scott called on the crowd to determine their fate. Someone yelled out, "Hang him!" and the Judge responded by saying, "You heard the motion, all those in favor, signify by saying 'aye'." And, of course, the "ayes" had it.

"This is no way to carry on a trial," said Andrew.

"The only thing in its favor is that it's quick," remarked Regina, with a sigh of resignation.

After the verdict was rendered, some of the men went to the jail, subdued the jailor Frank Carpenter, who refused to surrender the prisoners, took one of the prisoners up to the gallows next to the school yard on Fort Street, and in front of every man, woman and child in the pueblo, strung him up. The children had the best spot of all. They watched from the peepholes in the board fence in the yard where they played.

Someone in the crowd yelled out, "Before any more are hanged, let's send the children home. I see one peeping through that hole right now."

"You have a point there, sir!" said the Judge, and the children were hustled off to their homes.

"I'm glad Carrie doesn't attend that school," said Regina.

"I'm glad Frank is with Jessie and Arturo."

One after the other, the outlaws were hanged until the first batch was dispensed with; then the self-appointed executioners returned to their homes and waited for the arrival of the other banditos.

Chinese Camp Post Office

Chapter 18

San Francisco was filled with entertainment of all sizes and shapes. They came from the showboats of the Mississippi, from small theatres of Mobile, New Orleans, Galveston, Nashville, Cincinnati, and from New York. Actors, opera singers, musicians and circus performers came from all over the world. It was a melting pot, an exciting place to be; never before had so many great artists flocked to any one spot under such romantic circumstances in so short a period of time.

Tents and frame structures were being replaced by fine buildings of brick and stone. Many of the sand dunes succumbed to the new construction, and there were many gardens in evidence. Some of the streets now had sidewalks and were wonderfully improved. The city was taking on a metropolitan air.

The Great North American, as the Lee family now called their circus, performed at the American Theatre on the corner of Sansome and Halleck Streets on March 3, 1857. They featured Masters Eugene and Frances, tumbling; Miss Mary Ann Whittaker and Raphael as equestrians; dancing by George Peoples, and clowning by Frenchy Rochette.

In April, Lee and Bennett's North American Circus made plans to tour the northern mines. They were aware they were being followed by Rowe's Pioneer Circus. They were also aware that a wave of hard times had engulfed the country. Lee and his partner,

Bennett, knew that the diggings had been slowing down, that gold dust was not as plentiful as in prior years and many a miner had left the mines. The overall financial condition of the country was poor.

The miners were doing so poorly in the diggings Henry feared they wouldn't be able to afford the admission fare, making for poor gate receipts, but he still had to keep up his payroll to the previous standard of "good times."

Leaving Sacramento they headed east for the gold country, but their trip was doomed from the start. Hard times, plus the performers expecting the same high salaries, made a bad situation impossible.

Placerville was the first town where they planned to perform. Out of Folsom they traveled over the flat countryside up one fairly good-sized grade causing some slowing down. In the distance loomed the mighty peaks of the Sierra.

April 8—

Henry's new partner, Bennett, pumped money into the business and they were again traveling in style, but that money was now gone and they had to depend on the gate receipts to keep them going. Placerville was nestled in and protected by the surrounding hills. The miners watched them as they drove their string of wagons into town, a far cry from the two they had in '52.

In town, many new buildings were under construction. The town had been reduced to ashes the year before, and the only building Henry remembered was a rock building on the south side of Main Street.

They selected a spot on the outskirts of town to set up their tent. Despite having a larger and grander show, few miners attended, for the gold dust was scarce and prospects were bleak.

George Peoples, who had been with Henry since the early days in Stockton, decided to quit. One day he packed his bag and made ready to depart. Henry and George had little to say to each other, for Henry knew it was just as hard on George as it was on him. With a handshake Henry said, "I'll pay you as soon as I can."

"You can send it to me in care of the Pioneer Circus. I'm going to join up with them." Then he was on his way.

Their proceeds on that first night were in the neighborhood of three hundred dollars and the costs around five hundred. Henry felt they needed to reduce salaries to a level they could live with, but more performers threatened to leave, and so his hands were tied.

April 10th—

At Coloma they passed Bell's, a beautiful store made of brick. It had a shake-covered porch over a fancy brick sidewalk, and banners and signs were hung and merchandise was displayed outside, adding color to the front.

Jules Bekeart had another sturdy brick building where the man who first discovered gold, James Marshall, made the counters. All he could do now was get odd jobs after the discovery of gold had done him in.

April 13th—Gold Hill

Two of the great mines had been there: the Empire and the Gold Hill, both had all but petered out.

As they rode along, they still saw miners working along the side of the hills. They traveled over some poorly kept trails, carefully maneuvering their wagons, for a slip meant almost certain death.

Joseph Rowe and his Pioneer Circus were just a day behind the North American, breathing down their backs. Rowe's manager, Joseph Alexander, was trying to justify Rowe's skimpy receipts, for they were doing as poorly as the Great North American. Instead of crediting their problems to the poor financial condition of the country, he started knocking the Great North American.

Intense competition had already begun in the mountain regions. It was becoming more difficult to attract an audience, times were hard, the mountains were swarming with entertainers of all sizes, shapes and ability. Nearly all the well-known players from the San Francisco stage had been there on more than one occasion because that was where the money was. The miners were so familiar with the performances they could recite the lines before the entertainers had a chance to speak them. But now in 1857 if a performance didn't suit, a crackling shot was likely to dust the heels of an unlucky performer as he hurriedly left town.

Sitting on the wagon, holding the reins, traveling at a slow pace, Henry's worried look caused Jeannette to be concerned, "Henry, what's troubling you? You haven't said a word for the past several miles."

"Just thinking. Running a few things through my mind."

"You're very discouraged, aren't you?"

"Business is bad, but let's look on the bright side. I have you, and that's all I need to get me through."

"Being with child, Henry, how will we manage?"

"We'll manage somehow, my dear, we'll manage."

April 14—Auburn

On the way into Auburn they passed some miners still using rockers in the Auburn Ravine. Henry enjoyed performing there because the audience was more polite and enthusiastic. Hopefully the gold dust would be more plentiful in that quiet, prosperous law-abiding town perched high on the mountain top. Even the saloons were on a grander style and had more class, and the citizens were more genteel. In places, their sidewalks were of brick. The town still had a lot of Chinese, and many were walking around.

Mr. Armour had a butcher shop there. He had come from Hangtown and brought two hogs. While he was fattening them, he built his thick-walled adobe cabin. After he moved in he butchered his hogs and opened a shop. These sold so well he raised others, and soon he was the owner of a well-patronized shop.

The North American Circus set up their tent and performed before a good crowd. Their spirits improved, and they left with a little money in their money box. East of the mountain town, the land became flat, and the floor of the valley widespread. They passed through spacious country of live oaks. The spring wildflowers were abundant: ruddy larks sprang from the earth, pearly white convolvulus opened their spreading wheels.

April 16—Michigan Bluff

The entire area surrounding the town was deeply torn by hydraulic mining. Canvas hoses were stretched out along the hillside with their long iron nozzles lying braced against foundations of piled rocks like mighty cannons. The force of water was devastating, eating deeply into the earth, causing it to wash down, leaving ugly scars in the landscape. Tons of earth had fallen, bringing with it trees and grass, leaving an empty crater in its wake. The countryside that had once been covered with willows, pine and oak, where wild grapes, blackberry vines, snowy elder and wild roses flourished, was now a sea of destruction.

"Quartz smashing is very expensive, highly technical, and it takes a gold mine to run a gold mine," said Henry as they rode along passing many tunnels honeycombing the mountains around the old campsites.

"Even so, the countryside is still beautiful with the Sierra in the background," Jeannette said as they traveled along over roads no more than trails.

April 18—Camptonville

The weekly *Butte Record* declared that Lee & Bennett's "Great

North American Circus has come out with entirely new trappings, and performances. They have the largest canvas ever in the state and are spoken of as excelling anything ever before exhibited in the country." That every night they were performing at Camptonville. From there, they took the trail back toward Nevada.

April 20th—Nevada

The setting for the town was even more delightful, built along the banks of a river, with a backdrop of thickly pine-clad hills. One building was built with stone and had a brick facing; the assay office added charm to the hillside town.

They stopped to pay the toll to travel over the road graded by the turnpike company. At this stop, Lee again attempted to lower the salaries, and his performers again threatened to leave. When they got to Nevada, their boss groom served an attachment of $2,100.00 for feed and wages for his men. The local sheriff served papers on him so they made plans to return to Sacramento. Somehow, Henry would survive. In spite of Bennett's urging to the contrary, Henry decided to let his wagons go—the ones with minarets of bells of pure silver, and put his old wagons back into service. Even so, he didn't give up hope, for there was always another town, another place, but come what may, he would never part with his gold nuggets.

Henry somehow did survive that crisis; they were able to carry on. On May 13th, Lee and Bennett, with their great North American, were back in San Francisco. They arrived with an entirely new show which the critics applauded as original, brilliant, and diversified. This great company, by far the most complete in the United States, opened on the vacant lot next to the International Hotel, Wednesday evening. The ring department comprised of the greatest force of male and female equestrians, gymnasts, vaulters, clowns, acrobats, jugglers, rope performers, and tumblers ever concentrated in one establishment. They also had the most superb stud of highly trained performing horses and educated ponies in the world, enabling the management to present displays of dashing horsemanship and extraordinary athletic exercise in infinite variety and of the most wonderful character.

That magnificent new outfit cost a princely fortune. It was gotten up regardless of expense by their agent, Mr. Frank Rivers, who spent all of the prior year in the Atlantic States and in Europe.

The mammoth waterproof pavilion manufactured by Cas Amory, Esquire, of San Francisco, was brilliantly illuminated with gas, which was acknowledged to be a decided improvement over all former styles of lighting.

The band was made up of the best musical talent in California, comprised of a brass and string band under the direction of J. B. Parsons, the best coronet player in California.

Among the members of the troupe were the distinguished artists from the Atlantic States and Europe: Mary Ann Whittaker, George Ryland, William Franklin, Young Raphael and Master Hernandez, all world famous performers.

The managers took great pleasure in announcing that they had engaged the best clown in the United States, William Worrell, late of General Welch's Great National Circus with his juveniles, Sophia, Irene and La Petite Jennie. Worrell's name was sufficient, guaranteeing wit without coarseness, fun without vulgarity, and mirth without end.

William F. Wallett arrived in San Francisco and also joined them. He was one of the greatest performers of all time, having performed before royalty in England and booked as the "Queen's Jester," a fool of the Shakespearean School for a period of twenty years. Those were in his greatest days. Ducrow had sent Wallett to Paris where he was on the bill with the American, Robert Stickney, one of the best vaulters who ever appeared in the ring and one of the few able to do a double somersault on horseback.

William Wallett liked to reminisce about his early days in the circus. Both he and George Ryland, another young performer, had worked with Dan Rice, the great clown. He talked a lot about Dan. They performed together and had a lot of respect for each other. One day he cornered George Ryland, and they started talking.

"One time I went to where Dan was performing, and he showed me all through the circus. Then he took me into the ring and introduced me to the audience. In a speech he said he considered me a friend, and as long as he lived, I would never starve.

"Then it was my turn, and I said, 'As long as Dan lives there will always be a 'Wallett at his command'."

Theirs was the only company to furnish a good cushioned seat to every lady visitor, the only circus to perform everything as represented in the Bills and Advertisements. Prices of Admission were: Box, $1; Pit, 50 cents. There was a separate entrance for the ladies. The doors opened at seven o'clock p.m. and the entertainment commenced at eight o'clock. An attentive usher waited upon and escorted the ladies and family parties to their seats.

All their careful attention to detail, the effort they exerted to obtain the best performers in the country, was still in vain. The audience was sparse, the profits were nil, so they packed up their gear and headed back to the gold fields.

Their plan called for June and July to be spent exhibiting before the miners of the south. As they rode along, they saw the miners with their uplifted picks taking in the spectacle.

June 18th—Chinese Camp

Times did not get better. Lee & Bennett's Circus again preceded Rowe's, for they always tried to get the jump on the competitor to be the first in any town, but the situation was no better in the southern mining towns. Rowe's Pioneer Circus, too, was attached by the sheriff.

Jas. Hernandez, J. R. Marshall, Nat and Mrs. Austin, George Peoples were now all working for Joseph Rowe, but were not being paid. It was at this point that Mr. Rowe had to mortgage his Rancho Santa Anita. Both circuses were suffering greatly, neither was able to pay the wages of their performers, so at Chinese Camp, Henry in desperation sat down and wrote John Center, Joseph Rowe's manager, a letter.

He went to the post office, paid the clerk four dollars to mail it, four dollars he could scarcely spare.

Chinese Camp June 19th, 1857
John Center

Dear Sir:

I write to you according to promise regarding the salary and engaging of the people. We will not engage any man that was in your company at any price, and we expect the same of you in return. The salaries have been very exorbitant and we are now going to reduce all ours. We can have them if we both choose, at our own price, and at a price we can live at.

Franklin is not worth over $75 per week, Fisher $40. Nat Austin and wife we had two years ago when they were both new to the country for $100 per week, and they certainly ought not to be worth now over $80 per week. Hernandez ought to be worth I suppose about $90 or $100.

If all work at those salaries there will be a chance to live. If not, there is no use in employing our capital to build them up. The business has now got to be managed very economically to make it pay, the way the country is. We are not making a dollar for ourselves. I assure you. We have to pay it all out in salaries.

Please answer this directed to Columbia.

Yours with respect,
Henry Charles Lee
North American Circus

June 19th—Columbia

They paid a high price for hay and barley because of the high cost of freight. It cost about three dollars a day to feed the animals, another three dollars for room and board for the performers, not counting the high wages being paid out. George Peoples was still getting $305.72 a month from Rowe; Hernandez was commanding $922.57. Joseph Rowe was paying out almost five thousand dollars a month in wages alone.

Columbia had enormously rich deposits, burned down twice and rebuilt the third time with fine brick buildings. They had two theatres, dry goods and department stores, four hotels and a half dozen boarding houses, three drug stores, several laundries, carpenter shops, banks, tobacconists, wagon makers, doctor and lawyer offices, a printing shop, a brewery, a daguerreotype studio and a Chinatown.

Henry decided to take what little money they had to the assayer's office. The line was a block long, so he had a good piece to wait. He talked to another man in line.

"Just last year Mike Sherlock and his lady bought that lot over there and built a wooden boarding house on it for the miners. The year before there was a tent on that property that burned down."

The line moved a little, and they found themselves in front of the express office, where the gold dust and nuggets were weighed, the most beautiful of all the buildings in Columbia, draped with a bower of fragrant locust blossoms. It had a beautiful cast-iron balcony.

Noticing Henry was looking at it, he said, "That grill was shipped from Troy, New York, and hauled to Columbia by mule freight."

"It's beautiful."

"More than fifty-five million dollars worth of gold in dust and nuggets have been weighed here in Columbia alone."

Next to it was the Wells Fargo office, a low, brick-front building called the American Hotel, and on the corner was the D. O. Mills bank.

The man went on to say, "That large rambling provision store on the corner of Main and State Streets was completed this spring. The owner, Mr. Knapp did a rushing business selling supplies he brought in by pack train and sent on to the diggings and camps along the Stanislaus. It's that one over there where the poplar trees are growing in front of it and where that weeping willow is on the corner."

"I'm more impressed with Columbia than any other town I've seen."

"Yes, we're the largest in the gold country. We have a fancy 'tonsorial parlor' here, too. It's fitted out with elegant red plush chairs, trimmed with gold fringe and red tassels, and lined up behind the barber are rows of bottles on shelves all over the walls."

"Looks like I picked the wrong day to come here," interposed Henry.

"Yes, you sure did. Friday is the busiest day of the week."

The Great North American traveled through Jamestown, surrounded by lofty mountains. They passed through town, driving their wagons past beautiful trees along the narrow and canopied sidewalks of the main street.

It was now summer. The trip from Jamestown back to Stockton was slow. On the plains they found the heat to be intense, the vegetation already burned, and the wildflowers gone. They barely made fifteen miles a day and often only twelve. During the heat of the day they found shelter under the evergreen oaks. They traveled either early or late. The tule marshes, moist and green in the winter, were now dry and burnt. Finally tired and forlorn after having such a fruitless season, they arrived back at the ranch, and waited for the country's economy to improve.

George Peoples stopped by the ranch. "Henry, I'd like to buy one of your horses."

"I'll part with whichever one you choose."

So the men looked them over, and after George made his selection, Henry said, "Why don't we call it square, the horse for your back wages?"

"That's mighty fine of you, Henry. I'm much obliged."

"How is it going with Rowe's Circus, George?"

"He's in bad shape, Henry. At the end he paid me $30.00 a month, and I had to pay for my own food. I was glad to have a job."

"Oh! You're going back?"

"No. He's going to take another trip to Australia, taking John Marshall with him as agent, and I'm not too sure we'd get along."

"And you?" asked Henry.

"I'm heading on down to Los Angeles. I hope to pick up some work down there."

"The best of luck," said Henry. The two men shook hands and parted company.

On one of those summer evenings, while Henry was working on the ranch, word reached him that the Metropolitan in San

Francisco, less than four years old, around eight o'clock at night, had caught fire. By nine o'clock it was in flames, and by twelve o'clock it had been reduced to ashes. The Opera House next door was saved. Henry thought to himself, "I'll miss that place. It was grand, nice as any place back East."

Lee and Bennett broke up their partnership following their unsuccessful tour. Lee had no plans to perform at either Stockton or San Francisco. Jeannette was heavy with child, so they decided to stay at what was now her father's ranch in Stockton.

"What will we do, Henry?" asked Jeannette.

"We'll continue to work, do the only thing we know how to do." The only bright spot in the entire season was the birth of their baby daughter, Pauline. They called her Polly.

Ozro Childs

Chapter 19

In Los Angeles on January 19th in 1858, an article appeared in the local newspaper stating Pancho Daniel was captured near San Luis Obispo. The editor of the *Porcupine*, Horace Bell, the nephew of Alexander Bell, one of the first whites to come to town, was the first to announce it. Sheriff Murphy, with the help of others, rounded Pancho up and brought him back to Los Angeles.

After spending a few days in jail, Pancho got his lawyer to secure a change of venue to Santa Barbara, fearing the people of Los Angeles would take justice into their own hands and string him up for killing Barton and his comrades. Even so he wasn't safe. His worst fears were realized, for Pancho got his just reward. A group of irate citizens overpowered the jailer and hanged him on the gateway of the county jail.

Andrew and Regina were doing well, so Andrew went to put some surplus money in the safe at Joseph Downey's drug store. In Mobile, Andrew would have deposited the money in a bank, but this little Mexican village didn't have one. He walked in the door holding up his bag. "How about it, Joe? Can I put this money in your safe?"

"You certainly can, Andrew. Come in any time and pick it up."

"Much obliged," said Andrew, as he put the cash down on the counter.

From there he headed for Sonora Town, located north of the Plaza. Native Californians dozed under their sombreros in the shade of the wooden veranda overgrown with geraniums and heliotrope. In the doorway, he glanced at the fat señora as she sat smoking a cigarette while her half-naked children played in the dirt.

On the way home Andrew passed Stearns' Arcadia block, the most expensive building in Los Angeles, on the corner of Los Angeles and Arcadia Streets. It outshone all the others. Then he went over to the Temple Block. Daniel Desmond, the hatter, rented one of Temple's stores.

Andrew saw one of the new "stove pipe" hats in the store. He thought it quite handsome, walked over to it. While he was looking at it, Mr. Desmond stepped up.

"How do you like that, Andrew?"

"Very nice," he said.

"The Congressman from Illinois, Abe Lincoln, wears one just like it. This is the hat that replaced the beaver. Beaver you know is getting scarce. Very few are even being made today."

Andrew stood there a while and admired it. He tried it on and was impressed. Before he had a chance to change his mind, and feeling a little flush for having money in Downey's safe, he decided to buy it. On his way home he was aware people were looking at him and wondered if he hadn't made a rather hasty decision.

While he was walking along, he heard the sound of pistol shots, the sound of an alarm; so he quickly headed in that direction. The fire was in Ozro Child's tin shop. The bucket brigade had already formed a relay from the zanja, and the buckets were being passed briskly along from one person to another. By the time Andrew arrived, almost everyone in town was there to watch, including his own two children, Carrie and Frank. The flames spread so fast they were threatening both the Bella Union and El Palacio, but finally the fire was brought under control. Someone in the crowd piped up, "We need one of those fancy fire engines like the one they have in San Francisco."

Someone else replied, "You're right there," but that was as far as it got.

When Andrew reached Ozro, he was sitting on a crate nearby with his head in his hands, bemoaning his loss. Andrew went over to him. "What do you think Ozro? We should be able to save some of this. Let me give you a hand and we'll clean it up." That bit of kindness was all Ozro needed. The two men started moving around, clearing the debris.

When Andrew got home, Regina was busy stirring catsup. She noticed Andrew's new hat, thought it looked out of place, but refrained from saying anything.

"Why don't you let Jesse do that?"

"She has other things to do," said Regina. "The children went over to investigate the fire at Ozro's shop."

"I know, I saw them there."

"I felt so sorry for Ozro, having everything go up in smoke. What was the damage like?"

"We were able to salvage a lot, so it wasn't a total loss."

"That's good, I'll bet Ozro is relieved not to have to start all over again."

The next day in town Andrew walked in the direction of John Shumacher's grocery store. So many men wore guns and felt they had to use them. Gabe Allen, a Mexican War veteran, was no exception. While he was walking down the street, saw a man on a roof and took aim at him. The new Sheriff, Billy Rowland, saw Gabe and knocked him down before he was able to get a shot off.

"What do you think you're trying to do, Gabe?"

"I don't know what happened, Billy. I guess I was back in Mexico during the war. There we had to shoot the Mexicans off the rooftops."

Then Billy noticed Gabe had been drinking, so he hauled him off to jail. Andrew passed them as they were walking along. At first he was going to offer his assistance, but on seeing Gabe's condition, thought better of it and continued on.

Extending a block from the Plaza to the head of Los Angeles Street at Arcadia Street was an alley called Calle de los Negroes. Each side of the alley was occupied by saloons, bordellos and gambling houses. Its reputation for violence was unparalled. Criminals, murderers, bandits and thieves were living with or without the law. It could best be described as a "den of thieves," teeming with the lowest drunkards and gamblers of the country, where restless and reckless characters, disgruntled Mexicans, depraved Indians, and ruffians that had been driven from San Francisco by the vigilantes, spent their time. Nightly shootings kept the pitch of excitement at its height, and the gaiety of the fandangoes stirred the hearts of many. Liquor flowed in abundance and the sounds of guitars were heard throughout the pueblo.

When law and order became somewhat established, the jury system was inaugurated. Those serving conducted themselves rather informally in court. During the warm weather neither vest nor collar was worn. Each juror provided himself with a stick of wood and a knife in order to whittle away his time while he listened to a case. If by chance he forgot his stick, he whittled on the chair he was sitting in. Andrew was asked to serve, but knew nothing about the custom, so he had neither knife nor wood.

Sheriff Rowland, having the Gabe Allen near-shooting on his mind, got up before them and tried to pass a law to control the indiscriminate firing of pistols. That fell on deaf ears. One of the leading citizens on the jury got up and said the judges were not acting firmly enough in handing down sentences, he felt that criminals were being allowed to return to the streets to commit crimes over and over again.

One fellow was brought to court; the case was tried, and the prisoner was found guilty. The sheriff discovered that the prisoner was his brother-in-law, one he hadn't met, so he got the jury to recommend clemency. Judge Dryden, in announcing the verdict, said, "The jury finds you guilty as charged," then proceeded to give the prisoner a lecture, ending it with, "I now declare you a free man, you may go about your business." Someone in the room shouted out, "What's his business?" and the Judge replied, "Horse stealing, sir. Horse stealing."

One day while Andrew was serving on the jury, Regina and the children walked to town to meet him. They walked up to the town jail, a brick building at the corner of Franklin and Spring Streets. As they approached it, Frank jerked at his mother's skirt.

"Golly sakes, look over there. Those men are chained to logs. Why would anyone do a thing like that?" asked Frank.

"They've done something wrong, and don't stare, Frank, leave them be."

Just then, Andrew joined the family. It was election day. Passing by was the great Don Julio Verdugo himself on a beautiful mount, making a fine figure on horseback. On his head he wore a low-crowned black hat with a wide brim and a handkerchief around his neck.

As he rode along, he called out, "Come to my rancho for a rodeo and a fiesta on the first Saturday of the month."

A man standing nearby replied, "We'll be glad to come. We love your fiestas, but we're afraid of the bears that come down from the mountains."

"No need to worry. I'll have one of the vaqueros fire a gun and scare them back into hiding!"

"You'd never know he owed so much money, would you?" asked Regina.

"That's one of his problems. He doesn't take his debts seriously. Some day there will be an reckoning, and when that day comes, he'll be a sorrowful man."

Following Don Julio was his son, Victoriano Verdugo and his thirteen sons, coming to town to vote en masse for their father's favorite candidate. All were decked out in their fancy velvet clothes, pants slit up the side, ornamented with decorative braid, with silver buttons flashing in the sunlight. Following behind were other members of the family in the carreta.

"How do the men campaign for office here?" asked Regina.

"They go to the other side of the Plaza, Sonora Town, where the families Governor de Neve brought from Mexico lived. Those were the first buildings built in Los Angeles, now being used as places for drinking, and those gathering votes go there looking for men. They take them to the corral and offer them as much free liquor as they can drink, put them in one of Phineas Banning's stages and take them to the voting place. When they get there, they give them a ticket which they deposit into the ballot box, and because the influential Mexican candidates are Democrats, they control the elections."

"Why would they do such a thing?" asked Regina.

"They'll do anything to get votes. The white man has brought the Indians down to a state of debauchery. Drunkenness is a special curse for the poor Indians. They're sold the poorest line of liquor, which causes untold misery. Every Saturday night the streets are full of drunken men, scores of sodden wretches lying alongside the road and in the gutters. Some have been stabbed or bullet-ridden, the sheriff buries the dead and locks up the drunks."

"Oh! How dreadful!"

"Monday morning they line them up and sell them to the highest bidder and send them out to a rancho or winery to work. Saturday night they release them, they get drunk—survive or die—and get picked up or are buried. If they live, they go to jail. Monday morning they are sold again to the highest bidder. This takes place fifty-two times a year."

"That's slavery!" exclaimed Regina.

"That's true," said Andrew. "During early fall when the temperatures are at their highest, they use the Indians to make wine, pressing the juice out with their bare feet. The heat plus the incessant toil causes their perspiration to drip from their bodies into the wine."

"If it is made that way, I'm not going to buy any. My family specialized in fine wine in the south of France, and I don't think they used men to do that."

Another day Andrew, Regina and the children took a picnic lunch and went to Fort Hill, up above the town where they could look down on the church. Nearby was Vincent Lugo's adobe. Close by was the old Mexican adobe jail house, now falling into ruin, where Gillespie and his men held out against the Californios until their supply of water ran out, and had to leave town in a hurry. Later Mervine and Gillespie, together, tried to retake Los Angeles, but the Californios' four pounders were too much for them, wounding ten men. Shortly after that, four of the ten men died.

Andrew and Regina were enjoying sitting in the shade of the old adobe building, looking down on the town and out over the countryside. Vast grazing lands stretched before them, many acres planted to oranges and vineyards in every direction, and much of it belonged to William Wolfskill.

Wolfskill worked on a schooner fitted out at San Pedro to hunt sea otter and returned to settle down south of town in 1830. Before that he was a trapper in the territory. Both he and Antonio Maria Lugo set out grapevines, Wolfskill planted his in 1838. He was led to believe his vines would live a hundred years.

"Look down there! Andrew, you can see all the orange trees Mr. Wolfskill planted, row after row. I've never seen so many in all my born days."

"I had some in Mexico, wonderful tasting," said Andrew.

"We had them in France, too," replied Regina. "How long before they'll bear?"

"Oh, about five years."

"I understand some nice shade trees are going to be planted at the Plaza."

"We certainly need them," noted Andrew. "We only have that one pepper tree there now."

"Isn't this wonderful looking down on the town? You once told me that California was heaven on earth. Do you still feel that way, Andrew?"

"Yes, I do. It's just too bad some of those poor devils down there don't realize how lucky they are to be here. The beautiful clear sky above, the mountains in the background, the weather so mild."

Andrew remarked as he turned his back to the mountains and looked out toward the sea.

"It's strange Los Angeles isn't nearer the ocean. They must have had a reason."

"Perhaps this fertile land is the reason," said Andrew as Regina spread out a blanket and arranged their lunch. "Wouldn't it be nice to have a place of our own at the seashore? I love the salt water."

"You've had a bit of that in your lifetime, haven't you?"

"I certainly have. At Monte Carlo the water was so warm and clear. I know we'll never go back to Monte Carlo or even Alabama, but someday I would like to go back to San Francisco."

"As soon as our business picks up."

"I love the weather here; it's so soft and balmy, no winter, just perpetual spring and summer."

"We may not have the snow, but the rain or lack of it can cause a bit of havoc. This is where every prospect pleases and only man is vile."

"How true that statement is."

Just then the children came back from their chase through the mustard, and they ate a hearty lunch before going home.

The most patronized store in town was John Shumacher's grocery store. John, a good-hearted German, came from Wurtenberg, Germany, to New York, then with Stevenson's Regiment to California, making that long journey around the Horn. After his term in the Army, he settled down at Sutter's Creek to dig for gold and came away with one nugget that brought him eight hundred dollars.

While the Weinshanks were looking at his merchandise, John said, "I like dealing with the Mormons because they're so dependable and their vegetables and eggs are always fresh, even if it takes a few days to get here. I'll bet these turnips you're looking at were dug the day before they headed out."

"They are a hard working people, all right."

"Yes, and good businessmen."

"They're bound to succeed," said Andrew. "Look at the way they sell lumber in town, no place to store it, no lumberyard like we had in Mobile. They get it from the boat and just haul it around. Several frame buildings are going up already."

"The Mormons have done a lot for this town," John added. "Jesse Hunter, he's a Mormon, built that kiln farther down on Fort

Street between 2nd and 3rd and that brick building on the west side of Main Street. They do a lot for their own families. He let his son-in-law, John Burke, have his blacksmith shop in that building. Speaking of the devil, he's walking in the door. I'd like you to meet the Weinshanks, Jesse. Andrew was in the Mexican War."

"Glad to make your acquaintance. I guess you might say I was in it, too. Not as a soldier, though. The government wanted us to volunteer for the occupation of California. Our teams and wagons were to transport army supplies, erect forts in Indian territory, build roads and operate ferries. The government was willing to pay for the recruiting of volunteers. With this money we were able to buy the much-needed wagons, stock, supplies, clothing, and leave additional money for our main body of Mormons to make the exodus to the west. Then, too, as volunteers we would be the 'old settlers,' the first to arrive, we would be the ones to break the wilderness."

"Something you Mormons can be proud of," said Andrew.

"It wasn't easy to recruit men for the army, but when we were organized, there were about five hundred in the group made up of several large families, many wives and children and some grandparents. I was selected to be in charge of Company B, then we left Council Bluffs for Fort Leavenworth to be mustered into the service."

"Brigham Young had a big load to carry didn't he?"

"Yes, he did. We pulled out of Fort Leavenworth in the middle of August of 1846, and it was rough going from the start. We didn't go to Bent's Fort, as the army did. At the Arkansas Crossing we were taken down a shorter, thirstier route to Santa Fe. With twenty wagons loaded with goods and supplies, we went in search of a wagon road, one that could be used for a possible route to California. To do this we had to go farther south into the states of Chihuahua and Sonora. We came out on the Arizona desert. From there we crossed straight northwest to the Gila. From there on we followed Kearny's route. We crossed the desert during the winter. Water wells were twenty, thirty, even forty miles apart, and we had to dig a deep well before we could get a trickle of water. Mules began to die; most of the wagons gave out along the way. Our stout boots gave way, and we had to wrap our feet with rawhide and old shirts. When we arrived in San Diego at the end of January in '47, we had only five of the twenty wagons we started with.

"Then, after all the fanfare and praise, we were assigned

garrison duty at various places. Of those who remained, some were put on Sutter's payroll because Fremont had recruited the best of his workers and riflemen, and I was assigned duty here in town. That's just about it."

Regina joined the men. "We're going to need a lot of butter and eggs," said Regina. "Do they have cows and chickens around here?"

"On some of the ranchos, a few running around here in town, but we get our supplies from San Bernardino. They come in by wagon regularly. It's a three-day trip. You let me know what you'll need, and I'll get them for you."

"That will be fine; then I can count on it. I'll let you know how many."

After they left the store, they saw a carreta filled with watermelons. Several people had gathered around. An Indian bought one, sat down along the side of the road and ate with his face buried in the melon. When he was through, he tossed the rind on the road.

"Look over there, Andrew. Why do people do that? Don't they know that brings flies that carry germs? Oh, Andrew! Look over there, that horse is running away!"

As Regina made her observation, a caballero came toward them at full speed, lassoed the frightened animal and returned him to his owner.

"Regina, I'll be back in a bit. I'm going over to Peter Biggs'. I need a haircut."

"Fine, Andrew, but don't get taken in by any of his other services—cupping or bleeding or let him pull any of your teeth," knowing full well she was pulling his leg.

"I won't. I know better than that."

When Andrew walked into the shop, Peter Biggs, the town barber, was working on another man. Peter was a colored man, a good-natured fellow, had been a slave, sold to an officer at Fort Leavenworth and freed at the close of the Mexican War. Biggs came to California and opened his shop on Main Street near the Bella Union. In his shop there was one high-backed chair. The men sat waiting their turn. As Biggs called "next," he sprinkled his last victim with Florida water and at the same time applied his own concoction of bear oil as his finishing touch.

One man seeing a fellow customer being doused with bear oil, led Andrew aside and said, "Don't let Biggs put that bear oil on you; it stains the pillows! My wife gives me fits if I go home with it on." Andrew thanked him and sat down to wait his turn, trying to remember to have Biggs refrain from using the bear oil on him. As there were several before him, he dozed off. When his turn came, the man next to him gave him a nudge, and up he sprang.

When he got into the chair, the same towel that had been used on the man before him was put around his neck. He got the treatment of Florida water, and before he had a chance to object, Peter gave him a sprinkling of bear oil. As he stepped down, he looked around to see if Biggs was going to use the same towel on the next man, and sure enough, he did.

Back at the Plaza, Andrew rejoined Regina and the children. "Today we're having a treat. I'm taking my family for a meal at the Bella Union." Henry Hammel had added the second and third stories. It was the town's leading hotel, saloon, restaurant, and was their favorite meeting place. It was advertised far and wide as "one of the finest of all California."

The Weinshanks walked over and waited in line outside the door, listening for the shrill steam whistle on the roof calling both transients and regulars, letting the people know their meal was ready. People came scurrying from all directions, all crowding around the door to be the first to enter and to get a good place to eat.

Out on the street after dinner, the children watched a wagon-load of ice lumbering along. Water was dripping down.

"Mama, where does ice come from?"

"Up on the mountains beyond San Bernardino. See, those mountains way off in the distance."

"Where do they get it?"

"It's hard packed snow. They cut it up in big chunks and bring it to town. But if there is no snow, we do without. Of course, if we were wealthy like Don Abel Stearns, we could buy ice from the ships. Its brought down from Alaska in chunks packed in straw."

Suddenly, Regina felt faint, Andrew steadied her, and a man walking nearby hurried over, dipped his handkerchief in the water trough and put it on her forehead. As soon as Regina felt better, Andrew took her home.

It was the day after Christmas. Their third child was due momentarily. Regina and Andrew had agreed on the name of Regina if the baby was a girl, because the name had been in the family for five generations; however, they were going to call her Jenny to save confusion. If it was a boy, they were going to call him George. Dr. Griffin, who was always very busy, was on hand to help with the delivery.

"Oh, doctor, I'm so glad you're here," said Regina.

"I wanted to be here Regina. I have to take special care of you."

"It can't be too long now. The pains are coming closer together, only a minute or two apart."

"Just relax, Regina, it'll just be a while. Well, Andrew, if you would step outside for a bit, Regina and I have a job to do."

"I'm on my way, Doctor, but say the word and I'll come on the run," sensing he'd better hurry.

Regina began to moan. The doctor turned, went over to the bed. "Easy now, Regina, we're going to have that baby here before you know it."

Then she raked with pain, the sweat rolling down her face. The doctor grabbed her hands, "Push, push! Regina, push again! Now, one more time, it's coming. Keep at it, Regina, we're almost there. Now, here we come, here we come. It's a girl!"

"Oh! Doctor, thank you, what would I do without you?"

"Knowing you, you'd do just fine. Well, Regina, what are you going to name her?"

"We've picked the name of Jenny for her, Doctor," said Regina weakly. "I guess you're holding Jenny."

"Well, Jenny," said the doctor, "you're the second little white baby I've delivered in our fair city, if you can call it that. Emmalina Child's little girl, Emma, was the first, but being second is still pretty good. After I get this cord cut and clean up a bit, I'll tell Andrew to come in. You'll be in good hands with Mrs. Childs and Jesse to look after you."

The doctor went outside to give Andrew the good news. He found him in the shed, pacing up and down. Andrew, anxious to hear about the baby, rushed over to the doctor as he came through the door.

"It's a girl, Andrew. Regina's doing fine. I understand you're calling her Jenny. She's a beauty, all right."

"I'm glad its over with, Doctor. Does it ever get any easier?"

"I doubt it. Even after all my experience, the miracle of birth is still a thrill, but you never know what problems you may run into."

"How soon can I see them?"

"It'll be a little while, the womenfolk are finishing up a bit."

"Anything exciting happening to you these days?" asked

Andrew, still a little shaken but trying to think of other things to pass the time.

"Got a letter from Phillip Kearny."

"What happened to Kearny after the war?" asked Andrew.

"He returned to Fort Leavenworth."

"Oh?"

"Yes. He took the immigrant route via Sutter's, left the last day of May in 1847. They crossed the high Sierra and camped at the Truckee Lake. There they came upon the cabin where a party of immigrants, the Donners, had stayed the winter before, where many died of hunger. Their bodies and bones were strewn about. General Kearny instructed some soldiers to dig a single grave, he performed the rite and they headed on. They continued along the immigrant trail much of the way along Mary's River. After days of traveling they reached the Snake River, then came up on the Oregon road and on to Fort Hall.They followed the Platte River Road on to Fort Leavenworth, arriving August 2nd.

"They made the full circle. From Fort Leavenworth and back again, under terrible hardships with scant provisions and unmanageable mounts. They conquered a land that could have been had by the consent of its inhabitants had it been done the right way. General Kearny and Colonel Alexander Doniphan brought more stability to the people of New Mexico in two months than Spain in two centuries or Mexico after taking over from Spain."

The year was 1859. Lee's circus was at Jackson and Kearny Streets. In the the *Daily Alta* was an article that interested Henry.

"Listen to this, George, 'In Sacramento the Forest Theatre has cracked from dome to pit in many places and is fully expected to fall in on its own.' Here is another article that says the National Theatre built by Lee and Marshall was again sold, renovated, and is now called the Metropolitan Theatre.

"That's the one you built, isn't it, Henry?"

"Yes, it is. Last year it was sold by the sheriff for the paltry sum of eleven thousand dollars. I'd like to go back there some day, George."

"I would like to see it, Henry. I'd better go on back to the tent. There's lots to do. Are you coming?"

"I'll be right along, George."

George left to join the others, but Henry continued reading. He read about the four businessmen in Sacramento, Mark Hopkins,

Leland Stanford, Collis Huntington and Charles Crocker, who were entering into a partnership for the railroad. A man by the name of Theodore Judah made it possible. He was the one who got Congress to appropriate the money for the transcontinental railroad, but died before it was organized.

The four businessmen had already set their plan in motion, building track eastward through the Sierra to join the Union Pacific, working its way westward.

For The season of 1860 Henry again decided to continue on down the coast. Little Polly, now three years old, darted here and there, taking in everything there was to see. Their baby, Ellena, was beginning to walk and had to be watched carefully. Henry and George Ryland supervised the boarding of the wagons and saw that everything was carefully packed away.

Henry took his circus to San Pedro, then hauled overland to Los Angeles by wagon. They stopped at the halfway house for a bite to eat and a change of horses, then on to town traveling over the flat open country to the City of the Angels. They again chose Los Angeles for a January show because of its mild climate.

They set up their tent, one ring, on a lot south of the Plaza and opened their show on January 5th. Headlining the program were the outstanding riding of George Ryland and the Lee children in "The Sprite of the Morning Star," all the children taking part. Their acts were either biblical, educational or scientific in nature.

The Lees left Los Angeles by sidewheeler, continuing south along the coast of Mexico, remaining close to land. Henry and Jeannette stood at the rail, looking out over the horizon talking about their plans. Their eyes rested on the lofty mountains in the background, rearing their peaks above the clouds. The gentle breezes of the tropical climate felt good, and the voyage was a continuous scene of beauty and pleasure.

When they entered the harbor of Acapulco, a lively Mexican village on the coast of Mexico, they watched the boys swim offshore, diving into the clear placid waters of the bay to retrieve coins thrown by the passengers.

As Henry and his sons led their horses down the gangplank and sent their other equipment to shore, the sailors on the steamer were busy taking on coal and water, as well as other supplies for the trip ahead.

After getting the ladies and children quartered in a hotel, the men set about locating a lot on which to place their tent and made preparations for the show. The novelty of a traveling circus and the promise of watching bareback riding was enough to induce the people to attend.

During the day, Henry took his family to see the sights. Everywhere they looked were orange trees, laden with fruit. They ate their fill, purchased some chocolate, the best they had ever tasted.

After a couple of days, they broke down the tent, loaded the wagons and prepared to leave, again amid the acclamation and well wishes of those they left behind.

They continued on, crossed the equator, traveling along the coast of South America, both by steamer and then inland by wagon to as many towns as possible, to stay while their steamer was taking on supplies, only long enough to present a benefit for the town, another for themselves, then push on, following the pattern of the year before.

They stayed several days in Lima, Peru. There they saw the beautiful women, flashing of eye, trim of ankle, lithe in their walk and exceedingly graceful as they manipulated their corn-husk cigarettes. They continued on to Valparaiso, Chile. Jeannette was beginning to find ocean travel quite difficult because she was well along with child.

They entered the picturesque port of Valparaiso, with a population of about thirty thousand people, where their steamer would be holding over for a week. Here merchants from many nations sold their goods in white-walled waterfront stores. The fine homes behind the cliffs were handsome with their gardens laden with bright geraniums.

They enjoyed that coastal town with its adobe buildings and the streets lined with flourishing shops. When the circus was not performing or rehearsing, Henry and his family tramped the streets. He and his boys rode horseback on the more extensive forays. He took his family to the theatre, sampled the local drinks, and bought apples, almonds and curios. They talked to others and learned that the children there could read, as well as write and do sums.

Henry planned to stay on in Valparaiso, to await the arrival of the new baby. They continued performing, pleasing the crowd. On July 28, 1860, Jeannette gave birth to a boy, her sixth, and Henry named him Lavater. "If only he would follow in the footsteps of his uncle, the great rider at the Old Bowery Theatre."

At Gettysburg

Chapter 20

Twelve days after the attack on Fort Sumter, on April 27th, 1861, word arrived at San Francisco by Pony Express that the War of Rebellion had started. South Carolina had already seceded, and people were wondering what would happen next.

Some of the men were already making plans to go to war. Albert Sydney Johnston, whose wife was the sister of Doctor Griffin, set about packing to return to the South, by way of Warner's Ranch, over the overland route, to join the Confederacy. Another to go was Cameron Thom.

Andrew waited anxiously for each steamer to arrive, hoping for news in favor of the South. But, no matter what the news, the people gathered in groups in the streets and exchanged points of view. Some were elated, others were sad. Some started a war of their own. Sympathizers on both sides took to fighting, arguing about who was right or wrong, who would win or lose, and when they felt they were losing ground, some took well-aimed punches. Grown men rolled around in the dirt over a war they could do nothing about.

One day, while Andrew was in Ozro's tin shop, Sam Foy and Henry Hammel joined them.

"The South will win," said Sam. "There's greater wealth in the South and better leadership. Our own Albert Johnston is a general now, and Lee will get his turn one of these days. He did as much as anyone to win the war in Mexico. He's a southerner for sure."

"I can't imagine him on a losing side," said Andrew, trying to get his two cents worth in.

"But the North has industry," said Ozro, "and the munitions factory at Harper's Ferry."

"Now that the government has Drum Barracks in Wilmington to receive merchandise from Los Angeles for the war effort, this could tip the balance," added Sam.

"A lot of people aren't too happy about that," Hammel remarked.

"I'm not all fired sure Abe Lincoln's got everybody's confidence. We have over three thousand people living here now, and he only got 198 votes," said Sam.

"You men can carry on, but I've had enough war to last me all my days," said Andrew, and he walked out the door.

On Christmas Eve, it started to rain, and with only slight interruption, it lasted thirty days. The rivers rose and flooded the lowlands, but it happened so slowly the stock was able to reach the neighboring hills in safety. People in the country had to seek refuge on their rooftops. In Los Angeles, the town's water system collapsed, and many adobe walls crumbled.

It wasn't long before complaints that telegraph poles and wires had fallen to the ground, blocking thoroughfares and entangling animals, began to roll in. There were soon so many complaints that the city fathers had to decide to either "repair it or remove it, or better still, throw the equipment away." This was the state of affairs when Regina gave birth to a baby girl. They named her Elizabeth.

The year was 1862, the Civil War was well underway, and the nation was devastated. Tom Phelan's brother, Billy, wrote to the priests in Clonmel to keep their folks informed on what they were doing and how they were getting on.

Then, one day a letter arrived from one of their brother John's friends in Ireland, who was now living in Vermont. He wrote saying that if both Billy and Tom would fight on the side of the North they could earn some money. He told them of the bounty being paid for fighting and gave them the name of a man who was willing to pay one thousand dollars to someone who would take his place. If they were interested, they were to go to a broker in town, enlist and the money would be sent to them at Waverly.

Billy wasn't interested. He felt he was too old, but Tom was anxious to go. When word reached him that his money could be picked up at the broker's office, he learned he was to join a company in Vermont, a regiment made up of gentlemen and scholars.

It was a sorrowful day, the day Tom said "Good-bye" to his family and friends, but with money in his pocket, he again set out on another journey.

On September 25th Tom's regiment went into Camp Lincoln at Brattleboro, Vermont. Tom was issued his uniform, a hip-length dark blue coat, and light blue trousers; his buttons were adorned with a spreadeagle design.

On October 4th his regiment was reviewed by Governor Holbrook. That afternoon Tom was mustered into the service of the United States, and on the evening of the 7th his regiment left Brattleboro for Washington, D.C. He took the steamer at New Haven for Jersey City. They stopped in Philadelphia for supper and spent the night at Soldier's Rest. The next morning they went into camp on Capitol Hill; took part in various reviews where the regiment acquitted themselves so well, they received special complimentary notice from the commanding general.

The concentration of the brigade took place at Camp Casey on East Capitol Hill. Tom's regiment was then ordered to move across the Potomac over Long Bridge to the country five miles south of the city, to Arlington Heights. At Munson's Hill Tom's regiment camped on the edge of a stretch of oak timber in a field of fresh green grass. Alongside was a stream of clear water. This was a refreshing contrast to the barren surface and stifling dust-storms of Capitol Hill.

They then moved on south marching ten miles through Alexandria, on to a spot south of Hunting Creek, over the road to Mount Vernon and on to Centreville. After a hard day on the road, they bivouacked for the night. Tom got out his meager rations and made out the best he could. The next day they moved a mile and a half to the south to the spot where they had orders to stay for the next month.

They christened their camp "Camp Vermont," and its headquarters was established in a wing of the mansion of Mr. George Mason, who announced himself "neutral" on the war issue. In the shadow of the mansion the Vermonters found good camping ground with plenty of timber nearby for fuel. Their assignment was to picket that portion of the line encircling Washington.

Tom was assigned to help construct the barracks of oak logs for their winter quarters. It was good working alongside the men from Vermont who all pitched in and carried their share of the load. In the evening they sat around and talked about their dreams and aspirations and of going back home.

At this time, Lee's Army was in the Shenandoah Valley, and the Army of the Potomac, around Warrenton.

Tom's regiment, the Twelfth, was then assigned to some old rifle pits a half-mile east of the village, running across the Alexandria Turnpike. On the 20th of October they again broke camp and marched to Fairfax Station. They camped near Fairfax Courthouse, a short distance from the Capitol. There they drilled and learned the rudiments of warfare. Tom realized he would have to learn his lessons well; failure to do otherwise, could result in death on the battlefield.

The Lees went back to Sacramento where they planned to spend the winter at the Annereau Ranch. As they approached Sacramento by boat, they came in full view of the two-story brick buildings with their iron shutters, gaudily painted wooden structures with showy verandas and ornate carvings. They could see the church steeple in the midst of the market area. George Ryland stayed back and supervised the unloading of the stock and equipment, while Henry and the family went into town.

Henry hired a hackney. They passed gambling halls, restaurants, boarding houses, and a dry goods shop. They continued on to the outskirts of town where they pulled into the yard at the Annereau ranch. The ladies and children went into the house, while Henry unharnessed the horses and bedded them down for the night.

For Jeannette it was a tearful reunion with her sister. She was again heavy with child, and it was good to get back to the family to have her baby in the comfort of her own home.

At the ranch there was always work to do. After their baby Rosa was born on Christmas Day in 1862, Jeannette again began working out. Francis and Eugene were at the top of their profession and doing spectacular feats. Eugene was now a premier leaper. Polly at age seven was already performing, being postured by her father as they rode around the ring. They stayed on at the ranch for a while, working on their show and perfecting their acts.

In the evening they gathered around the big table in the dining room and later sat around the fireplace exchanging stories and talking, making plans for the future.

"I was in town today," said Henry. "Still evidence of lots of damage from that flood."

"It rained for over two weeks here without a let up. Water flowed like a river all over town. Boats glided up K Street. Crafts of all kinds were gliding in and out of low-arched doorways, and water was in the first stories of the hotels."

"The levee just doesn't hold the water back as it should," said Jeannette's father.

"They've worked on it, but the powers that be said either raise the levee, or the town. They've already started raising the town."

"That will cost a lot of money." said Henry, "And the town will be disrupted for a long time."

"They had to do something! The women and children had to be taken to the Agricultural Hall, that dismal, bleak place for meals and a place to sleep. The countryside over was flooded, and only the roofs of a few farm houses were visible here and there. Wagons were stranded, moving wherever the tide would take them."

A few days later Henry went to town. He found it hard to go from place to place because sometimes the sidewalks were raised in front of one store, nothing in front of the next one, so he had to walk up and down crude stairways or ramps as he went from store to store.

He walked along Front Street near K. Nearby, men were laying tracks for the railroad. Men were everywhere putting the ties and planks in place. As he paused to look, a man said, "This is the one that's going to hook up with the railroad coming west, making it transcontinental. That's what I call progress."

Lee, Worrell and Sebastian's Great Circus performed at the Metropolitan Theatre, San Francisco's finest theatre on May 1st. The Metropolitan was on Montgomery Street and was built with the same lavishness as the first one, a magnificent temple of the drama, unsurpassed in elegance and completeness of its appointments by any other structure in the state. There was a generous use of gold leaf throughout. The tiers of boxes were in a horseshoe and the cushions were elegantly upholstered in red velvet, and the drop curtain was made of the same velvet material.

Henry again met and had a chance to talk to Mr. Maguire, the lessee.

"This is a magnificent building you have here, quite an improvement over the third Jenny Lind."

"Yes, it is," said Maguire. "Who do you have in your show?"

"We have Madame Sebastian, the graceful danseuse and equestrienne; La Petite Mary Ann Whittaker, the pride of the profession; Signor Sebastian, the premier Rider of the World. Also appearing in his great somersault and vaulting feats is Mr. George Henrie—the famous one- two- and four-horse rider. We have a magnificent stud of trained horses, diminutive ponies and educated mules performing."

"You know I'm interested only in the best. You have a few performers in your own family, don't you, Henry?"

"Yes, my sons, Eugene and Francis, are now accomplished riders, and Masters Harry, John, and James are our infant performers and are following the family profession with great promise. Polly and Ellena are doing gymnastic events, and later on in the program their mother performs her equestrian act."

"You have quite a family, don't you?" asked Maguire.

"Yes, nine children, all performing, adding to the family coffers."

"Yes, I'm sure they're an asset. Never thought of it that way before. On the 24th of August I want you to perform at my Opera House, a special event."

"Be glad to," said Henry.

Tom Phelan's regiment commenced the year at Alexandria, Virginia, guarding government property and patrolling the streets. Tom was assigned duty every other day, standing out in the cold, night after night, wondering what he was doing there. The only consolation was the thousand dollars he had tucked away.

Tom was transferred to the Seventh Regiment, performing continuous service as part of the garrison of Washington. He was assigned to Company F under Captain Darius Thomas. At one time, the regiment guarded twenty-five posts in the city. One-third of the men were constantly on duty.

The snows and severe weather lasted into April in Virginia that year and made spring a trying one on the health of the brigade. The sick list rapidly increased, and the picket service became more arduous. Tom had spent much of his time out in the rainy, windy, wintery streets doing guard duty. He caught a cold that stayed with him for days on end. Finally realizing that he was not getting better, he decided to see the company doctor.

"I don't like the sound of your cough, Private. I hope you wear warm clothing while on duty."

"I tried to get warm clothes, but the quartermaster can't see his way free to part with them."

"Keep after him, Private, or you won't be fit to fight in any man's army."

"I'll keep on it, sir, and maybe the weather will warm up a bit. Is that all, sir?'

"Carry on, soldier, and lots of luck, and don't forget to get that underwear."

They broke up camp and moved on to another assignment. Heavy rain set in on the night after they moved out. The bottom dropped out of the roads, so in addition to picket duty, Tom's company was assigned to make the road passable for the loaded army wagons. The soldiers worked all through the night in pouring down rain. Tom got the chills and had to take to his bed.

About the 10th of April the weather became more settled. General Hooker's preparations for the Chancellorville campaign were in progress. By early May, Tom regained his strength. His regiment was being assigned to guard the railroad at Warrenton Junction. Here the drilling lasted five hours a day. The exercise, plus the weather improving, did wonders for his health.

Tom's regiment left for Chancellorville, traveling by train. Alongside the tracks were the remains of a train burned in Pope's campaign. The battle of Chancellorville was then in progress. No time was wasted for the Vermont regiments, for they were immediately ordered to storm Mary's Heights. Three men from Tom's regiment, the Seventh, were captured and taken away.

On the 23rd of June the entire brigade was attached to the First Corps of the Army of the Potomac. They concentrated at Union Mills and starting at three o'clock in the afternoon, marched eight miles and bivouacked a mile beyond Centreville. Tom spread out his blankets, thankful for a chance to rest and slept well.

The next morning they marched into Hendon Station, along the line of Alexandria and London Railroad to Guilford Station and another day's march into Maryland. They crossed the Potomac on the pontoon bridges at Edward's Ferry to Poolesville. At eight o'clock the following morning, the brigade continued on. They crossed the Monacacy at its mouth at noon. The hard marching caused many of the men to discard their knapsacks and blankets, but Tom had remembered the doctor's warning. He knew if he discarded his, he wouldn't get a replacement. They bivouacked two miles beyond Adamstown, on the Baltimore and Ohio Railroad.

Tom's regiment was being driven by forced marches, pushed along by the officers, suffering from the sweltering heat and heavy dust. Then came the rain which lasted all day of the 29th. They halted at Frederick City for three hours. Tom sat down, his breech loader at his side, waiting for the rain to stop. He looked down. His shoes were without soles. The chief quartermaster had already refused him new underwear, so there was no use asking for shoes. They continued on. The march was telling on him, as they covered 120 miles in six days.

General Meade replaced General Hooker, and from the commanding general to the youngest drummer boy, they knew they were about to engage in one of the greatest battles of all times. The two great armies were converging on the little market town known as Gettysburg in Pennsylvania, lying amid rolling hills and broad shallow valleys.

On July 1st the guns opened up. For the Federals the day started well and ended in disaster. As the day progressed, they were greatly outnumbered, making it nearly impossible to hold the line. They waited for the rest of the army of the Potomac to reach the scene.

July 2nd dawned hot after a windless night. Most of the army had come up, and the Federals held good ground on Cemetery Ridge. The fight continued, again the guns roared, then quieted down, and they went at it hand to hand. By the grace of God, Tom was spared.

By the end of the second day, word had passed through the line that both flanks had held. All during the moonlit night, Tom rested on his musket, dozing fitfully, waiting for the dawn.

Early the following morning, Tom got up, tended to his chores, ate his meager rations and sat down to wait his fate. At one o'clock in the afternoon, the Confederate Army began a thunderous attack and was answered by the Federal guns. For two hours the shelling continued; then the Federals slackened off.

The Confederates, thousands of them, came at the middle of the Union line, from the direction of Emmitsburg Road. The Union batteries again opened up, doing terrible damage to the Confederates.

All around him, Tom heard the men swearing and cursing. The ground was covered over with the dead and dying. Soldiers were carrying their battle flags, darting here and there, officers on horseback with swords in hand, shouting directions.

In the midst of the battle, Tom thought he heard someone call out his name, an officer, perhaps his brother John's friend. Just as he turned his head to hear the order, a bullet whizzed past his ear, in the space where his head had just been. Hearing nothing more, he turned back to the task at hand, fighting side by side his fellow comrades. All around him the men were at their awful chore, bayonet-thrusts, saber strokes and pistol shots and Tom was in the thick of it. His uniform was in tatters, blood streamed down his arm, from some wound, his or a comrade's.

Then, suddenly, it was over. The charging column had been broken to bits, and the Confederates retreated. Tom fell to the ground exhausted, not caring whether he lived or died. After a few moments rest, Tom struggled to his feet, pitched in and did his share. After the dead had been buried, the wounded tended, he could see in the far distance the Army of Northern Virginia moving out, leaving the battle scene.

The next day, troops arrived to make the city secure. Tom's regiment got orders to move out. He left that devastated, desecrated battlefield with its dead and dying strewn in every direction, a sight he knew would haunt him for the remainder of his days.

Tom returned to New Haven, back to Brattleboro, and then on July 15th he was mustered out of the service. He went back to Waverly, Illinois, to his family and friends where he got a job in a broom factory. He continued working for the next two years, teaching broom-making to the blind, just enough time to build up his stake so he could head out for California.

In Los Angeles, yellow flags marked the stricken adobes, where the epidemic of smallpox had broken out. Los Angeles was hit especially hard, killing off most of the Indians. Many died at the ranchos and in town as well, as many as fifteen to twenty a day. It spread like wildfire through town, taking a large toll in Sonora town.

Deaths were so frequent the city fathers asked the padres to stop ringing the church bells for the souls of the departed. Baptisms had to be postponed because the priests were too busy burying the dead.

The smallpox wagon, the Black Maria, moved slowly down Fort Street, a frequent sight in front of the Weinshank adobe. Funeral processions were attended by men on horseback and by women on foot. Their trip was a long and fatiguing one.

Regina left the chores for Jesse and Arturo to do and worked from morning till night going from house to house supervising the care of the sick, for most of the patients were treated at home. For this she earned the title, "The Angel of Los Angeles."

Regina was assisting in births and took it upon herself to baptize the babies for fear they, too, would contact the dread disease and die before the padres had time to perform the baptismal.

The Sisters of Charity established a hospital in the quiet airy part of town in a small adobe belonging to Cristobal Aguilar north of the church, and many of the townfolk were taken there.

Dr. Walter Lindley had Mr. Downey get a serum to vaccinate those who would let him.

"What is this, Doctor?" asked Regina as she watched him inoculate a patient she was caring for.

"It's called a vaccination, serum taken from those who have already had the disease. Having this vaccination causes the body to become immune to smallpox."

"Would you be able to come by our house and vaccinate my family?"

"The sooner the better, if you're leaving now, I'll be right over.

"I'm leaving here in just a minute, Doctor."

As soon as Regina walked in the door at home, she said, "Gather around children, the doctor is coming to scratch your arm and put a drop of serum on it." The doctor followed her in.

"I'm going to put it in their hips, Regina. It can leave an ugly scar."

Carrie looked to her mother for reassurance. Regina walked over to her and held her hands while the doctor lifted her skirt and administered the shot. Little Frank sent up a howl before the doctor got near him. The neighbors the country over could hear him. Andrew stepped up, and then it was Regina's turn.

"Doctor, do you think I should be vaccinated, nursing the new baby and all?"

"Yes, you're just as susceptible as anyone, Regina. You'll surely get smallpox if you don't. I worry about you, taking care of others with a baby at home."

"I don't stay long, I just drop in on them. Someone has to show the womenfolk what to do. Go ahead, Doctor. I just hope it doesn't affect my milk."

Days following the vaccination, the family felt slightly ill and moped around the house. A crust formed over the scratches and left big ugly scars.

When Regina had a chance, she talked to the doctor. "We all felt so bum after that vaccination, doctor."

"That was a good thing, Regina. That means that if you had gotten smallpox, you could have died from it. You're very lucky."

Tom Rowan stopped by to deliver bread from his father's bakery. As he walked through the door, the doctor called to him.

"Tom, get over here and let me give you a vaccination."

"I don't need that, sir. I'm not sick," answered Tom.

"Get over here anyway. That's when it's effective. This way we'll feel better about it, and anyway, working in the bakery you are more apt to spread germs."

"All right. I'll do it, but promise first it won't hurt!"

"Well, not too much at any rate."

The great floods of the previous winter were followed by several dry seasons, bringing on the drought, giving Los Angeles the appearance of a desert wasteland. Cattle perished, leaving the hillsides littered with thousands of sun bleached carcasses. The lean long-horned cattle staggered across the barren hills dying from the lack of water. Many of the rancheros lost their land because the countryside was dependent on rain for their cattle and crops.

Don Able Stearns had to mortgage his Rancho Los Alamitos, and Ricardo Vejar lost his property by foreclosure. Many of the ranchos were broken up into small parcels, and many small towns began to spring up.

In town, the merchants became downhearted. The collector of taxes was unable to collect a single cent.

The romantic era of the ranchos had peaked in the 1830s, the 1840s, and the 1850s, but they were now doomed in the 1860s. The drought, the squatters, the money lenders and the farmers moving in, all took their toll.

Tom and Mary Phelan

The Brother Jonathan

Chapter 21

The Lees began 1865 with a performance at the Mechanic's Pavilion in San Francisco. The Lee family and George Ryland combined their acts. They also presented chariot races, hurdle and Roman racing. William Vincent was their ringmaster.

By the latter part of March, Lee and Ryland performed at the Metropolitan in Sacramento, Henry's former pavilion. He couldn't help feeling regret for having to give it up.

Henry again made arrangements for the engagement with the lessee, Tom Maguire. While he was talking to him, Henry said, "I'd like to present Mazeppa in 'The Cataract of the Ganges'."

"Sounds interesting."

"I'm sure you've heard I once owned this building with my partner. I had to sell because of the depression of 1857. My partner invested in stock and we lost everything."

"Yes, I knew that. John Marshall was his name, wasn't it? I heard he had speculated heavily and the sheriff had to take over."

"Yes, I'm afraid so. But there is no use crying over spilled milk. How is it doing now?"

"Can't complain. As you can see, I've fixed it up, put a lot of money into it. We've had a lot of performers on this stage in the past few years, some good, some not so good. Mark Twain was one of the more prominent ones."

It was good to get back to the pavilion. The children were thrilled to perform in the theatre their father had built, but after a short engagement, it was time to move on. They again toured the mines, ending up in the mining camps at Virginia City, Nevada, on May 14th.

The circus moved on. They headed north for engagements in the towns along the coast. Their plan called for stopping at Portland, Oregon, to travel as far north as Victoria, British Columbia. Jeannette was again about to give birth, so she stayed on at the ranch in Sacramento, intending to join the family as soon as possible. Everything was going according to plan.

Jeannette Lee took her three-week-old baby and set out for San Francisco. On July 28th she booked passage on the "Brother Jonathan," an old side-wheel steamer owned by the California Steam Navigation Company.

Traveling light, with only the necessities required for caring for her baby, named Tom after Henry's brother, and a change of clothes for herself, anxious to join her family, she went up the gangplank. All her costumes and other paraphernalia had gone on ahead.

She was not the only celebrity who boarded that day. James Nesbitt, ace reporter for the San Francisco *Bulletin* was heading north. In show business, his word was law. If he praised one of the actors at the opera house, Maguire upped the performer's wages entirely on his own. Another to board was William Logan, the Indian agent, accompanying a very large shipment of gold. He had been assigned to distribute it to the Indians for payment of treaties made by the U. S. Government.

The most famous of its passengers was a survivor of the Mexican War, Brigadier General Wright. He and his wife made a handsome couple, the General dressed in a fine sealskin coat. They made their way up the gangplank and headed for their stateroom. Also boarding was Mrs. J. C. Keeman, a "businesswoman," her fingers heavily laden with diamonds. Boarding with her were her seven "soiled doves." Heads turned in their direction as the ladies of the oldest profession in the world walked up the gangplank. There was no mistaking their identity, as they displayed their wares for all to see. The more sedate among the passengers appeared shocked by this exposure to the seamier side of life; but some of the male passengers and members of the crew exchanged knowing winks and smiles. They were on their way to Portland and Victoria to alleviate the shortages there, and no doubt their arrival would be welcomed by many.

After Jeannette settled in, she took the baby and went on deck for fresh air, and awaited their departure. She watched as the passengers were boarding the ship. Below them, the captain and the ship's agent were supervising the cargo being loaded from the dock. She overheard a hot argument between the captain and the agent. She heard the captain say, "Stop receiving any more cargo. She's already grossly overloaded and it's too dangerous to take on any more. This ship won't run safely under such conditions."

That statement infuriated the arrogant freight agent, so he shouted at the captain. "Either follow orders or we'll relieve you of your command." Then he turned his back, making the captain even more furious.

On board the "Brother Jonathan" were 116 passengers and a full complement of crew. At the stroke of noon the captain gave the order to cast off her lines, and she slipped through the Golden Gate.

There was a persistent headwind and a heavy sea which caused Jeannette to be confined to her quarters with her baby. The usual gaiety aboard ship was noticeably absent as it headed out to sea.

Two days out, on July 30th,the old leaky sidewheeler encountered a terrific gale. Progress was difficult. The gale reached full proportions about sixteen miles north of Crescent City. The ship was taking a terrible pounding. The sea was running mountainous swells. Jeannette became frightened by the storm. She gathered up her baby and hurried to the dining room. Then, all of a sudden, the ship was put about and they headed in the direction of Crescent City. Jeannette was afraid, so didn't return to her cabin. It was clear enough where she was, but foggy and smoky on shore.

They had logged about six miles in the opposite direction and were in the area of the dreaded St. George Reef when suddenly the ship struck something with a terrible jolt. People started screaming, running in all directions and Jeannette was knocked down. She lay there her arms around her baby, unable to move. All around her pandemonium had broken loose. The ship began to roll, then a terrible thump. A part of the keel came up alongside. By the time Jeannette got to her feet, the wind had tossed the ship around, her head came to the sea, and she worked herself off the reef a little. Destruction was everywhere, the yard was resting on the deck. The passengers were running toward the lifeboats.

Jeannette could hear the captain shout, "Look for your own safety. I'll do all I can for you." She, too, started running for the lifeboats. Carrying the baby, she couldn't move as quickly as the others to get through the crowd to the boats, where she watched the harassed crewmen trying desperately to get them lowered. All around her people were pushing and screaming. The next lifeboat was lowered, it was filled before she could get in, it capsized and everyone went down.

Jeannette watched, horrified by the sight. She was afraid to get into the second boat, but Mrs. Keeman and her seven doves got in quickly and without panic. As the crew lowered the boat, the Brother Jonathan lurched to starboard and swung the lifeboat out of the water. The steamer took a severe lurch. The lifeboat fell into the water and swamped. At that very moment, a wave crashed through the deck and before her very eyes, washed several overboard.

Five women and three children got into the next boat. Jeannette moved in that direction, but before she could get in, the fireman, came running up screaming, "She's about to go down!"

"Take my baby! Take my baby!" Jeannette cried to the quartermaster as he rushed past her, ignoring her plea, looking out only for his own safety. The baker and a waiter pushed her aside and got into the lifeboat. Then came a cabin boy, and a steerage steward, both pushing and shoving, both converging at the same time and jumped in before she had a chance. The third officer, Patterson, was pushed along with all the others and against his orders the crewmen lowered the boat. This was the last of the lifeboats. Jeannette watched Patterson's surfboat pull away, clutching her baby to her, looking out at the small boat as it tossed about like a chip on the wild waves. One moment it chip bobbed high on a crest and in the next second, it fell from sight in the sea's trough. She could faintly hear Patterson call out, "Good-bye and good luck."

As she turned around, the ship split wide open and began spilling its screaming occupants into the rolling sea. Jeannette watched helplessly as the mate grabbed the chain plate with one arm and two women with the other. . . he held on until the men on deck rescued them. One was Mrs. Wright. Below her in the water was Mrs. Keeman, amid debris, swimming in desperation trying to save her seven young beauties. The churning water held her prisoner. Mrs. Keeman was thrown a piece of planking from the upper deck. The board hit her in the head, and she sank beneath the waves, her doves floundering around her.

The baby was startled by the cannon exploding nearby, the last desperate signal for help. The towering smokestack came down with a crash.

Jeannette moved in the direction of the crowd who had gathered around Captain DeWolf, pleading for help and all she could hear him say, in total despair, "Tell them that if they hadn't overloaded us, we would have gotten through all right. This never would have happened."

Knowing all hope was gone, Jeannette sat down by James Nesbitt, the reporter. He was sitting on the ship's forward cover. She watched him as he wrote his will in his notebook, wrapped it neatly about his waist, and waited for his death. General Wright wrapped his coat about his wife, their arms wrapped around each other. Jeannette, holding her baby tightly, sat quietly reciting the rosary and waited for the waves to engulf them. In less than an hour, the "Brother Jonathan" was gone.

The circus was in Portland, Oregon, when the word arrived that the "Brother Jonathan" had gone down. The entire story was in the newspaper. When Henry read it he broke down and cried. The children whimpered for their mother, not knowing the full impact on their lives.

The story was told and retold day after day, adding to their agony. But sad as it was, the circus went on. Everything appeared as though gaiety and lightheartedness prevailed. Henry suffered on in silence. During the days that followed there was a job to be done, a performance to give. While riding around the ring and posturing his children before an audience, his attention was on them. But after the show was over, he took the children back to the hotel, and gloom set in. Henry sat in stony silence, grieving for his little French equestrienne. He missed her by his side, her tiny body, her soft skin. Oh, God! Why did this have to happen to him, when he loved her so? Francis and Eugene shared his grief, for they loved performing with her.

One night while they were in their room, Eugene spoke up. "I've been thinking of the night when mother and I walked the rope as we ascended the pavilion, and how she hugged me when we got down safely."

"Yes, a beautiful performer, and she thought a lot of you, too. Oh! Why did we leave her home this time to have the baby? If she had been with us this never would have happened," Henry said over and over as the tears came streaming down his face.

"Don't blame yourself. How were you to know?"

Henry now had nine children to raise and look after. The younger ones depended on his strong body to carry them around the ring, and this gave him strength. With a heavy heart, he carried an emptiness that could not be shared. His first inclination was to leave his family and go to Crescent City to stand vigil while the bodies of Jeannette and the baby were recovered, a baby he would never know. But he knew his duty was to care for his other children, for that was what Jeannette would have wanted him to do.

Days and even weeks later, seventy-five of the bodies were washed ashore. Most of them were unrecognizable. One body was that of Mrs. Keeman; her stiffened fingers were grotesquely ablaze with $5,000 worth of jewels. Mr. Nesbitt's body had his notebook still attached. The bodies of Jeannette and the baby were never found. There was nothing from the ship except the wheel, which was taken to be hung over the bar at Scovill's Saloon in Crescent City. All the gold was gone. Either by miracle or the capabilities of Officer Patterson the boat carrying nineteen occupants, five women, three children and eleven crew members, was able to reach shore. They were the only survivors.

Henry and George Ryland made plans to take the children back to Sacramento, where Jeannette's family lived and where Rosa was born. Polly now eight, was followed closely by John, then James, Harry, Ellena, Lavater, and little Rosa, who was less than three years old. Henry's two older boys, Eugene and Francis could manage on their own. Their plan was to work and train the children so they could carry on the profession their mother loved so well.

The circus returned to Sacramento and to the ranch. It was a hard thing for Henry to do, but he knew he would have to face it some day, seeing the family, knowing they were sharing his grief.

When they pulled into the yard, Jeannette's mother, father and sister were there to greet them.

"Welcome home, Henry," said Mrs. Annereau, as she gathered up little Rosa. "Let's get the children inside. We'll get a nice hot meal ready for your famished brood."

Henry embraced each one in turn, thankful that no mention had been made of Jeannette. After supper the children were sent to bed and the others sat around talking.

"Surely you'll continue to make your winter quarters here, Henry?" inquired Jeannette's father.

"I certainly hope to. I'll need help with the younger children, Rosa especially. The older ones can manage quite well on their own."

"I'm glad that's settled." Then Mr. Annereau walked out of the room and brought back a small, black velvet sack and handed it to Henry. "Jeannette asked me to keep this. She said it contained the gold nuggets you collected in your early days in the gold country."

"Yes, it does," said Henry in wonder. "I thought perhaps it had gone down with her, but I should have known she would have left them in your trusting hands. She knew what they meant to me. I was going to have them made up into a chain, but never got around to it. Now, I wonder if I ever will."

"I'm sure you'll change your mind, Henry. There must be days you don't feel you can go on, but you have the children to think of, so don't give up hope."

Henry took George Ryland on as his new partner. George had proven himself with several seasons of great performances and they prospered. He was a hard working man and very talented. Again, they went to the Sandwich Islands, Mexico and Central America, always on the move.

George was about ten years younger than Henry, a very small man, clean-shaven with a small mustache. His hat was always too large for his head. He was a juggler and rider. He could do the principal riding act, go into tumbling and the leaps, juggle and spin on the ground or horseback, be ringmaster or clown, break and perform animals, teach others, as well as turn a dollar and keep going. He was billed as "The Olympic Ball Thrower."

George had been a partner of Dan Rice, the great clown who had been a close friend of Zachary Taylor, the then presidential candidate and a hero of the Mexican War. Taylor had seen a lot of Dan's shows and praised him for his performances.

Dan Rice, had suffered from yellow fever and Taylor was well-versed in the treatment of the dread disease and so gave Dan some much-needed advice. Taylor enjoyed the long talks he had with Dan during his recovery and was able to relive the battle of Buena Vista, the surrender and the importance of the battle and its effect on the war.

Dan was a good listener and was able to visualize how the scene of battle could be portrayed in the arena. He gathered together the necessary costumes for both the American and Mexican armies, adding sound effects, and the battle scene provided a very moving experience. The audience enjoyed it immensely. At the conclusion of the act, he spoke in glowing terms of the accomplishments of Zachary Taylor and suggested the audience support him in his candidacy for the Presidency of the United States. Because of this, Dan was invited to represent the state of Louisiana at the Whig convention.

On April 22nd the circus performed at Hayes Park in San Francisco. The Lees and George Ryland were featured. Again, Henry's two little girls, Ellena and Polly, pleased the crowd.

The Cosmopolitan Circus, as they were now called, pitched their tent at the corner of Montgomery and Jackson on May 3rd. That part of town had been built on pilings, for the bay came all the way up to Montgomery. Life and activity centered down the street at the corner of Washington and Montgomery. Here were all the first class business houses: the banks, the express office and dance halls. All night long they could hear the strains of music, the rattle of the ivory chips. Down the street they could see the El Dorado overlooking the Plaza, along with several French restaurants, hotels and lodging houses.

The circus of Messrs. Lee and Ryland performed at San Andreas, one of the small mining towns, on June 14th. On their program was William Franklin, the greatest equestrian artist in the world. Books had been written describing his daring and skill. While Franklin rode the trotting horse around the ring, two men stood on small platforms facing each other, each holding the end of a piece of cloth. Franklin accomplished a backward somersault from a standing position, over the cloth and landed in an upright position on his horse. Such agility and grace could not be equaled.

On that same program little Polly performed on the tightrope with Señor Cordejelli and was the admiration of the spectators. Miss Ellen Bolton was the equestrienne in the show.

All through the mining country they went. Gold mining had slowed down, but many people stayed on, living in the small towns along the way. As as they rode along, they enjoyed the countryside, the clear mountain air and the blue meadows of mountain iris. On the steeper grades, they all got off the wagons, the ladies leading the teams while the men pushed from the rear, then back on. From the gold country they went home to Stockton, then back to San Francisco.

The Lees had their Grand Opening Night on Monday evening, November 5th, on the lot adjoining the International Hotel on Jackson Street. They continued to improve their show and added many new acts. This was the first appearance of the favorite comedian, Harry Jackson, in San Francisco, as Jester the Clown, who had been received in Oregon, as well as California, with shouts of laughter and applause nightly giving him the title of Rex Jocindi, King of Clowns.

Ducrow, the world famous two horse rider, joined the show. Astride two galloping horses he rode while four more entered the ring in succession, galloping between his outstretched legs, stooping he snatched up their reins as they passed under him.

At each and every performance there was a grand change of races. This new and splendid pavilion, the largest erected on the Pacific Coast was gotten up expressly for that engagement at immense expense, after the style of the great hippodromes of London, Paris and New York. They gave a series of new and magnificent entertainments consisting of chariot racing, hurdle racing, steeple chasing, flat racing, ladies racing, foot racing, trotting matches, racing in sacks, and pole climbing, and all kinds of amusements which heretofore had never been introduced in the Modern Hippodrome. John Marshall stopped by, and Henry hired him on to help manage. Nothing was mentioned about John's investing their money on worthless stock, for Henry felt that bygones should be bygones.

Harry Lee

Polly Lee

Lavater Lee

Rosa Lee

Robert Lee

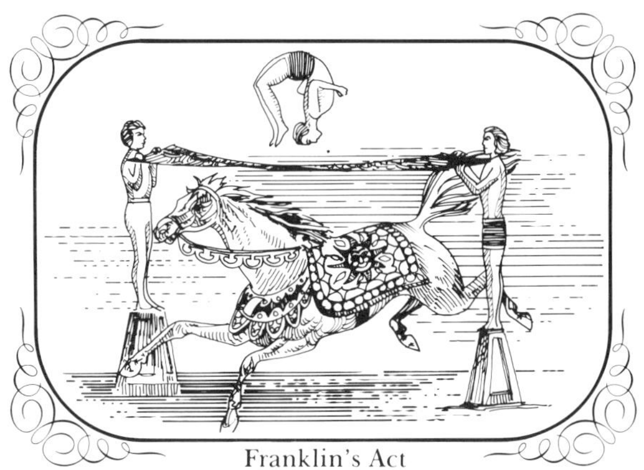
Franklin's Act

Chapter 22

The Weinshank's adobe at 744 Fort Street, had been damaged by an earthquake and from time to time by floods, so they went in search of a new place where they would have a little land and be away from the dust and traffic. They wanted to get away from the flocks of sheep, bands of horses, trains of long-eared burros, wagons loaded down with implements and provisions churning up the choking dust as they lumbered along on their way to Fort Tejon past the old adobe.

They found a nice two-acre piece with another old adobe, but it was larger and in better condition, on Second Street, between Los Angeles and San Pedro Streets. In the distance they had a clear view of the San Gabriel mountains and the surrounding land covered with grapevines. Andrew purchased the property from Bishop Amat, one of the most highly respected men of all California, the alcalde of Monterey.

Across from them, in an adobe that had been built in 1819, lived the illustrious Lugo family. It was Don Antonio Maria Lugo's father, Salvador, a soldier at the Mission San Gabriel who came to the pueblo with Felipe de Neve in 1771. Don Antonio Maria became Judge of the Plains and his son, Don Felipe, followed in his father's footsteps; traveling out into the country to the various ranchos, one of which was the Workman-Rowland rancho, acting as majordomo at their rodeos. He had been, on more than one occasion, the alcalde of Los Angeles and was considered the best rider in all California.

Young Frank Weinshank, now thirteen years old, loved to cross the street to listen to the older Lugo children talk about their grandfather and the old days when he was the Judge of the Plains. Whenever he left the house, he could always count on being followed by his little sister Jenny.

The children sat on the ground under a shady oak, listening in rapt attention to one, then another tell about Salvador and Antonio Maria; how in the old days before they built adobes, they lived in brush shelters made of tules; how the rancheros rode their horses into saloons rather than dismount; and how sometimes when the horses were left tethered outside, they would break away and run pell-mell down the street. No matter how often the stories were told, the children asked to hear them again and again. Their eyes grew big as saucers as they heard the stories of the old days when the dons roamed the great ranchos, hunting their cattle in the tall mustard, hosting thrilling rodeos where the skills of the horsemen were tested publicly. The great names of Verdugo, Dominguez, Palomares, Vejar, Yorba, and Nieto became as familiar to them as their own neighbors', and the storyteller waved his arms letting them know his stories took in all the countryside.

Carrie never accompanied the younger ones. She stayed at home doing her studies or her needlepoint, and anyway, she thought she was too old to take part in their childish fun. While at school, she worked on a cross-stitched picture of George Washington. It had such fine detail and shading it took her that entire school year to complete it.

Across the street while the children were engrossed in their stories, Andrew and Regina walked to the City Hall, an adobe building, to record the deed to their new property and to transfer the home and lot on Fort Street to its new owner. They walked down the hall within its whitewashed, tobacco-spattered walls, passed several dingy, smoke-filled rooms, peeked into one room where the city council sat on benches and where the mayor was holding court for the drunk and disorderly. They walked past that door and into the next room and up to the desk.

The recorder read Andrew the description of his deed. It called for one of the boundaries to end at a peach tree.

"What happens if it dies?" asked Andrew.

"You don't need to worry about that; the tree will last a hundred years," answered the recorder.

"Not if I decide to chop it down. I'm planning on putting in oranges on that land."

"Suit yourself, but you'd better put an orange tree on that very spot and come in and we'll change the deed."

They moved into their single story adobe on Second Street, long and rambling, with thick walls. It was cool in the summer and warm in the winter. They moved in the lovely furniture that came around the Horn. It looked handsome in its new setting, made of dark cherry wood embellished with intricate carvings. On the hard-packed, dirt floor they laid a rug Jesse had just finished which greatly enhanced the beauty of the furniture.

For use during the day, they had a privy out back. At night a pot was kept under the bed, a chore Jesse tended to, for she washed them out each morning. For wipers Jesse was careful to keep the family well supplied with corn cobs.

Dr. Hammel lived next door. He had come to Los Angeles after the '49 gold rush. They could never understand why it was "Dr." Hammel. He didn't do any doctoring; he ran the Bella Union.

Regina was glad to get settled in her new house because she was again expecting a child. On September 23, 1866, four months after moving, Regina had a little boy, and they named him George.

On Second Street the Weinshanks were surrounded with vineyards and the already burgeoning orange groves—the Wolfskills to the south had their large ranch planted to citrus, and Mr. Forster's vineyard went all the way to the river.

When Andrew wasn't making barrels, he set about clearing the land. He was able to get small orange cuttings from his friend, William Wolfskill, and they soon became his pride and joy. When it was time to irrigate his trees, Andrew used the water from the Zanja Madre that ran along the edge of his property. The main ditch of the Zanja was on the north side of town, and the water came from the Los Angeles River. If Andrew needed to irrigate, he got a permit from the Zanjero which allowed him to use what he needed during a twelve hour period. The cost to him was the same, no matter how much water he used, and if he couldn't get the water turned into his ditches early enough during the day, he was allowed to continue on through the night.

There was a constant flow of wagons in the Weinshank yard to pick up the foodstuffs to be sent off to the mines and to the merchants in town. Once a year a wagon came from the Church of Our Lady Queen of the Angels to pick up their year's supply of foodstuffs in lieu of a donation.

The "ladies of the house of ill repute" also got their foodstuffs from the Weinshanks. The "madam," a handsome woman somewhat past her prime, did the shopping for her "girls." She dressed in clothes of the very finest material and was heavily doused with toilet water, lip rouge, and makeup. She wore several expensive rings on her fingers and an expensive necklace hanging down over her full bosom. She moved around looking at the various foodstuffs the Weinshanks had, bought some and always had some small trinket to leave for the children. Regina had a way with people, able to put them at their ease, but Andrew felt uncomfortable in the madam's presence and stepped out of the way. Even though Regina sold foodstuffs to the prostitutes, whenever she was on the streets of Los Angeles going about her business of shopping and the "madam" happened to pass by, out of respect for her, the madam gave no sign of recognition.

Andrew was a meticulous man when he made a barrel. He made them entirely by hand, and he wasn't satisfied until the inside was sanded as smooth as glass. His final touch was to hammer on the brass rim stays because he didn't want them scuffed.

Regina, too, was constantly on the move, taking care of many of the household chores. One day their friend and neighbor, Julia Breer, took her bundles of clothes over to the Weinshanks, and together she and Regina, with Jesse along for help, went down to the Zanja Madre to do their wash. They hung their clothes on a rock to dry. Then there was time to sit and talk and enjoy the sunshine.

"I hear a man by the name of Germaine Pellissier, a Frenchman from the Hautes Alps, has come to town. I understand he's raising sheep and that he plans to import them from both France and Australia to improve his herd."

"I wonder how the rancheros will like that," said Regina. "Of course Don Able Stearns has always had a lot of sheep on his rancho. Some people say that sheep eat the grass down so it won't grow the following year."

"Apparently cattle and sheep shouldn't graze the same land," replied Julia.

"There have been a lot of changes here in the short time we've been here," Regina remarked.

"What's Andrew been doing lately?"

"He's been pretty busy. He attends German Club meetings once a week. The other day he told me some of the fellows were trying to get German taught in the schools because there are so many of us here."

"Are you for that, Regina?"

"No, I feel if the schools catered to all the nationalities, the schools would be taking up languages, neglecting other subjects."

"I agree."

Regina liked those lazy relaxing times, especially when she was with Julia, for she liked to talk about her boys, Carl and Willie, and what they were doing.

"Always up to something," Julia would say. "All Carl can think of is making parts for this contraption he's building. He says he's going to build a horseless carriage one of these days. Do you think he could be 'touched,' Regina? A bright boy, but do you think it would be possible for a buggy to go running around without a horse to pull it?"

"Don't discredit him, Julia. You can never tell about these boys. I never cease to wonder about some of the things Frank tells me about. He thinks we'll have running water in our houses one of these days and gas lights, too. No, it doesn't pay to hold them back. Give them the reins. I'm not too sure these things won't happen."

"I read in the papers the other day there now are ten thousand Chinamen working on the railroad over the Sierra. If they can accomplish that, I guess anything is possible."

"This country is full of enthusiastic, enterprising men, Julia. You can't stop progress."

The year was 1867. Andrew took time out from making his rounds to stop in at Desmond's hat store on Main Street opposite the El Palacio. "I see Rinaldi's furniture store is empty. How come?"

"Oh, he sold it," said Mr. Desmond. "I heard he took his family and moved to San Fernando."

"I wonder what happened to all that beautiful furniture he carried?" mused Andrew.

"I really can't say. One morning I came down to the store, and it was empty. Everything was gone—lock, stock and barrel."

"Well, can't get any work done here, so I'd best be getting along."

Andrew walked on down the street. When he reached the Bella Union Hotel, he arrived in time to see the new Concord stage as it pulled up. Most of the town's people had never seen one before and had gathered around to watch the passengers get off the stage. The driver blew his trumpet to warn the pedestrians, causing the chickens to scatter and the dogs to bark.

"This stage line came all the way from San Francisco," said the man next to Andrew. "It stopped at San Jose, San Luis Obispo, Santa Barbara, Santa Buenaventura before hitting Los Angeles. It'll soon be on its way down to San Diego. Doesn't that beat all? I never thought I'd ever live to see anything as grand as this."

As Andrew was admiring the stage, he looked up to see the Great Cosmopolitan Circus as they entered town in their gaily painted wagons, loaded down with tent and all their paraphernalia, a glorious sight to be sure. So he hurried home to tell the family of its coming to town.

Henry Charles Lee was driving the lead wagon. As he looked around, he noticed that a second story had been added to the Bella Union. There were other new two-story buildings near Main and Spring Streets, a few lamp posts, the type used for the burning of gas, but the streets were still unpaved, and the sidewalks were still dirt held in place by boards, and the tar-stained adobe houses looked shabbier than ever.

Henry wasted no time in meeting with some of the town's leaders at Lodge No. 42. They held their meetings upstairs at Mr. Potter's store, a fine brick building, on Main Street, opposite the Bella Union. The hook and ladder company had been trying to get people to contribute to a new fire engine when Henry Charles Lee came to town. Henry got up to speak to the gathering, "I'm more than willing to offer a circus performance to help pay for your fire engine. In return I would hope you would spread the word so people will attend a benefit for us." And the men nodded in agreement.

Sam Prager, "Uncle Sam" as they called him, a good-natured and benevolent man, having a deep interest in Masonic matters, along with Rabb Edelman, Thomas Rowan, Judge Mallard and Uncle Billy Workman took control of the benefit. They planned a very gala affair at the pavilion in Stearns Hall near the Plaza on Main Street located across the street from where Rinaldi's furniture store had been. The floor was decorated with Masonic emblems under the artistic care of Dr. Hayes, giving it a patriotic appearance.

The lodge men went out spreading the word that from the proceeds, Los Angeles would soon be able to buy the new fire engine so important to their town. The people would only have to attend a benefit performance, pay the regular fare, and the fire engine was practically theirs, no more bucket brigades.

A committee was nominated to collect the proceeds and make arrangements for the purchase of the fire wagon. There was lots to be done, spreading the word for good attendance, supervising the pavilion itself.

A parade was planned to make the day a very special one, a grand event that would give the people of Los Angeles a chance to see all that was in store for them.

On the day of the big event, early in the morning, all the roads and trails leading into town and all the main thoroughfares were filled with wagons and carretas carrying families, people on horseback, many on foot, all heading for town. Long before the parade started, the streets were filled with throngs of people milling about waiting for the big event to start.

The floods of the previous December had washed out all of the telegraph lines, and the roads had turned into swamps and quagmires. When the weather cleared in mid-January, the first mail in over a month arrived.

The rains continued to fall in January, but in spite of the muddy streets, elegantly dressed ladies went with their families to be thrilled by the grand parade of the incomparable Lee and Ryland Circus. The spectators headed back to Main Street. The Grand Cortege was forming on the circus lot, and there was a scramble for good places to see it pass. It was an excited crowd that waited along the route. In the distance came the faint clop-clop of horses. Somebody down the street yelled, "Here it comes!"

The band in the distance struck up a tune that sent shivers up their spines. The people along the road were thrilled to see them pass and watched the performers as they marched along carrying American, French and Spanish flags.

That evening as people approached the pavilion, their faces were alive and happy. They waited outside. Finally, a man appeared, dressed in a fancy suit, to sell tickets. It was his job to open the door.

They were all there—all the townfolk crowded in that one small room. The Weinshanks were there, too, Andrew, Regina and little Jenny, Carrie, now a lovely young lady of seventeen, and Frank, a handsome boy with dark hair like his father's and flashing brown eyes.

The program presented that night was one most appropriate for the small hall and one that would be most pleasing for the more refined audience. On the bill were the classical positions and gymnastics, but the best act of all was the one performed by William Franklin, taking the part of an American sailor. He rode bareback, performing his great leaping act over a banner of cloth, a feat that could be performed by few living performers. Another principal act was the riding of George Ryland and the Lee children in "The Sprites of the Morning Star."

The pavilion was crowded, and the audience enjoyed the performance. On the program Polly had her first starring role standing on her father's shoulders as he played the part of Dick Turpin, the renowned highwayman. Henry, mounted on Black Bess, carried his weeping Polly to the free booters' den, an act that electrified the audience, depicting a story that would be told and retold by those who saw it.

On their way home, the Weinshanks relived what they had seen and heard.

"What did you like the best, mother?" Carrie asked.

"Oh, Carrie, I liked it all. Such a fine performance. Never in my life have I seen such skill and daring, and all so exciting, and I did like the music especially well. It was such a fine band."

When the Weinshanks walked home that night Carrie was flushed for thinking that for one fleeting moment, she was certain Mr. Lee's eyes had rested on hers.

The next day Carrie went with her mother to the new United States Hotel to deliver a small order of foodstuffs. Louis Messmer, the proprietor and friend of theirs, had come to Los Angeles in 1858. He brought with him a tidy sum of money which he had made cooking for the Hudson Bay Company Troops. There, in the lobby, was the same Mr. Lee. A crowd had gathered around him.

Mr. Messmer was behind the desk, and while they put their packages down, Mr. Lee walked over.

"May I help you?" he asked.

"Oh, no," replied Regina. "Thank you, anyway. We're not delivering much today." But it was obvious he was not looking at her; it was Carrie who caught his eye. He was looking down at the beautiful young lady with long sleek black hair, worn in a bun at the nape of her neck, a style which complimented her large, lovely dark eyes and rosy cheeks.

Mr. Messmer came around from behind the desk and said, "Miss Weinshank's quite a seamstress, Mr. Lee. Perhaps she would like to help you with the wardrobe repairs you were mentioning."

Yes, I'd like that very much," said Henry, unable to take his eyes off her. "That would be most helpful. If you have the time, please consider it. I can send a buggy for you."

"I don't know, Mr. Lee," Carrie began, looking at her mother. He nodded to her mother then went back and resumed talking to the people gathered around.

The next day, Carrie and her mother went to the circus grounds where they saw Mr. Lee making arrangements for the day's performance. When he saw them enter, he left his work and joined them.

"Hello, Mrs. Weinshank, Miss Weinshank. Would you like to look over our wardrobe?"

"Oh, yes, Mr. Lee," and he took them to the improvised dressing room.

"Oh, these are lovely! I couldn't possibly do this kind of work," said Carrie.

"I don't mean for you to make costumes. Several of these need repair."

"Oh, I can do that. Would you let me work on them?"

"Yes, by the way, you didn't ask me who did make these costumes."

"I didn't think it any of my business."

"I'll tell you anyway, Miss Weinshank. I did. I make all the costumes for my children, even their shoes."

"I'm sure it was a labor of love on your part."

The circus was well-received that year. But, their schedule required they continue on. Carrie had been caught up in the excitement of the circus and the attention paid to her by Mr. Lee, and she dreaded seeing the circus leave. The performers of the great Cosmopolitan Circus had other places to go, other things to see, and Carrie would be left behind in that little Mexican village, letting all the excitement go by.

Then Mr. Lee walked in where Carrie was working and said, "A penny for your thoughts, Miss Weinshank."

"I was just thinking what it will be like after the circus leaves."

"It need not be that way, you know. You can come with us."

"Oh! My parents would frown on that Mr. Lee. They're very strict."

He walked up to her, put both hands on her shoulders ever so tenderly and said, "Then, let me speak to your father of marriage, Miss Weinshank, and the rest of your life will be a fairyland of adventure."

"But to go so far away. I don't know if I'm up to it, and we've only known each other for such a short time and . . ." she whispered, hardly able to breathe.

"Oh! We'll come back. I promise you. We'll come back to Los Angeles every year. This would be a wonderful place to settle down. I'll purchase a ranch nearby and raise horses. Would you like that?"

"Oh yes, Mr. Lee, I'd like it very much."

"Do I have permission to speak to your father?"

"If that's your wish, then come tomorrow at two."

"I'll be there." Then suddenly he was gone.

As soon as Carrie walked in the door at home, she was called in to supper. All through the meal she sat quietly, scarcely eating.

"Carrie, is something wrong?" asked her father.

"May I talk to you and mother after supper?"

"Yes, of course you may," said her father, not knowing what to think.

After they finished eating, they all went into the sala. Andrew quietly closed the door as Regina and Carrie sat down.

"Yes, Carrie. You have something to say?"

"Yes. Mr. Lee wants your permission to marry me."

"Mr. Lee? Who is he? No man in this town is named Lee."

"He's the circus man, Andrew," said Regina. "The one that put the program on for the lodge."

"Oh! I didn't catch his name. How did you meet him?"

"I was with mother when we took the foodstuffs to the United States Hotel. Mr. Messmer introduced us. I've spent the last few days repairing costumes for him."

"But, how long have you known him? He looks older than I am. Doesn't he have a lot of children? Seems to me he had several in that program, and aren't some of them young? And doesn't he have a couple of boys older than you?"

"I know all this, and I still want to marry him."

"You'd be going off to God knows where! Don't those circus people keep on the move? They're like gypsies; they never put down roots."

"I've invited him to come here tomorrow, Father," said Carrie.

"I'll speak to him, but I'm sure your Mother and I both heartily disapprove."

Carrie ran sobbing from the room. Her mother followed her. When Regina got to Carrie's room, she knocked on the door.

"Can we talk a minute, Carrie?" asked her mother.

"Yes, but please don't ask me to change my mind. I love him. I still want to marry him."

"I know your father was a bit harsh, but he only has your best interest at heart. We both want the very best for you. We were so hoping you would marry some nice man here in Los Angeles."

"There's no one here but Mr. Workman, and he's so old," wailed Carrie.

"He could make a wonderful home for you, and I don't think he's any older than Mr. Lee," responded Regina, managing not to smile at her daughter's reference to Mr. Workman's advanced years. "He's already spoken to your father."

"Mr. Lee seems young by comparison. The way he performs, and he's so exciting to be around. And every time he comes over to me, the way he looks at me, the feeling I get inside. I don't think I could bear to go on living, not knowing if I'll ever see him again. If you drive him away, I'll waste away for sure."

"Your father is thinking of all those children he has to raise. What will they do to you?"

"But they're not like other children. They're all so independent. He has trained them to stand on their own two feet."

"I'll have to agree there. Dry your tears and I'll talk to your father. We only want you to be happy."

"I do so hope father will give in. I love Mr. Lee and I can't bear to see him leave."

"Now, don't you fret, Carrie. Get some sleep and I'll see you in the morning."

The next afternoon Henry arrived at the adobe on Second Street. Andrew invited him in. Carrie was excused while Andrew and Regina conversed with him in the sala. At first Andrew was very much opposed. Regina said nothing, but pleaded with her eyes. Then, when they asked Carrie to join them and she was so teary-eyed and fearful they wouldn't give their blessing, the conversation ended with Andrew agreeing to talk to Father Mora and getting his advice.

Henry Charles Lee and Carrie Weinshank were married on Febuary 11th, 1867, at the Plaza Church, Our Lady Queen of Angels. Henry was fifty-three, fashionably dressed in a frock coat with wide slanting lapels. His trousers fitted snugly to show his boots, which to him were the most important part of his attire. Under his frock coat he wore a ruffled shirt, which had a high collar, about which a cravat was wound twice and tied in front. His waistcoat was embroidered in forget-me-nots. Caroline, a beautiful young lady of seventeen, was dressed in a gracefully flowing brown taffeta gown with numerous tiny tucks in the bodice. Father Francisco Mora officiated, and Andrew and Regina stood up with them. George Ryland was their witness.

There was little time for a celebration; just a simple little get-together at the house on Second Street and a few close friends in attendance. Henry's children were everywhere, darting in and out. Regina walked over to Andrew. "I hope we did the right thing. I'm sure they're very happy, but I hope the children won't be too much for Carrie."

"That was her choice, Regina. We made our stand. Now we have to let her live with it."

There was a performance to give, work to be done. After the wedding reception they left for the harbor and headed north. They traveled along the coast to their new winter quarters at Hayward and started working on the show they planned to take to San Francisco.

At the winter quarters, circus life was hard, the training strenuous. Henry took Polly into the barn, instructed her to get up on a beam, placed hay on the ground and ordered her to throw a backward somersault. Henry had a whip in his hand to crack if she decided to balk; he was a hard taskmaster and a perfectionist, working hard himself and expecting the same of others.

As Carrie watched the exquisitely-formed child perform, her father urging her on, making her repeat the same stunt time and time again, Carrie cringed. Henry noticed and suggested Polly take a moment's rest, while he walked over to Carrie.

"Why is she having to do it so many times, Henry?"

"To build up her muscles. Hardly a week passes but what some member of the circus is injured to a greater or lesser extent. Please understand I'm only using the whip to keep her attention. I'm not going to beat her."

"I know you're far too kind for that, but I can't imagine my children doing that. I don't see how I could stand by and watch that kind of training."

"Let's wait till that time comes, Carrie."

"Henry, what happened to your little Ellena, and your boys, John and James? Did something happen while they were performing?"

"Yes, we had an accident. But having circus in their blood, they wouldn't have been happy doing anything else." He turned his head and again went back to work.

Polly was working with a new horse. Henry named the young colt "Mazeppa" after the leading man in the show "The Wild Horse of Tartary" produced when he first came to San Francisco in 1851. Polly rode around the ring balancing. Then she put her weight on one leg and extended the other out to the side.

Henry again turned to Carrie. "Polly is one of the few performers able to stand up on a horse and do what she's doing now, without a pad."

On May 13th the Great New York Circus and Animal Show opened for a short run on a lot adjoining the International Hotel on Jackson Street in San Francisco. They featured Mr. William Kennedy, the celebrated clown from New York, a wonderfully trained buffalo and his Indian rider in a thrilling performance excelling in novelty anything ever introduced on the coast. This was followed by the horse, General Grant, and a troupe of trained horses and ponies. The Lee children were featured in the fairy interlude "Sprites of the Silver Shower."

This was a number taught to the children by George Ryland. His partner, Dan Rice, the world's greatest clown, was the first to introduce it. The act consisted of several young children performing an aesthetic dance on a tarpaulin ring.

The magical pattern of light enveloped the tent. Equestriennes entered the ring riding sidesaddle. They wore long, velvet gowns, each of a different color, their horses prancing around the ring, executing intricate steps, changing style, manner and pace as the music changed tempo. All the while, the audience sat entranced in ecstatic rapture, witnessing the scene of fairyland splendor.

When the act was over, the equestriennes left the ring. The appreciation of the audience was so great they returned for an encore. This time, they circled the tent between the audience and the ring, giving the people a better view of the horses, bringing gasps of admiration from the ladies in the crowd.

After the Wednesday matinee, Henry took Carrie to have her picture taken on Washington Street next door to Maguire's Opera House, which was diagonally across the street from the saloon called the Exchange. In the days of the Gold Rush, it had been the most prestigious place in town. As they walked along the street, Henry nodded to the passers-by. Many recognized him and were grateful for the acknowledgment. Carrie noticed sometimes he spoke, sometimes lifted his hat. "Why do you do that, Henry?"

"If I pass a lady, and you can tell the difference, I nod my head and tip my hat, recognizing she is a lady. If she's one of the other kind, which is quite common here, it's customary only to nod."

Carrie blushed. "Oh, Henry, I didn't realize it was done that way. Of course our little village of Los Angeles isn't sophisticated like San Francisco."

They paused in front of the Bank Exchange. All along the front of the building was a wrought iron balcony. They walked the short distance to the bay to see vessels of all sizes and shapes anchored nearby. It was a delightful afternoon, good for Carrie to have Henry to herself. They walked up and down the wharf looking in the shops.

"It's beautiful here this time of year. In the early evening a heavy fog creeps steadily into the bay and toward the city. Then later it moves out to sea again, only to return."

"The glow from the lights gives me an eerie feeling, but it's very beautiful. I never thought I would ever see anything as grand as San Francisco," said Carrie.

"You should have seen this when we first came here in 1851. My, how this place has changed! All this section was covered with shanties and tents with only a sprinkling of brick buildings. Now it's a regular metropolis."

They walked into the daguerreotype shop next door to Maguire's Opera House. Across the street was the city hall, farther on down was Sam Sample's Saloon and Robert Tiffany's store. Carrie had on her brown taffeta dress, her hair sleeked back, the bun arranged neatly at the nape of her neck.

"Before you sit down, I have something for you," said Henry. Then he brought out a small velvet bag and from it he took a gold chain holding it up for her to see, "After everyone left the arena, I collected the gold nuggets thrown at our feet while performing before the miners in the gold country. I should have had it made up years ago, but always put it off," he said as he put it around her neck. He wrapped it around her head once, gathered the longer strand up, put a knot in it and let it fall to her waist.

"Oh, Henry! It's exquisite! I never dreamed I'd have anything as grand as this. It's a work of art. Threads of gold wound together. And it makes it even more precious knowing the nuggets came from the gold country."

"All through my sorrow and grief, the gold nuggets made into this chain have stayed intact, and I hope it will always stay in the hands of my family; that some day some one of my descendants will take it out of a box and say as she puts it around her neck, 'Henry Charles Lee, my great-, great-, great-grandfather, the circus man, came to the gold country in 1851. He traveled from town to town in the foothills of the Sierra, set up his little tattered canvas tent with all the dingy tinsel he could scrape together, his few scant properties and wardrobe and performed before the gold miners with such skill and daring few men could ever boast."

"Oh, Henry! I'll never let it out of my sight."

"I know you will take good care of it my dear."

"I will, Henry."

"Are you folks ready?" asked the impatient photographer.

"Yes, sir, we're ready now," said Henry.

After they left the shop, they went into Peter Job's the Sherry of the Pacific. It was fitted up in Louis XIV style with gold gilded chairs and silk hangings. The patrons were tastefully dressed, the men in ruffled shirts and frock coats; the women in their high lace bodices and their hoop skirts ballooning about them. On the table before them were sweetmeats of every description, beverages chilled with snow from the high Sierra floating on top, cakes and dried fruit, hot meats and pies in great abundance.

George and Emma Lee

Carrie Weinshank

Jenny Weinshank

Frank Weinshank

San Gabriel Mission

Chapter 23

The year was 1868, and people were still heading for California. In Waverly, Illinois, Tom Phelan was working, saving his money, looking forward to the day when he could go to California. He wanted to purchase land as other members of the family suggested, "Get land where there is plenty of water nearby." Now that he had a stake, he was eager to be on his way.

He sent passage money to Ireland for his little sister, Ellen, to join him, for he planned to take her with him to San Francisco.

While working in the school for the blind Tom met Mr. Woodward. He, too, had been in the war, and had fought in the battle of Bull Run. A formal, quiet sort of man, much older than Tom, he kept pretty much to himself. He was a hard-working man and very steady.

"Would you be wanting to go to California with me, Mr. Woodward? My sister, Ellen, is coming from Ireland. I'm to meet her in Boston and we'll go on from there. It's around the Horn we'll be going, for I'm thinking it well safer and cheaper."

"You're a fine man, Tom, but I'm getting along in years. I'd probably be in the way. Perhaps I'd better stay here."

"We're friends, Mr. Woodward, and I've a hankering to take you with me. My sister, Mary, lives in San Francisco and she says the climate there is mild, and I'll always provide a roof over your head."

"I know you will, Tom. You're a man of your word. If you don't think I'd be in the way, I will go with you."

"Then, it's settled. We'll be heading out in a few days."

Tom had not seen his sister, Ellen, for seven years. She was only five when he left Ireland, and she was too young to remember him, but he would know her, of that he was sure. The two men stood on the wharf looking up. Then Tom spotted the little red headed, blue-eyed girl walking down the gangplank. He called out, "Ellen," and she beamed back. As she came up to him he grabbed her up and hugged her tightly. "You're no longer the wee one underfoot I left in Ireland. How are Mama and Papa, Ellen?"

"They're making it, Tom. Not good on the farm, but they're getting by."

"I wish they would come to this country, Ellen."

"They'll never come, Tom. They won't leave Ireland. They'll be buried there."

Ships were leaving daily for California. Tom booked passage for Mr. Woodward, Ellen and himself. While they were waiting on the dock, ready to board, Ellen looked at her brother and said, "I'm sure you know what you're talking about, Tom, and I'm willing to do anything you say, but I'm not happy about another long voyage."

"It's all we can afford, Ellen, and it will take less time than going across by land. You can't begin to imagine how large this country is, and before you'd get to California by wagon, you'd cross a desert so hot that people die by the score." He picked up her satchel and they walked up the gangplank.

They touched at the few ports below the Mason-Dixon Line, continued on through the West Indies and on down to Rio de Janeiro, where they had a short stop-over to pick up coal and other supplies. It was a beautiful harbor, safe from storms with a fine anchorage for many ships.

They spent the day in town, walking down the narrow, dirty streets, Ellen walking between her two protectors. They paused to watch a Negro carrying a heavy load on his head. They saw several mules so loaded down that only their heads and ears showed. There, mingling on the streets, were people from all walks of life, the prince and the pauper in close harmony.

As they neared the region of Cape Horn, icebergs were everywhere, many being visible at one time, great, glassy islands, grand and dangerous, frightening yet beautiful to see. They plunged into the bleak passage around the Horn.

When in sight of the outer rocky point, a terrible gale came up. They were at the mercy of the storm; the waves were running mountainhigh. Heavy swells came rolling in, pounding them with walls of grey angry water. They got their taste of Antarctic cold. The boat pitched about so violently that table meals were a rarity. Tom, Mr. Woodward, and Ellen all stayed below deck in that dark and dingy place, the men holding on to little Ellen for fear of her being pitched around, for the boat tossed and rolled with great force.

"This is worse than my coming across the ocean," cried Ellen.

"Even worse than my crossing, but that went on for weeks. This won't last long, wait and see." It was only after several days of gallant fighting by the captain and his crew that they did round Cape Horn, and what a relief it was!

Following that horrible experience, they were often becalmed and had to wait. Then a puff of wind came up and sent them on their way. Whales swam alongside as they sailed along, each sending up a column of water, as if trying to determine the greatest blower.

Once fairly upon the Pacific, they headed for the port of Valparaiso, Chile, a beautiful seaport town. They took on water, flour, potatoes and a few head of sheep and cattle, then continued along the coast of South America heading north. At Panama they took on passengers as well as cargo. Another stop was made at Acapulco and then at long last, the best sight of all, San Francisco.

It was a tearful reunion when they saw their sister, Mary, on the dock, for their coming had been posted on the board at the harbor. Ellen hadn't been born when Mary immigrated to America and Tom was no more than a toddler himself. They met her husband, Sheily, a big strapping fellow, full of fun, ready for adventure.

That evening Mary and her Sheily, Tom, Ellen and Mr. Woodward all sat down to a fine meal prepared by Mary and ate their fill and talked of Ireland.

"Ellen says our folks will never leave Ireland, Mary."

"Let them be, Tom. That is their land. Let them die in peace. But our place is here. They knew that. They knew we could not stay in Ireland. Praised be to God they cared enough to let us go."

"Truer words have never been spoken, Mary," said Tom. "What do you think of my doing a little prospecting while I'm here?"

"Oh, Tom! That's a thankless job and few rewards. It's back-breaking work, and the gold has dwindled to a trickle."

"The folks back in Waverly say I should look for land, land where there's plenty of water nearby."

"Follow their advice, Tom," said Sheily. "They know what they're talking about."

While in San Francisco, Tom enjoyed the sights. He attended the performance of Lee's Great New York Circus and marveled at the great feats he paid to witness. Tom met some very fine people at a social gathering he attended with Mary and Sheily. Among them was a man by the name of E. J. Baldwin, a tall, stately man of aristocratic bearing and striking good looks. He had invested money in a Comstock Lode mining concern, went to South America, and while he was gone the stock went up. By the time he got back, he was a millionaire.

Tom talked to him. "You've been around, Mr. Baldwin, where is there good land to buy?

"Call me 'Lucky,' everybody does. If you're interested in either raising cattle or farming, you want to settle in the countryside near Los Angeles."

"Is there lots of water?"

"Yes, all you can use. The cattle have been grazing there in the valley for more than a hundred years, and land has become more fertile every year. It's covered with wild mustard so high you can sit in your saddle and not see over it. The fruits and vegetables grown around the mission are the best I've ever tasted. The padres brought cuttings from Mexico, orange trees, lemons, and thousands of acres are planted to grapes. Yes, I've been a lot of places, but none as fine as there."

"I'll make arrangements to go by steamer."

"There's a cattle drive heading for Los Angeles. Why don't you go with them? That way you can see the country and be able to spot some good land to buy."

"Thank you, 'Lucky,' I'll look into it."

At the same social gathering, Tom met Stephen White, a law student who was thinking about Los Angeles as the place to set up his law practice. They took an instant liking to each other.

Tom and Mr. Woodward had no difficulty finding a group going down to Los Angeles. Ellen stayed on with her sister Mary and her family, and Tom and Mr. Woodward again set out on another journey.

A group of Mexicans was heading south after having delivered cattle to the San Francisco market, so Tom and Mr. Woodward joined up with them. They were starting their journey homeward with a few cows that had calved on the trip north and a few stragglers that didn't sell which they planned to butcher for food along the way. They traveled over open range, following the countryside along El Camino Real, through swollen streams and across miles of semi-parched desert, driving the cattle up steep inclines and sharp descents over which the animals were often hard to handle. They passed by country inns, saloons and stage stops. Between the missions they saw a few adobe houses with doors and windows protected by iron bars. Each night they made camp in the open. Tom wanted to talk to the vaqueros, but they spoke no English, so he and Mr. Woodward kept pretty much to themselves.

The vaqueros drove the cattle through the center of Salinas down the main street of town. Keeping to the outskirts of San Luis Obispo, they made camp near Santa Barbara, a small town noted for its saloons, gambling houses and billiard parlors. The men had been warned to keep to themselves, tend to their own herds, stay on the outskirts of town whenever possible. This was so they would be more apt to get home safely. As they traveled along, they kept a sharp eye out for desperadoes who stalked the highways for prey, striking in the passes or canyons, only to vanish into the mountains where they had their hideaways.

Then finally they reached the valley of San Gabriel. As they closed the corral gate on the last steer, they felt good, knowing they had at last reached their destination, after many a long, hard day in the saddle—the better part of a month.

Tom and Mr. Woodward looked over at the mission. Tom said, "You can tell it once was a beautiful building." All around were workmen making repairs. And though it would never be the splendid building it once was, it was comforting to know there was such a place of worship. If this was where he chose to settle, he would surely have his priests.

It was here the party broke up. Tom and Mr. Woodward continued on along El Camino Real, over country with many tiny lakes, keeping close to the river. It was in this valley they were able to get work at a ranch.

"Just call me O.P.," said the rancher, "everybody does. I have no money; nobody around these parts has any, but if you're willing to take out your wages in broom corn, I can use your help."

"That suits me fine," said Tom. "I hope to settle down, get some land of my own. We'd like to make brooms here."

They bunked in the barn and had their own place at the table. In the evening they sat around and talked. Mr. Woodward, a quiet man, had very little to say, but one night after a little prodding, they were able to get him to talk about the Civil War and the battle of "Bull Run."

"A farce it was," he said. "All those important people—those congressmen and their ladies dressed in fancy clothes, riding out to the scene of battle in their fine carriages, trying to get a look for themselves, making a picnic of it. Then them 'rebs' came in from nowhere, swarming all over the place, doing terrible damage. Them Congressmen learned in a hurry we were engaged in a terrible bloody affair. I'll never forget it for the remainder of my days."

"People do strange things," said Tom.

"How did you come to California?" asked O.P.

"Around the Horn. I wouldn't wish that on anyone. How'd you come?"

"Through Mexico, heading for the gold fields. We were captured by some Indians, but they let us go. We had to walk all the way from Yuma, in the territory."

"Don't know where that is, but I guess it was quite a piece."

"Yes, quite a piece, all right. You have to walk it to realize how far it is."

The men worked hard that year. They had a good crop, and O.P. was well pleased. When Tom was ready to move on, he decided to talk to him about buying land.

"I bought my one hundred acres from Bernardino Guirado," said O.P. "He was one of the early ones to come in—came in 1833. His land had been part of the Paso de Bartolo Rancho owned by Juan Crispin Perez, before that it was part of the Santa Gertrudes. At one time the The Nieto family owned all the valley. They also allowed Don Juan Ramirez to graze cattle there, and he, too, applied for a grant.

"Bernardino Guirado bought seven hundred acres from Perez in '43. Don Pio Pico, too, bought land from him and is selling some of his off. As far as I know, Bernardino Guirado and Don Pio Pico are the only two that have land for sale. Just a couple of years ago Don Pio Pico sold some land to a family by the name of Strong. If I were you I'd talk to him."

"I thank you for your advice," said Tom. "We'll go see him the first chance we get."

"It wasn't too long ago when the Don was fighting hard to keep the 'Yankees' out, but now the Don himself is welcoming them with open arms."

"I hope he'll sell to me."

"In the early days his adobe was the focal point for the area. Many a time that adobe along the river was the meeting place for plans and strategy for him to gain the governorship."

"Is he friendly, easy to talk to?"

"The Don is very hospitable and down through the years has spent lots of money. In the early days he went in for gambling and horse racing. The Don is a small man, loves fancy clothes, wears huge gold rings set with rubies and diamonds. He built a brick hotel in Los Angeles, calls it the Pico House; it's now the city's finest hotel. It has walnut furnishings, indoor plumbing, stairs striped with the best quality Brussels over oilcloth. It's complete with its shady ladies and gambling tables, and in the courtyard is a waterfall and cage of beautiful birds."

"He sounds like a wealthy man and wouldn't need to sell, but I'm hoping he'll be feeling kindly toward me so I'll be getting the land I need."

Thousands of Chinamen laying track for the Southern Pacific were working their way east, while the workmen employed by the Union Pacific, most of whom were Irish, were laying track westward across the prairie from Omaha. Because the federal subsidy yielded the owners a handsome profit on each mile of rails they laid, each company was trying to control as large a share as possible of the completed line.

And so it was on May 10th, 1869, at the windswept village of Promontory Point, on the northern shore of the Great Salt Lake, while a crowd of Irish and Chinese construction workers, Indian camp followers and visiting dignitaries looked on, a band played and the final rail was put in place. Leland Stanford hammered down spikes of gold and silver. The East was now linked to the West. Cabrillo had found California, Portola had explored it, Father Serra had planted the cross and the big four: Huntington, Stanford, Crocker and Hopkins, had bound it with rails.

Trains began to run from Los Angeles to Wilmington, and the San Pedro Railway depot was built on Alameda Street. More freight was transported than passengers. William Wolfskill was one of the biggest users of the freight cars because he shipped most of the oranges out. In fact, the facilities for passengers were rather meager. Many people were opposed to the railroad for fear it would do away with horses and the need for barley.

In Los Angeles Andrew heard the sound of pistol shots, the warning of a fire. Andrew joined the bucket brigade that formed a relay at the zanja. The men passed the buckets of water briskly along from person to person, but in spite of their efforts, the building burned down.

Thus, the day the new fire wagon, the Amoskeag second class steamer arrived in Los Angeles, was a day of great rejoicing. Some of the leading citizens sent to San Francisco for uniforms and a steam engine, and Fire Company No. 1 was formed. They staged a trial run on Main Street and a crowd gathered to watch. Regina and Andrew and their children were there watching the big event.

"I wish Henry could have been here today, Andrew."

"Yes, it would have been nice for him to get a little recognition. He and George Ryland worked hard on that performance, and the parade they put on must have been quite a lot of work."

"Oh! look, Andrew, what a beautiful fire engine. I don't think I've ever seen anything so grand. The pump doesn't seem to be working. Look how angry the mayor appears. I do hope nothing is wrong." But something was indeed wrong and the word was passed along that the men couldn't start it.

"Oh, dear!" said Regina. "Now we'll have to wait some more."

"We still have the bucket brigade, so I guess they'll still have need for me."

It was some time before another gleaming red engine was unloaded. The firemen spent the entire day polishing her iron plating and brass trimmings, and then dressed up in their red shirts, black pants and fire helmets and staged a trial run. Regina and Andrew were again there in the crowd of onlookers. The new Amoskeag was pulled onto Main Street and the firemen fired her up. She was attached to the hydrant at Main and Commercial Streets. When her steam gauge indicated one hundred pounds of pressure, they sent two streams of water rocketing over the flagstaff on Temple Block. One of the hoses burst and sprayed a bystander, causing quit a stir.

Now if only they would have a fire! Then all of a sudden there was one. Sparks from their own Amoskeag landed on the awning of the hardware store. The nozzle was turned toward the flames which were soon overwhelmed by the sheer force of the spray. So the firemen put out their first fire with their own fire wagon, the one made possible by the circus men, Henry Charles Lee and George Ryland.

Because of its age, the Weinshank adobe, built in early 1800's began to crumble. Regina had a hankering for one of those beautiful Victorian homes. Since their business was going well and since they could well afford it, they made plans to build it.

The construction of the house got underway. Ozro Childs was doing the plumbing, and Frank was anxious to learn a trade.
to take the time to go to the local saloons.

The plans called for plenty of bedrooms upstairs with the parlor and dining room downstairs and a kitchen at the back, with a sink and running water.

There were other nice frame houses going up on Fort Street. J.M. Griffith was building a beautiful two-story frame house between Second and Third Streets. Judge O'Melveny was building his on the corner of Second and Fort.

Ozro and young Frank worked side by side, piping in gas and water, running the pipes along the surface of the walls and ceilings. They installed gas fixtures consisting of ornamental drops from the ceiling.

One day, while they were working, Ozro said, "Say, Frank, after we get your house built, why don't you come work for me as an apprentice?"

"Oh! I'd like that very much. You're sure now?"

"Yes, I like your work very much."

After the furniture was moved into the big frame house, the adobe was used for storage and as a workshop for Andrew to make barrels. As Andrew walked in each day, he got a whiff of the pleasant smelling wood shavings and sawdust. Barrels of all sizes lined the walls and hung suspended from racks hanging from the rafters to be used later for their foodstuffs. He walked over to one sitting on the shelves and rubbed his fingers down inside. "I haven't lost my touch, smooth as glass," he thought to himself.

The Great New York Circus closed their season in San Francisco and Henry Charles Lee booked passage on a steamer for the north, for their plans included Canada that year. They traveled along the coast by sidewheeler, performing at the coastal towns along the way.

Carrie was heavy with child and found the constant movement of the boat a great discomfort. The children were managing on their own, the older ones looking after little Rosa, but still Henry and Carrie had little time for themselves, for Henry kept busy overseeing the children's, training most of their waking hours.

The next port was to be Victoria, and Henry hoped they would make it in time for the birth. Two weeks before they arrived, however, the baby was born. Carrie named her Emmelina Victoria, after her mother's dear friend Emmalina Childs, and Victoria after the town of their next engagement.

They stayed on in Victoria long after their engagement ended to give Carrie a chance to rest before taking another long voyage, their most ambitious tour yet. This time it was to be the Sandwich Islands.

Henry and Carrie were on the deck as they rounded the point called Diamond Head. "See over there?" asked Henry. "That's actually a volcano. It no longer erupts, but it once did. It won't be long before we drop anchor. The harbor is just around this bend."

"I can't say I'll be unhappy. I'll be glad to get my feet on dry land."

"Look, over there! They've come out to greet us. There's King Kamehameha, all dressed in his regal gown."

"Does he do this every time the boat comes in?"

"He certainly does. Well, I have lots to do. I'll go help the others get the horses ready to land."

"I need to nurse the baby and help the smaller ones so they won't hold you up," and Carrie hurried back to their cabin.

Henry was the first to walk down the gangplank, where he was warmly greeted by the king. George followed closely behind; the natives gathered around him to get a closer look at such a small man under a hat that was much too large. They headed out toward the circus grounds, and the men began setting up the tent.

They were invited to stay in one of the little huts on the palace grounds and pay a visit to the royal court. They entered the palace and were escorted into the long narrow room where the regal family entertained guests. The King was seated on his throne. Nearby were the ladies of the court. They all gathered around Carrie.

Queen Emma asked to hold the baby and Carrie beamed as the queen fondled her little fingers. She bounced her on her knee to keep her entertained, held her up for all to see and settled her on her lap. Little Emmalina, feeling the warmth of the Queen's body, fell off to sleep. Later, the Queen felt something warm in her lap, only to look down to find her mumu had been soaked. Little Emmalina was then unceremoniously handed back to her mother.

The circus was invited to go to Lahania, on the island of Maui, to perform before the natives there. The climate was heavenly with its warm tropical breezes. No matter where they went, there was a delightful view of the ocean. They enjoyed their stay surrounded by the lush, green tropical growth so unfamiliar to them, with wild orchids growing in the forest of fern trees.

After a lengthy stay, made memorable by their gracious hosts and appreciative audiences who had never before witnessed such entertainment, they regretfully left their island paradise and sailed for home. Their pockets were full of coins; for not since the gold mining days had audiences demonstrated their appreciation so tangibly.

The circus returned to San Francisco, then back to Los Angeles. They now were under the title, The Great Paris Exposition Circus. They drove along Spring Street passing wooden verandas along the way, heading toward the Plaza. While the men set up the tent, Henry and Carrie went to the house on Second Street where Andrew and Regina were able to see their little grandchild for the first time.

Those were good times for Carrie, for she loved being home. She was especially close to her sister, Jenny, who was beginning to blossom, having just celebrated her eleventh birthday. She got to visit with her brother Frank and Lizzie, and see and hold her baby brother, George.

There were now 172 Chinese in the City of Los Angeles. Many of them were concentrated in the adobe hovels on the north side of town. They took over much of Calle de Negroes for their opium dens, shops and laundries. They opened washhouses, peddled vegetables and gradually ousted the Indians from the family kitchens.

On October 21st, 1871, war broke out near Calle de los Negroes between two rival factions of Chinese over the forcible abduction of one of the female members. A bunch of Chinamen came down from San Francisco, arriving on the steamer "California" to retaliate against the abductors. Two days later some were arrested, taken to the local jail known as Hotel de Burns, named after their school teacher turned fighting sheriff. They were taken before Justice Gray and released on bail.

Later on that day, trouble again broke out, and the officers again attempted an arrest. Two of them were wounded, and Robert

Thompson, going to their aid, was shot and killed for his efforts. The news spread like wildfire. A mob gathered with pistols, guns, knives and ropes to avenge the murder.

One Chinaman was caught and strung up. Others ran down Los Angeles Street to the south side of Commercial. There near Goller's wagon shop, between two wagons stood on end, they were hanged.

Harris Newmark, Cameron Thom and John G. Downey all hurried to the scene. Judge Whitney displayed courage in facing the mob, but he couldn't do anything with them. Thom then tried to address the crowd, but they wouldn't listen to him.

Henry Hazard was lolling comfortably in Peter Biggs' shaving saloon, all lathered up, when he heard that Thompson had been killed by a Chinaman. He rushed to the scene, got up on a barrel to talk to the people to calm them down. He was pulled down by his friends, fearing he might be shot.

A.J. King had been called to supper. He grabbed his rifle and two revolvers. He tried one of the guns and in so doing shot off the end of one of his fingers, which put him out of commission.

People everywhere were hell bent to take matters into their own hands. They rushed out to kill a Chinaman, any Chinaman they could find, shooting as they went. Everyone ran every which way. Chinamen were scurrying around, running in all directions, looking for a place to hide. Some ran past the circus tent. Henry and George heard the commotion and ran outside.

"We've got trouble here, George," said Henry. "You stick around and watch things, while I see if the others are all right at home."

"Go ahead, Henry, I'll take care of things here. There's a horse saddled over there, ready to go."

Henry went by the way of Calle de los Negroes, then stopped to see what was going on. Sheriff Burns was now on the scene. He was up on the barrel trying to talk to the crowd, but his two hundred pounds were too much for it. The barrel gave way and he fell to the floor. He tried to get up a posse, but no one responded. He then tried to get everyone to go home, but they wouldn't go. But he did talk the crowd out of burning down the chinese quarters. Cameron Thom, again tried to take over. He wasn't getting anywhere, so Henry continued on.

By the time he arrived at the house on Second Street, Andrew was outside trying to find out what happened. He heard shots and figured the situation was out of hand, Chinamen darting around and white men after them. Then Andrew saw some Chinamen running through his orchard. By this time, Henry was at his side.

Andrew ran over to the adobe, opened the door and waited for them to go inside.

"We have to hide them, Henry, no matter what they've done. They'll be safe here. They can stay all night."

"You're right," said Henry, and the two men hurried to the house.

It was a week before the smoke of the battle had cleared. Each day, Regina saw to it that they had plenty to eat. Then, finally, the day came when Andrew felt free to open the door of the adobe and send the hapless Chinese on their way.

After that disgraceful incident, a jury was impounded. Their report stated nineteen bodies were in evidence, their deaths due to a strangulation by persons unknown.

The Lees stayed on in Los Angeles. At the circus grounds they started each night's performance by sending into the ring eight mounted cavaliers, prancing around. The Don Van Brothers did their great muscular act. Alla Pashe, the Arabian horse, was shown by George Ryland; Eugene Lee performed in the role of leaper and somersault thrower. Rosa Lee, only seven years old, was a beautiful bareback rider. Polly was outstanding by any standard, performing amazing feats of grace. Lavater was performing on his own. Henry was everywhere tending to small details. Regina and Andrew, with the younger ones, attended as often as they could and enjoyed the show. Every night there were changes on the program. At one performance, they featured the Great Buffalo Hunt.

The Lees spent Christmas Day at the house on Second Street, and that was an especially happy time. Regina, with the help of Jesse and Arturo, busied herself in the cookhouse preparing Christmas delicacies of all types.

During that month they took the Great Champion Circus to other small towns that had sprung up in the area, such places as Santa Ana, Florence, and Compton. They also had a Zoological Institute for the people to view, then headed back to Los Angeles.

Carrie and the baby stayed on in Los Angeles while the others continued south. They hauled their tents and trappings by wagon to San Pedro and took the steamer to San Diego, a little town situated in a bay farther down the coast, consisting of a few houses, some grog shops and scattering of other buildings.

They began showing on Sunday, January 20th. The show held the audience spellbound in its execution. The parade downtown was a spectacle to behold, and the people came from miles around. They returned the following Wednesday to Los Angeles.

In Los Angeles the announcement in the local paper stated that the Lee and Ryland "Great Champion Circus and Zoological Institute" had a great variety of acts. Eugene was getting star billing as the premier leaper and somersault thrower on their opening on May 6th. Once again they left by steamer and headed north.

On July 10th Lee and Ryland's Great Champion Circus and Zoological Institute performed at the Oakland Town Plaza.

It was there Eugene was offered another position, by Menkley's Constable Circus and decided to go on alone.

I'll miss the family," said Eugene, "but you have the others coming up. Lavater will be a great acrobat one of these days and, of course, Polly's a star already. With Harry and Rosa and the others, you won't need me."

"I'll miss you, Eugene, but I won't stand in your way. This sounds like a great opportunity."

That night Eugene gave his last performance for his father and then continued on his own. Henry's family again made ready to head south for the City of Angels.

El Ranchito

Chapter 24

After the crop was harvested and in, the broom corn divided, Tom Phelan and Mr. Woodward crossed the river, rode along El Camino Real to "El Ranchito." They were met by Don Pio Pico himself, a small portly man, standing out in the open courtyard of his beautiful adobe nestled in among the willows along the San Gabriel River.

"Buenos dias," said Tom, his hand extended. "Mr. Passons tells me you might be willing to sell some land."

"Si, señor, I have land to sell." Let's sit down and rest a bit, then I'll show you around. How much land do you want to buy?"

"Just a small piece, just enough to get me started," replied Tom. "Were you here when they fought the battle on the bluff?"

"Oh! No, señor, I was in Mexico trying to get help, but they would not help me, not a peso would they spare. When I returned from Mexico, I was going to take up my duties as governor, but I was told to surrender myself, and was no longer governor."

"Mr. Passons was telling us the Workman and Rowland families came in very early."

"Si, Señor, they were fur traders. Their friend, Kit Carson, who had been here, was in the merchandising store in Taos, New Mexico, one day talking to Workman. He told him about the grants given to men who lived in Mexican territory, who were Roman Catholic or married to Mexican women. He also told them of the sea otter and other furs to be had for the taking. Workman's partner, Rowland, heard the men talking and wanted to come see for himself."

"And with good cause," said Mr. Woodward.

"Rowland came to our fertile valley in August of '41 and settled on the other side of the hill. The only other rancheros here were the soldiers from the mission. Then Rowland returned to Taos and brought Workman, his family and two other men, B.D. Wilson and Lemuel Carpenter, back to California with him."

"That must have been some trip."

"A long way, señor, they stopped at the mission, gave the padres a thousand dollars in gold, signed papers to take to Monterey to get their grant. The next year, my friend, Juan Matius Sanchez, arrived from New Mexico. He was a trapper, the son of settlers who immigrated to this country from Spain. He, too, was interested in a land grant. Later on I helped him get one."

"Did you think others would follow Workman and Roland?"

"Si, señor. And they did. I was afraid they would be cultivating farms, establishing vineyards, erecting mills, sawing lumber, and so I asked if these incursions should go on unchecked until we became strangers in our own land. Even then I decided on a plan. I urged secession from Mexico and annexation by France or England. Either way we could have kept the gringos out."

"You have quite a spread here," said Mr. Woodward.

"Oh, no, señor," said the Don. "I call it my 'El Ranchito' because it's so small. Only nine thousand acres and the only place I could find. I bought it from Juan Crispin Perez. At that time he was the only one who had land for sale. I wanted to be near town but still live in the country.

"When I was a boy, my father was a soldier at the mission. He came with de Anza in 1776. I was the second son of ten children, born in a brush shelter, near the mission. When my father died, he left us not a vara of ground, nor a mule. So, I had to work to help my family. Later I became governor and ruled all of California.

"My Santa Margarita was the largest of all the ranchos—thirty thousand acres. Señor Forster married my sister and took it over because I wanted to spend the rest of my days in Los Angeles and here at 'El Ranchito'."

"One could never go hungry here. In Ireland we were never out from the shadow of starvation. Each year there were more people. Our farms became smaller, the land became overworked and finally it played out. It's hard for me to imagine so much land belonging to one man."

"It's getting late, Don Pio Pico, and we must go. Would you show us the land you want to sell?" The Don pointed out the boundaries and with Tom and Mr. Woodward went to look it over.

"Look at this soil, Mr. Woodward. This is land that has never known the feel of the plow. We'll be the first to till it, not at all like it was in Ireland."

"Don't they have a lot of rocks in Ireland?" asked Mr. Woodward.

"That they do," said Tom. "That they do. All through the countryside you see rock walls. When the soil is turned each year, the rocks are loosened and gathered up. The English made government grants and hired work gangs to build rock walls to seal off the land for their wealthy land barons from us poor people, so we called them 'famine walls.' How much are you asking for the land, Don Pio Pico?"

"Thirty dollars an acre. This piece has sixty-one acres. You can pay me four hundred dollars and the balance after you harvest your first crop."

"I'll be back with the money in a day or two and we can sign the papers," replied Tom.

"Gracias, señor."

After making the down payment, Tom and Mr. Woodward got right to work clearing the land, Tom's piece of "El Ranchito," that was once part of the Jose Manuel Nieto rancho, "Santa Gertrudes." For a house they found a small grain storage building and moved it onto the place, and with tools Tom borrowed from Don Pio Pico, the two men set out to plant their first crop of broom corn.

Whenever they went down to the zanja to let the water in to irrigate the land, Tom took his breech-loader, the one he carried in the Civil War. "You never know when trouble will crop up," he said to Mr. Woodward. "Maybe it will prevent someone from trying to take the water from us."

The zanja, built by Indian labor, ran along the property. Tom let the water in on to his land, checking it from time to time, the way the Mexicans had done for hundreds of years, and his crops flourished.

Close to Tom's house was a long strip of soil of solid clay. The two men talked it over. "You know, this might work out to our advantage," said Mr. Woodward.

"What do you mean?" asked Tom.

"With a little work we ought to be able to make our own brick, like those in Waverly."

"And wouldn't it be grand to build a house of brick right here?"

"We'll need a kiln. It will take a bit of doing, but it should work out. You can't use the ground for anything else," remarked Mr. Woodward.

At the end of that first year, after the crops had been harvested and sold, Tom was able to pay Don Pio Pico the balance of what he owed him.

When Tom went to pay the Don, they walked out by the river bank.

"In '67 the San Gabriel River ran very high. See over there, where it's all washed out? You have to be careful with this river. Don't let it wash your land away."

"Does it rain a lot here?"

"Sometimes it rains for days on end; sometimes we have dry years and the cattle die and we have to borrow money to tide us over. Don't let that happen to you, my friend."

"Where do you sell your cattle?"

"In Los Angeles now, but during the Gold Rush, we drove our cattle to San Francisco. We no longer make that long drive, and if we're not careful, sometimes we glut the market in Los Angeles."

"Isn't most of this land under grants?"

"Yes, but the story of the grants is a long and black one. Your government has much to answer for."

"It's your government, too, now," Tom pointed out.

"Si, señor, sad to say. But there was neither reason nor justice why those claims should have taken so long. Rowland and Workman waited sixteen years before theirs was finally settled."

"Didn't the rancheros own their grants?"

"No. At first, the soldiers, Verdugo, Nieto, and Dominguez asked permission to graze their cattle. Then, later, they went to Monterey and were given grants, but when the United States took over, the rancheros had to apply, again, through the Land Commission. In many cases the lower courts failed to award clear title, and they had to go to the higher courts, and in some cases clear up the Supreme Court of the land, and all this cost a lot of dinero. Had those titles been good, the rancheros would have sold for as little as twenty-five to fifty cents an acre, but with this, they couldn't sell. They had to borrow to keep going. Julio Verdugo was forced to put a mortgage on his share of Rancho San Rafael for a little more than three thousand five hundred dollars, but he was not able to pay it back, and before he died all his land was taken from him. This is why I feared the Yankees coming in. I knew they would put the plow to the land. When the iron horse came in, I knew it would bring the end to our rancho days. I spoke up about it, but what is one voice among so many?"

"There was nothing they could do about it," said Tom.

"Lemuel Carpenter purchased the Santa Gertrudes Rancho from Josefa Cota, the daughter of Manuel Nieto. When Josefa's father was granted his Rancho Santa Gertrudes, he brought Indian helpers from the mission to build his adobe. He followed the River San Gabriel along El Camino Real. His rancho included all the land from the hills to the sea between the old San Gabriel and the Santa Ana Rivers," said the don as he waved his arm to take in all the country. "His small adobe, twenty feet square, had thick walls and a thatched roof and earthen floors. His windows were covered with oilcloth, and cooking was done outside. He ruled over his land and his slim-bodied, longhorn cattle roamed the hills and could be counted in the thousands. Each year hundreds of calves were dropped and his herd grew larger. Later when Lemuel Carpenter took over, he had dry years, he too borrowed money and was unable to pay it back. Then Lemuel's wife died, and he was left with many children to raise. He became downhearted and one morning he put a pistol to his head."

"What a pity."

"Now his poor family can barely eke out a living."

"I've met them," said Tom. "A proud people from good stock."

Tom held back part of his crop for making brooms, so he went to Los Angeles in search of cheap labor. While he was there, he talked to a man by the name of Swainvain.

"Get some Chinamen," he said. "They're willing to work hard, and for less, and their living needs are very simple. Chinese women are scarce, so the men go off in groups and live off the land."

"Thank you for your advice. I'll look into it," said Tom.

"You'll find them in Calle de los Negroes."

Tom continued riding along the dirty street. At one place he stopped and inquired for men who were looking for work and he was directed to a little clapboard house and found three Chinamen who were willing to go with him. They quickly gathered up their few possessions, mounted the extra horses Tom had brought along and went back to the ranch.

Two hundred miles north of Los Angeles, in the Owens River

country, was a silver camp called Cerro Gordo. It was situated two miles above sea level at the crest of the Inyo Range where a swarm of miners was digging into the side of the Buena Vista Peak. Mexicans smelted the silver and lead ore in crude rock ovens. Word of the strike was heard throughout the East.

Mortimer Belshaw came to California during the gold rush in 1852, a man of medium height, his husky frame, his suntanned cheeks showed a lifetime of mining. Belshaw and his partner, Judson, graded the wagon road up the rugged eight mile ascent to the mine from a nearby lake. Belshaw decided to build a smelting furnace and with this scheme, talked his way into a one-half interest. Because of this, long trains of mule teams pulling heavy wagons carrying as much as $50,000 worth of silver and lead pulled into Los Angeles almost every day and the boom was on.

The mule skinners shouted and cursed as they headed their wagons up Spring Street, their mules snorting, raising clouds of dust, causing problems for the storekeepers.

At the Commercial Street railroad platform they unloaded their cargoes, then on to the wholesale houses to pick up bales of hay, kegs of wine, sacks of potatoes, everything they would need from frying pans to crates of live chickens.

After leaving the wholesale house, the wagons pulled into the Weinshank yard on Second Street and picked up a good supply of catsup, pickled turnips and sauerkraut. As soon as their wagons were loaded, they headed back to the mines.

The Weinshanks were doing well and felt they should move their money from Downey's safe at the drug store to the new Merchants Bank. John G. Downey was president; W. Hellman was secretary, and their good friend, Ozro Childs, was on the board of trustees. After making a deposit, they went to the other bank on the corner of Spring and Main Streets, the one built by F.P.F. Temple. Temple had sold his ranch near Fort Tejon to enter the banking business having had no previous experience. Regina and Andrew went to the grand opening. Inside the furnishings were elaborate, and the counter was made from native cedar. Temple's father-in-law, William Workman, had full confidence in his son-in-law's ability and being very old didn't take part in its management.

"I think we should open an account here, Regina," said Andrew. "One shouldn't put all his eggs in one basket."

"I think you're right, Andrew, but I'll leave that up to you. I have my hands full as it is."

On their way home they stopped at Ozro's tin shop. Andrew spoke to him about putting money in the Temple-Workman Bank.

"I don't know if that's too good an idea, Andrew. Many an immigrant farmer coming to town without means to buy land was sent to Temple's bank. Harris Newmark was telling me that one farmer from Oregon went there to ask for a loan. Temple asked him what security he had, and the farmer said if he would step out the door, he'd show him. The man asked Temple if he could see through the window and he said, 'Yes.' Temple looked out in the direction of Spring Street and saw the farmer's wife and six children and a pair of ancient horses. The man walked back in the bank, and Temple handed him the money."

"I see what you mean," said Andrew. "Well, at any rate, we only opened a small account."

From Los Angeles, in the spring of 1872, Henry made plans to cross the continent. His plan called for going by rail. Before leaving there were axles to grease, boards and wheels to replace. The tents were unrolled and examined for tears and mildew. Chairs and ropes had to be tested. There were stakes to be cut, for the old ones were too short after a season's use. Wagons needed repainting. Horses needed to adjust to the harness before the season began, and because the name was changed, the new name had to be painted on the wagon.

As soon as the wagons were ready, they headed out in the direction of the depot where they were placed on flat cars. The family had a nice warm place in the car. They went to San Francisco, continued over the Sierra, then on across the flat prairie to the more populated areas. If a small town was near the depot, they unloaded their wagons and headed for an open spot to set up their tent.

The wagons and the teams faced twenty-eight weeks of trouping when they left in the spring, weeks in which there would be rain and high winds and runaways and bottomless roads, moving at the speed of a walking horse. If the towns were close together, they went from village to village, and each night except Sunday gave a performance.

They arrived in one small town having traveled all night by wagon that creaked over mile after mile of lonely wilderness, passing dwellings that were few and far between along the way. Their only light was from the torches carried by the weary, plodding men in front of them. For Henry the problem of securing food and lodging was a constant concern, especially when touring the smaller towns.

At three in the morning the sleepy, weary performers roused themselves, got ready for the parade, and headed for town.

For the children who saw the circus pass by, it was the most exciting thing in the whole wide world and a day to be remembered for the remainder of their days.

After the parade was over, they went to a vacant lot to get ready for the performance. Crowds stood and watched from afar as they hoisted the canvas tent. The lot that had been selected was always within easy walking distance of the town, fairly free of stumps and boulders. Local workmen made the "mud pie circle" of clay. With spades and water they patted a rim for the giant-sized pie and the men filled it with four inches of tanbark.

For this one-ring show, Henry needed a male and female rider, a clown, an acrobat, and a ringmaster. The pipe, the drum and the horn were music enough.

At sixteen years of age, Polly was the star of her father's show as the principal bareback rider, juggling and also working the two horse tandem cart. As Henry watched his little Polly, he was reminded of her mother riding bareback as she circled the ring, mounted on a beautiful white horse, thrilling the audience and taking their breath away. Rosa was next, juggling eight flaming torches as she rode around the ring, tiny, graceful, wearing a beautifully appliqued dress down to her knees, tights and soft slippers on her feet. She first performed on one horse, then on two and tandem cart.

After the show, the performers gathered up their gear, broke down the tent and continued on to another town, another place.

When they reached the Mississippi, Henry booked an engagement aboard the "Robert E. Lee," a showboat, performing up and down the Mississippi and Ohio Rivers, stopping at various places along the way. They were staying at a hotel in one of the smaller towns when Carrie gave birth to a boy, naming him Frank after her brother. They performed for other circuses, just as Henry did in the old days when he first came to America. It was while they were staying at a hotel when a baby was left on their doorstep.

"Oh, Henry! We can't put him in an orphanage," said Carrie. "I have more than enough milk. I can nurse two babies as well as one."

"I wouldn't be at all surprised if his parents were performers. So, if you're willing to raise him, I'll train him. What will we name him, Carrie?"

"Oh, I have just the name. Lets name him Robert E. after the showboat, and we'll give him the name of Lee. Robert E. Lee."

"You're very kind to do this Carrie. Not many women would take on this kind of responsibility."

"I'm sure you'll do your part, Henry. With you as his trainer, he's bound to succeed."

In January of 1873 Thomas Hackett Phelan felt he was ready to take a wife. He was now a strong, hardy man, with a big mop of black curly hair that never saw a comb; he just ran his fingers through it. His shaggy whiskers made him look well beyond his twenty-eight years. He was carrying part of the stake from the money he earned as a bounty soldier in the Civil War. His property paid for and a house to live in, now he needed a wife to cook for and comfort him.

When Tom went to Los Angeles, he went to see his Irish friends, the sheriff's deputies, and always visited the Sister's of Charity at the orphanage. One day he asked Sister Maryanne, "Do you know an Irish girl who would like to live in the country?"

Sister Maryanne thought for a minute. "Yes, as a matter of fact, I do. She's a big strapping girl from the homeland, fresh off the boat. Even the saints can't make her out. She's working in the house of a banker. If you wait a minute I'll let you know just where." Sister Maryanne walked out of the room and returned with a slip of paper with the address on it, and handed it to Tom.

"I'm beholden to you, Sister, thank you, I must be going."

"Goodbye, Tom."

When Tom arrived at the banker's house, he knocked on the kitchen door. It was Mary who opened it, a large girl, with light red hair and blue eyes, large coarse features, not at all pretty, but big-boned and hefty.

Mary took one look at the Irishman standing on the back porch and mistook him for a vendor. Before she had a chance to chase him away, he spoke up.

"You're Mary, aren't you, Mary Ryan? I'm Tom—Tom Phelan. Sister Maryanne said I would be finding you here." Then Tom looked past Mary, for he had already smelled the hot bread ready to be taken from the oven.

Without saying a word Mary had him come in, seated him at the table and put a cup of hot broth and a piece of freshly baked bread before him. She sat across the table while he ate.

"And is this your cooking, Mary?"

"That it is, Tom Phelan."

"And you'll be making a man a fine wife. What part of Ireland are you from Mary?"

"Temple More. My father was a banker. He had an important position, had his own desk there, he did."

"Why did you come to this country?"

"I wanted to, didn't need to, mind you. We lived in a great big house, had plenty to eat. My Auntie Wade sent me the money, one hundred dollars, she did. Oh! what a terrible storm that caused. I didn't tell my mother 'bout it till the night before I left. Oh! You never heard such wailing in all your life. Oh! Did she plead with me, but finally she gave in. But she made me promise one thing, that if anything happened to me in America, that if I were to die, someone would get word to them in Ireland so they could pray for me."

"You should thank your blessed mother for that, Mary. Did you come alone?"

"Oh, goodness, gracious no. My cousin, Wade, came with me. Our priest booked our passage on the ship the S.S. Tanpa, and we had a terrible crossing, we did. Captain Michael Murphy, if that isn't a good Irish name, paid little heed to us in the steerage section but couldn't do enough for those in the cabin class."

"I'm afraid that's the way it is and always will be," said Tom as he sat there eating his bread, looking at Mary, sizing her up. Mary wasn't the prettiest girl Tom had ever seen, surely no more than eighteen, but there weren't many to choose from and he wouldn't have found her had it not been for Sister Maryanne.

"Would you be wanting to attend Our Lady Queen of the Angels, and after mass we could take a stroll through the Plaza?"

"I'm a-thinking that would be fine, Tom. Then we can come back here for a bite to eat."

After several Sunday outings, Tom's mind was made up, so while they were sitting at the kitchen table, Tom spoke up.

"I have a nice place in the country, Mary, a house on it, and it's all paid for. It's not as if I were just starting out, so I'm thinking of taking on a wife. So, Mary, if you're willing, is there someone I could speak to?"

"I think Sister Maryanne would talk to you about it, Tom. She's the one who placed me here, and if she is willing, you can go ahead and make the plans."

Tom didn't expect such a hasty answer, so in a dither he grabbed up his cap and rushed out the door. Then it dawned on him and he turned back into the kitchen. "Mary, I'm sure'n Sister Maryanne will give us her blessing and we'll be very happy." Then his face got firey red. "Shall we seal our bargain with a kiss?"

"Don't you be taking such liberties with me, Tom Phelan. You'll wait till we get married. I'm a proper girl, I am, and I've got work to do, so be off with you."

After Tom visited Sister Maryanne and got her blessing, he went to see Father Mora at the church and made the arrangements, then back to the banker's house. After telling Mary the plans, he made the long trip across the mesa back to the ranch. The first thing he did when he got home was to go see his friend Gary Lynch, his neighbor to the south of him.

"Gary, I'm going to marry an Irish girl. Her name is Mary Ryan, and I want you to stand up with me."

"I'll be glad to Tom, and I'm sure John Ourly will want to be there too. Are you going to be married at the Mission or at the church?"

"The church, The Plaza Church in town, and Father Mora will marry us after mass."

"When does this wedding take place?"

"We're going to be married on January 20th. Just a simple wedding, Gary. Then we'll come on out to the ranch."

"Who else will be going with us?"

"Pete Serrano will be there, but not Mr. Woodward. He doesn't like those affairs, so he'll want to stay and tend the ranch."

"Let's all come back to my place, Tom, and Katie will have a nice supper waiting for us, and we'll go up and get Mr. Woodward and we'll invite all the neighbors to meet her. I'll get someone to play the violin and we'll get the two of you to dance the reel and make a grand affair of it."

"That sounds fine with me, Gary. It's all settled then."

Tom Phelan

Irish Dan

The Phelan Homestead

Chapter 25

In 1873 showmen stood on the threshold of the greatest era intheir history. They left the one-ring, one-rider, one-clown, family-run circus; the wagon-mounted show was now on its way out, and the 2- and 3-ring extravaganzas were making their appearances, resulting in greater receipts.

Henry Charles Lee sold all his circus equipment and hired on with George de Haven to be his manager. Together they hoped to put de Haven's circus on a profitable paying basis by using labor-saving and cost-cutting techniques.

Henry had devised a system of starting to pack at the conclusion of each number. As certain performers and props were no longer needed, the performers themselves packed their props and sent them on their way. By the time the tent came down, everything else had gone on ahead, and the tent was taken down simply and easily.

Life was easier now, for they were traveling entirely on rails. No longer did they stop, get a few hours' sleep, then head on into town early in the morning.

Carrie was seeing the country as she had never expected to see it. As they traveled along on rails Carrie watched the farmers while they did their early morning chores, stopping long enough to see the circus train as it came rolling in.

All the little boys and girls who were lucky enough to live along the route, were there to see the slow-moving circus train as it came lumbering into town. There were cars for the animals, for the tent, and one for all the gear. Some cars were set up for sleeping quarters, others for the men who owned and managed the circus.

Henry kept the books. Wages remained high. A good bareback rider commanded anywhere from three hundred to five hundred dollars a week.

On August 11th, the Lees were in Jerseyville, Illinois. Henry's children Harry, Lavater, Rosa and little Charles, their youngest, were all on the program.

On August 27th they opened at DuQuoin, Iowa. The advertisement announced that it was a combination circus, museum, and menagerie coming in on its own special train. Rosa and Lavater were the stars of the show, receiving top billing both on the program and on the handbills.

Charles, only a baby, performed with his father. Henry, while riding bareback, held him first in one position, then another. Henry was getting too old for this sort of thing but still wasn't ready totrust Charles' safety to Lavater or Harry. Carrie didn't like her little one performing because she was fearful of Henry's training tactics, but the boy was strong and loved being carried around the ring by his father. The season was progressing nicely, without a problem.

Henry sent out the billing crews who worked from two weeks to a month ahead of the circus, carrying paper brushes, ladders, raw material and paste. Handbills were their most common form of advertising. Small boys were paid a few pennies each to distribute an armful. Some were tacked up in hotel lobbies, livery stables, and taverns for people to see. Newspaper advertising was begun ten days in advance of the showing.

The circus lot was selected in a vacant spot on the edge of town, preferably at the end of the car line. It needed to be fairly level, dry and inexpensive to rent. If it had grass, that was a bonus. The contracting agent made the arrangements for the land, but Henry saw to it that the rent was not paid until the tent was set up.

Henry supervised the work of putting up the tent. As the king pole was put in place by the elephants, straining against the heavy chains, the tent slowly billowed out. While the roustabouts shouted, "Heave it, weave it, shake it, break it," the side walls flapped like sails. They drove the stakes for the guy ropes with their heavy sledge hammers, taking them as long as two to four hours to raise the tent.

Henry and George supervised while the men set up some special equipment and they talked about the past. "When I had my first tent, John Marshall and I put it up ourselves," said Henry, "nothing like it is today. We used side walls and had a canvas top, a center pole, just a small one, and, of course, just one ring."

"Yes, there have been a lot of changes over the years. You either keep up with the big ones like Barnum or you're out."

"George, have you ever heard of a man by the name of John Glenroy?"

"Yes, he was a bareback rider, worked for me ten, fifteen years ago. I was in just about as much financial trouble then as I am now. I gave him and his friend, Bell a couple of good ring horses because I didn't have any money to pay them."

"I know what that's like," said Henry. "I had that trouble in California."

"That night the sheriff came by, but they had already gotten away. They sold the horses and got part of their money at any rate."

"What did the circus men do about serving in the war? Were they called?"

"Yes. Doctor Thayer had to pay three hundred dollars for a substitute. He thought it better to pay rather than run the risk of losing his own life on the battlefield."

"I doubt if this country will ever get over that war."

"I'm sure you're right, but talking about Glenroy, he worked for Dan Rice. Dan was a friend of Old Zack Taylor."

"Oh! I heard about Dan Rice. My partner, George Ryland, worked for him. From what George told me Dan and Taylor were close friends, and Dan presented one of his battle scenes of the Mexican War."

"Yes, he did. It was 'The Battle of Buena Vista.' John Glenroy was performing in it, and he received a flesh wound when a musket held too close to his arm went off and blew away four or five inches of flesh along his right arm. That's what caused him to be exempt."

"I missed the war altogether, being in California."

"John Glenroy was telling me he was in Chicago on April 15th of 1865, the day President Lincoln died. Chicago was very shaken up by the President's death. That was the day Glenroy joined up with Frank Lee, the tumbler and vaulter. Is he related to you?"

"He certainly is. He's my son," replied Henry. "That's one thing about the circus—you can pretty much keep tabs on your own."

While the two men stood watching the men, a roustabout rushed up to George. "Look at this," he said, handing him a handbill.

George read it aloud to Henry. "'Don't attend any other circus that might come your way. Barnum's Circus will follow, and we will have The Greatest Show on Earth." He crumpled the bill and threw it away. "That does it for us. We can't compete with him."

Barnum's posters were effective, and the crowds stayed away, so much so that de Haven couldn't meet his payroll. So Henry decided to take his family back to Los Angeles.

Henry decided to travel to Mexico to check out the possibility of taking a circus there, just a small one made up of his own children. Little Emma was ill, under the doctor's care, and Carrie stayed home to care for her.

One morning while Carrie and her mother were in Emma's bedroom, little Charles was bothering, getting underfoot. "Rosa, will you take Charles down to the kitchen and look after him? Emma's not well and I want it quiet."

Rosa picked him up and started for the stairs. Charles didn't want to be carried, so he struggled to get free. Just as Rosa started down the steps, he lunged out of her arms and went tumbling down, landing at the bottom of the stairs. By the time she reached him, his body was limp. Carrie, hearing Rosa's scream rushed to her aid and carried Charles up to bed. Carrie rushed to the adobe, found her brother Frank working on some cuttings, and sent him for the doctor.

In Mexico, Henry discovered the towns were too far apart; the expenses would be too great to risk taking the circus there, so he booked passage for the north and home.

When he arrived back at the house on Second Street, he found his little Charles in bed requiring constant care; it upset him greatly. He looked down at his son, tears forming in his eyes, seeing a bright child, eager to learn, so full of life with unusual skill and daring, his beautiful little boy in long curls who showed such promise as a performer, was lying there motionless. Henry put some things he brought from Mexico on the dresser and sat down at his son's bedside. After a while Regina walked in.

"Henry, you've been sitting here for hours. Can I get you some tea?"

"Don't worry about me. I'm all right. Has he been lying like this long?"

"Several days, but the doctor says he'll get better, will probably even walk, but what he needs now is rest."

"Mother Weinshank, that box over there, contains the things I brought from Mexico, but this is no time to bring them out. Would you put them away for the time being?"

"Yes, Henry. I will. You let me know when you want them."

One day, while the doctor was checking Charles he said to Regina, "I'm afraid this boy will never make it to maturity. His back is seriously injured. I think I can get him on his feet, but we'll just have to wait and see."

The Lees stayed on in the house on Second Street. Charles did not get better, but there were others to think about. Henry again purchased wagons and again made plans to take the circus East.

He worked from morning till night, personally organizing all the packing procedures. Henry had little to say, for he knew he should stay in Los Angeles to look after Charles and Emma, but Carrie felt it would be better if he got back to the glitter of the arena, so leaving Emma and Charles behind, they headed out in the direction of the depot.

Emma finally recovered, color returned to her cheeks, and again she was up and around. For her first outing, Regina took her to St. Vibianas to light a candle for her brother Charles and on to Hamburg's department store. Regina's eye was taken by a stylish black cape lined in red silk. She rarely acted on impulse, but this time she did and bought it.

On the way home on Main Street, a parade was in progress so they stopped and watched. Gay caballeros, decked out in colorful costumes, mounted on beautiful caparisoned horses adorned with saddles covered with pure silver, passed by.

"What's the parade for grandma?"

"I really can't say, Emma, but Los Angeles is always celebrating something. There goes John Goller's hackney coach. Isn't it beautiful?"

"Oh! Yes, Grandma! I wish I could ride in it."

"Maybe some day you can," she replied.

While they were watching, Andrew walked up. "I'll see you in a little bit, I have some things to do in town."

He walked into Ozro's tin shop on Commercial. They were now carrying some hardware items. He was in business there with a man by the name of Hicks. Both men were there when Andrew walked in.

"What about those bands I ordered?"

"Oh, I'll have them done in a few days. You ordered fifty didn't you?"

"Ya, I did," said Andrew. "I'm going to a store on Main Street. Will you deliver them as soon as possible?"

"Be glad to," said Ozro, so Andrew left to join Regina and Emma.

When they got home, Regina took the cape out of the box. Andrew noticed the lining and much to her chagrin, said, "Red isn't a color for a lady. It's for the other kind. Put it away."

Regina felt the tears coming on, so she quickly turned so Andrew wouldn't see them form. She put the cape back in the box and put the box on the shelf with a resolve never to look at it again. The joy had been taken out of it.

On February 18th of 1874, Andrew Weinshank was working in his grove picking oranges when suddenly he slumped over, then came tumbling down. From the house, Regina saw him fall. She ran out to help him, dropped to the ground beside him, lifted his shoulders and put his head in her lap, stroking his beautiful dark brown hair.

She sobbed as she held him, swaying back and forth. Where could she turn? Carrie was on tour, Frank was living in San Francisco, and Jenny was staying with the Devlins, teaching in Sacramento. Young George, only eight years old, came running out to join his mother and started to cry, followed by his sister Lizzie and little Emma.

Regina was goaded into action by their presence. The children needed her strong will. "George, go to the house and get help and take the little ones with you." But before he could, Jesse and Arturo came running from the kitchen and carried Andrew to the house. George was sent to fetch the doctor, but Regina knew it was too late. She knew he was dead.

Later in the day, Father Mora called to make arrangements for the burial. That night they recited the rosary in the parlor in front of Andrew's casket.

The following morning, Father Mora joined the family and their many friends, and with their hired help, followed the wagon carrying the casket to the Roman Catholic Cemetery on Fort Street. They passed through the gate to the family burial plot.

Following the service, Ozro came over to Regina. "Just the other day Andrew was in the shop to get bands for the barrels. I was going to bring them by today and pay him a visit."

"I still don't believe it, Ozro" said Regina. "He was only 49, and he seemed to be in such good health."

"You'll never know what a toll the war took on him, though, Regina. I'm sure he went through a lot, much more than we'll ever know."

When the people were ready to leave, Regina turned suddenly to her friend, Mary White and said, "I hate this cemetery. That old wall enclosing it, and when it rains this land is under water more often than not. I don't know what I'll do, but I can't leave him here." She then broke down and sobbed, and Mary helped her back to the buggy.

Regina took little George with her when she went to see Stephen White, the young attorney, to settle Andrew's estate. Stephen, born in San Francisco, received his law degree at Santa Clara and had been admitted to the bar.

"Before we can settle Andrew's estate, we'll have to locate all of Henry's family," he said. "All of Henry's children from his former marriages are to receive a share. That's the way Andrew set up his will."

"I'm not too sure they can be found, or whether they are even alive, for that matter, but my business is doing well, so we'll manage."

As Regina was about to walk out the door, Stephen spoke up, "Regina, why don't you apply for a pension? You're entitled to it, you know, for Andrew serving in the war. You'd get at least seven dollars a month. Not much, but it all helps."

"I don't need the money, Stephen. I'm well-fixed. Plenty to last me the rest of my days."

"But Congress set that aside for all the families of the soldiers, not just the poor ones."

"If you think it is the proper thing to do, the next time I come in perhaps you can help me fill out the papers."

Regina and George walked over to see the new dentist, Dr. Crawford, at his office located in the Downey Block. He looked at George's mouth, while he was doing this, he said to Regina, "I hate to say this, but the people around here don't know a whole lot about dentistry, do they?"

"I'm afraid you're right, Doctor. Most of the people in this town let their teeth rot in their heads before letting Peter Biggs, the barber, pull them out. I can't say that I blame them."

"Regina, everything looks fine with George, something stuck between his teeth."

"That's good to hear."

"I'd appreciate it if you would spread the word that I work as painlessly as possible. It might help bring a few patients in at least."

"I certainly will. I'm sure you will do well in time. Thank you for your time, Doctor, and we will be back."

A few days later Regina returned to Stephen White's office with the pension papers. After Mr. White filled in all the answers, he broached another subject, "What do you think about the prostitutes here in town?"

"Why, I don't know what I'm supposed to think. They buy my products. They pay their bill promptly. I have no quarrels with them."

"I think they should be legalized. Then they can be checked by a doctor and regulated. This way they can be inspected."

"I never thought of it that way, but I guess it is a business, and surely all businesses need regulating. But why not just send them out of town? They certainly don't improve its reputation."

"Some feel there is a need for them. This way the men don't have to bother their wives as much, so they do serve a purpose. You know women, they're always afraid of getting pregnant."

"You may be right. I didn't think of it that way. I've seen many a city official either going in or coming out of one of those houses, and I ought to know—I live close enough to them. In fact, one of our more illustrious town officials married one, and that takes a bit of nerve."

"The thing that worries me is that a man can catch a dreadful disease and take it home to his wife."

"You're right. They really do need to be checked by a doctor."

"That's why I want to have them regulated. Think about it, Regina. I may need your support. Not too many women around here are as open-minded as you are."

"I will, Stephen."

Regina took the Main Street line, the horse railway, home, one horse pulling a bob-tailed car, seating eight to ten passengers. The adults paid ten cents, the children five cents. At night the horse and car were housed in a barn at the end of the line.

June 10th, 1874, Mary Phelan's labor pains began. She set about doing her usual chores. She waited until they were rather close together before she set out to call Tom.

"You better get Auntie Wade, Tom. It can't be too much longer and I need her good hands."

"Why in tarnation does a woman have to wait until the last minute?" he said to himself while he fumbled with the harness. Luckily Mary's Auntie Wade lived on the ranch and he didn't have far to go.

From the time they got back to the house, Auntie Wade took over. "You stay out of here, Tom, but first get some water and stoke up the stove, and I'll do the rest. And keep out of our way."

The time went by slowly. Tom knew Auntie Wade wouldn't let him stick around, so he tried to make the best of it. He went out where the Chinamen were making brooms and worked with them a while. Later on, Auntie Wade walked out onto the porch holding their baby, wrapped in a blanket.

"It's a boy, Tom. A beautiful baby. Come look at him. What are you going to name him?"

"Daniel," he said, "Daniel, after my own dear father."

Auntie Wade stayed on a few days to look after Mary. In the evening they sat around and talked while Mary nursed the baby.

"How did you come to California, Auntie Wade?" asked Tom.

"Oh, we came by covered wagon, we did, and oh! what hardship we suffered. The dust kicking up in our faces, the cold nights on the prairie, and when we got to Salt Lake, the worst of all happened. Some Mormons stopped us and said we had to stay. They put us to work, servitude, they called it. I don't know why. Maybe for passing through their land, but they wouldn't let us come on to California. Pete had to herd cattle and it was Pete, praise be to God, who helped us get away."

"That Pete's nobody's fool."

"One day he asked us to join him, and when we got there, he said, 'We're going to California.' 'When?' I asked. 'Right now,' he said. 'The cattle can look after themselves,' and on we came. It took us weeks to cross the desert, through the San Bernardino Mountains and into the valley, but on we came."

A few days later Tom made arrangements with the padres at the mission for their baby to be baptized on the following Sunday. They were called to Mass by the sweet sound of the mission bells in the early morning hours. Tom got up, hitched the team to the buckboard, and off they went, traveling along El Camino Real.

The only house they saw before arriving at the mission was the Garvey house. They traveled along over the dusty road through the countryside covered with mustard and barley. Mary covered the baby so the sun wouldn't burn him. They enjoyed the warm, gentle breezes and the sun beating down on them, and finally they arrived at the mission.

The Padre was there to greet them, as were their neighbors and friends. After Mass, they gathered around the baptismal, listened while the priest chanted the prayers and sprinkled the holy water over the baby. When the ceremony was over, they went out to the courtyard.

"What a beautiful spot this is," said Tom. "Peaceful and quiet. What are those rooms for, over there?"

"Oh! They were the rooms where the Indians worked." After showing them around, they walked through the courtyard back to their wagon.

Again, Tom shook his hand, then said, "Thank you for your kindness, Padre, for showing us around."

"God go with you, and I hope you'll soon return."

On one of Tom's trips to Los Angeles, he stopped at Luis Vignes' Vineyard to rest his team and sit a spell before heading on to the Plaza. Don Vignes told him he had chestnut cuttings for sale and talked Tom into buying some.

"But will I be able to sell them?"

"Oh, yes. Chestnuts are great eating, and you'll be the only one beside myself to have them." Tom thought that over a minute; that sounded pretty good, so he had him load his wagon.

"While you're at it, put on some of those grape vines over there. I'll plant a few around the house," then he headed on.

While riding back to the ranch, Tom thought about the vein of clay running through his place. When he got home, he found a neighbor, a man by the name of Bowman, who was willing to build a kiln on his property, so with some Mexican help, they hauled willows from the river in the big wagon to use for fuel.

The Phelans were prospering. As soon as the kiln was finished, the Mexicans started making brick. They cared for the stock, planted the crops and cared for the chestnut trees, but it was the Phelans, Tom and Mary, who really kept things going and everyone at his task.

Tom's sister and her husband Sheily visited the Phelans on the ranch. It was Sheily who decided they needed a fireplace, now that they had a good sized stack of brick, "What about it, Tom, why don't we build a fireplace?" So the men got right to work. "While we're at it, let's make it large enough to do the job right!" said Sheily.

"Whatever you say. I'll leave that up to you."

When the fireplace was finished, they all sat around the crackling fire, watched it as the logs dwindled down. The family talked about the old days, of Tom coming to America, fighting in the war.

"That whole war was a terrible calamity," said Sheily.

"Oh! what a war that was," declared Mary. "I'm glad my Tom fought for the North, if he had to fight, for I hold no kindness for slavery, and I'll hate them southerners for the rest of my days for what they've done to my poor Tom. Now he has a cough and I'm sure'n he got it from the war. Coughs all the time at night."

Tom wanted to change the subject, so he said, "Sister, you remember Phil Sheridan, don't you? He was born close to our farm at home."

"Yes," she answered. "I remember the family."

"Well, one night while we were in camp, he came riding up mounted on his big, black horse—all foaming with sweat. Phil was a fine figure of a man and I wanted to step up and speak to him. But his being so important and all, and being in charge of the calvary, and seeming to be in a great hurry, I let him be, but it was pleased I was to see him."

"I'm sure all the folk in Ireland are proud of him, Tom," said Sheily.

Tom's sister, Mary, spoke up, "Tom, now that you have the little one, you need a bathtub, a nice one like those they have in Los Angeles."

"You're right," said Tom, "and my Mary would put it to good use. I'll go get some tin the first chance I get."

Whenever it rained neither the San Gabriel, nor the Rio Hondo Rivers were safe to cross. The only bridge across the San Gabriel was the Sanford Bridge and it was too far downstream to be of any use.

So, the first time Tom started to Los Angeles to get the tin for the bathtub, his wagon bogged down. He was able to uncouple his horses and lead them to safety, but he had to leave his wagon to the mercy of the flood. He was able to save his own skin, so felt himself lucky in the bargain. When he reached the bank, he looked back and watched his wagon sink then went home, riding one horse and leading the other.

When the waters had drained away, Tom again started for Los Angeles. He bought the tin, a piece large enough to make a good sized tub, and took it back to the ranch. While Mr. Woodward was making it, he dropped his ax, cutting a hole the length of the blade, which he had to solder before they could use the tub. It wasn't too smooth, but the tin cost so much, they had to make do. Now Mary had a tub to bathe her little one.

The country suddenly plunged into a depression. Banks all over closed their doors, including the two banks in Los Angeles. They went from the greatest prosperity they had ever known, to the lowest depths, and property values fell. The Temple-Workman Bank on Main Street, opposite the Bella Union was hit hard. When Regina heard about it, she dropped everything and went over. People came from all directions, down Aliso and Arcadia, up Main and Spring Streets. Angelenos converged on the tottering institution and crowded about its great iron doors. Inside the bank was crowded; the tellers were slow in transacting business.

At exactly three o'clock a bank official stepped to the door and put the "closed" sign on it. Regina hadn't made her way inside. The crowd dispersed, but the uneasiness remained; and she resolved to return the next day.

Early the next morning, Regina, again, went to the bank and waited in front. But at ten o'clock when the bank was scheduled to open, a sign was put up, "Closed for thirty days until loans can be arranged."

The story got around that Hellman of the Downey-Hellman Bank was in Europe and was to be called home. Temple of the Temple-Workman Bank was in San Francisco, trying to arrange a loan with E. J. "Lucky" Baldwin, the Comstock Lode millionaire. Temple arrived back in Los Angeles with the $200,000 he had managed to borrow and the people were able to transact their business. But confidence waned, and people began to question Temple's money lending principles, so much so that many withdrew their accounts. Regina took her money out and transferred it to the Downey-Hellman Bank.

Temple went to see his father-in-law and his good friend, Juan Matis Sanchez, to get them to put up more money. Juan was uncertain as to what to do, so he said he wanted to think about it and he would let them know.

Juan was concerned because he could neither read, nor write. So, a few days later he asked Temple, "If I sign, will it be for all my ranchos, or for just one of them?"

"Only one, Juan."

"I need a little more time to think about it." He went to see his old friend, Harris Newmark, for advice. Harris thought about it for a moment or two then said, "I feel relief would be only temporary at best. I don't think you should do it, my friend."

Matis just said quietly, "No quiero morir de hambre. I do not wish to die of hunger." When Juan left the store, Newmark thought the matter was settled.

But this was not to be the case. Juan felt the pressure for a decision. He wanted the help and advice of his two sons, Tomas and Frank, but they were away at school, so the next time he was pressured to sign, he weakened and put his "X" on the document.

The Downey-Hellman bank had been founded on sound principles and good management and was able to stem the tide. But this was not so with the Temple-Workman Bank.

Business did not pick up. Baldwin lent them another $100,000 and this too dwindled to a mere pittance. The Temple-Workman Bank closed its doors for the last time. Baldwin filed foreclosure on all the property covered by the loan. Juan Matis Sanchez learned that all three of his ranchos, Rancho Chico, Rancho Merced, and Rancho Portero, had been put up as security and so was stripped of most of his holdings, twenty-two hundred acres of the finest land surrounding the old mission. Temple was reduced to a pauper, and Workman put a gun to his head.

Nell and Dan Phelan

Joe and Annie Phelan

Weinshank Beach Cottage

Chapter 26

Jenny returned from Sacramento because she felt she was needed at home after her father's death. She tried to get her mother interested in new activities. A man by the name of J. P. Jones was selling lots at Santa Monica. He went to San Francisco to spread the word and he put an ad in the Los Angeles paper. Jenny saw the ad and the idea of having a cottage at the seashore was most appealing, especially because her mother had always loved the ocean so.

Jones arranged to have the steamship "The Senator" transport 150 eager buyers from San Francisco to participate in the land sale. It was on July 14th when the sidewheeler chugged into the harbor and dispatched its passengers.

At daylight the next morning, the road from Los Angeles over the hot, dusty mesa was a continuous line of Angelenos driving their buggies through the wide-open pasture lands, as stages and hacks began shuttling citizens to the auction sale. Los Angeles livery stables were empty by noon, and the horse cars were the only moving vehicles on the streets.

Jenny and her mother stood in the crowd, along with all the others, waiting for the bidding to begin. Then the auctioneer, Jim Fitch, mounted the platform, stood with his back to the ocean.

"Just visualize, if you will, several wharfs projected out in the bay, a gigantic smelting works erected to refine the Cerro Gordo and Panamint ores. Think of all the activity this will bring."

One man from the crowd asked, "What about drinking water?"

"You can dig an Artesian well. Fresh water is close to the surface," answered Jim. "Now, can we get on?"

Nearby stood a temporary bar, a row of beer kegs with a sign on it saying, "Grand Palace Saloon."

Jim Fitch got right down to business. "We'll start with the first lot. Can I hear 'two hundred.?' Fine, how about 'two-twenty-five?' and now, who will give me 'two-seventy-five?" and so it went.

A few moments later, one of the kegs of beer exploded, the beer sprayed out over the spectators. One of the witty onlookers remarked, "One of the Artesian wells just came in," and the crowd howled. It took a little doing to get the crowd back under control, but when the day was over, four thousand dollars' worth of lots had been sold, and Regina had hers.

The Weinshanks built a beach cottage along the ocean front, just a bungalow with a porch facing the water. The children waded within easy vision of those in the house.

Regina took every opportunity to go there for a few days. Phineas Banning had purchased land from the Dominguez family and built a landing nearby. While they were staying at the beach cottage, Regina always loved to get up early in the morning and walk down to the water's edge. Then, no matter what the weather was like, she swam around the pier. She would be back at the cottage before the others got up. But, if anyone thought they were good enough to join her, she always came back with the same answer, "You go have your fun, but when I swim, I swim alone."

One time, as they were riding along at a leisurely pace on the way to their beach cottage Regina spoke up, "Jenny, one of these days Los Angeles is going to be a great city like San Francisco. I can feel it in my bones, and one of those who will make it possible is our own dear friend, Stephen White. Yes, the railroad is important. It brought us where we are today, but the harbor they're talking about—that's many times more important. With a great harbor we're bound to have a great city. Mark my words, Jenny, maybe you will see it; it won't be during my time, but surely the little ones will, and it will be a far cry from the little Mexican village your father and I came to."

"It's like you say, mother. Men like Stephen White, Phineas Banning and William Mulholland, are men of vision. They'll all make their mark and go down in the history books of this city. Of course, we're partial to Stephen White because they're such good friends."

"Yes, this city will grow to be one of the great ones some day, but only by the efforts of men like them."

"Phineas Banning did as much as anyone to promote the town. He hauled the poles out for the telegraph lines, built the railroad into town, and now he's transporting people from Los Angeles to the beach."

"The day we arrived in town, our driver said Banning could handle the ribbons better than any other driver in the country."

"Yes, mother, and I think Mr. Mulholland is right. We do need other sources of water for Los Angeles as well as the river. Sometimes the river has plenty of water and sometimes it doesn't. I read an article the other day in the *Los Angeles Star* about the water situation and what Mr. Mulholland is trying to do to promote it."

"Stephen feels the harbor should be at San Pedro. I hope he wins out."

"He will, he's a fighter, Mother."

"Oh! I'm proud of him all right. He has done a fine job for the town and has worked so hard. I take a great deal of pride in what Stephen has been able to accomplish."

"Maybe some day they'll erect a statue in his memory, when he's dead and gone," said Frank.

Regina added, "They should recognize his greatness now. He'd never know about the statue."

At "El Ranchito", Don Pio Pico made plans for a grand fandango. When all was in readiness, the servants were sent to spread the word to all the neighbors. The evening of the great event people the countryside over arrived in buckboards and buggies.

It was with great pomp and ceremony the Don greeted his guests at the door. He was dressed in a short black velvet coat and tight black pants, slit up the side and adorned with braid. Around his neck he wore several heavy gold chains and his fingers were laden with jewels.

Mary, with her arm on Tom's, felt awkward as the Don bowed and reached for her hand. He kissed it ever so tenderly. She looked to Tom for reassurance.

They went into the sala. On a table was a guitar, hinting at later entertainment. Three big chairs were stuffed with horsehair and covered with brocade material; on either side of the door were large glazed urns, and a goatskin rug covered the bare wood floor.

The Don escorted them to the courtyard, where they saw his gaily colored parrots in ornate cages. They watched the Indian servants making the last minute preparations. Nearby was a room used to store jerky, flour and other food.

"The Don has many peons working for him and many mouths to feed," Tom said to Mary.

Many of the neighbors were there, all dressed in their Sunday best. Tom and Mary made the rounds talking to them. When all was in readiness, they sat down to a feast of tamales, carne seca, and the delicious wine made from the Don's own grapes. Then they adjourned to the ballroom overlooking the San Gabriel River, and danced to the sweet sounds of guitar and violin. But Mary didn't join in. She felt awkward in this strange surrounding. She was again heavy with child, so after watching a while, Tom took her hand and they walked outside to the river's edge.

"A few years back, in '67, the flood washed away the old Nieto adobe on down the river. The Carpenters were living in it then. When the flood waters were at their height, Christian Sorenson brought out his boat and went around rescuing people. The Kings barely escaped with their lives. Mr. King saw a wall of water washing toward them, helped his wife and daughter on to the back of his horse, grabbed his two-year-old. A neighbor grabbed his six-year-old and they made it to safety.

"What a near miss they had!"

"On the bluff over there, Mary, is where they had a battle before California became part of the United States. General Kearny and Commodore Stockton came up from San Diego with three hundred men and fought the native Californios there."

"Did the Don fight?"

"No, he wasn't here; he was on his way to Mexico to get help from the Mexican government and he didn't get back in time."

"When did that happen?"

"About thirty years ago."

It was good for Tom and Mary to have a chance to be by themselves, as they watched a bird perched on a rock near the edge of the river. Up on the bluff on the far side of the Rio Hondo was where the battle took place.

Stockton took charge because Kearny was still weak. Kearny had lost an arm at San Pasqual. The Californios were on the far bank, high on the bluff. The Americans crossed at Passo de Bartola. The artillery stopped to fire at the Californios. Kearny's men charged. Then all of a sudden, one of Flore's aides panicked and called, "Halt." The Americans took the hill unopposed.

Mary turned to Tom, "Did you see the Don's saddle, and his spurs and bridle? His saddle has so much silver on it you can hardly see any leather!"

"Yes, it's ornate, all right," replied Tom. "But don't let all that fool you. The Pico House in town, that saddle and jewels are probably all he has left besides his land, and he's selling it off fast. This adobe is spacious, but it didn't cost him anything. It was built by the Gabrielino Indians from the mission. Some of the Indians now are sharecropping with him."

When they returned to the house, Tom took Mary back to visit with the ladies in the patio, while Tom went to join the men.

A few days after the grand affair, Mary had her second child, a baby girl born on September 28, 1875. They named her Nell, a wee one with red hair and light blue eyes. A new baby didn't keep Mary from her chores. She was up at dawn the following day, working, cooking for the family and hired help. Tom, all the while, was as unconcerned as could be. He went spreading the word the country over, telling his neighbors and friends that a christening would be held at the mission as soon as he could make the arrangements.

The Weinshanks not only had social and church events to attend, but civic matters as well. Regina, being in the business of shipping foodstuffs, was interested in the railroad because much of her business was out of Los Angeles. A woman being in business was very rare indeed, but she felt she had no other choice than to attend a public hearing about the railroad coming to Los Angeles.

The big four railroad magnates had offered to include Los Angeles on the main line. Los Angeles was expected to put up a considerable amount of money as well as pay the rates set by the big four.

Crocker was sent down to speak to those gathered in the council room. Regina and Jenny were there. With all the smoking and tobacco chewing, both the atmosphere and floor were in a disgraceful state.

"Mother, do you think we should be here? All the others are men," Jenny whispered uncomfortably.

"I'm just as interested in what's going on around here as they are. George is too young, Frank is living in San Francisco, and now that your father is gone, I no longer have him to lean on, so it behooves me to take an interest."

After the audience quieted down, one of the councilmen got up and said he felt Crocker should only be permitted to address the people if and when it was his turn and not before.

Harris Newmark, one of the largest, if not the largest, shipper of goods, and Judge Widney were in the audience. They were embarrassed by the rudeness, for they were two of the more prominent figures in the local campaign to have Los Angeles included on the main line. Otherwise, they were afraid Los Angeles would be bypassed and the town would shrink in size and fade into oblivion.

After a while, Crocker was allowed to speak. He had hardly started when one man popped up from the audience and said, "I'd like to tell a story." Then the man walked to the front of the room and started talking. "Seems as though a man built an expensive hotel in the middle of the desert. Being so far out, he had no guests. Then one day, a lone traveler rode across the burning sands, saw the hotel and spent the night. The next morning, he was presented with a bill for seventy-five dollars. When he inquired why it was so much, the owner said it was because the hotel cost him so much to build, and because the man was his first and only guest, he had to pay his part of the interest on his investment."

Many laughed, but Regina and Jenny just looked at one another. When the crowd quieted down, Crocker got up to speak. By this time he was shaking with rage. "If this is the spirit in which Los Angeles proposes to deal with the railroad upon which this town's very vitality depends, I will see grass grow under your streets before I'll lift a hand to help you."

Then he relaxed and continued talking, "It's up to you. We're willing to divide $250,000 needed to build the track, a tidy sum, to include Los Angeles on the main line; otherwise we're going to bypass your town and go several miles inland. Yes, we can. Then if you want to take advantage of the railroad, you can build your own branch to connect with the main line and forget about being a railroad center."

By this time, he had everyone's attention. After he concluded his speech, he sat down, and they started filing out. It was a sober bunch of people who left the council room that night. "These men have met their match, a man with whom they dare not trifle," said Regina as she and Jenny walked out. "I have a lot of respect for that man, Jenny."

The City Council was busy making street improvements. Main, Spring and Fort Streets were being paved. The Wolfskills had already donated a strip of land, 300 by 1900 feet in size, fronting on Alameda between Fourth and Sixth streets for a train station. Soon after that, the remainder of the Wolfskill property was subdivided. Regina, too, had a decision to make. The City wanted her to donate some land to the City for the widening of Los Angeles Street, and she was glad to have Jenny home to help her decide what to do.

Jenny always helped her mother with business matters. Regina could read and write in German, but not in English. Jenny was needed to go over all their papers since all her mother's property was in her name, she had to be there to sign. After they got that taken care of, she turned to other matters.

In Los Angeles, church activity was an important part of the Weinshanks' lives now that Andrew was gone. Charles, too, had died—that dear little child who had circus in his blood.

Regina, to keep herself busy, was taking part in more and more church activities. On Palm Sunday, 1876, the Cathedral of Saint Vibiana opened its doors for service. In Los Angeles the new cathedral was planned to be fashioned after the Iglesia de Puerto de San Miguel in Barcelona. Bishop Amat left for Europe and Bishop Mora went on with construction plans, Louis Messmer was in charge of the work.

The Weinshanks attended a money raiser at the church. Regina made a couple of her specialties for the big event. As they walked into the courtyard, women were busy setting up the tables, making everything attractive. Emmelina walked up to Regina and took a look at what she had. "Oh! You brought my favorite dishes. Your potato salad is the best I've ever tasted. Let's put them here where I can find them later on."

"You certainly are entitled to whatever you want, Emmelina; after all you gave the church the land we're standing on."

The people began to arrive in great numbers, and when it was all over and they were clearing the tables, one lady said, "I think half of Los Angeles was here today."

Regina insisted on attending the parade, for forty-two battle-scarred veterans of the Mexican War were scheduled to march in the Los Angeles Independence Day parade in 1876. Regina and Jenny were among the crowd watching with tear-filled eyes.

"Andrew should have been in that parade, Jenny, wearing his tattered Mexican clothes."

"I know, Mother."

After the veterans marched by, the crowd assembled outside the Round House on Main Street to hear speeches commemorating the day, while the band played "Hail Columbia." The Round House, an adobe that George Lehman, a former neighbor, had fixed up as a German Wine Garden, was the Weinshanks' favorite place of entertainment when Andrew was alive. Many a time Regina and Andrew and the children went there for a pleasant afternoon. At the front door were statues of Adam and Eve beside an apple tree.

Regina and Jenny walked inside and out into the courtyard where a large crowd was milling around. On the balcony men were playing the familiar German strains. They sat at a table and drank the refreshing beer served at the bar, nearby the Bell Sweep. All around them George had his plants and flowers growing, making it a pleasant setting very much like the old country. They knew many of the other people there, so they had a pleasant time talking and waiting for the program to start.

Then Phineas Banning got up and began to speak about the war and about the men who fought in it. Regina's mind drifted back to the day on the wharf in New Orleans when she saw Andrew for the first time. Then she heard his name, how he had been a hero in the war. It did comfort her to know that he had been remembered. After Banning had finished his speech and the band struck up with "Yankee Doodle," she began to shake, so Jenny gave her a little hug, and they went home together.

Most often the Phelans attended mass at the Poyorena adobe in Fulton Wells, just a short distance south of the ranch. The Poyorenas had set up a small alter in the parlor where the neighbors gathered to recite the rosary and take part in the Mass. On occasion, a wedding was performed, as well as christenings.

Sometimes the priest came from Mission San Gabriel, sometimes from Los Angeles. As he rode into the yard at the Phelan place, Tom greeted him with, "Father, you surely will spend the night; we have plenty of room."

The padre had his answer ready, because he knew he would get some of Mary's fine cooking. He was especially fond of her homemade bread. "I'll be happy to stay, Tom, and mighty fine of you to ask me."

In the evening after supper, Mary put the little ones to bed and they sat in front of the fireplace—whiling away the hours, talking of the old days and of Tom's and Mary's childhood in Ireland. The priest told stories about the mission and how they had once been great places of worship, the center of trade, and of the great ranchos that surrounded them.

"Los Angeles is certainly growing, isn't it?"

"Yes, I think around four thousand people live there now!"

After the logs burned down, the padre said, "Better hit the hay, morning comes mighty soon."

Early on the Sabbath the padre got up, thinking he should have gone to bed earlier the night before. Tom had his horse saddled, ready to send him on his way.

"I'll see you there, won't I, Tom?" asked the padre.

"You can count on it, we'll be along as soon as everyone is ready."

In Los Angeles, Billy Rowland was again running for sheriff. It was his father, John Rowland, who came to the Puente Valley in 1841. Billy's sister, Nieves, was married to John Reed, who came in with Stephen Watts Kearny and the Army of the West.

After Billy was made sheriff, he was an important figure around town. He loved cigars and purchased them a box at a time; he wrote his name on the lid and always left it in the store. That way he could slip in by the rear door and help himself.

Tom Phelan had a high regard for Billy and knew the family well, for many a time the Phelans went to the Workman-Rowland rancho. He was more than happy to work on Billy's behalf to help get him elected sheriff, going around the countryside talking to people, soliciting votes, for he felt Billy was a square shooter.

Tom gave a barbeque to introduce Billy to his neighbors. Some people came from as far off as Los Angeles. The guests looked on while the men participated in the horse races on the dirt road in front of the ranch, for nothing was more important to a man than his horse. Tom had posts marking off a mile in front of his place. Just have someone say how fast his horse could go, and Tom would say, "Let's go out and try it." They would mount their favorite, someone would send them on their way, and the matter was settled on the spot.

Mary, with the help of the ladies, spread food out on long tables in the yard, and after all had their fill, the children again went back to playing in the yard, and the grown-ups sat around in the shade visiting. In the evening, everyone was invited into the parlor, while Angel Rameriz played his violin, and the people stood around and sang.

On election day, Billy being a good Democrat, got the majority vote, so it was a great day. They celebrated with a victory barbeque in town that lasted far on into the night.

Billy was very much impressed with Tom and thought he should become a lawyer.

"I don't have any schooling in that, Billy."

"You don't have to. You just get someone to let you represent them, then go to the courthouse, ask the judge for a time to hear the case, and you're in business."

"That's it? It's that easy? I don't have to go to school?"

"No, just do as I say, and you're on your way, and anyway, there's no harm in trying. Doctors don't do any different here. If they know the names of the medicines the womenfolk have on their shelves at home, they hang out their shingles."

"Well, in that case, maybe I'll give it a try."

One day while Tom was at the courthouse, he saw a familiar face. "Stephen White, good to see you! The last time I saw you, you were in San Francisco."

"I've come to live here, Tom. I'm a lawyer now. I've opened an office in town."

"I've been trying a few cases myself, and have had pretty good luck, but I don't have a degree like you do, though."

"I'm sure you'll do very well."

"Why don't you bring your family and come visit us on the ranch? We can sit and talk about some of our cases."

"One of these days Mary and I might just do that."

In no time at all, Stephen and his wife, Mary, were driving into the yard at the ranch.

"That was a fine meal, Mary," said Mary White as she was pushing herself away from the table. "But, you have so many to cook for. We really shouldn't have come."

"I cook for so many men, two more certainly doesn't bother me, Mary. Tom and I were talking it over and we would consider it an honor if you and Mr. White would act as godparents when our baby comes."

"We would be the honored ones, Mary. Let us know when and we'll be there."

A short time later, on June 22nd, 1877, Mary's third child was born. Tom went to Los Angeles to see the Whites and let them know of the date of the baptism, which the padre set for July 8th.

For the Phelans, the baptism was a big event, as their activity centered around the church. They had a social gathering now and then, but weddings and baptisms were most important. Other than that, life went on in its own uneventful way.

Tom and Mary, their children Daniel, Nell and the baby, along with Stephen and Mary, from Los Angeles, attended Mass. Following it, the priest performed the baptism.

"You have a fine family there, Tom," said Stephen.

"That we do, Stephen, and we're growing."

When the baby was just beginning to walk, but still a bit unsteady on his feet, he walked into the barn where the Chinamen were working. He picked up a bottle of clear liquid and drank it. Then he started screaming at the top of his lungs, throwing his arms in the air. Then he collapsed on the ground. By the time Mary got to him he was more dead than alive.

Mary ran to the chicken house, grabbed a couple of eggs, poured them down his throat, and he threw up. Then she stuck her fingers down, but still he screamed. She put him up on her shoulder, but he continued to toss and squirm. Then she went over to where the bottle was on the ground, picked it up, dropped a speck on her finger and tasted it.

"Why, this is lye. What in the name of God is it doing here? God help the person who put it here."

The baby continued whimpering, so Mary held him sitting in the rocking chair for several nights. During the day, when she had a meal to cook, she carried her little one around on her shoulder. After a week or so passed, he began to do better and was able to get around on his own.

"I'm afraid the damage will stay with him the remainder of his days," said Mary to Tom, as the tears streamed down her face, "and only God knows who left that lye there. If I ever find out who did it, I'll send him packing for sure." But, try as she did, she never found out.

They called the baby Joe. He was born with three thumbs, and because all the doctoring had to be done at home, Mary had to take care of him herself. She went out to the barn, pulled one of the hairs from the horse's tail and wrapped it around his extra thumb. Each day she tightened it a little more, and after a few days it dropped off.

Mary had all sorts of things to tend to on her own because Tom spent much of his time in Los Angeles, tending to other people's business. One time he offered to take a prisoner to San Francisco for trial, boarding the train in Los Angeles. He handcuffed the prisoner to himself. It was comfortable enough with the warmth generated by the coal burning, pot-bellied stove, but his seat was hard. From time to time Tom got up and walked around, which meant taking the prisoner with him, or locking him to the seat. The other passengers didn't like it, so Tom stayed pretty much put most of the time.

When the train stopped to let the passengers eat at selected places along the route, Tom and his prisoner got off the train too, but this, too, was inconvenient, because the poor man had difficulty eating with his left hand. Then Tom decided to let his prisoner eat first, and then he ate.

After Tom delivered the prisoner, he stayed with his sister, Mary, and her husband Sheily for a few days and they talked of Ireland and of the family there.

During the season of 1878, the Lee's were performing in the East, working for the Campbell Circus. They traveled along the Mississippi and Ohio Rivers. Those navigable rivers gave them easy access to the growing communities of the various towns and plantation landings. During the winter they toured the lower stretches of the river system, moving north as spring arrived. The show exhibited principally on land, under tent, and the performers and family members were again staying in hotels.

They were in Louisville, Kentucky, when Carrie gave birth to a baby girl. They named her Edna Nettie Laura Pauline Beatrice Lee.

But there was a job to be done, a performance to give, so Carrie was left in the care of a hired lady, and the others left for the glorious street parade which was scheduled to begin at ten o'clock in the morning, complete with two full military bands, and golden chariots.

That evening the program began with the grand entry. The band struck up. Around the hippodrome track came all the performers—elephants, bareback riders, clowns; the whole procession swept past to the circus march.

Into the ring walked Henry, an erect, elegant man in black pants, a red coat, top hat, and polished black boots. The whole timing of the circus depended on him. No waits, no breaks, it would have to go at a pace that would make the next two hours seem like just a few short minutes.

His voice boomed out, "La-dies and Gentlemen—the show is about to begin!"

As the crowd quieted down, Henry introduced the acts as they came along.

"In the ring on your right is Miss Rosa Lee juggling three flaming torches as she balances on the revolving globe."

Henry watched this wonderfully graceful, fairy-like creature as she captivated the audience. She then did her juggling act with rings and knives as she stood mounted on a beautiful horse, circling the ring at full speed. She followed that by riding two horses around the ring and again balancing torches at the same time. She then leaped from her horse, skipped to the center of the ring, and took her bow before a delighted audience. Henry's little Rosa Lee was now a premier equestrienne, justly styled the Empress of the Arenic circus.

While the acts were changing, the audience was amused by the clown, who was sure of foot and graceful in delivery so the public might gaze and thrill, wonder, laugh and cry. Then Henry again stepped into the ring and introduced Lavater Lee, the dashing and graceful two-horse rider.

This act was followed by Rosa and Harry doing their two-horse riding act. Then, all four—Henry, Lavater, Harry and Rosa performed a specialty juggling act. Henry then introduced Linda Jeal, the beautiful equestrienne; such outstanding horsemanship the audience had never seen before.

The performance seemed to be over almost as soon as it had begun. The crowd wandered out at a leisurely pace all full of wonder.

Following that engagement, the Lees, signed on with the Orrin Brothers, one of the most outstanding circuses. So, Henry, Carrie, and their children, Rosa, Lavater, Harry, Augusta, Robert, Frank, and the baby Edna, left their comfortable quarters and made ready for another journey. They sailed from Charleston to Havana, Cuba, arriving a few days later at one of the finer seaports. They were moored at the wharf, having easy access for the horses. The view of the city from the harbor was most magnificent.

They set up their tents at the outskirts of town and performed before fair crowds. The elite of the city enjoyed seeing the horses and admiring their beauty. Their performances were well attended, especially on Sundays.

From Havana, they continued on to some of the more inland towns. After spending several weeks, they completed their stay at Regulas and returned to Havana. All of Cuba would have been a wonderful fairyland, had they not buried their own little Augusta there. She caught yellow fever, and her frail little body couldn't throw off that dread disease. For them, the trip became one of sorrow and disappointment. They were scheduled to return to the United States, so they continued on, another place, another town.

The Lees returned to the States; they again hired on with Campbells, and exhibited at Coulterville August 26th, Carbondale the 29th, St. Louis and back for a one week stand commencing August 19th. But by the end of the year, they were back in Los Angeles.

Henry wanted a new and spectacular act for his show. His brother-in-law lived in Australia, and had written him about the Australian Bushmen who threw lighted torches into the air and to each other. Henry presented the idea of importing them for a visit to the city council. They insisted upon his securing a bond for bringing them to this country, which Henry was willing to do. Henry then wrote to his brother-in-law in Adelaide and waited the arrival of the Bushmen. When they arrived, it caused quite a stir, and while they remained in Los Angeles their act was quite spectacular and well worth Henry's effort to bring them to Los Angeles.

The Lees were living in the house on Second Street. Henry felt Rosa needed some formal education, so he enrolled her with the Sisters of Charity, but her education was short-lived. Joseph Chiarini with his Royal Italian Circus was in San Francisco; he heard that Henry was in Los Angeles, so he wrote asking if he would like to join him on his world tour. Carrie wanted to stay in Los Angeles, but Henry wanted to accept Joseph's offer, and Lavater, Harry, Robert and Rosa were all eager to go.

They had crossed the country three times during the seventies. Carrie had so hoped they would settle down, but this was not to be the case. The night before they left for San Francisco, Carrie called her brother, Frank, aside and gave him a little, black velvet bag.

"Please keep this for me while I'm gone, Frank. I just don't want to take the chance of something happening to them. Be especially careful because the gold chain and small cuff links are in it, and they mean so much to us."

"I will, Carrie. I wish you didn't have to make this trip."

"I must, Frank. Henry needs me, but when we get home, he promised me he will buy a ranch and settle down. The children will then be able to go out on their own if they wish to stay in the business."

Henry asked for the box he had Regina put away. After supper, the family went to the parlor. Henry brought out a frame he had made in Mexico; a beautiful gold gilt frame that cost him a princely fortune. Frank put Carrie's picture of George Washington in it and hung it over the mantle.

Then he brought out the water jugs, placed them on the mantle. "These are for the family to enjoy while we're away." Then he brought out the elk-horn cups. "See, one fits inside the other and this little one on the inside has a lid."

"They're all very beautiful to be sure," said Carrie, "but we best go to bed, Mr. Lee. We have a long journey ahead."

Robert, Edna and Frank Lee

The New Yorker

Chapter 27

The Lees joined up with Joseph Chiarini, the owner of the Royal Italian Circus. Chiarini opened in San Francisco on August 7th for a two-week stand. The Chiarinis, along with the Wallenda and Knies families, were among the greatest circus families of all time. They showed in South America all of 1878. It had been the only circus to show in California in '79 and touched only the one base.

Chiarini made all the plans for his large company for an extended tour of New Zealand, Australia, India, British Burma, before returning home. It would take many months, so he engaged space on a sailing vessel, extra services, and extra help from its crew. "I'll need sleeping quarters in cabin class for the ten members of my staff and their families," he said to the captain. "The others can make do in steerage section."

"I'll be able to accommodate you," said Captain Cobb.

"And we'll also need to bring on our fancy show horses."

"It's up to you, Mr. Chiarini, as to how many you bring aboard, as long as you don't overload the ship."

"We'll have other equipment, too."

"I'll have everything ready for you."

"Thank you, Captain, and good day."

The Lees performed for Chiarini in San Francisco, both Lavater and Rosa having starring roles. The company was large and they had many animals to care for. Harry was more interested in management and wanted to become the equestrian director. Polly and her husband, August, were also back with the family and going on the tour.

One night after a performance, the family went back to the hotel. Henry asked Lavater and Polly to look after the younger ones while he took Carrie out to see the sights at Portsmouth Square, where the older buildings of the earlier mining days were. As they walked around, all the streets were lit by gas lamps. The fog rolled in, sending an eerie light from the places of amusement and over the glaring torches carried by the small vendors and card tricksters. When they reached one of the famous old restaurants, they stood outside and looked up at its wrought iron balcony and ornate doorway. They sniffed at the luscious aromas of broiled quail, fine game, delicate punch and succulent French cooking, then walked inside.

"See why I like this town, Carrie?"

"Because of all the good food?"

"Yes, San Francisco has wonderful places to eat, a truly cosmopolitan city, one of the greatest of the world."

"The discovery of gold certainly made this part of the country famous, didn't it?"

"Yes. People came here from all corners of the earth. Those early days were very exciting. You can't imagine the activity here. It was wild. It was a wonderful place to be."

They left the harbor on October 23rd, 1879 aboard the "City of New York." Henry planned to have Carrie and the little ones visit his family in Australia while he continued on with the circus. Their oldest daughter, Emma, stayed on with her grandmother in Los Angeles. The two little ones, Frank and Edna, were on tour with them. Frank could look after himself, but little Edna had to be watched constantly, for she was just learning to walk.

As the anchor was pulled, a salute was fired; they slowly left the harbor and with fine weather, put out to sea.

On board ship, the Lees were busy from morning until night, but for many passengers on board there was nothing to drive away the dull monotony of the voyage but quarrelling and lovemaking.

One evening on board ship, after the animals had been fed and bedded down, Henry and Joseph, a small man, with dark hair and mustache, found a rare moment to sit and talk.

"Well, Henry, it's good just to sit and enjoy the sunset."

"Yes, Joseph, it is."

"What did you think of my wife's performance in San Francisco?"

"One of the best! Beatrice is lovely on horseback.

"I've heard your family goes back a way in the circus business," remarked Henry.

"Yes, around 1603."

"The Lees go back a long way, too. In England there was a Lee and Harper stall at Bartholomew Fair as early as 1721. On one occasion, Lee's partner, Harper, was arrested for vagrancy and taken before the magistrate for performing at Southwark Fairs, Bartholomew and Drury Lane. He appealed the decision on the grounds he was a householder of Westminster, a freeholder of Surrey, an honest man who paid his debts and injured no man. Harper was discharged on his own recognizance to be of good conduct. He left Westminster Hall amidst the acclamation of several hundred people."

"How many performers in your family, Henry?"

"Lavater, Hercules and two other brothers, Tom and Theodore. Theodore, while riding one or more fiery steeds, can make extraordinary leaps, gaining the admiration of the audience. I'm also pretty proud of my own two girls, Polly and Rosa. Not too many people can ride bareback, especially without using a pad, but they can."

"I'm sure I can count them on one hand. I once worked with a man by the name of John Glenroy, never used a pad. Said he knew your brother. That was in 1855."

"Yes. That must have been Lavater. The last time we were together he had two girls."

"Well, his family has grown. When John was with him he had his wife, two girls and two boys."

"I'm glad to hear he has a couple of boys."

"Yes, your brother and his family were working with John at Santo Espiritu, Cuba, but left the company at Cardenas. They were only with him a few days. Then John and his partner joined up with us. John was one of the proprietors of the company, a small man, didn't weigh much more than a hundred pounds, but he certainly could ride! They supplied the wagons, twenty horses and themselves; we supplied five ring horses and ourselves."

"We were in Cuba just last year," said Henry. "Beautiful country, isn't it?"

"But hot," replied Joseph. "We were at Puerto Principie on April 2nd of that year. We started on horseback for Havana, a ride of three hundred fifty miles, and one of the worst rides I've ever undertaken. John lost seventeen of his pack horses and the horse he rode in the ring. I lost my best ring horse, all because of the heat and the poor roads. When we got to Havana, we engaged ox carts to carry our baggage. Then my wife, daughter, our groom, and I, all got yellow fever. Our groom was so bad he was taken to the hospital. The rest of us got all right on our own."

"You fared better than we did," said Henry, thinking of the child they lost. But Henry turned his head and Joseph didn't pursue it.

"The heat in Cuba was very hard to bear at times. We were in Havana six weeks and never slept indoors, always outside in a hammock, swinging from the trees. If we couldn't find a tree, we put up stakes and slung the hammocks there."

"Reminds me of our early days in the gold country," said Henry. "Sometimes we used to sleep in hammocks there, too."

"Far cry from what we are planning now, isn't it?"

"Then Glenroy went to work for George de Haven and that was the last I ever heard of him."

"Over the years you've worked with the great ones, haven't you Henry?"

"Yes, Ducrow, Wallett, Worrell, Latrop, Whittaker—they all had a whirl in the gold country."

"I'm sure nothing has had a greater impact on the world than the discovery of gold."

"I wonder how historians will write about what took place on the stages and in the arenas—I'm proud to say I was a part of that great scene."

After their long voyage, the country of New Zealand was wonderful to behold. While the circus performed, Carrie and the small children stayed in hotels. Henry divided his time between family and the performances. Carrie had time to relax and write to her sister Jenny in Los Angeles. She had been on the high seas when Jenny celebrated her twenty first birthday, so she sent her a belated letter with a poem printed on it:

Birthday

Another year has brought again
The cycle of thy birth
Adding a new link to the chain
That binds thee to the earth.

Oft may this day with joy return
With nought a care or sorrow
Till happy age at last may yearn
For hope's eternal morrow!

My dear sister:

You will not receive this until about the first of January. Nevertheless, I send to you for your birthday a hope you may see many more and may they be brighter than the past.

Mr. Lee has sent for you for your birthday a collection of school books which they use in the schools of New Zealand. It will be quite a little library for you. I hope you will be pleased with them. Mr. Lee says that when we go to Australia we will send you some of their books. You will pay nothing for we have paid all.

Enclosed you will find a few postage stamps for your collection that we had left and will have no earthly use for.

Have they ever found my prayer book at home? You have no idea how much I miss it. I'm surprised to discover how many Catholics there are here, all the elite are Catholic.

Frankie was seven years old on the 27th of November. You remember the rash he had that made him so sick? I had a good English doctor and he cured him. He is now in splendid health. I hope and trust to God he will not be sick anymore.

Dear sister, answer this to Melbourne, Australia, care of Chiarini Circus.

Good bye and God bless you all. From your affectionate sister,
Carrie Lee

When they arrived in Australia they anchored at Hobson Bay, afterwards landed at Williamstown, a distance from the city of about eight miles. Henry hired a hackney for his family, and they continued on into town. Melbourne was built of brick and stones and the landscape very much like that of England. The handsome granite fronts of many of the houses would be considered an ornament in either London or Paris. The use of the city was most striking and thoroughly English. They continued on out into the suburbs.

"This is what it was like, the same kind of countryside where I grew up," Henry said to Carrie. "These beautifully laid out grounds and superb scenery are just like our old English domains."

"It's a far cry from California, our desert country where we have no trees and barren hills. This is beautiful, Henry."

They went to Sydney, which was the largest as well as the oldest city. It had the most magnificent of all the ports in the world, even more handsome than San Francisco, and Carrie thought that could never be surpassed.

They made their second Australian landfall at the Heads, with the long blue harbor behind them and headed toward the city that turned her smiling face to the sea. Henry and Carrie were on deck as they entered a break in the coast, a narrow passage, hardly a mile wide and through it they entered the harbor. All around them were ships everywhere. In the background their eyes fell on the bright green verdure of the surrounding country, the terraced garden walks, the city stretching along the shore and on the heights in the most magnificent manner. Henry pointed in the direction of the lower portion with its many churches, cathedrals, and public buildings.

An enthusiastic passenger standing next to them as they stood at the rail looking at the sights, said loud enough for them to hear, "In summer, these waterways are an intense blue, and the air is a golden haze. In the winter and autumn under cloud, the water is opal green, and the shores seem to flow into it."

"He must live here," said Carrie.

"I'm sure he does," Henry agreed.

After docking, Carrie waited while Henry made arrangements for a hackney to take her and the children for a drive, for he wanted them to see as much as possible of this beautiful country, so very much like his own. They saw gardens laid out in the most attractive manner, passed fountains spurting forth their refreshing streams. Their hackney shook as it crossed one of the many bridges. Windmills dotted the countryside. "There's a great deal of trade going on here," said Henry.

They passed flashy equipages with their coachmen and footmen with armorial bearings tawdrily painted on their carriages.

"Those are decorated more than my circus wagons," remarked Henry.

"Yes, they are flashy."

"To think many of these people had been the dregs of society in England," said Henry. "I wonder how many of them had been caught stealing sheep or were released from a cell in Old Bailey to be sent here. But, don't ever mention that. You don't know whose corns you might step on."

They passed the Lunatic Asylum, a magnificent structure of granite, several storys high.

As they rode along, Henry again spoke up, "Carrie, I've been thinking, it's time for me to step down, look after the careers of the younger children, especially Robert and Rosa. They're beginning to show great promise."

"I think you're right, Henry. It's time Harry had his chance at being head equestrian director. This way, he will get more recognition.

"I'm going to speak to Joseph right away," said Henry.

Harry beamed, for this was one of the most prestigious jobs in the circus and he was anxious to have a chance to move up.

Henry made plans for Carrie, Rosa, little Frank, and the baby Edna to go to Adelaide to stay with his brother-in-law at his country estate while the circus toured. Carrie was expecting and Henry thought she needed the rest. Rosa was with them because Henry wanted her to have some formal education, the Burtons having a governess who could help her with her studies. Henry took them to the train station and left to join the others at the circus grounds.

Carrie and the children arrived at Adelaide on March 3rd. Henry Burton, Henry's brother-in-law, was beautifully attired, huge diamond hanging from his watch fob, was there to meet them at the train. They rode through town. Adelaide was decidedly a handsome city and had more the appearance of a quiet, well-organized, regularly built English town, of all the towns they visited. Henry Burton pointed out the government house which was very imposing, situated in the center of magnificent grounds, tastefully and elegantly laid out. They passed several handsome churches, two theaters, and several stylish public buildings, and continued on to Burton's Red Banks estate, a quarter of a mile from the train station. As they rode along, Carrie's brother-in-law started talking.

"Soon after Margaret and I arrived in Australia, I went into business for myself. With three of my associates we formed a vocal quartet and opened at the Royal Hall in Sydney in January of 1850, all under vice-regal patronage. I had mostly equestrian events and introduced the first hippodrome track here."

"That was some feat."

"Yes, it was. In '73 Bird and Taylor, another group of performers, bet two hundred pounds on the best of seven events to be judged by three Adelaide gentlemen. I took him up on it. We had all sorts of acts: bareback riding, gymnastics, juggling, vaulting, clowning, acts using our trick performing dogs and monkeys, and we won. Then they wanted to challenge again, and we won that time too. Margaret died right after that."

"Henry told me you hadn't been here long before she died."

They arrived at Red Banks, which was located along the run of the Murray River.

"This is where we winter and train our horses," Henry Burton said as he pointed out the horses grazing in the pasture.

"Beautiful animals," said Carrie as they pulled up to the house. "I guess Henry has trained a few horses in his day."

"Yes, he trained some for the military."

"Were they for the servicemen and used in the Civil War?"

"He didn't say, but it was around that time. It's incredible what his horse Mazeppa can do."

"Was Henry ever held up by bandits?"

"Not to my knowledge, although it was a constant concern because the California mining towns were noted for them."

"We were, when we toured the Victoria diggings. We were held up by brush-rangers near Queanbeyan, but they released us after the ladies gave an equestrian display for them. We were stopped a second time on the Lachlow when we were mistaken for a gold escort, but we were allowed to go through when they found they were mistaken. If the truth were known, we were probably carrying more gold than was in the mail bags carried by the coach they planned to hold up."

"That must have been frightening."

"Yes, it was. Have you ever heard of Lola Montez, Carrie?"

"Yes, I have. She was performing in Grass Valley when Henry's circus was there."

"She was here too. Did a spider dance, kind of odd, people didn't care too much for it."

They pulled up to the house which was set back from the road, a large, three-story house with a wooden veranda in the front and several small trees. Carrie thought their orchard and flower garden showed signs of bygone beauty and were sorely in need of work. It made her think they were not quite as prosperous as she had been led to believe.

They were greeted at the door by Fanny, Henry's second wife, and shown the lovely home. It, too, showed signs of neglect and an absence of servants, but the hospitality was most sincere and inviting.

"You have a wonderful variety of fruit trees on your property, Fanny."

Yes, we do. Almost any kind you'd like. We also have a winery."

"How much property do you have?"

"Sixty acres in all," she replied. "The Murray River runs out behind the house. I'll show it to you later."

"You call your estate 'Red Banks'; an interesting name."

"Yes, we called it that because of the color of the soil," said Fanny as she was showing Carrie to her room.

"Why don't you lie down and relax a bit, and I'll take the children to the kitchen for refreshments."

"Thank you, Fanny, I could use some rest."

"How many children do you have, Carrie?"

"Henry was married twice before, so he had a large family when I married him. Seventeen in all."

"My Henry even has him beat. He was one of twenty!" Then she closed the door.

The following Thursday, Henry Burton took his wife, Fanny, their three girls and Carrie and her children into the bush to visit the Swiders. The girls all danced, and Rosa sang while Mrs. O'Hagen, the Swiders' governess, played the piano.

At eleven, Henry drew the social gathering to a close. He went out to get the team, but they had been turned loose in the paddock and could not be caught. The Swiders lent him one of theirs.

Because it was very cold, Fanny insisted that Carrie and her little one, Edna, stay overnight.

Mr. Burton and Rosa and Frank returned for them the next morning. On the way home, Mr. Burton took them farther into the bush and showed them the kangaroos.

The following day, they again went riding in the country. Carrie saw the Bushmen and was rather shocked to see they scarcely had any clothes on.

At Red Banks estate, they spent their time entertaining each other. Fanny enjoyed reciting verses; they walked to the bond, to the back water of the river, where there were many lagoons. They gathered cockatoo and parrot feathers and watched the Svec, both black and white. The white ones were considered sacred.

After dinner they sat in the parlor and talked.

"Mr. Lee told me you left England for Australia near the same time his family left for America. Why did you choose it? A fine choice I might add."

"We stayed in England because of our engagements; then we learned of the gold rush in Australia, so we came directly here. I trained as a ringmaster under Charles Cook in England. We arrived on December 23rd, 1849. Then we went to Sydney in January of 1850. We played at Melbourne, Launceston, and Hobart town, then toured Parramatta, Liverpool and as far as Goulburn. I opened a riding school at Sir Joseph Bank's Hotel in Botany Bay."

"Henry told me Charles Cook was famous."

"Yes, he was. We opened our first circus in an amphitheater that seated two thousand people, a grand equestrian fete-a-la Vauxhall. We had Maitland-bred ponies and several horses that I trained."

"Mr. Lee uses ponies in his acts."

"In Parramatta we performed three times a week, doing 'Billy Button's Ride to Brentford.' Have you heard of that?"

"Yes, I have."

"When is Henry going to settle down, Carrie?"

"This will be our last trip for sure. We hope to go back to Los Angeles. My family is there. Mr. Lee plans to purchase a ranch and raise horses. We have wonderful grazing land there, some of the most fertile soil in the world. Great herds of cattle have roamed the hills for over a hundred years."

Henry Lee returned to Adelaide, and a ball was planned in their honor. Sunday evening was spent with a moonlight walk and reading aloud, then time was given for the preparation for the social, a gala to introduce Henry and Carrie to the Burton's many friends. A string quartette was hired, the food prepared, and the garden put in good order.

When the evening arrived, Fanny rushed up to Carrie's room holding a small box. "Carrie I want you to wear my diamonds."

"Oh, Fanny! Are you sure? Shouldn't you be wearing them?"

"No, Carrie, this is your night. I won't take no for an answer.

"I'd be honored, Fanny. You're so kind."

In the next room little Edna was being dressed in her pink dress, with ruffles trimmed in white lace, pink stockings and gold boots. Her hair was done up in a French roll, puffed in front with a little sprig of oleanders and white jasmine. The older girls took Edna downstairs to the music room. It was no wonder she was called "The Belle of the Ball," darting around, happy because her father was home. He picked her up and held her in his arms. Then with the exuberance of youth she wiggled to get free. Henry walked over to Carrie, took her hand and as they moved on to the dance floor the dancing began. After staying a few more days, enjoying the rest and relaxation Henry announced they were leaving.

Lavater's Leaping Act

Chapter 28

From Australia, the circus went to India. As they headed toward the shore at the coastal town at Madras, they were tossed about by the fearful force of the waves, making it a dangerous place to land. At Madras they gave magnificent performances, then continued on to Calcutta, the "City of Palaces." Standing on deck they caught the first view of it from a bend in the river. As they approached the shore, their eyes took in the matchless beauty of the city itself. About a half-mile from the anchorage, the whole splendor of the city burst into sight.

Standing on deck, Carrie held little Edna's hand and Henry kept a watchful eye on Frank. They looked over the vast domes of the government house, with its superbly ornamented gates. They gazed at the lofty towers of their many places of worship. In the distance were public offices and magnificent mansions of purest white stucco. Nearby the many fine landing places were surrounded by a forest of masts and barges lying ready for hire.

After landing they proceeded to the palace itself, passing a well-watered plain, called a "maidaun." On one side ran an aqueduct, on the other, a fine wide road crowded with every style of vehicle and many horsemen as well.

The family was invited to stay within the palace walls during the time of their engagement. As soon as they arrived, they were shown to their quarters overlooking the Indian Sea. The gracious living, the exotic food and the elegant quarters were more than Carrie had ever dreamed of.

The Indian pages couldn't take their eyes off Rosa, now seventeen years old, her lovely tiny fairylike body of perfect proportions, her poise and charm, her fair complexion, her lovely, light brown hair, curling softly around her face and falling to her shoulders.

Frank's eyes were as big as saucers, as they walked across the courtyard looking at all the beautiful sights around him. Edna holding her mother's hand ever so tightly, was all full of wonder. Her mother, too, was enthralled by everything she saw.

In their private quarters, Carrie's every wish was her command. She never had such pampering in all her life. At home her mother had Jesse and Arturo, but they were like members of the family. They had always gone about doing their own chores, not standing around waiting to respond to her every wish, as did the servants here.

One day while Carrie was walking across the courtyard, she saw a young prince. He caught her unaware. She smiled at him; he smiled back. She curtsied and he bowed and then she quickly walked back to her private quarters. She was embarrassed. Had she responded correctly, or had she made a fool of herself? She couldn't speak to him, for she didn't speak his language, nor did she have Henry to lean on, for he was in town looking for a Masonic Lodge. He had been told the Masons were very active in Calcutta, and he wanted to make arrangements for setting up performances for Robert and Rosa.

The circus was doing a fabulous business; people were coming from miles around to view the grand affair. They were well received, and the gate receipts far exceeded even their wildest dreams. The highlight of their stay was their command performance before the Maharajah. The performers were all decked out in their very best.

With the fanfare of bugles and the roll of the drums, the arena doors were opened and the chariots came dashing around the track, followed by the Grand Cavalcade, led by Lavater Lee, while their beautiful ladies and handsome gentlemen followed. Following the overture, the clowns entered the arena, executing somersaults, cartwheels, handstands, talu flips, somersaults from a standing position, feet to feet, until performers were doing fifty to sixty at a time. Then Harry, the expert horseman, came driving in behind thirty-five horses dashing around the hippodrome track at top speed, a spectacular event. This was followed by a trapeze act. Added to the company were a tiger trainer and his clan of Bengal tigers.

Then Robert and Rosa entered the hippodrome track juggling and riding bareback. Polly's husband, August, the clown, kept everyone laughing with his funny tricks, presenting a performance impressive even to the Maharajah.

Then finally the grand finale was about to begin. Lavater the leaper, stood at the top of the incline board, ready to leap over fourteen horses standing side by side, one of the most daring, graceful and thrilling acts in all circus entertainment. Lavater was now at the height of his career, among the elite of the acrobats. With the aid of the incline springboard, he was about to leap over the horses, execute two somersaults in mid-air then land on the pad beyond. All eyes turned toward him. The crowd quieted down.

All his family, his parents, his brothers and sisters, stood below, not moving, giving their full attention to the act. Then he glided down the board, picked up speed, and went soaring over the horses. He executed the two somersaults, cleared the last horse and landed in an upright position before a wildly cheering crowd.

This whole fairyland adventure would have been a dream come true had it not been for the epidemic of smallpox which caused havoc over the countryside and invaded the palace grounds. One of the circus men, Charles Warner, became very ill and died, so they left him in Calcutta, but the circus had a schedule to keep, so they continued on their way to another town, another place.

They went on to Rangoon, British Burma. They weren't always invited to stay at the royal palace as they were in India, but accommodations were always comfortable, if not lavish. Henry made arrangements for a suite of rooms at the Hotel Burma.

While in British Burma, the heat became unbearable, and the crowds were too much for Carrie, so she stayed pretty much to the hotel with the two younger children, Frank and Edna. Carrie started feeling poorly. This was most alarming because her time was at hand to give birth, and unexpected because up until then she had been in robust health.

Even though Carrie rested much of the time, she didn't feel at all well. Then she came down with the chills and had to take to her bed. Henry became worried and called in a doctor. After the doctor examined her, he went into the parlor where Henry was waiting,

"Sit down, Henry, I need to talk to you." Henry sat on the sofa and gestured for the doctor to join him.

The doctor lowered his heavy body next to Henry. There was no mistaking the concern on his face. "I'm afraid Carrie has more than just carrying the baby to worry about, Henry. Carrie has Bubonic Plague."

"How can you be sure?" Henry blurted out, losing all control.

"She has a boil under her arm, it's plain, as plain as can be," his voice rising.

"Oh, no!" he cried out. "I thought because she's carrying the baby, she was just tired. Is there anything you can do?"

"There is nothing that can be done, Henry." Now the doctors voice was barely above a whisper, "There is no cure. No, Henry, I'm afraid she's going to die."

"She hasn't even been out. She's been here all the time!" he cried.

"She could have gotten it from anyone, someone here at the hotel."

"Oh, my God! Oh, no. I love her so!"

"I know, she's such a beautiful young lady, and I'm sure she means the world to you."

"I don't know if I can go on without her, but I must. We have two small children."

"And you need to keep the little ones out of her room. It's very contagious."

"I'll see to that."

"I know this is a frightful time to mention it, but there are so many cases of the plague in the city that caskets are very scarce; they're hard to come by. If you don't get one right away, when the time comes it won't be available."

Henry sat there, with downcast eyes, muttering to himself, "I understand. I'll take care of it right away." The next day Henry purchased the coffin, knowing the gravity of his wife's condition and kept it in the hallway. Each day Carrie grew weaker. Henry sat at her bedside hour after hour, holding her hand, not talking, just sitting there. Small native boys waved large palm leaves over her to keep her as cool as possible. Little Frank and Edna peeked in at their mother and were in awe of the palm leaves going back and forth and wondered about the box in the hall outside.

Then on May 10th, 1881, Carrie gave birth to a baby boy, a

stillborn, and being so weak she died. The box was brought in from the hall and placed on a drape-covered stand in the parlor.

"That's the box that was in the hall," said Edna.

"Yes, dear. It's a coffin," said Polly. "Your mama died. She has already gone to Heaven, just her body is in it," she said as she stroked little Edna's hair, tears streaming her face.

That night the family knelt in front of the coffin. There was: Rosa, Harry, Lavater, August and Robert all reciting the rosary. Little Edna sensed something was wrong though not comprehending its importance, not knowing the impact on her life. Next to her was her big sister, Polly, who was ever so kind and loving with her arm around her. Her brother Frank, was nearby whimpering and calling for his mother. Her father was off in the corner by himself kneeling, his head buried in his hands. When Edna started to go to him Polly held her back, "You stay with me, Edna, let Daddy be; he needs to be by himself."

The rosary went on and on, the priest standing near the coffin, his eyes closed, reciting, and the mourners joining in. Finally when it was over, Polly said to her, "Edna, it's time you went to bed. I'll sit with you a while. You come along, too, Frank," and they left the room.

At half past seven the next morning, Polly and Rosa dressed Edna in her pink dress with ruffles trimmed in lace, pink stockings and gold boots, and checked with Frank to see that all was in good order. Polly fed the children and later stayed with them in the parlor while they waited for the others to join them.

Their father walked in, walked over to the coffin, and touched it ever so tenderly. Tears streaming down his face, he walked over to little Edna and picked her up and held her in his arms.

Just then the priest came in with Harry and Lavater and other men from the circus troupe. They picked up the coffin and carried it out. Her father handed Edna over to Polly and followed, then Edna and Frank, their hands held by Polly, were next, then Rosa and Robert behind.

Outside the hotel a wagon holding the coffin draped with a black cloth and two fancy carriages were waiting. Her father helped them in and they headed for the town Roman Catholic Cathedral for Mass. The men who had carried out the casket were in the second carriage.

After the Requiem Mass, Polly took the children back to the

hotel, and the others continued on to the Roman Catholic Cemetery.

That afternoon a performance went on as usual, but after it was over they returned to the hotel and sadness again fell over the household.

Carrie was thirty-one years old when she died, and Henry grieved for his lovely wife. Henry was in his late sixties, getting along in years. He worried about his two little ones in case something should happen to him. He talked it over with Lavater.

"I'm willing to look after them, Father. I plan to go to England. I want to live in Southampton, with other members of our family. I'd make a good home for them there."

"Thank you, Lavater, but I'm in good health, and I plan to keep them as long as possible. I just need to know they will be taken care of, should I be unable to see them through."

Joseph Chiarini wanted to return to America and made arrangements for the circus to make the homeward circuit. Lavater, Harry, Rosa and Robert wanted to stay on performing with other troupes. August and Polly wanted to return to the States so Polly could have her baby in America, but Henry felt he was only getting in the way. They were all now fine performers and ready to be on their own.

"Well, Henry, what do you plan to do?" asked Joseph.

"I think I'll part company. I plan to return to Australia, perhaps join up with my brother-in-law. Circus is all I know, and I could work in management."

When it was time for Henry and the children to take their leave, Lavater again approached his father about taking over the two younger children.

"You know I'd take good care of them, Father."

"I know you would, Son. but, you have your own career. That's enough for you to worry about. They're my responsibility and I'll manage for the present." The two men shook hands. Then with a warm embrace, father and son, said their last farewells. Lavater and the others left British Burma. They continued on. . . another town, another place.

When Henry was up to it, he wrote to the family in Los Angeles to tell them of Carrie's passing, and also to his brother-in-law, Henry Burton, with the intention of returning to Adelaide. Henry didn't hear from the family in California and feared they blamed him for Carrie's death.

The letter Henry received from the Burtons carried the news that they had lost everything in an unsuccessful tour. All their belongings, all their jewels, their diamonds, the gold they had saved from the diggings and Red Banks Estates, all were gone. Burton would have to look elsewhere for a situation and would be on the road. When Henry finished the letter, he put it down, the thought running through his mind, and said to himself, "At least Carrie didn't have to hear this. She was so fond of them"

Henry returned to Australia, taking Frank and Edna with him. On reaching the city of Sydney from the Heads, Henry and his children settled down. He hired a lady to keep house and prepare their meals. And so, three years passed. Henry again began enjoying the peace and contentment of the relaxed life, met friends with whom he could enjoy hunting and fishing. He missed the circus life, but he had two small ones to look after.

It was on a hunting trip that Henry was accidentally wounded. His friends wanted to take him immediately to the hospital, but fearing the worst, he insisted on returning home to make arrangements for the care of his two young children.

Covering his wound so the children wouldn't be alarmed, he helped the hired lady get them ready for travel. He put their few possessions in a handbag, some clothes and a couple of keepsakes for Edna, her mother's diary and her beautiful black fan, and helped them into the waiting carriage, getting in after them.

Frank was inquisitive, but he father was evasive.

"Now, Frank," he said. "I'm going to the hospital. I shouldn't be gone long. I'm going to leave you at the George Street Orphanage. You're to take good care of your sister and I'll be back to get you in a few days, so please don't worry about me."

They continued on, traveling in the direction of Parramatta, the first settlement beyond Sydney Cove, fourteen miles west on the arm of the harbor. As they rode along, Henry absentmindedly gazed at the countryside, looking out at the mellow bricks and placid greens, the jumping off place to the great advance into the interior.

They headed in the direction of the oldest public school, the King's School, that had a church that remembered the chain gangs, and was now being used as an orphanage.

Henry instructed the driver, "Please go down George Street," he said. His pain becoming unbearable. He knew if he left the children at the gate of the institution they would be cared for, and

Frank was now old enough to tell the head matron of their father's condition. They pulled up to the gate, and he helped the children out.

As Henry rang the bell, Frank held his sister's hand. Then Henry talked quietly to Frank.

"Now, Frank, as soon as I get better I'll come back for you. Take good care of Edna and I'll get you as soon as I can, and speak right up when someone answers."

"I will, Father." Then Henry got back in the carriage. Edna looked back at her father, and waved, too young to really understand what was happening—yet sensing she would never see him again. She held on tightly to her brother.

The gate was opened. They walked inside and through the big door into the office and up to where a bespectacled clerk was standing at the desk. "I'm Frank Lee and this is my sister, Edna. My father left us because he had to go to the hospital. He'll be coming after us as soon as he's well."

"Strange that he wouldn't come in and tell us himself," mused the clerk. "Well, never mind, but I do need to know more about you. Where were you born?"

"In America."

"How old are you?"

"I'm twelve. My sister is seven."

"The matron is here and will show you where to go. So, this will do for now."

A woman in a uniform stepped up and separated the children and Edna began to cry. Their hands were parted and Edna was led off to another part of the building. When they got to the dormitory, everybody gaped at her and she found little friendliness or compassion on the part of those in charge. Edna sensed this and it added to her fears.

The children had many chores to perform. The older girls looked after the younger ones. Edna, being seven, was not considered old enough to work, so she was allowed to play in the courtyard.

Frank, on the other hand, had many duties to perform, many of which were too hard on his frail body. He was now expected to work long hours scrubbing floors, for cleanliness was their prime concern. No sooner had he settled in than he was assigned to carry heavy buckets of water, scrubbing from morning till night, day after day, under the watchful eye of the matron.

Days passed; Frank was not allowed to see his little sister and mourned deeply for his parents. After having lost his mother, not knowing the condition of his father weighed heavily on his mind. Now he was left to fend for himself after a life of pampering and living under the best of conditions; if only he could get word to his Uncle Burton, but he was too far away and Frank didn't know how to reach him. Why hadn't anyone come for them? He remembered his grandmother in Los Angeles. Why hadn't she come?

Frank was a forgotten child in a strange land, timid, sensitive, insecure, a handsome boy with dark brown hair and mournful brown eyes. When his father did not return as he promised, Frank feared he would never see him again.

When word reached San Francisco that Henry Charles Lee had died at the Prince Alfred Hospital in Sydney, Australia, the announcement passed by the editor's desk. He called in one of his reporters.

"I want a nice article about this man. He owned a hippodrome here in San Francisco and performed in this city for years. He built the Metropolitan Theatre in Sacramento and toured the mines. I wonder what has happened to his family? Get on it, please." Then he went on to other matters.

The Devlins read about Henry's death in the *San Francisco Star* and wrote to Regina, enclosing the article. It ended with, "He was generous to a fault and no one ever appealed to him in vain. Not withstanding his troubles, hard work and disappointments, he reached a ripe old age before the Reaper garnered him." And so it was said that "Of all the circus men on the Gold Coast, Mr. Henry Charles Lee was the longest lasting and the best liked."

When the family in Los Angeles learned of the death of the children's father, they waited for the letter from Carrie that never came.

"I can't understand this, mother. Carrie wrote me regularly. Why haven't we heard from her?"

"Let's not judge her too harshly," said Regina. "She must be grieving so. We'll get a letter; we must just be patient." And still no letter arrived.

Polly was at the winter quarters in Columbus, Ohio, when she received word that her father had died. She returned to California, went to Stockton, back to the ranch where she was born. It was her job to settle her father's will, but the ranch had been sold. It was still known as the Lee and Marshall Ranch after its illustrious owners, but many changes had been made.

She went to Sacramento only to find that the pavilion had been put up at a sheriff's sale. She had never been told her father had lost it. It was now known as the Metropolitan Theatre. Through years of use it was still being used nightly and considered Sacramento's most important theatre.

When she got to San Francisco, she found the hippodrome had been replaced by another building. The only thing left for her to claim was Mazeppa. She found him in Hayward where her father had made arrangements for his care.

Sell's Brothers Circus was wintering in California and wanted Polly to work for them. This was a happy arrangement for now Polly was at the top of her profession.

The circus was coming to town. Jenny read one of the posters. On the bill was Pauline Lee riding bareback with Bud Gorman the champion hurdler.

They were going to be in Los Angeles on April 24th and 25th. It didn't say anything about the others.

Jenny was so excited she ran home to tell her mother, and they made plans to attend.

When the circus arrived, they were on hand to greet Polly. They found her in her dressing room close by the tent. Polly introduced her husband, Bud, a small man, not an ounce of fat on his body. After meeting Regina and Jenny, he left them, for he sensed it would be a tearful reunion.

"What happened to August, Polly? Did he die?" asked Jenny.

"No, he left. He never wanted the responsibility of a family and after our baby died, he just wandered off. I got a divorce and married Bud."

"How sad!" said Regina. "What did you have, Polly, a boy or girl?"

"A girl."

"I'll light a candle for her. What was her name?"

"Paula," said Polly. "She only lived six months. It just broke my heart. I don't think I could ever have another."

"What of the others?" asked Jenny.

"Oh! Didn't you know? Our mother died in British Burma five years ago."

"Oh, no! Polly, we didn't know," cried Regina. "We've waited all this time for a letter from her. She wrote regularly to Jenny, then nothing."

"I wrote to her in care of Chiarini Circus, but they must have been on the move and being in India the letters were never delivered. We didn't dream she had died before your father." Jenny then gave way to uncontrollable sobs and the women put cold compresses on her forehead.

"Our father had the two smaller ones with him, but I don't know what happened to them. Didn't he write to you about our mother?"

"I'm sure he did," said Regina, "but we never got the letter."

"While our father was with us, he spoke to Lavater about the younger ones. Lavater wanted to take them, but our father wasn't ready to give them up. They must be in Australia somewhere, perhaps with Uncle Burton."

"Oh dear! We must do something about this right away," said Regina, anxious to make arrangements concerning the children. "We must go now, Polly. Write to us, won't you?"

"I will, and I won't rest until you write and tell me the little ones are safe and sound."

It was two sad ladies who left the tent that day to return to the house on Second Street. As they walked along, Jenny said as she kept dabbing at her eyes, "I can accept their father dying, he was old—seventy-one—but Carrie was so young—only thirty-one. She had so many years ahead of her."

Their dentist, Dr. Crawford from the Downey Block, was going to Australia, so Regina went to see him.

"Dr. Crawford, is it true, are you going to Australia?"

"Yes, Mrs. Weinshank, I am."

"Would you mind trying to locate my grandchildren? They could be at Adelaide with my daughter's husband's family, or possibly in Sydney, but I'm terribly worried about them. Do you think you can help?"

"If you have Jenny write down all the addresses where I should inquire, I'll make the rounds. I'll do the very best I can, Regina, and I'll write as soon as I know something."

"Oh! Thank you Dr. Crawford. I'll always be grateful."

"I'm glad to do it. I won't forget your helping me. When I first came to Los Angeles you encouraged people to come to me instead of that barber, what's his name?"

"Peter Biggs."

"That's the one. I always shy away from his place for fear of losing my own teeth. Well, I'll be sure to write. Good-bye, Regina."

"Good-bye, Doctor."

At the orphanage, whenever Edna saw her brother Frank, young as she was, she could see he was getting weaker. Then, finally, she didn't see him at all.

His health deteriorated, he became weak and was finally moved to the infirmary. Even there he made no progress. He had no will to live. A doctor was called in, gave him a good examination. "This boy is exhausted, but I want to look into it more thoroughly," he said. But before the doctor had a chance to study the case, Frank died. The doctor wrote death due to "exhaustion," his only choice of words, for his examination indicated no other cause. The head matron of the orphanage was incensed, but the doctor held to his guns.

"I don't care what you say, this is my opinion, and I'll stick by it." And so he left.

Little Frank was buried in the Catholic Cemetery at Roakwood, without family or friends to say good-bye, only a few short words uttered by the parish priest. His little sister was told only that he had died.

Edna was now eight years old and had many chores to do as well as look after herself. Her life at the orphanage was hard; the work was as strenuous as it had been for Frank. She was timid and shy, and whenever possible kept to herself. All she had in the world was her mother's little brown diary and a beautiful black fan. The fan had a small picture on it outlined in silver and a design of flowers throughout. Her mother had always worn it on a ribbon around her neck. Now that her brother was gone, she had no idea what would become of her.

Back in Los Angeles, each day Jenny or her mother went to the post office in search of news from Dr. Crawford. Finally, one day a letter arrived. Jenny opened it with nervous fingers. "Oh, dear! Listen to this. Our little Frank died in the George Street Orphanage—and from exhaustion. Oh, how dreadful," she said with tears forming in her eyes. Her mother handed her a handkerchief as she continued reading to herself.

"Oh! Mercy me! How can a child die from that? What have they done to him?" Regina kept asking herself over and over while Jenny read on.

Jenny interrupted her thoughts, "But listen to this. This is wonderful news—little Edna is alive, and she is doing well. She's in the same orphanage in Parramatta."

"Thank heavens for that," said Regina. "I'm not wasting any time. I'm going to the church to get help to get her out of there."

"Wait, Mother, I'll go with you," said Jenny as they hurriedly left the house.

They walked into the cool chapel at St. Vibiana's, lit a candle for the children and headed on to the rectory.

"Father, we've heard from Dr. Crawford. My dear grandson has died of exhaustion, if you can believe anything so horrible. His little sister is alive and well, and I want you to make all the arrangements to get her back. Dr. Crawford inquired about the passage, and it will be five hundred dollars."

"Five hundred dollars; isn't that a lot of money? Are you sure you can spare it?"

"I'm well fixed, Father Mora, I'm not concerned about the money. I want that child back here safe and sound in the United States. Money is of no importance when a child's future is at stake."

"All right, Regina, calm down. I'll make all the arrangements. I'll write the church at Parramatta. They'll arrange to get her out. But this all takes a great deal of time. You and Jenny go on home, and you'll know the news the very day I get a reply, I promise you."

Regina gave the priest the passage money. There was nothing more they could do, so they went home.

The headmistress called Edna to her office. A stern woman, but not unkind, "Sit down, Edna," she said as she handed Edna a small bundle of clothes, the ones she wore when she first arrived. "You're going to be leaving. Two men will come to get you—one will be a priest to guarantee your welfare. You're to go with them without question." Mutely Edna accepted the bundle and returned to the dormitory.

Several months passed before the summons came. Late one night she was awakened and told to ready herself. She dressed quickly in the clothes her father had made, too small, but they would have to do. The shoes she couldn't wear, so she bundled them up with her possessions and slipped on the orphanage shoes, hoping they would understand, then quickly left the room. The two men outside the door merely nodded and they were on their way.

The orphanage stood at the foot of George Street near the steamers' wharf. Edna's new guardians took her to a small boat at the wharf, helped her in. Edna put her head in the priest's lap as he rowed and finally fell asleep. It was daybreak before they arrived at the huge ship, with its sails gently flapping in the wind.

The three were greeted on the deck of the ship by the captain and his wife, a plump, motherly-looking woman.

"This is the little girl I'm leaving in your care. Her grandmother, Regina Weinshank, will meet you in San Francisco. I'll write and give her the particulars. This is all costing a lot of money, and I trust you will give her the best of care."

"That I will, Father," said the captain. "That's why I brought my wife along; so she can cook and care for her." Then the priest left in the rowboat, and Edna was left standing on the deck of a strange sailing vessel under the care of the captain, a handsome man with kind blue eyes, set deep in his crinkled face. He took her hand and led her to their quarters and a nice hot meal. After they ate, the captain's wife showed her her bunk, tucked her in, and she quickly fell asleep. The captain gave the order to pull the anchor, and they headed for the open sea.

The captain was busy on his rounds, and Edna seldom saw him. Many times Edna and the captain's wife had meals by themselves, but no matter how tired and overworked he was, the captain was careful to see that all her needs were met.

For some days the trip was pleasant, the sea calm and the wind gentle. Edna ate at the captain's table where she was treated royally. On the warm days the captain let her play on deck. She was beginning to feel a freedom she never expected to find. She helped in the galley, set the table, helped with the bunks, and swept the floor. She took an instant liking for the captain and his wife and expected to live with them always.

At first the wind was still, but as time went on the winds came up, the waves broke over the deck and she was told to remain inside.

Then one day a terrible storm came up, and the water slapped against the boat. The boat rolled. Everything had to be fastened down. The captain and his wife strapped Edna down in bed, and with sorrow in his heart he left the weeping child and returned to the deck to take command, for all his thoughts were on the saving of his ship.

As Edna lay there, whimpering for the captain, she looked up and saw water rushing through the porthole.

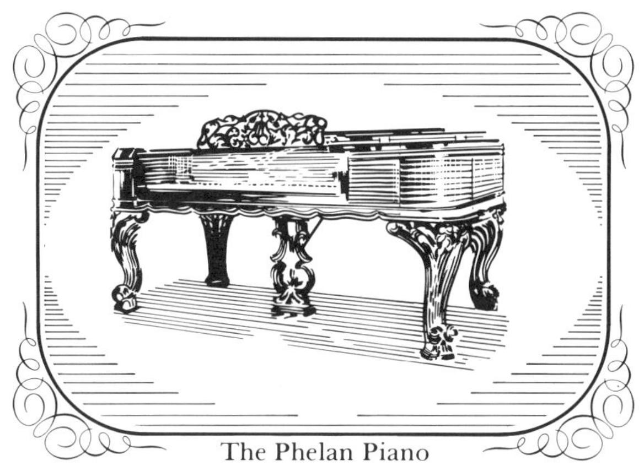
The Phelan Piano

Chapter 29

Little Billy Phelan was only three years old when he started failing. Mary did all she could. She used what medicines she had in her medicine chest, cared for him night and day. While Mary busied herself with the baby, Nell, still a young girl, took over even more of the household chores. In spite of all Mary's loving care, Billy died.

Mary and Tom fixed him up and put his little body in the coffin Mr. Woodward made from lumber on the ranch. The family got into the buckboard and made that long, silent ride to the mission.

There, they were greeted by the Padre, and after the recital of the mass, they took Billy's little coffin into the courtyard, lowered it into the ground. There were Tom and Mary and their children, Dan, Nell, Joe, Annie, now seven, and their little one, Tom, all listening to the priest as he recited the graveside service.

After it was over, Mary said, "I carried that baby nine months, tended to him when he was sick, and now he is gone. No more will we see the likes of him, running around the house, giving the family so much joy."

Tom, knowing how Mary was grieving, said "Come, Mary, let's go home."

On the way back to the wagon, she said, "I'll always miss that little one, but the Lord above must have had a good reason to take him."

"And that's the truth of it, Mary. We must accept God's wishes, and this is the last that will be said of it, for there is work to be done, a living to be made, others to care for, and as time passes, the memory of this heartache will fade. I'm thinking of homesteading a quarter section of land at Castaic, Mary" said Tom trying to get Mary's attention on other matters as he got back into the wagon. "To keep it, I must build or move in a house. I'm thinking that little white frame house on the ranch, the one the Nicholsons live in, would be just the one. We can build another for them. We'll haul it up there and set it down on a secluded spot among the trees."

"What will you do with all that land, Tom?" asked Mary.

"I'll buy cattle and herd them up."

"What will we do for money?"

"Borrow."

"Borrow? Never in all my born days have I heard of such a thing. Just like that, you 'borrow'?"

"Yes. I'm thinking of borrowing enough to buy six hundred head. Marius Meyers wants me to go in with him and put in a hay crop on his ranch."

"Who is Marius Meyers?"

"He's a sheep herder, he was a native of the high Alps near the Franco-Italian border. Before coming to this country, he worked for a man by the name of Bixby and took his wages out in sheep."

"I thought sheep shouldn't graze the same land as cattle," said Mary.

"It's better if they don't, but there are a lot around in this part of the country. Gracian Arranbide and Peter Itcairia have a herd of sheep up on the hill behind us. But getting back to my plan, Pallette, too, wants more grazing land and he wants me to go in with him on that. We're thinking about the high desert country at Rock Creek. Lots of wild horses are up there. The Pallettes are going to file on two sections, I'm going to file on one."

All the Phelan children went to the Ranchito School and were in the same room. One evening while the family was sitting around the table, having supper with the hired hands, Mary started in, "I saw your report card today, Joe, and your grades aren't too good, are they?"

"No, I guess not," he answered.

Mary went on to say, "If you got your marks in clod-throwing you'd be getting much better grades than the ones I saw today."

Everybody laughed. Joe hung his head, his face almost the same color as his flaming red hair.

Right at that moment, Nell stood up to stab a piece of bacon from the far side of the table, and Joe pulled her chair out from under her, thinking this might take the pressure off him. When she went to sit back down, she fell to the floor. Nell went crying from the room. This really got Mary's dander up.

"That does it, Joe. Out to the tank house, and be quick about it. And, Tom, get out there and give him the switching he deserves. I don't want to see either of you back in this house until the job is done, and done proper, now." So, Joe bawling, with his father behind him, hurriedly left the room.

Because all the grades were taught in the one room, the children of all their neighbors—the Richlings, the Pattens, the Pallettes and the Dunlaps—were in the same classroom. The Judson boy, Dan and Nell, were like grown-ups, compared to Joe and his little friend, Jack Lane. It was Jack who thought up most of the devilment. Jack had his little four year old sister, Lulu, with him. The family sent her to school to take care of Jack.

One day, Mrs. Bowers, their teacher asked, "Jack, how old are you?" While he was giving it some thought his little sister jumped up and said, "Jack is six at school and five at home." Then everybody laughed. They knew the family sent Jack to school just to get him out of their hair. Even Mrs. Bowers turned around and snickered to herself.

School was close to the river, and while they were at recess, Jack said, "Hey, Joe, Let's go for a swim!"

"I'm game," said Joe, "when?"

"Right now," Jack replied, and off the two boys went. When recess was over, Mrs. Bowers sent the Judson boy to the door to call them in.

"Hey, you guys had better get on in here—Mrs. Bowers is mighty mad."

The boys acted as if they didn't hear, and they didn't go back to the classroom; instead they picked up their clothes and found another place to swim. After they got tired, they dressed and went home.

On the way to school the next day Joe and Jack decided to go for another swim at the afternoon recess. But, when they got in the classroom and sat down at their desks, Mrs. Bowers had something else in mind. She walked over to the door, locked it and put the key in her pocket.

Then she walked over to Joe. He noticed she had something in her hand.

"Joe, stand up. I'm giving you a switching right here and now, in front of the whole class."

Joe's older sister, Nell, sitting at her desk nearby could have died of embarrassment. Dan, sitting at the back of the room, a big strapping fellow, felt sympathy for his little brother, but knew Joe was getting what he deserved. His sister, Annie, snickered and Tom, a little first-grader, hung his head; he wasn't up to watching such a horrible ordeal.

Joe started to cry, but he got a whaling anyway, one he would never forget, knowing full well he would get another one to match it when he got home. But, as for Jack, it was a different matter. He took his whipping very much in stride.

Several months later, the cattle at the ranch at Castaic were ready to sell. Tom asked, "Joe, would you be liking to go with us to bring cattle down from the ranch? Your ma wants to have Mr. Levi look them over. It'll be rough, sleeping on the ground at night under the stars, but it should be to your liking. We'll be leaving bright and early in the morning because we need to get to the ranch before dark."

When Joe went to bed that night, he was so excited he could hardly sleep. Early the next morning he was up at dawn for breakfast before the others.

All that day they spent in the saddle and stayed over at the ranch that night. The following morning, they were ready to start the drive with 105 in the herd, heading back to the ranch.

Wherever the cattle damaged a fence, it had to be repaired on the spot, which slowed their progress. By the time they reached the valley of San Gabriel, after a week on the trail, the stock was poor and the men were weary. They drove them into the corral at the mission into a large feed lot and closed the gate.

"Well, that's done, but I'm afraid those poor devils lost a lot of fat on the way down, and I'm not too sure they'll bring much of a price," said Tom, "but we'll see." Then they rode on home to the ranch.

A few days later, Dan and one of the Mexicans rode over to the mission and cut out some of the better stock and took them back to the ranch. Joe didn't want to go, he was still too sore from that long hard cattle drive. In fact, he was so sore, he couldn't sit down for a week, and had to take his meals at the sideboard.

Times were hard and Mr. Levi knew how to take advantage of them. So a few days later, when he drove into the yard, after putting his sack of cheese in the barrel on the wagon under the tree he and Mary got down to business, haggling over the price of steers. He purchased some, and left others. The men then cut them out for a later delivery. Mr. Levi then picked up his cheese, got into his buggy and headed back to Santa Ana.

There was always a lot to contend with on the ranch, with such a large place and so much to do. Tom wrote other members of the family in Waverly and invited them to join him on the ranch. His brother, Dan, his wife Ellen and their children, Dan, Jim and Maryanne all arrived. Billy's son, Dan, was with them.

"You know, Dan, your father brought me to this country when I was a lad. It would make my heart glad to see him."

"I know, Uncle Tom, but he said he was too old to come, but wanted to be remembered to you."

Then Tom turned to his brother. "Dan, how do you and your boy keep yourselves apart?"

"They call me Big Dan and my boy Little Dan."

"With Uncle Billy's Dan, that's three and my Dan, that's four. Well, I guess we'll manage."

Tom asked his brother, Big Dan, and his family to live in the little white house on the ranch at Castaic. Near the house was a natural corral that hemmed the cattle in, a protected spot between two hills. The men built a gate and the cattle and horses were securely boxed in.

Tom went to the ranch frequently, mostly by train. Big Dan would meet him with an extra horse, and they rode back to the ranch together. Tom would always spend a few days before returning home.

When the chestnut trees were old enough to bear nuts, they had to be picked every day and put in trays to dry. Mr. Thompson, the postmaster, made up some trays, the first in the valley, so Tom got some from him. After the nuts dried out, they were shoveled into sacks of one hundred pounds each, and Tom had ten sacks.

Tom and Dan loaded them on the wagon and took them to the market in Los Angeles. When Tom went back a few weeks later, he found that few chestnuts had been sold.

"What's the matter?" he asked.

"You flooded the market. There aren't that many people in Los Angeles who eat chestnuts. You better take the rest home, or better still, I know a man by the name of Patrite who says the Italians in San Francisco will buy them. Why don't you talk to him?"

Tom wasn't doing any good there, so he decided to look him up. Patrite was a decent sort of fellow, and friendly. He told Tom, "I have a friend who will sell them all right, in San Francisco, but you'll have to take them to the harbor."

A few days later, Tom and Jack Nicholson loaded the wagon again, drove down to the harbor, made arrangements to place them on a flat boat that took them out to the sailing vessel, waiting in the harbor.

Some weeks later, Tom got a letter at the Thompson house, saying all the chestnuts had been sold.

Tom said, "Joe, let's go see Don Pio Pico. I need to borrow some things." This meant a happy day for Joe. After breakfast, Tom, Dan and Joe went out to the barn and saddled up the horses.

"El Ranchito" was a piece down the road. It wasn't long before they rode into the yard. While Tom and Dan were out by the corral, Joe was left to amuse himself. Joe loved to go there, look around while his father talked to Pete Serrano and the other men. There were always Indians working in the fields to watch. Joe went back to the patio and looked longingly at the womenfolk as they set about doing their chores, and maybe, if he was lucky, they would treat him to one of their buñuelos.

Joe went out to see the huge mill stones by the river that had been used to grind corn in the early days of the ranchos. He found them in the same place they had probably been for many years. Each stone was about three feet in diameter, like an enormous plate, with a hole in the middle to attach it to a beam. The oxen were driven around in a circle, revolving the stones.

After throwing a few pebbles into the river, Joe again went back to the patio and stood around, "Se gusto buñuelo?" asked one of the servants.

"Oh, yes," said Joe, his eyes lighting up. "I'd love to have one. Thank you very much. Muchas gracias." So with buñuelo in hand, off he went to the corral.

The great Don Pio Pico himself was there, talking to Pete and his father. Dan was busy inside lassoing the horses and tying them up. He could hear Don Pio Pico tell his father in Spanish, "Take as many as you like, keep them as long as you need them, and when you are through, just bring them back."

"Gracias, Señor, and I'll take good care of them."

Dan gathered the horses together. He had them haltered to lead back to the ranch. Joe jumped on his horse and tagged along behind, reluctant to leave such a pleasant place, hoping he would soon return.

When they got home, Dan turned the horses out in the corral. They kept a box of loose hay nearby. Joe lured a horse over, gave him a handful of hay, then jumped on. About one bounce and off he went, only to get a face full of manure for his efforts. His dad and brother, Dan, had a good laugh, then Dan stepped in and went to work in earnest breaking the horses.

After the crop had been harvested, Dan haltered the horses to return them to "El Ranchito." As he was doing this, Jack Nicholson came over and Tom took the opportunity to ask for help.

"I need to get some pigeons out of one of Don Pico's rooms and could use some help. Can you give me a hand?"

"Glad to, Tom. When do you want to do it?"

"Right now, if that's all right with you, and Joe, if you want, you can tag along. Jack go on ahead. We'll see you over there."

This proved to be quite a job. The pigeons were nesting and managed to find their way into the adobe through large cracks in the walls. It took a little doing, but finally they chased them all out and boarded up the holes.

After Tom and Jack got the job done, Jack had other chores so he left. Tom went out to the corral. Pete Serrano was branding cattle and the Don was helping him, each holding a reata on a calf. After they released the calf, they walked over to the gate where Tom was standing.

"No tengo sacate para los caballos," (I have no feed for the horses), he told the Don.

"Bien, venga usted por los caballos otra vez cuando usted quierar plantar." (Good, come for the horses again when you need to plant), said Don Pio Pico. Joe was standing there, leaning against the corral gate, taking everything in. "We need to go, Joe," said Tom. "We have lots to do. Muchas gracias, Don Pio Pico."

They had other errands to do, so they drove on, lumbering along with their wagon loaded with sacks of grain. They followed the hills along the river, through the tules and large patches of mustard, to the grist mill.

"You never talk about the saloon you owned with the Don, pa. Why not?" asked Dan.

"I'm not too proud of it, Dan. It was a mistake from the start. The Don wanted me to go in with him and open up a saloon in Bernardino Guirado's grocery store across from 'El Ranchito.' The Don furnished the building, I bought the liquor, and Joe Anderson was the bartender. It was a rowdy bunch of men who went there, and they had cock fights out back. Some of the neighbors complained, so we just shut it down."

"Who built those buildings?"

"The Indians from the mission; after they built Don Pio Pico's adobe, they stayed on; had quite a settlement there."

When they arrived at the grist mill, Dan helped his father unload the grain. They stacked the sacks on the ground near the stones for grinding. Joe waited while his father talked to the man. Then they all headed for home.

As they rode up the driveway at home, his father said, "Joe, you had better go get the wine."

Joe slid down from his horse and headed for the house. He always found the jug in the same place on the back porch, strapped it over his horse, then jumped on himself and off he went.

As he headed out for El Camino Real, he passed the Isbell place. This was where his father came when he needed to borrow equipment. When the Isbells came to California, they were traveling along El Camino Real and stopped at "El Ranchito." Isbell asked if they could stay a few days while his pregnant wife rested. The Don insisted they stay on. All that winter she was cared for by the Don's Indian servants, for not until after her baby was born did her health improve. The Don sold them some property and gave them a start of corn.

As Joe rode along El Camino Real, he looked up and saw an Indian up on the hill. The only ones he had ever seen were the ones at El Ranchito. He continued traveling along over the dirt road.

The Phelans had gotten their wine from Christian Sorenson for years. When Sorenson first came to California, he settled in Los Angeles, went into partnership with Don Abel Stearns and William Wolfskill in building ships, a skill he learned in his native land of Sweden. Later he bought land from Don Pio Pico, settled down farming, made a little wine on the side and started trading with his neighbors. Tom bought his wine from him and Joe went there once a week to pick it up.

As Joe rode into the yard at the Sorenson place, their three little girls were playing tag. Joe went up to the tank house, and the girls followed him. "Can't you stay and play, Joe?"

"I'm afraid not. My ma would skin me alive if I didn't get this wine right back." He didn't want to play tag with little girls anyway, for he looked upon himself as a boy doing man's work.

Christian opened the door to the tank house and let Joe help himself. "I'll just put it on the book, Joe; you'd better get along home."

"Thank you Mr. Sorenson. I saw an Indian up on the hill above the road," blurted out Joe.

"Nothing to worry about, Joe, the Indians around here won't hurt you. But, anyway, go straight home."

Another one of Joe's chores was to get the mail, and this he also did once a week, collecting it at Samuel Thompson's house. Sam kept the mail in the back room. As Joe walked in, he noticed all the mail had been sorted and laid out on a long table. He recognized his father's *Irish World* newspaper. As he picked it up, Mr. Thompson walked in.

"How are you, Joe?"

"Fine, Mr. Thompson. Is this all there is for my pa?"

"Afraid so."

"Well, I guess I'll be going now."

On his way home, Joe thought about Mr. Thompson the postmaster. His father had told him that he brought his family across the plains by oxtrain to the Monte in '52. They were escorted to the river by the vaqueros of Rancho La Puente because Mr. Workman was afraid Indians would attack their wagon. He thought about the Indian he had seen the day before and was glad that Indian wasn't like the ones on the Rowland-Workman Rancho.

As he was going along, his horse stumbled in a chuck hole, and he fell off in front of Bernardino Guirado's blacksmith shop. Andy Broadbent, a big, husky fellow working in the shop, saw Joe, walked out and picked him up and brushed him off.

When Joe got home, Bosco Mills and his wagon laden with goods of all sizes and sorts was in the yard. Joe was in awe of all the wonderful things Bosco had on his wagon. He didn't come around too often, but when he did, his ma stocked up.

"Is your ma home?" asked Bosco.

"She always is. She's in the kitchen," said Joe.

"Don't bother to call her. I'll go in. Maybe I can get a cup of coffee and a bite to eat." And he went in the back door, leaving his team unattended.

Life was peaceful and not very exciting, but for this one

exception—the day the piano arrived. It wouldn't go through the front door, so Tom had some of the hired hands take out a window and put it through that way.

It was a grand instrument, very large with ornate legs, a work of art. Mary selected a spot for it at the end of the parlor.

Word was spread to all the neighbors that the Phelan piano had arrived, and if they were so inclined, they could attend a "sing feast" at the Phelans' that very evening.

People came from all around, driving up in horse and buggy. Mary had plenty of wine and cakes for everyone. It wasn't long before the parlor was full and overflowing. Many had to stand outside on the porch and in the yard.

The man who had sold the Phelans the piano stayed on for a while to teach Nell how to play. He, himself, played beautifully for the folks that night, playing "Silver Threads Among the Gold," "Sweet By and By," "Wait for the Wagon," "When You and I Were Young, Maggie," "My Old Kentucky Home." He played on and on and on, far into the night. It was late when the people got back into their buggies and buckboards and headed for home.

For days following the big event, neighbors stopped in to say how much they enjoyed the music, and the answer was always the same, "As soon as Nell learns to play, we'll have you over again."

"We'll be looking forward to it."

After the man who sold them the piano left, the Phelans made arrangements with Mrs. Hudson to teach Nell. They furnished her with a horse and buggy. They had given her one of their best sorrels which pleased her very much because she came all the way from Pomona, and it took her most of the day to get there. She would spend a night or two, working with Nell during the day. After her stay, Dan would hitch up her horse and buggy, and she drove out of the yard to pay a visit on her next student.

Nell hated the long hours she had to practice, but her mother kept her at it. She really didn't want to play, but with Mrs. Hudson's skill in teaching and Mary's determination to have a pianist in the family, she learned in spite of it.

One day while she was playing, she noticed her father running his fingers up and down on the wall, then slip something underneath the wallpaper. She thought it rather strange, but if her father had a reason for putting something there, the secret was safe with her.

Some weeks later while Nell was practicing, she saw her mother looking at the bulge in the wall. Her mother walked over to it, pulled the wallpaper off and found some money. That night Mary was waiting for Tom and ready for bear.

When Tom walked in the door from Los Angeles, she started in, "And what do you mean by hiding this money?"

"Give it back, Mary. I'm giving it to my sister, Mary, to pay Dan's passage from Ireland."

"We need the money here, Tom."

"She has always been the one to send the money, Mary, and this time I have a mind to help her. Now turn it over and be quick about it."

"Hail, fellow, well met, that's what you are. You're always worrying about the other fellow. Then take your money and get out of my sight!"

"That I will, Mary and I'll come back when you can keep a civil tongue in your head." Then Mary lifted her broom, but Tom was on his way out the door.

A few months later, there was a note posted on the bulletin board at San Francisco harbor, "The long expected 'Daniel Phelan' has arrived" Tom Phelan made the trip to visit his sister, Mary, and to meet his big husky strapping nephew. "Come back with me to my ranch in the San Gabriel Valley, Dan, there's lots to do and you can join the other Dans on the ranch."

"How many Dans do you have?"

"Four right now, you'd make number five. We have my younger brother, Dan, he's there. We call him Big Dan, and his son is Little Dan. Then we have your Uncle Billy's Dan, and my son is just Dan."

"And if I join you, what will you call me?"

"Well, being fresh off the boat, we'll call you 'Irish Dan'."

"Sounds all right to me."

"Well, Irish Dan, I have to head for home. You think it over, and if you want to join us, you're certainly welcome."

Tom had only been home a short time when he got word that Irish Dan could be picked up at the station at Fulton Wells. Tom was so excited he went himself, rather than pass the job on to someone else. Tom was so proud, he went around to all the neighbors saying, "My nephew from Ireland is here," and everybody had to go to the ranch to take a good look at him.

There was always plenty of work on the Phelan place, thicket clearing, post hole digging, walking behind the plow, calf flanking and horses to tend to. The Phelans always kept a lot of help.

From time to time, Tom worked the fields with the hired help, driving mules. He used four of them to make ditches in order to irrigate the crops, getting his water from the zanja that ran along the ranch. If there was going to be a dispute over who was to use the water and for how long, Tom wanted to be able to keep it, so he always picked up his breech loader on the way out the door.

After irrigating, the weeds sprouted. Tom took a bunch of Mexicans out to the fields and worked, hoeing the weeds. Every time they came to the end of the row, the Mexicans sat and smoked their cigarillos and Tom listened and joined the conversation. Sometimes Tom would get one of his coughing spells.

"Señor, what is the matter?"

"Oh, Alex, I've had this cough a long time, ever since the war."

There was always a lot to do on the ranch. Many men were hired, but it didn't mean Tom's children had it easy. Dan took care of the livestock, Nell helped her mother in the house, and Annie had little chores to do. It was Joe's job to knock the kernels off the broom straw to get it ready for the brooms.

To do this, Joe drove a horse in a circle, turning a spiked wheel that cleaned the straw. Then he scooped it up and put it in bins where it could be used later to feed the fowl on the ranch. Joe hated this work because a lot of dust was raised and it caused him to itch all over.

There was one barn that was used only for broom making, and the Chinamen stayed in it, working from morning till night. It was a forbidding place and the children were told to stay out. It was Mr. Woodward's job to supervise the Chinamen while they made the brooms, a job he learned at Waverly.

When a load of brooms was ready for market, they loaded them on the wagon and took them either to El Monte or Los Angeles. When they went to El Monte, Joe was never allowed to go. There were too many killings there, at least one a week, sometimes more. His father was afraid he might be hit by a stray bullet. El Monte was settled by the Texas Rangers, a tough bunch of men, quick to pull the trigger. Whenever there was more trouble in Los Angeles than the sheriff could handle, it was always the "Monte" boys who were called upon to help. They were always ready for a good fight.

The Chinamen were in the barn making brooms, the Mexicans

were handling the brick, there were those who cared for the stock, planted the crops, cared for the trees. But it was the Irishmen, the Phelans, who kept things going, kept everyone at his task.

The Chinamen kept out of the way of the Mexicans; the Mexicans pretty much tended to their own business, so in spite of the different nationalities and customs, all went smoothly.

But poor little Joe didn't fare too well. One day after he finished cleaning the broom straw, he climbed a tree, hoping to tease the Chinamen when they came out of the barn. He didn't have long to wait. Beneath him walked two, their long black braids protruding underneath their skull caps, wearing their padded jackets, cloth slippered feet and pantaloons. Joe started out making funny faces. One of them didn't like it and grabbed a pole. He didn't care if he was the son of his boss man. He gave Joe a terrible jabbing, making Joe jump from limb to limb to get out of his way. He kept after him, giving him blow after blow.

Then Joe kicked up a terrible storm and started crying. The Chinaman finally gave up and left, and Joe got down. He ran for the house, knowing full well it would be the last time he would ever tease them.

When he got to the kitchen, his mother was busy baking bread. Nell was stirring at the stove, leaning over to put a chunk of wood in the fire, and Annie was churning the butter. They all looked up at Joe, red-faced, his pants torn, tears streaming down his face.

Mary spoke up, "I knew that would happen some day, Joe. You've been teasing the Chinamen, haven't you?"

"One of them kept poking me. I thought he'd never quit."

"Well, serves you right. You got what you asked for. Now maybe you'll leave them alone. Get along now and clean up. We'll be eating before long."

Joe didn't want to go back to the pump house, so he walked outside, rubbed his face on his shirt and went back to the kitchen where his little sister, Annie, was struggling with the butter. Mary turned around from the stove, "Don't just stand there gaping, Joe, give her a hand."

When he took over the cream, it was still swishing around inside the glass container; the little yellow chunks of butter were beginning to appear. He took over just when it got harder to turn the crank, turning till his arm ached, but knew he couldn't quit.

Mary walked over to the table, "You young ones don't know how lucky you are, having all this butter to eat. In Ireland, a man's wealth is determined by how much butter he can spread on his bread."

"It's done now, Ma. Just one chunk. I get to quit now, don't I?"

His mother took over, squeezed out the water, washed it off and wrapped it in a tight container. "Here Joe, put this butter in the barrel out by the side of the house under the tree. See, Annie, you were lucky your brother walked in at just the right time."

The Jonathan Bailey Home

Chapter 30

There was always something to do at home. The chores were never all done, and Mary saw to it that everyone was always busy. There was water to carry from the river, apples to be stored away in the pump house and culled over from time to time, discarding the spoiled ones. There were nuts to pick, livestock to feed, eggs to be gathered, and Mary had to oversee it herself. It was Mary who really ran the ranch. She did all the business, kept the books, borrowed the yearly expense money and made many of the decisions.

In the kitchen Mary would be busy baking bread. Nell, yet a young girl, worked alongside her mother, from early morning until late at night. The boys were never expected to make their beds or pick up after themselves, for that was all left up to Nell.

One spring morning, Joe went with his brother, Dan, to get Marianna Exarat at Puente around the hill, to sew for the family. She always stayed a few days at the ranch and made all the clothes they would need for the following year. She traveled light, didn't need a satchel, for she kept her nightgown in her bustle and was satisfied with the clothes on her back 'til it was time for her to return home.

Mariana got right down to work. She threaded the sewing machine and started out by sewing for Mary. Other women wore their skirts to the floor, but Mary wanted hers to clear the ground, which was unheard of in those days.

The only one Marianna didn't sew for was Tom. He wore store clothes. As always, he was off somewhere. This time he was with Ory Isbell, putting a homestead on land up on the hill above the Thomas Ranch. They went to look the property over.

"Beautiful up here, isn't it, Ory?"

"Yes. And look at the ocean way out there."

"Just a while back, this entire valley was under water."

"How are we going to use this land, Tom?"

"We'll have to do something, at least put a house on it. That's the requirement for all homestead property. It's so peaceful and quiet up here, I hate to leave, but we'd better head for home.

If Tom wanted to go to a convention in Los Angeles, he just picked up and went. There was nothing Mary could do about it, no matter how much work there was at home.

Tom's neighbors trusted him and followed his advice. He pleaded cases in the Los Angeles courtrooms and was very much sought after. But Mary looked at him quite differently. She always said he was a "jolly fellow, well met," always taking on everyone else's problems, but leaving all of theirs to her.

Tom loved going to Los Angeles to help his Irish friends at the jail house. One day when Tom was there and talking to Stephen White, he told him of his humble beginnings, of the hardships he suffered and his want of food in Ireland. "When we came to America, we came by steerage and I'm not too proud of that."

"No one should think different of you, Tom, from which part of the boat you came."

"You're right, Stephen, and I'm thankful to my sister Mary, for making it possible. What case are you working on now?" asked Tom.

"Don Pio Pico's boy, Romulf, is accused of shooting a man. Another new case I'm working on is Andrew Weinshank's will. I'm running into all sorts of problems there."

"Oh? How come?"

"Can't locate all the heirs. Some are circus performers, traveling all over the world."

One day while Tom was at the courthouse, two men came galloping into the yard at the ranch. On seeing a little boy, with firey red hair playing with his hoop near the house, one of the riders inquired in a loud voice, "Where's Tom Phelan?"

"My pa ain't home from Los Angeles yet," said Joe.

"Then fetch me your ma," he ordered. He sounded gruff, so Joe high tailed it to the house. Mary followed him outdoors.

"We need Tom Phelan right away. We've got ourselves some trouble at Fulton Wells."

"My Tom hasn't come home yet," she said. "I expect him any minute. You can wait if you like, suit yourself." And she went on back inside the house. Joe stayed outside, watching the men.

A few minutes later, Tom turned off the road into the place, the men galloped out to meet him, they exchanged a few words, and they all left together. They headed south at a gallop and after the men were out of sight, Joe went into the house.

At Fulton Wells, the three men pulled to an abrupt stop just outside a saloon. It was a nervous bunch of men milling around that greeted them. Standing in a wagon under the lone tree was a pitiful man, head bowed, fearing to look up at the angry mob. He had a noose around his neck.

The men had arrived just in the nick of time, "What's this man done?" Tom shouted at the man who held the reins, waiting for the command to pull the wagon away.

"He shot a man."

"What provoked it, did the other man pull a gun?"

"Sure did, had every right to. This man's a half-breed, and Indian at that. He has no right to be here."

Tom Phelan, still mounted on his horse, in a loud voice addressed the group. "This is no way to deal justice. Cut this man down!" he said, struggling to keep his horse under control, for the excitement of the crowd had telegraphed itself to the high-strung animal. "He should be tried in a court of law. If he's guilty, they'll hang him. I'll even take him to jail myself."

There was a howl of dissension, for the angry crowd wanted no part of that. Tom sat nervously in his saddle, knowing the destiny of the poor defenseless man was in his hands. After several moments two men jumped up into the wagon, took the noose from around the man's neck and released him. He jumped out of the wagon and onto the back of Tom's horse and hurriedly they headed back to the ranch.

The next day Tom took him to Los Angeles. After sitting it out in jail a few days, his trial was held. It was a speedy one. The facts were brought out. They found Jap Reynolds, the half-breed, had killed in self-defense.

At the ranch at Castaic, Big Dan was having trouble with the neighbors who had the adjoining section. They thought the Phelans were trespassing over their land. Word reached the ranch, so Tom and Dan went up to see what could be done about it. When

Tom and Dan arrived, Big Dan was there to meet them at the train, with two extra horses. As the three men were riding along, Tom was a little ahead of the others. He heard a shot; as he turned around, he saw Big Dan falling from his horse. Tom and Dan quickly dismounted. By the time they got to Big Dan, he was dead. Dan ran over to where the shot had been fired and the rifle was still in the fork of the tree. He looked around in the underbrush, but found nobody. When Dan got back to his father he said, "Whoever did it got away. There's no one around."

"Oh, Dan! Why? He wouldn't hurt a fly, and to die like this. This was the work of a coward."

They put Big Dan's body on the back of his horse and walked the rest of the way to the ranch house. They stayed over that night. The next morning they put Big Dan in the wagon, covered him with straw and headed for home.

The Keays family also had a ranch next to the Phelans at Castaic and were visiting the Phelans. The children were playing in the yard—Harold and Mabel Keays, Jim and Joe, Annie and little Maryanne. First it was roll the hoop, then kick-the-can and a little clod throwing on the side, to while away the time waiting for supper to be served.

About dusk, just as the sun was about to set, Joe spotted the wagon. It was his father who was holding the reins, instead of Dan who usually did the driving.

His father didn't have his usual jovial expression, and Joe all of a sudden felt sick, as if something had fallen to the bottom of his stomach.

Tom didn't pull to a stop as he usually did, to give the kids a chance to hop on for their ride to the barn. Instead, he looked straight ahead, his head bent. Dan was sitting beside him with the same downcast look. On the wagon was a pile of hay.

Then Tom pulled the team to a halt, looked back at the children. "Run get your ma, Joe, and Aunt Ellen. They're needed in the barn." Joe dropped his clod and ran for the house, opened the back door. He had sensed something was wrong from the start and held back.

"What is it Joe?" his mother asked, knowing something horrible had happened, for his face was ghostly white.

"Ma, you and Aunt Ellen are wanted outside." The women dropped what they were doing, ran out and followed the wagon into the barn and closed the door.

The other children gathered around; then Mary came out.

"Come on in, Jim, we need to talk to you. As he walked in, Mary closed the door, "It's your pa, Jim, he's been shot. He's dead."

That night, as they sat around the supper table, it was Tom who broke the silence.

"We'll be needing to go to Los Angeles tomorrow. I'll need you womenfolk to help pick out a burial plot."

"We'll be ready when you are. I'll tell Ellen she's lying down upstairs," said Mary, and they continued eating in silence.

After a few moments, Mary spoke up, "What's to be done with the man who shot him, Tom?"

"I'm not sure it was a man, Mary. In fact, I'm thinking it was a woman."

"Someone we know?" asked Mary.

"Yes, someone we know."

"Have we been doing something wrong?" asked Mary.

"We had no right to cross their land, that's true, and they had a right to protect what was theirs, but I don't think I could ever kill a man for that."

The next day Mary, Ellen and Tom made the long hard trip across the mesa to Los Angeles.

The following day the family, Dan's family, his wife, Ellen; his sons, Dan and Jim, and their daughter, Maryanne, in the company of the priest, made that long hard trip again, again over the mesa, to Los Angeles to the Roman Catholic cemetery on Fort Street, this time with Dan's body in the coffin made on the ranch. Following behind were Tom and Mary with their five children.

As soon as they got back to the ranch, Ellen told Tom she wanted to return to Waverly, back to her family and friends.

"Ellen, you do what's best. Waverly is a grand place, and if that's what will make you happy, Mary and the girls will help you pack. I'll take you to Los Angeles in the buckboard and put you on the train."

"The children will hate to leave the ranch, but everything here is a sad reminder of my poor Dan, and I'll just waste away for sure!"

Soon after Ellen and her children left to return to Waverly, Tom decided to take the Chestnuts out.

"If we can't sell the nuts, then it's best we take them out," said Tom. "We'll set aside forty acres for hay to feed the cattle."

"What will we put in place of them, Tom?" asked Mary.

"Walnuts. That's what everyone else around here is planting, walnuts. I'm running for a place on the Walnut Association Board, which goes to show what faith I have in them."

Tom being away so much, Mary being left to run the ranch gave Mary more reason for concern.

By this time Mary had five living children. She felt very dragged out, but there wasn't too much she could do about it.

Tom was always happy when a new one was on its way, but it was Mary who had to carry them around for nine months and nurse them when they got sick. Dan was the oldest, then Nell, then Joe, Annie, and Tommy, Billy already in his grave and Mary had lost a set of twins along the way.

Tom would say, "We can always use more hands," and Mary would appeal to the priest for help, and he would always say, "Oh, Mary, it's your duty to have children. That's what you're here for. Food should be no problem on your big ranch."

"I'm not concerned about that. I'm the one who has to carry them, feed them, care for them when they get sick. What does Tom do? He goes off somewhere."

"Just think," Father Lilly would say, "later on they can be a lot of help and comfort in your old age. Think along those lines."

During the great flood of 1886, 35 inches of rain fell, causing flooding conditions throughout the county. In Los Angeles, the rivers rose and overflowed the lowlands, but the water level rose so gradually there was no loss of lives and the cattle had time to get to the neighboring hills in safety.

By January 19th, the waters had risen so high, people were marooned in the upper floors of their homes. Tom kept the windows open in their upstairs bedroom, just in case he heard cries in the night and was called upon to rescue people.

In the valley the flood waters were again rising so rapidly many people were marooned, and they began to worry about the river bank. One young man, Seaborn Reynolds, the young fellow married to Sam Thompson's daughter, had just purchased lumber for a new room he was going to build onto his house. He heard cries in the night, so he hurriedly built a raft and set out to rescue people that had found refuge in the trees.

The Sorensons spent a week in a tree with their little girls before they were rescued, living all that time on dried beans.

In Anaheim, the water was four feet deep in the streets, and people had to take flight to the uplands or to the rooftops of their houses. Vineyards were partially ruined with deep layers of sand. For over a month, it rained so steadily the sun scarcely shone.

Whenever it rained several days in a row, the Los Angeles River was sure to overflow its banks. It was raining so hard that Tom said, "I think I'll head for town. If I stayed here, I'd just have to sit around the house."

Mary came back with, "You think all there is to do is outside. What about all the things I have to tend to inside? I could use a little help from you."

"Oh, I would only be in the way," and before she could think up an answer, he was out the door and on his way, but not before grabbing one of her freshly baked loaves of bread. He then went to the barn, saddled up a horse and headed straight for town.

In Los Angeles, Tom worked night and day helping Sheriff Gard move the women and children to safety, just catching a bite to eat on the run and a few winks in the town's jail at night. One fellow by the name of Martin Aguirre, a deputy, threw himself up on his horse and rescued more than twenty people from drowning, almost losing his own life.

Tom returned home after spending a week in town. It had been raining hard all that day. Mary met him at the door of the barn. She had picked up one of the brooms and headed for him, hitting him time after time, her swollen body a reminder to Tom that he had no other course than to take her wrath. Usually he could soft soap her and calm her down, but the harder he tried, the more she swung. Tom knew his Mary well, so he left in double quick time, not bothering to look back.

"Not even the archangel from heaven could get along with her," he said to himself as he saddled a fresh horse as fast as his nervous fingers could manipulate the buckle and strap, jumped on and sped out of the yard.

He headed in the direction of El Camino Real, forged both rivers, the San Gabriel and the Rio Hondo. His horse bogged down, he was soaked to the skin, but was able to make the crossing. He continued on for several hours He stopped to wait for the rain to subside at a farm house on the Paiute River and left his horse to rest at a squatter's ranch house. He had to sit for nine hours in wet clothes before the people returned so he could get a fresh horse. By the time he reached the ranch at Castaic, he had the chills and had to take to his bed.

The men on the ranch at Castaic were able to get word to Mary that Tom was very ill and was in need of nursing care. Mary sent Nell up to care for him, even if Tom would speak to her, her time was near and the trip would be too much for her. Nell was there for some time before she could get her father to allow her mother to come see him.

On July 13th Mary had the baby. She named him Edward. Mary was finally allowed to make the weekly trip, taking Joe with her, to talk over the problems on the ranch. They either took the train or went by buckboard. If they went by train, as they were nearing the ranch, Joe jumped up and pulled the cord just at the right moment to bring the train to a halt in front of the ranch. Because there was no station nearby, and no one there to meet them, they walked the six miles to the ranch house.

A lone buggy, carrying Aquilla Pickering and T. E. Newlin and two other Quakers, Hervey Lindley and Jonathan Bailey, rolled along El Camino Real one bright April day on their way to the Thomas Ranch in search of land for their new colony. The land was located on the southern slope of the Puente Hills behind the Phelan Ranch. There were more than one thousand acres, priced at fifty-five dollars an acre.

As they traveled along, they passed the decaying adobe of Don Pio Pico, continued along the dirt road and up to the Thomas Ranch house. There they sat on the porch of the little white frame house on the property, overlooking the valley nestled serenely at the foot of the Puente Hills. The men liked what they saw, so Pickering decided to call a conference of the Friends.

On the 3rd of May, 1887, the purchase was completed, and the Quakers made plans to build their settlement on land that once belonged to Manuel Nieto, the great ranchero, who owned all the valley all the way to the sea.

A few days later, on May 11th, Jonathan Bailey and his wife, Rebecca, moved into the ranch house up on the hill among the pepper trees. The following Sunday, they held a religious service on their front porch. The men met with other Quakers: John Painter, William Coffin, Dr. Grinnell, and Eleager Andrews— all of Pasadena. Later the first Friends Meeting House was built and paid for. The Pickering Land and Water Company donated the land and built the building, and Hervey Lindley presented the church with bells.

The Friends planned originally to sell the land in ten-acre parcels, but decided to break it up into smaller pieces. Though Whittier was founded by Friends, all fair minded people were invited to settle there. Baldwin and Jessup got the contract to survey and lay out the townsites. Walter Keen graded the roads.

Sales began on May 19th at nine o'clock in the morning in Hervey Lindley's office in Los Angeles at 75 North Spring Street.

Jenny Weinshank saw the ad in the paper. Town lots were one hundred dollars each and the five-acre parcels outside of town were a thousand dollars. Jenny thought it would be a good investment, so she went down to Lindley's office and stood in line long before the door opened. Finally, Mr. Lindley opened it and the rush was on. Jenny purchased three lots that day, a few blocks from the center of town.

When the doors were locked that night, after the crowd dispersed, Hervey Lindley and Jonathan Bailey were two tired men. They had taken in $34,000, getting back more than half of what they paid for the land and still had much more land to sell.

A few days later Jenny and her mother hired a horse and buggy and went to look at the lots in Whittier. After a dusty drive across the mesa, they turned on Philadelphia Street. A short distance up the street Jenny said, "Look mother, that sign says Pickering; the lots are on this street. The map in the office shows them down here a ways so let's turn to the right. All the lots are marked."

As they rode along checking each number on the way, in the second block Jenny spotted her number, "A fine choice, Jenny," said her mother, "A fine choice indeed."

Letters were written to other Quakers in Iowa, letters telling them of the wonderful land that could be theirs, of the beautiful countryside covered with wild mustard, and of the mild, hospitable climate. So many made plans to make the trip to California.

Early in July, a party of Quakers boarded a train in Iowa. They occupied a touring car, carrying their provisions in baskets. The trip west took two weeks with the train stopping twice a day to allow them a chance to rest. They crossed the prairies of the Middle West, climbed the rugged Rockies, dropped down into deep canyons. They had a good rest in Denver, then continued on to the Mormon community at Salt Lake.

As they traveled along, it was like a dream come true. On the roadsides flowers were in bloom and along the way inhabitants were living a carefree life on their land. They thought about the fears of those they left behind. Those at home weren't sure everything would be sunshine and honey. They were sure those going would be killed by earthquakes.

The Quakers began arriving late in the afternoon of July 18th. The first trainload reached the township of Norwalk and was pushed onto the siding for the night. The next morning, bright and early, Jonathan Bailey and his friend, William Cooper, were there with their spring wagons and two extra ponies for the trip to the new town. Two of the girls mounted the ponies, and all the rest got in the wagon. On the floor of the wagon was a box of delicious apricots William Cooper had brought for them to enjoy.

The wagon party headed for the hills. They stopped at Fulton Wells for a drink of sulfur water. They continued on along the dirt road, passing a few scattered houses along the way. At one place, they saw a strange looking Chinaman sitting out under a tree, and a big brick kiln being fired up, Mexicans carrying bricks. All the people in the wagon turned to look.

William Cooper said, "An Irish family by the name of Phelan owns that ranch. They make brooms as well as brick and will have one of the largest walnut orchards in the country; see, the men are planting now."

They followed the foot of the hills until they reached another dirt road that led up to higher ground. "This street is Philadelphia," Jonathan said as they rode along. "This is my house and we just passed Milton Street." On the opposite corner was a large tent. He stopped the wagon, "This is where we eat," and they all piled out.

That evening some of the party returned to Norwalk, where they found better accommodations; for others, it was time to pitch their tents across the street. In no time at all, they began building their houses and Whittier became a beehive of activity.

The kiln on the Phelan ranch was kept fired up around the clock, for brick from the ranch was in great demand to accommodate the construction for the new town.

Walter Vernon started a lumber yard on the corner of Philadelphia Street and Pickering Avenue. Later a grist mill was built. The Vernon brothers convinced the Southern Pacific Railroad to come to Whittier, using a box car as the depot. J. H. Gwin built a livery stable on North Milton and a broom factory went up.

Water was brought in by barrel from the San Gabriel River. The wagon pulled up at the corner of Philadelphia and Greenleaf so the people could fill their buckets. Later water was brought from the springs at Turnbull Canyon, but it had an oily taste. A group of businessmen purchased the Rameriz ranch of two thousand acres, hoping to break it up into smaller parcels.

Whittier began to look like any other little country town, with its boardwalk and frame buildings lining the rain-rutted main street, for the newly graded streets were soft from the recent rains. The country over was a sea of mustard, no sidewalks, a few houses, many families living in tents and barns, the only light being carried by hand or tied on the buggy or wagon.

When people went to Los Angeles it was over the mesa, or by stage to Norwalk then by train. Mail was being delivered to Whittier and could be picked up at Doty's store at the corner of Greenleaf and Philadelphia Streets where it was distributed in little pigeonholes.

The children went down to the Evergreen school house on the County Road.

The one aspect that made Whittier unique was the appearance of its people. The leaders dressed in plain, dark colors, unadorned by frills of any kind, wearing garb as simple as nature's self. All adults, without exception, wore some head covering.

One day a white tent mysteriously was erected in town. Word was spread that it was to be a meat market, but turned out to be a saloon. One day a drunk was hanging around the tent, the proprietor tried to chase him away but couldn't, so he shot him dead, then fled town. The next day, the townsmen got together, pulled down the tent, set fire to it and smashed the bottles. The saloon-keeper sued and collected damages, even tried to set up elsewhere, but a crusade was on the new location where the townspeople stood praying. One saloon keeper was converted, the others left town.

When they first settled on their land, their only means of making a living was by raising crops and marketing them in Los Angeles. They delivered their produce by horse and wagon— a hot and dusty trip in the summer, rough and muddy in the winter. Their first crop was barley, which was harvested at Greenleaf and Philadelphia Streets. Mr. Reynolds threshed and Mr. Cooper baled it.

The greatest boom known to history hit during that year of 1887. It started with the rate war between the two transcontinental railroad lines, the Union Pacific and the Santa Fe, to get homeseekers to visit the Pacific Coast. The rate war raged so hotly that on one day tickets were sold from Kansas City to Los Angeles for one dollar per person. The trains were crowded not only with potential homemakers but with undesirables as well, the "boomers" as they were called; tricky, smooth, out to make a killing. Towns began to pop up all over. Before the close of 1887, twenty-five towns from Los Angeles to San Bernardino sprang up.

One night, one of Whittier's leading citizens, C. W. Harvey, in a lamp-light inspection, purchased some lots on Greenleaf Avenue. He was a promoter in every sense of the word. He was one of those who would go into a town, buy up land, build a building or two and move on. On this project he got his friends, Hervey Lindley, George Mason and Moses Ricker to go in with him.

He had heard the Phelan's had a yard full of brick on hand, so he decided to pay them a visit. He was able to talk to Mary herself, for she was now in charge of the entire operation.

"Well, Mrs. Phelan, how about it? I can use most of your bricks, if the price is right. I plan to build four buildings on what I hope to be the four corners of Whittier. I'm willing to pay six dollars a thousand, but you must haul them for that price."

"We've already made a lot of brick, Mr. Harvey, and we can continue on for some time. As you know, most of the houses in Whittier have been built by Raymond Hunnicut and he used the bricks from this ranch for his foundations; then too, we supplied the brick for one of the first stores near the corner of Philadelphia and Greenleaf. I'll have to think about it. We were going to build our own home with that brick. My Tom still has his heart set on it."

"Well, you think it over and let me know."

"I'll send one of the boys, as soon as I've made up my mind." Mary knew Tom didn't have too much longer to live. He had been getting weaker with each passing week. She realized that building the house would be up to her, and that it would be just another sad reminder of her Tom's dream, his dream of building a house ever since he first found the vein of clay, the day he and Mr. Woodward first looked over the ranch.

"I don't think I could ever live in it," she thought to herself. So, without consulting Tom, she said, "Dan, go tell Mr. Harvey he can have the brick. We'll get them up there as soon as possible. We'll use the big heavy wagon and let's use two teams on it. That hill won't be easy and, Dan, go get Ned Powers to help."

So, Ned with the Resegos and the Castillos, all worked from morning to night, only resting when they rode along on the wagon on their way to Whittier. There they unloaded the brick, carrying six at a time, then headed back to the ranch, working day after day until the job was done.

Construction got underway. One building was intended to be a bank, but instead became the first meeting place of the newly-organized Methodist Church. The upper floor was the living quarters of the pastor. Another was to be used as a school. With all the building going on, Whittier was becoming a boom town.

Then came the bust. Land prices went down, many could not meet their payments, there were no jobs. Sunday suits became shiny, socks were darned until no longer darnable, shoes were patched until no longer patchable. Whittier was struggling, the people were unable to pay for their land, some up and left in the middle of the night taking their houses with them and went on to cheaper land to begin anew. In order to save their tomato crop, someone suggested they start a cannery which they did out in the open on Comstock Avenue, cooking over an open fire. Mr. Hiatt took charge. This gave the town a boost, providing work for everyone.

Land could not be sold at any price. Mr. Simon Murphy advanced money for the development of the Ramirez property, securing it with land. He decided to plant citrus, but because no water was available he planned to build a ditch from the Artesian wells near El Monte, skirting Whittier Hills, sending the water through a wooden flume to his ranch, with the idea of selling water to the Pickering Land and Water Company, to serve as a source of water for Whittier. Even so there was little enthusiasm for the project, but construction proceeded anyway. The wooden flumes skirted the base of the Whittier hills to the ranch. After the water line was completed and water came flowing through, the people changed their tune and began singing the praises of Simon Murphy and A. L. Reed, calling them the Saviors of Whittier.

When Mary Phelan and Joe, now eleven years old, went to the ranch at Castaic by buckboard, Mary didn't have to worry about whether or not someone would be waiting at the train for a ride to the ranch. They always went up one day and returned home the next, taking the baby with them.

No sooner had Mary gotten in the door at the ranch house than she announced, "Nell, I'm leaving Edward with you. He's only underfoot at home."

"But Ma, I have so much to do."

"Oh, you'll get by. I have him weaned."

"But, Ma, he's two years old, going on three. . . "

"If you get too busy, tie him to a chair and go about your business."

"Well, if there's no other way, I guess I have to." Joe just hung his head.

The next morning Mary sat down by Tom's bed and started talking about the problems at the homeplace and the things that needed tending to. She didn't tell him about the brick. She knew he wanted her to hold on to them.

"Tom, Irish Dan is now in charge and we have Ned Powers working, too.

"They'll be able to handle things, Mary." Then she produced her bills and they went over them item by item. After they had talked it out, Mary said to Tom "Come on home, Tom. I want you home."

"I'll think about it Mary. It's getting late. Now you and Joe had better go on home. I'll see you next week."

Los Angeles, 1888

Chapter 31

It was on March 4, 1888, Edna Lee's 10th birthday, that the "Belle of the Ball" arrived in San Francisco.

Edna was happy whenever the ship arrived in a port to take on fuel, because then she could go on deck to play and pretend while the captain went about his business. She had grown to love the captain and his wife, and thought of them as her parents. She considered the ship her home.

Standing on the wharf below them were two ladies, apparently related. They were anxiously awaiting something, and after a while, they walked up the gangplank to speak with the captain.

"Good morning, Captain," said the older woman, a small lady dressed in black, "I'm Regina Weinshank. I'm here to meet my granddaughter, Edna Lee. She is with you, isn't she?"

"She is, indeed, Mrs. Weinshank, and I can tell you this, I'll miss that little one, I will. We've come to be great friends. She likes to play on deck; she should be around here somewhere. Let's find her."

Edna was sitting down, playing pretend behind some gear on the bow of the ship, unaware that anyone was looking for her. Then Jenny, the younger woman, with beautiful hazel eyes and soft curls around her face, spotted the pretty little girl wearing handmade clothes that were much too small. Jenny knew instantly she was her sister's daughter.

"Edna, you're Edna Lee, aren't you?"

"Yes, ma'am, I am."

The captain walked over to Edna and took her hand. "Edna, these ladies are here for you."

"I'm your Aunt Jenny, and this is your grandmother. We're going to take you back to Los Angeles to live with us."

"But I don't want to go. I want to stay with you," looking up at the captain with pleading eyes. "I won't be any trouble." Then he put his arms around her and gave her a farewell hug.

"I know, you've been with him a long time, Edna, and he has taken wonderful care of you, but you need your own family and home. You need to go to school. Now it's time for us to go, so say 'good-bye' to the captain."

The ladies gently took her by the hand and walked her down the gangplank, not daring to look back.

"Oh! Ladies!" The captain called, his wife at his side, with tears streaming down her cheeks. "You left these in the cabin." He handed Edna a little brown diary and a lovely black fan. Timidly she took them, then rushed over to the captain's wife and threw her arms around her for that last final embrace.

From the wharf they took the cable car back to town. On the way in, Regina said to Jenny, "We must buy this child some clothes." Jenny agreed, so they headed for a department store. But once inside, their agreement dissolved. Edna's grandmother had eyes only for the dresses to the floor, but Jenny felt otherwise.

"But mother, small children don't wear long dresses any more."

"I think they're more proper, but you may be right, Jenny. You know more about what the youngsters are wearing these days. I still think it rather indecent." So they settled for shorter skirts and heavy stockings to the knees.

Back home in Los Angeles they rode along Main Street. The road was torn up. "They're paving this, Edna," said Jenny to their quiet little charge, trying to make conversation. "Isn't it wonderful? Our skirts won't get so muddy. They're also paving Spring and Fort Streets. We'll be home soon," she said as they neared the house on Second Street. They walked up the steps of the beautiful Victorian home and into the front door. The other members of the family were there to greet them.

"This is your Uncle Frank and your Aunt Hattie, and this is your little cousin Tootsie. They live here too. Your Aunt Hattie helps me with the foodstuffs."

The ladies took Edna into the parlor. She walked around, admiring the beautiful horsehair furniture, the sofa with its black silk cover, the beautiful marble topped table and the clay pots on the mantle.

"These are pretty," said Edna meekly, looking up at the pots.

"Do you like them, Edna?"

"Oh! Very much! They're interesting, where did they come from?"

"Your father brought them from Mexico many years ago."

"And that picture up there, the frame is beautiful."

"Your mother made that picture at school. The Sisters of Charity taught her needlework. It's of George Washington, our first President, and it's all in cross stitch. Your father had that frame made for it," said Jenny, looking over at her mother, knowing Edna was pleased to be in the presence of her mother's things.

They took her into the kitchen where she met Martha, their colored housekeeper. Edna looked around, then noticed a strange contraption hanging on the wall.

"What is this?" she asked.

"It's a telephone," said her grandmother. "We've had it for some time. It's a help in our business. Mr. Newmark was one of the first to subscribe. He has Telephone No. 5."

Then Jenny said, "Perhaps we can make arrangements to have your sister come visit, and we'll do something special."

"I didn't know I had a sister."

"Yes, She's a young lady now. When she was little, she wasn't very strong, so she couldn't travel with the circus. She's always lived with us. You had a brother, too, Charles; he died when he was five. Now it's just you and Emma and your adopted brother Robert. But of course you have lots of half brothers and sisters."

"I don't remember them either. I guess I was too young when our father left us at the orphanage. He was always supposed to come back to get us, but he never did."

"He died right after he left you there, Edna. He couldn't get you."

"I never knew," said Edna.

Edna heard loud noises coming from outside the house in the yard. They walked over to where the foodstuffs were being prepared in large kettles on the wood stove. Then Edna noticed a wagon had pulled into the yard.

"What are they doing here?"

"They came to pick up the barrels of foodstuffs for the mines.

Some are north of here, some in Virginia City. Most of our food products are sent to the mining towns, but now, let me show you to your room, Edna. Don't bother about your bundle. Martha will take care of it. Let's go upstairs."

The next morning when Edna woke up, she went to her grandmother's bedroom. She found her propped up in bed with a high headboard with fancy carving on it eating her breakfast. Along the opposite wall was a massive dresser. On her grandmother's lap was a shining silver tray with serving pieces on it.

"What do you think of this, Edna?" motioning to the tray, "Martha cooks my breakfast and brings it up every morning."

"That's very nice of her. She brought milk and cookies up to my room before I went to sleep last night."

"Yes, she's just like a member of the family. We used to have Jesse and Arturo, an Indian couple, and we were very fond of them. Now we have Martha and she takes good care of the house. Did you sleep well?"

"Oh, yes, I love my bed. What's that big fluffy bag on it?"

"That's called a feather tick. That came with us from the South. Everyone there has them. When we came across the Isthmus of Panama to California, your grandfather put it on the back of our donkey, and that's how we rode from Cruces to Panama. But hurry along, I need to get up. Isn't this a beautiful day, Edna?"

"Yes, it is, grandmother. I'll see you downstairs."

"Yes, I'll be right down."

After breakfast, Jenny took time to show Edna around the place. They went to see the adobe where they had lived with its dirt floors and thick walls. Edna entered through the low doorway where a deep shadow and an agreeable coolness fell upon her, as sudden and grateful as a plunge in cool water.

Edna walked to where the chouncer was standing and picked it up. It was no longer in use, just a log of wood attached to a stick that was serving as a handle.

"That's what your grandfather made so Arturo could press the cabbage down in the barrels, Edna. Can you imagine what it was like in the old days, trying to sell food to people who only ate tamales, frijoles and beans?"

Later on in the day Edna went with her Uncle Frank to see the new hotel he built farther on down Second Street. It was a fancy two-story affair, with living quarters upstairs and a row of shops downstairs, a fine-looking building.

"Unfortunately, Edna, the stores aren't renting well. So far mother has picked up the loss."

Edna was beginning to appreciate Los Angeles and was happy living in the house on Second Street and going to school with her Aunt Jenny. It was on their way to school one day that Jenny told her about their friend, Stephen White and another man by the name of Hervey Lindley who were working on a plan to help the little town of Whittier out in the country to return to solvency. Stephen was now Lieutenant Governor for the State and was in a good position to know about the various projects being proposed. He learned that the third correctional institution of the state was going to be built and because the first two had been placed in the northern part of the state, he felt it was only right that southern California should benefit as well.

Edna enjoyed watching the people as she rode to school on the horse-drawn cable railway. As they rode along, they watched the wagons heavily-laden with produce as they headed out of town. She loved watching the fancy hackney coaches and their beautiful high-spirited horses.

"Aunt Jenny, how long have you been teaching?"

"Oh, dear! Several years now. I was very young when I started. From the 8th grade I went to normal school and was in one of the first classes attending Pound Cake Hill. When I completed my two years I qualified for teaching, but I wanted more background, so I went to San Jose for more work. I taught in Sacramento and boarded with our friends, the Devlins, for a year before returning to Los Angeles."

"Why did you come back? Didn't you like teaching there?"

"I liked it very much, but when father died, I decided I was needed at home.

Edna was pleased to be in the same school as her aunt. That year she was in the fourth grade. The boy sitting behind her was Leo Carrillo, whose father was a very important man in Los Angeles, and whose grandfather had fought in the Battle of San Gabriel.

"Several Saturdays each year we're required to attend institute, Edna. Our principal feels we should learn more about what's going on in town. I want to take you with me, you'll benefit by it. Next week we'll go to tour the opium dens near the Plaza."

Bright and early the following Saturday they left the house. They went down a tunnel-like pathway below the street level. When they got to a dimly-lit room, several Chinamen were sitting in a corner huddled together, smoking strange-looking pipes, just sitting there with a far-away look in their eyes.

The smell was stifling and upsetting to Edna, so she pleaded with her Aunt Jenny. "Please take me up to the street. I'm getting sick."

Back in the fresh air, she felt better. "I'm sorry you had to go down there, Edna. I didn't realize it would be like that. I don't even understand why we had to go, but I guess we've seen enough. Let's walk on home."

Jenny's favorite spot to pass the time of day was at the public library. Jenny and Mary Foy sat and talked quietly, exchanging fond memories about the good books they had read. While they were talking, their friend, the Howard girl, came in and joined them. Her parents had a nursery on Figueroa Street. Edna thought she was the most beautiful lady she had ever seen. While the women visited, Edna had fun browsing around and reading while she waited for her aunt.

The Los Angeles school administrators transferred their teachers frequently, so no matter where Jenny taught, the plan called for Edna attending the same school. Teaching positions were hard to come by and harder still to keep.

One day she was talking to one of her school teacher friends. "Listen, Jenny, the challenge of hanging on to one's job depends entirely on what embarrassing evidence you're able to accumulate on the principal. You either keep up with what's going on, get the goods, so to speak, or before you know it, you're transferred."

"I don't think I could do that."

"Then plan to be transferred every year."

"I guess that's the way it will have to be. Each year a different school, a different place, and I'm sure Edna will want to be in the same school, so she'll transfer too."

That night sitting at the supper table, Jenny brought the subject up. "I guess I'll be transferred next year. I was hoping to stay put because of Edna, but I'm afraid that isn't possible."

"What do you mean?" asked her mother.

"One of the teachers, and I'd rather not say which one, said I had to get the goods on the principal if I wanted to stay at the same school."

"What do you mean 'goods'? I'm not familiar with that word."

"Who he's been sparking up to!"

"That word I know. I learned that from the madam. What is this world coming to? What did you tell her?"

"That I'll just have to be transferred, that's all."

"You made the right choice. Edna can get along wherever she goes."

Frank excused himself and left the house. While Jenny and her mother were walking into the parlor, Regina said, "Ozro was telling Frank the other day that John Goller has been sending wagons all over the state, a far cry from what it was like when we first came here."

"Talking of Frank, one of the teachers saw him going into a saloon the other night."

"Let him be, Jenny. He has a lot on his mind with the hotel not renting well, and he's just trying to show a little independence," replied Regina, with a worried look on her face.

Often Regina would leave the house to take care of the sick. She packed her bag with castor oil, ipecac, black draught, and calomel from her medicine chest, as well as some night wear, for seldom did she make it home without staying a few days.

Regina had been home only a day or two when some men from the town council came to see her about widening Second Street, and wanted Regina to pay her share. Just as Jenny and Edna walked in the door from school, Regina was waiting there to talk to Jenny. "This disturbs me very much. I donated part of our property for Los Angeles Street, but now that Second Street is being widened, they want me to pay for the work being done on it. I wouldn't mind paying," she said, "but if I had held out like the others and was paid for the property I donated before, I could use that money to pay for this."

"That's true, Mother, but at the time you didn't think of yourself, only what was good for the town. If the same people were in office, they surely would take that into consideration."

"The next time they come around, I hope you'll be here to talk to them."

"I hope so too. At least you deserve an explanation."

A few days later when the men returned, they presented the papers for Regina to sign. Jenny looked them over, signed for her mother, made out a check and returned them. "We have no choice, Mother. These men mean business, this is all legal and binding. There's no provision here for past generosity."

One day Jenny took Edna to the main part of town, which was within easy walking distance from the house over dirt roads held in place by wooden boards. There were a few lampposts which the city dwellers were required to light at dusk, using asphaltum from the tar pits on the outskirts of town.

When they got to town, they took a ride on the new electric street car drawn by poles whose huge arms stretched into the middle of the street.

"See those things up there, Edna? They're called gallow poles."

"What are they?" asked Edna.

"They named them that because they look like the poles they used to use to hang men from in the old days."

"Strange looking," said Edna.

"You should have seen them two years ago. All this was under water, and those huge arms looked funny sticking up."

They came to Robinson's Department Store. Before going in, Jenny said, "This is quite new and the most popular dry goods store in town." Just inside the door, she saw something which took her eye. "Oh! Look at this, Edna, a pink bow. Isn't it pretty?"

"Yes, it is."

"Would you like to have it?"

"Yes, I would."

"In that case we'll just ask the clerk to wrap it up."

"What's that strange smell?" Edna asked as they walked back out onto the street.

"Oh, that's Mr. Armour's butcher shop. He does all his butchering out back. Someday they'll make him go farther out of town. He was one of the early ones to go to the gold country. He first settled in Hangtown—, its Placerville now. Then he moved to the little gold mining town of Auburn. He got his start with just two hogs, built his own adobe and sold pork to the miners."

When they got home, Edna ran upstairs to again admire her beautiful pink bow. She put it with a blouse and took it to her Aunt Jenny's room to show to her. Her aunt was writing at her desk. Edna walked over to her and saw the bow was listed as an expense. Jenny noticing the disappointment in Edna's eyes comforted her with, "I'm sorry you're disappointed, Edna, you thought it was a gift from me, didn't you? But, you're really very lucky. Your grandfather set up a trust for you. He provided for all your care."

"Did his money pay my passage back?"

"No, Edna. His estate wasn't settled then. Your grandmother paid for that."

On January 1, 1889, early in the morning, Edna and her grandmother went to attend the first parade held in Pasadena. They got up early as they wanted to be there in plenty of time. Martha packed them a lunch and they started out. They stopped by John Goller's and hired one of his rigs.

When they got out on a stretch of flat land, Regina said to Edna, "Would you like to take the reins?"

"Oh! Yes, I would like that very much."

"And remember, Edna, pass on the right."

They rode along a short distance; then Edna said, "But Grandmother, two buggies are coming toward us. What do I do now?"

"If that's the case, give me the reins, Edna."

"Yes, of course. Did I do something wrong? Am I going to get to try again?"

"I'm sorry, Edna. I'll have to check with the doctor first. There was only one buggy coming toward us."

When they arrived at the parade grounds, they sat in their buggy on the side of the road in the open field waiting for the parade to begin. Edna couldn't help but feel uneasy for fear something was seriously wrong with her vision. But as soon as the chariot races and other sports began, she became distracted. The principal event of the day was a parade of vehicles of every description which moved along under the graceful burden of beautiful floral decorations. Carriages, wagons, floats, buggies, carts, bicycles—every conceivable vehicle—was smothered in flowers all done with taste in design and skill of execution.

The next day, Regina took Edna to see the specialist.

"What do you think, Doctor?" asked Regina. "Why would Edna see two buggies coming toward us when there was only one?"

"She obviously has astigmatism, Regina. We can help her all right, but it means she'll have to wear two pairs of glasses."

"You mean two pairs at one time?"

"That's the only way we can do it, but I'll see to it they'll look good. Is that all right with you, Edna?"

"I'm sure they'll be fine, Doctor."

Edna's Uncle Frank's wife Hattie died of consumption, so Edna's grandmother took on the task of raising Tootsie, her son's little girl, for her father paid little heed.

Tootsie attended school with the Sisters of Charity. Being a very belligerent child, her grandmother felt the nuns could quiet her down so she would have more peace of mind.

It was hard on Tootsie growing up without a mother. She was a beautiful child, with baby-fine, blond curly hair, but she was very headstrong. She had a habit of throwing herself on the floor in a dead faint when her wishes were thwarted. One day Edna started over to help her up, but before she could her grandmother, without saying a word, walked to the sink, pumped a glass of water and threw it on Tootsie. At first it frightened Edna, but when she saw Tootsie "come to" so quickly, she knew her grandmother had done the right thing.

Tootsie attended school at Macy and Alameda. On the afternoon trip home, the horse was so reliable that Charlie Parker, the driver, tied the reins to the bar, let his horse continue on, while he sat reciting poetry and telling stories to the children.

Tootsie's father, a good-looking man, with dark hair like his father's, and big round brown eyes, became so distraught when his wife died, he stepped up his drinking. Every Friday night he went off to the saloon. One Friday night after Frank had frequented several, he got out his gun and started up Second Street acting as if he were going to shoot up the town. He made such a racket he could be heard the county over. Edna went out and helped him into the house. In her quiet way, she said, "Oh, Uncle Frank, you don't want to disturb the neighbors, do you? Why don't you just give me your gun?"

"All right, Edna. Now don't shoot yourself. It's loaded."

"I won't, Uncle Frank, now let me help you up the stairs. Now that wasn't so bad was it?" she said as they got up on the porch. While she was opening the door, her grandmother joined her.

"Grandma, get on the other side, and let's help him up the stairs." Jenny stood below with a look of scorn on her face. They made their way up the stairs to his bedroom. Together they got him on the bed, pulled off his pants and shirt and Regina helped him into his nightshirt. "Oh, Edna! Why do I do this? I swear I'll never drink another drop," then he dropped off to sleep. The very next Friday night he started out at Henry Dockweiler's Castle Dome Saloon on the corner for starters, and went from one saloon to another.

The next day when Edna was walking down the front steps on her way to gymnastics school, Willie, a boy several years older than

Edna, drove up in his horseless carriage, and invited her to take a ride. Willie didn't like school, so he didn't go, but he did enjoy tinkering with mechanical things and had built himself a horseless carriage.

"I'm on my way to gymnastic school," Edna said as she approached his contraption. "Grandmother insists I have physical training every day. It only takes an hour, and if you'd like you can drop me off."

"I'll do better than that. I'll stick around and bring you back."

"Oh! Thank you," she said as she hopped in.

As they rode along, Willie's contraption startled a team of horses coming toward them pulling a large wagon load of goods heading in the direction of the harbor.

When Edna got home she ran into the house. The first person she saw was her grandmother, "I had a wonderful ride in Willie's horseless carriage, at least that's what he calls it. He hopes to sell it someday."

"Yes, I know, his mother says his brother, Carl, is the brains of the family and has made most of the parts," said Regina.

"Carl says someday horses will be part of the past. This upsets his father because he works from morning till night as a blacksmith, and if the horseless carriages take the place of horses, he won't have a way to make a living."

"Yes, I feel sorry for him in a way," said Regina. "The rancheros hated to see the railroad come, for fear it would do away with the need for barley."

When the Wards came to stay at the big house on Second Street, coming all the way from San Fernando, Emma was with them. She lived with the Wards in order to care for their young children. She and Edna, followed by little Tootsie, would go up to Edna's room and talk by the hour. Emma was nine years older than Edna and very pretty. They always ended up by talking about school.

"Emma, what is normal school like?" asked Edna.

"Oh, I guess like any other. It's over on Pound Cake Hill. Have you seen it?"

"Yes, I have. It's beautiful," remarked Edna.

"I studied to be a teacher. I like the little ones best. This way you get a chance at them before the others do, and you're the one who teaches them how to read."

"Do you like living in San Fernando?" asked Edna.

"Yes, I like it very much. I take care of Aunt Lizzie's children, but I really haven't much to say. She dresses her girls in fancy clothes with lots of hand-drawn work and lace and then lets them play in the barn. I don't quite understand that. I wouldn't let them do that, but I'm not their mother."

"Would you rather be here or up in the valley?"

"I would like it here with you, but I met a nice young man in Lancaster. He did own and operate a stage coach there, but his partner was troublesome, and they had a falling out. They decided to divide the rolling stock which was easy enough, but the barn they owned together. That was a different matter. They ended up by cutting it into two parts, each taking half."

"What a clever way to solve the problem. What is your friend's name?"

"Francis Bacon. He isn't very strong, has asthma, but he is wonderful to be around, always jovial. He is a descendant of Sir Francis Bacon, the great English writer from a family of great wealth. He can live in England on the family estate and be supported by them, but the climate there is too hard on his health. He was told if he would come to Lancaster in California his condition would improve. Then we met and fell in love."

"You won't be living here, then," said Edna.

"No, I'm sorry. I'll be living in San Fernando, but we'll see each other from time to time. It's lovely up in the valley. The air is dry and pure, it's quiet and peaceful, not at all like Los Angeles. Before you came back from Australia, I stood at that window and watched some Chinamen being shuffled along on Second Street, herded out of town on their way to the waterfront. Behind them, prodding them along, were armed men on horseback."

"That's awful," said Edna.

"When I was your age, I went to school right next door to the jail where they hanged men. We peeked through the fence, but when the sheriff found out about it, he saw to it that we were let out of school just before they strung them up."

"Just before the excitement, huh?"

"But listen to this—this is a funny story that grandma loved to tell. A long time ago she saw a black cape with a red lining at Hamburgs and bought it. When she got home and was taking it out of the box, our grandpa noticed it, and said she couldn't wear it. She fussed about it, but he held his ground. 'Regina, I don't want you to wear it and that's final. Red just isn't worn by a lady of culture. That's left for the other kind.' Well, anyway, she put it away and didn't take it out of the box until a couple of years ago when I was here with the Wards."

"Poor grandmother."

"Like everyone else, we threw our discards in the yard and one day grandma and I heard shouting and laughing outside. We went to the window and saw some men out there kicking grandpa's stove pipe hat like a ball, the one he bought when they first came to Los Angeles, and they had grandma's black cape with the red lining in the center of their burning pyre."

"Oh! My goodness!" said Edna.

"Then grandma went steaming out to complain, one man shouted at her, 'Hey lady, Los Angeles is no place for these refinements,'" and both girls began to giggle.

"Why didn't you go with us when we went to Australia?"

"I think our father was only concerned about those who were talented and could perform; and because our mother was so close to Polly, she had her to keep her company. My being a bit sickly they decided to leave me home with our grandmother.

"The only one I knew was Frank because he was in the orphanage with me, but I didn't see him very often. Then he died there. I don't remember any of the others."

"Then you didn't know I was even here?"

"No, I didn't. How many children did our father have?"

"From what our grandmother told me, he had sixteen, and they adopted one, Robert, making it seventeen. Father was married three times you know. His first wife died from an accident in the Gold Country, fell from a wagon. She had three children, Eugene, Francis and Theodore. His second wife went down on a ship off the coast, in northern California. She had eight. Polly, Ellena, John, James, Harry, Lavater and Rosa, and had a baby with her when she went down at sea. Then our mother had Charles, and me, the adopted one, Robert, Augusta, Frank and you. That makes the seventeen. When she died in British Burma of Bubonic Plague, she delivered a stillborn boy, but because he didn't live, they didn't count him."

"What happened to them all? I only knew my brother, Frank."

"Of our brothers and sisters, Robert, our adopted brother, is still living and performing. He was the one left on their doorstep when our brother Frank was a baby. Our father thought he was from a circus family because he was so easy to train. From his second wife Polly, Harry, Lavater and Rosa are still living. The children from his first marriage, Eugene and Francis, could be living, but the others didn't reach maturity, so I guess they died of smallpox, cholera or whatever or by accident while they were performing. Our brother, Charles, showed great promise for the circus business. They started him in when he was a baby— balancing him. Charles loved it, but when Rosa was living here at the house, she dropped him and he fell down the stairs. He died from the fall about three years later. I don't think our father ever got over it. He had such high hopes for him."

"Why didn't they live here? Our grandmother told me she wanted them to settle down on a ranch nearby."

"Our father was one of those restless ones, and the circus business was the only thing he knew. Our grandmother would always quote him, 'Another town, another place, another fortune to be made'."

"Emma, one day Aunt Jenny took me to Robinson's Department Store and bought me a pink bow. I thought it was a gift, but I found it was paid for out of our trust. It hurt me very much."

"Yes, that was taken from the money our grandfather set up in trust for us. For those days it was quite a lot. When he died, grandmother went to see our friend, Mr. White the attorney, and he told her our mother's stepchildren would have to sign off in order for us to get it. The girls, Polly and Rosa, were willing to sign, but the boys weren't, so they all had to get a share. There were so many of them, seven still living, there was less for us. Just last week I had to sign a paper releasing the remainder of my trust back to grandma."

"We didn't do well by our father either," said Edna.

"No, our grandmother learned very little about what happened to all his money, except that his partner cheated him out of a great deal of it. At one time he was wealthy, but when Polly came to California to settle his will, there was very little left to settle except our father's horse 'Mazeppa.' She did get him. The Sells Brothers were at their winter quarters in the area, so Polly put Mazeppa through his paces. She got rich and Mazeppa became internationally famous."

"So our father did well by her after all. Our grandmother says our father was a thirty-second degree Mason. When would he ever have time to do that?"

"I certainly wouldn't know, but she always seems to know what she's talking about. Are you glad to be back in America?"

"Yes, I am now. At first it was hard. I thought I would be living with a captain and his wife, the ones who brought me to this country. I loved being aboard ship, when the weather was nice, but one time we were in a terrible storm, and it frightened me out of my wits. I didn't see the captain for days, but finally the storm passed and we made it to port. I didn't even know our grandmother had sent for me. When we were in the Hawaiian Islands, they treated me to ice cream—the first I ever tasted! It was wonderful. I'm getting sleepy, Emma."

"In that case, its time for bed."

In Whittier, construction got underway on the state school. The bricks were made at the brick yard on Hadley in Whittier and six hundred people were employed there. They began construction on the big, four-story administration building, a magnificent structure, complete with bell tower. On the second floor was a carpenter and paint shop and the printing shop was on the fourth floor. It also had shoe and tailoring shops. It had a plunge, shower baths, and lockers. In fact, the building was the best outside Los Angeles in southern California. Men were also hired to work on the grounds, in the agricultural program, and on the building used to house the girls, on down the road on the corner of the County Road and King's Lane.

On February 12, 1890 the state school had its dedication, and the Weinshanks attended. On the platform was Stephen White, whom Regina watched with pride as he got up to speak. After the program a picnic was held and they all took a tour of the buildings.

Regina took Emma, Edna and Tootsie to Mr. Steckel's shop to have their picture taken. As they were patiently waiting, they looked in awe at all of his fancy equipment. Then he walked over to where they were sitting.

"Emma, you and Edna sit together," he said as he placed Edna's head touching Emma's cheek. Emma was dressed in a lovely long brown dress, Edna wearing a white blouse and her pink bow.

"I like this," Mr. Steckel said to Regina, "Emma being older than Edna gives it a pleasing effect." Then he took their picture.

But when Mr. Steckel saw little Tootsie in her long dress, he said, "This isn't right, such a natural beauty with her soft blond curly hair. I don't want to hurt your feelings, Regina, so I'll go ahead and take her picture just like this." But when he finished he said "Regina, go home and get Tootsie's nightgown and bring it back."

Regina didn't know what to think but figured he knew what he was doing, so she did what she was told. She walked all the way from Spring to Second Street and back. She put Tootsie's nightgown on her, John put some flowers in her hands, scattered some on the floor by her bare feet and took her picture. She looked like an angel, and he was thrilled with what he saw through the lens.

"If it's all right with you, I'm going to enter this picture in competition at the World's Fair in New York." This took Regina by surprise and she just nodded her head in agreement, and they all started out the door.

Weeks later there was a knock on the door of the house on Second Street. When Martha answered it, Mr. Steckel was there. She invited him in. The family gathered around him. "I won first place for the picture of our little Tootsie at the World's Fair. Can you imagine that—First Place!"

Tom stayed on at Castaic. Nell took care of him as well as her little brother Edward, and Tom kept getting steadily worse. After he had been in bed several months, it was obvious he would not get well. His long wet journey to the ranch, his exposure during the cold while he was in the Civil War and the hardships he suffered aboard ship in coming to America caused him to fall victim to consumption.

It was a long time before he gave in, but he felt so sorry for Nell and the baby, he consented to go back to the ranch. They fixed up a bed in the buckboard and made the long journey home. Nell continued to care for her father. He lasted only a month; on June 1, 1889, he died.

The priest from St. Mary's Church came to the ranch. The family joined in, reciting the rosary around the casket in the parlor. At church the next morning the mass was recited and his coffin was placed on the buckboard.

His family and friends joined him on that last long ride to the Roman Catholic Cemetery on Fort Street in Los Angeles, traveling over the hot, dusty road, over the mesa.

Tom's body was in the wagon covered with a black cloth. Dan was at the reins, little Tommy at his side. Joe drove the buckboard with his mother. Alongside her sat Annie. In back Nell held the baby sitting alongside the priest from St. Mary's. They were followed by several wagons carrying the workers from the ranch. They entered the gate at the Catholic Cemetery surrounded by a high adobe wall. They drove over a narrow lane to the family plot that Mary and Tom had selected but a short time before when they buried Tom's brother, Dan.

When they got there, the priest led them in prayer. Family and friends stood near the casket, Mary, Dan, Joe, all with heads bowed, young Tom, Nell and Annie nearby, holding the hand of little Edward. Behind them were other neighbors and friends.

Mr. Woodward, Pete Serrano, Jack Nicholson and Orly Lynch gradually lowered the casket into the ground, each holding on to a rope, letting it out as the casket went lower and lower down till it reached its final resting place.

After it was over, Joe walked away, trying to hold back his tears. No more would he go with his father to Don Pio Pico's El Ranchito or the grist mill or hear his father talk about the old days.

He looked up at a lone tall monument nearby. On it was a single inscription "Weinshank." At the top were pictures of a rifle, a boat and a cannon. He felt a hand being placed on his shoulder. It was his brother, Dan. "I wonder what those pictures mean?" asked Joe.

"Seems as though they represent a battle. He probably went to war."

"What war would that be?" asked Joe.

"The Mexican War." And they turned and joined the others.

The priest comforted Mary, and she remained silent, for she knew she had sent her Tom away.

"Mary, Tom was esteemed by all who came in range of his strong and dominating personality. He was a self-made man who never lost track of his laborious rise in life and was always there when asked to lend a helping hand."

After those words of comfort, they got back into the buckboard and headed for home.

Tootsie Weinshank

Emma (left) and Edna Lee

The Guirado Victorian Mansion

Chapter 32

Several years passed. The Wards were staying at the Weinshank house on Second Street, Lizzie, James and their four children, Marguerite, John, Regina, and their baby, Andrew. This made four Reginas under the same roof.

James worked for the Blimm Lumber Company in San Fernando and sold jewelry around town on the side. He sold it on time. It was inexpensive and rather gaudy. One day he cornered Edna. "I have some business to attend to, would you mind collecting from the ladies on San Pedro Street?"

"I don't know, Uncle James, grandma doesn't like my going there."

"It won't take long, just this one time," he said smoothly, turning on his famous smile.

"All right, Uncle James, I'll do it," said Edna, unable to resist his charm. She didn't even take the time to change from her school clothes and was still dressed in her loose fitting blouse and skirt with stockings to her knees.

She went to one little white frame house after another, each identical to the last; they were small and simply built each with a white picket fence around it. Each house had a red light in its front window. Edna didn't know what the lights were for, but they made her feel uncomfortable so she wanted to collect as quickly as possible and head for home.

At every house, the door was opened slightly at Edna's knock. She quietly announced the amount owed. A soft voice said, "Wait a minute," or "Stay right there," and the door was closed. At one house, she recognized her uncle's jewelry on the lady's hand who opened the door. She looked down at her own bare hands, remembering her grandmother's warning they were to go unadorned until a wedding band was slipped on her finger. In a minute or two it was again opened, just a crack, and the money was put into her outstretched hand.

There was a long row of houses. All the houses had the same heavy draperies hanging in the windows, all pulled closed. Edna thought she saw the faint outline of a man scurrying around so she turned her head. Every one had accounts to be collected. This caused her to be late for supper. Her grandmother was waiting at the door when she returned home.

"Where in the world have you been, Edna? I've been worried sick!"

"I've been out collecting for Uncle James. There were so many houses to go to, I couldn't help but be late."

"Go on in and eat, Edna. Your supper's getting cold."

Edna put her uncle's money in her grandmother's outstretched hand. Her Uncle James was summoned to the parlor and the door was closed. A while later Regina and Edna's Uncle James came out and joined the others at the table. Edna looked over at her grandmother. The look on her face told Edna she would never again be asked to collect on San Pedro Street.

Soon after that little incident, the Wards hurriedly left, taking Emma with them. The house seemed empty. This pleased Jenny for she now had more room to herself and the peace and quiet which she dearly loved, as well as a chance to do her class preparations without the patter of little feet.

Every year Grandma Weinshank traveled by steamer to San Francisco. From there she went to visit her friends, the Devlins, a well-to-do family in Sacramento. She especially liked San Francisco because of the climate. She loved the fog and the cool ocean breezes. After staying a few days, Regina said to her granddaughter, "On the way home, we'll take the train and go by Lancaster and invite your sister and the Wards to your birthday party next month."

"That will be nice. I can talk to Emma by the hour. We always have such a wonderful time."

"It'll be good getting home. I always like it when your Uncle Frank surprises me by fixing up one of the rooms. He likes it this way too, because he knows I can't stand to have the house torn up. Then, too, I can always expect a lovely surprise when I get back home."

At Edna's sixteenth birthday party, her grandmother, her Uncle Frank, Emma, Aunt Jenny, Uncle George, Aunt Lizzie, Uncle James, and their children, were all enjoying Martha's cooking, sitting at the dining room table watching Edna open her packages. First, her grandmother gave her a beautiful set of dainty gold ear drops inlaid with black jade. Edna put them on, smiling as she did, feeling a special closeness to her grandmother. Then her Uncle Frank left the table and returned with something in his hands. First he handed her a set of elk horn cups.

"What are these, Uncle Frank?"

"Your father brought them from Mexico. They're for you, Edna. See, one cup nests inside the other, and the very inside one has a lid."

Then he handed her another gift. "These cuff links were made from gold coins your father bought in Mexico. He also brought back the jugs on the mantle and the frame for the cross stitch picture your mother made. This is a periwinkle your father had made into a pin for your mother. Isn't it lovely?"

Then, with a flourish, he fastened a gold chain around her neck. "Your father had this made from the gold nuggets thrown at his feet while performing before the miners in the gold country."

The chain was exquisite, and Edna caught her breath. Made from many strands of gold, twisted together in a delicate rope, it caught the light and sparkled along its entire length. It was so lavishly long it was necessary to wind it around her neck a second time and then knot it.

"As far as we know, this is all that is left of his fortune."

Edna sat in stunned silence. Up till then, the only things she had from her mother and father were the little brown diary and a beautiful black fan she brought back from Australia.

"Your mother left these with me for safekeeping because they meant so much to your father. She never dreamed that neither of them would live to collect them."

"Thank you, Uncle Frank, I'll treasure them always."

It was a sad day when Don Pio Pico got into his buggy, left his beloved El Ranchito and rode across the mesa to Los Angeles to live out his remaining days in the home of his sister. Hard times had engulfed the country. Rancheros had to borrow to keep going. Many could not keep up with their payments. Don Pio Pico had borrowed from a man by the name of Cohen and let his payments lapse. When he finally accumulated enough to pay him, Cohen would not accept the money and foreclosed on his "El Ranchito."

On hearing the news, Mary remarked, "Poor man, I wonder what he'll do now."

Joe loved the Don and was noticeably moved at the news and said, "He was a kind man, didn't hold malice toward anyone."

"He was too generous, always doing for other people," said young Tom.

"Look what he did for the Isbell's and all the things he did for us," Joe retorted angrily.

But Tom paid no heed to Joe and continued on. "And anyway, Joe, what about all the mission land he took and gave to his family and friends. That's why the missions deteriorated, why the weeds took over the vegetable gardens and their aqueducts crumbled. Even Juan Matias Sanchez got one of his ranchos from the Don and it was mission land. If it hadn't been for President Lincoln the missions would have been torn down. And what about the poor Indians? They were herded down to San Juan Capistrano because all their land had been given away."

"I'm sure there are good sides and bad," said Joe. "But he was colorful and he lived during the great days of the ranchos and my happiest days as a boy growing up were at 'El Ranchito'."

"You're so sentimental, Joe," Tom said with a disgusted tone. "You never worry about what is right or wrong. I liked him too, but that doesn't mean I have to overlook his faults. Someday I want to be a lawyer like our pa. That's why I study all the time. I want to make something of myself, and I have to work at it. It's not like it was with our pa who just up and decided one day he wanted to be a lawyer and started pleading cases. Now you have to pass a test."

Then Nell walked over from the stove, handed Tom a glass of water, sank down in a chair and joined them in the conversation. "I don't think there ever was a more generous man in this valley. Mr. Levi was telling me that when little Nora Passons and her friend, Stella Robinson, were looking at the dolls in a store window in Downey, Don Pio Pico happened by. He picked up the two little girls, one on each arm, took them into the store and bought each a coveted doll."

The walnut trees came out, and Mary borrowed the money to plant oranges. By the time the job of planting three hundred acres of oranges had been completed, the family was well satisfied, for it had been a monumental task, preparing the soil and planting the trees. With a large loan on the place, a lot was at stake. The Mexican laborers kept the weeds out, fertilized them and made large basins, making it possible to flood the grove, a system that had been used in Mexico for centuries, for water was plentiful.

After Tom died, Mary worked even harder. All she could think of was accumulating property and wealth. The ranch at Castaic was too far away, and since it held only sad memories for her, she decided to let it go, in favor of developing the home place.

Their home place, as they called it, now contained 416 acres. Mary wanted to buy the property across the street called the Judson Place. On it was a lovely three-story Victorian home. She'd had a falling out with the Judsons, so they wouldn't sell to her, but this didn't hold Mary back. She sent for Gus Gregg, a man who dabbled in real estate and was always trying to turn a dollar.

"Gus, I want you to buy the Judson Place."

"I don't have any money right now," he said.

"You don't need any. I'll advance you the money. You buy it; then turn it over to me. He won't sell directly to me."

"If that's the way you want it, Mary, I'll try to make a deal."

"Thank you, Gus, and be quick about it. I'm not one to stand around and wait."

Several days later Gus returned. "I'm sorry to disappoint you, Mary; they're not ready to sell."

"I guess I'll have to wait. I don't know when, but someday I'm going to own that place, just mark my word."

"I'm sure you will," said Gus. "You're a very determined woman."

Mary bought the Ott place, forty acres to the south of them, then the Hickman place. In fact she purchased so much land, salesmen stopped by and tried to make a deal. "I'm not one to take anyone else's figures," she said as she squatted down, smoothed out the dirt and did her own figuring.

"It never ceases to amaze me, Mary, watching you do that," said the salesman.

"I've done it this way all these years, I'm not going to change now."

Annie was the maverick of the family. When she got a turn at the reins, she spurred the horses on, giving everyone a thrill. Mary would get agitated, raise her voice, and yell out to young Tom, "Tom, get those reins away from her. She's a wild one, she is." And she would continue muttering to herself, "It's not easy raising children by myself, and Annie is the most difficult one of all."

Young Tom would take over; Annie would sit and sulk and remain unhappy the rest of the way. Tom at the age of twelve was a good driver, wouldn't let anyone bluff him; was steady and dependable.

"I have lots of confidence in your driving, Tom," his mother would soothe, "I hope some day Annie will change her ways."

Joe was smitten with Victoria Meyer, the great-great-granddaughter of Jose Antonio Yorba, a soldier who came to California with Gaspar Portola and Father Junipero Serra of Vera Cruz who with his seventeen, grey-frocked padres was ordered to found the missions in California. A courier overtook them between Guadalajara Road and San Blas with news that the Russians were moving southward, through Alsaka toward California in considerable numbers.

The soldiers and padres worked their way through Baja California and arrived in San Diego July 1st, 1769. California, for the most part, was desert waste, over which there were neither trails, nor pathways. The soldiers were to provide military protection for both the missions and the roads that were to be built. The men were Catalonians, who hailed from the city of Barcelona and other ports in the Mediterranean, as well as the Basque Provinces of Spain.

After his term of duty guarding at the mission and on El Camino Real, Jose Antonio Yorba wanted to remain in California and so was awarded a rancho, Rancho Santiago. His rancho was so large he could travel all day on horseback in any direction and never leave his land.

After he died, Victoria's great-grandfather, Bernardino Yorba inherited the land. He built an adobe of more than fifty rooms. Bernardino's daughter married a Cota and their daughter married Marius Meyer, the immigrant Basque who, when he got off the boat in the New York harbor, had only a ten dollar gold piece in his pocket. That he made on board ship.

Joe was always eager to attend the dances at Bernardino Guirado's home at Fulton Wells, for he would surely see Victoria, the great-great-granddaughter of Jose Antonio Yorba, the soldier at the mission. Everyone the countryside over would be there, dressed in their finest clothes.

Before the Phelans left the house, their mother said, "Now, you children eat a good meal before we leave home. I don't want you acting like a bunch of starving waifs just off the boat from the old country. I don't want folks to think I can't afford to feed my own."

So after a bite to eat, they all piled into the buckboard. Dan took the reins, and they trotted down the dirt lane to the little town of Fulton Wells for an evening of gaiety and fun. They pulled up to the Guirado home, a big three-story Victorian home, the likes of which Mary would give an eyetooth to own. The veranda had an ornate rail with gingerbread galore on the upper floor covering the porch beneath. Bernardino, whose father had come to the valley in 1833, greeted them on the porch, "Well, Nell, are you and Annie going to play for us tonight?" beaming from ear to ear.

"We'll be happy to, Mr. Guirado," Nell started to answer, but before she could get the words out, Annie darted away, lost in the crowd. "Is Angel Ramirez here?" asked Nell.

"Oh, yes. He walked in just a few minutes ago with his violin."

"That's good, Mr. Guirado. There is no one in this whole country that can play like Angel can."

Bernardino escorted Nell to the piano, and she played the whole night through, Annie accompanying her only for an occasional duet, when her mother brought her to the piano, but best of all was when Nell played the piano and Angel his violin, even the dancing improved. When the waltz quadrille was called, Joe and Victoria went to the head of the square. This was followed by a waltz and a polka, Joe not wanting to give her up.

Joe had a way with the ladies. He didn't care if they were fat or thin. He had a dance with each and was a favorite for it, dancing to "Oh! Them Golden Slippers" and "'Little Brown Jug." Then Angel played a tune that Joe especially liked—"I'll Take You Home Again, Kathleen."

Mary sat with Mrs. Guirado, and they talked about their children, little Edward playing at her feet. Dan found some fellows to talk to, for he didn't care to dance. They talked about horses or farming and caught up on the local news, for no matter what went on, Dan was always the first to hear it.

Young Tom played with the other children, for he was too young to dance. Annie sneaked out of the house without a wrap and sat on the porch, flirting with the boys—anything to keep from playing the piano, but she started coughing; her mother heard her, and called her in.

Later in the evening they went into the dining room and had a bite to eat. At the end of the long room was a massive fireplace with an inviting crackling fire. The food was piled high, but the Phelans ate little, for Mary kept a watchful eye on them. Then it was time to head for home. Dan and Joe harnessed up the team to the buckboard, and with a crack of the whip, they were on their way. It would be in the early morning hours before the team reached the barn and the Phelans would go to bed, for time meant nothing to them when they had a chance to socialize with their neighbors.

Each year the family piled into the buckboard and headed for the Puente Hills, traveling north along El Camino Real. They were on their way to one of their favorite outings; the yearly rodeo at the Rowland-Workman Rancho. These were always grand affairs.

By the time they arrived, the rodeo was already in progress. The men watched as the vaqueros cut out the steers; lassoed and threw them to the ground. Then the hot branding iron was picked out of the glowing bed of coals and it was pressed against the poor critter's rump.

Mary and Nell, with the little one, went down to the stream where the picnic tables were, to help arrange the food. After supper the musical instruments were brought out. Mary and Nell helped clear the table, with Edward tagging along. Dan sat around and talked with the men, as usual; Tom played nearby and Annie and Joe danced the whole night through.

One time the Phelans were invited to the Gracedas for a barbeque and dance. Dan and Joe hitched the team to the wagon, and the family was ready to go, but their mother was nowhere to be found. Joe went to call her, anxious to get going thinking Victoria might be there. He found his mother in the pump house apparently indulging in more than a few nips of wine. She was muttering about her Tom leaving her with all the work at home and Joe could hear her say, "He had no right to up and die."

"Ma, we're ready to go. We're waiting for you. Let's go have a good time. Nell has Edward in the wagon and Annie and Tom are waiting too." Mary was a little unsteady on her feet, but with a little help from Dan, who joined them, they helped her into the wagon.

They followed El Camino Real in an easterly direction, skirting the hills. Mary rode along looking first at one, then another, but with nothing to say for fear it might be the wrong thing. Young Tom kept his eyes to the road ahead, pretending not to notice;

Annie started to snicker, but Nell reached over and put her hand over her mouth.

When they got to a long stretch of flat land, Dan pulled over to the side of the road and stopped.

"Ma, why don't you walk a bit? It'll make you feel better." He got down and helped her out. She pulled and tugged and was reluctant to budge, but with a firm hand Dan was able to get her out of the wagon.

Mary walked slowly alongside, sometimes unsteady on her feet as they drove along at a slow pace. Joe, sitting next to Dan, spoke up, "Dan, did you hear ma in the pump house, when she said our pa had no right to up and die?"

"Don't pay any attention to that, Joe. Every time I went to the ranch I had to cut out one of the best steers in the herd so she could give it to Sister Maryanne for introducing our pa to her."

Joe answered with, "I should have guessed there was a soft spot in her heart. But woe be on the person who lets that secret out." After a while Mary felt better and got back into the wagon.

They slowly headed up into the hills over the winding dirt road and finally descended into the Puente Valley to the Graceda Ranch.

When they got to the house in the late afternoon, they washed up. Joe went in search of Victoria, but couldn't find her. The ladies took a nap while the men sat around and talked. The food was spread out on the long table, and they all had a bite to eat. Joe and Annie danced all evening long, Joe dancing with the lovely señoritas. He didn't forget the older ladies, knowing they too were anxious for his attention, dancing far into the night. After the dance was over the men found a soft spot in the loft of the barn; the ladies bedded down in the house. Bright and early the next morning they made the long journey home. It was late in the afternoon before they pulled up to the house.

The family, along with the hired hands, were just sitting down at the supper table, when Alex came running in and announced, "Don Pio Pico just died and is going to be buried in a pauper's grave." A hush fell over the entire household. As Nell passed a bowl of vegetables, she said, "To think that once he had that beautiful adobe, those fine clothes and expensive trappings, only to spend his last days living on the charity of others."

Hearing this made Joe especially sad, because he loved the Don. "If I ever get rich" said Joe to his ma, "I'm going to see he has a proper burial place."

"You're just like your pa, Joe, always thinking more of the other fellow than of your own. Hail fellow well met, like I've always said You'd best spend your money on your own and let his body be."

Tom sat with downcast eyes, reading as he ate, then looked up at Joe. He too had loved the Don, but he saw the problems of the Don more clearly. "He spent his money and didn't give any thought to his old age. If he'd been more frugal, he wouldn't have had to borrow, and he wouldn't have lost his property."

It was true. No one could deny it, so they continued eating in silence.

Joe had a good sense of humor and since the ranch hands were a happy-go-lucky bunch of men, Joe got along well with all of them. So Mary kept him home. He really wanted to attend business college and was willing to drive the buggy into Los Angeles every day, but his mother always had reasons for him to be there on the ranch, so he finally gave up the idea of going on to school.

Dan was now boarding at St. Vincent's College in Los Angeles. Joe thought Mary sent him there because only the wealthy could afford it and she thought Dan was doing well because he sent such wonderful letters home. Then she learned the priests had written the letters. She accused the college of only wanting her tuition money and took Dan out of school.

The Phelan's buckskin horse was stolen from them. The man who returned him had another horse for sale called Dick. Horses meant a lot to the Phelans. They weren't so interested in the high spirited ones but those they could depend on.

They dickered for a few minutes, made the deal and the Phelans had themselves a fine horse. He had a knee injury but was gentle.

Mary always depended on Joe to liven things up. Whenever the Whites came to visit, Mary felt a little uneasy because they had such fine manners and she was a bit shy. So when the buggy pulled in, she called to Annie, "Go get Joe, the Whites are here."

From the time Joe walked through the door and into the parlor, until it was time for them to leave, he kept everyone laughing. He told them the story about the Chinamen poking him and about the time he got a switching at school for going swimming at the afternoon recess. Though Joe didn't intend to be funny, he had a fine sense of humor.

"He reminds me of Tom, Mary," Stephen said as they were walking out to their carriage.

Uneasy at this reference to his father, Joe took his leave, "I must get back to work; Stephen, Mary, hope you come back soon," and headed back to the barn.

"We'll be back, Joe. Thanks."

"Yes, he is like his pa. His pa gave out with lots of blarney, Stephen! Always doing things for other people. Everybody respected him, looked up to him, called on him for help and he was always off somewhere. If he wasn't pleading a case, saving a hanging or rescuing some poor soul he wasn't happy. He always left the ranch to me. I'm the one who carried the load."

"Try not to be bitter, Mary. People know you had the brunt of it, but they couldn't help liking Tom Phelan for the man he was," Stephen replied as they settled themselves in the carriage. "By the way, Mary, did they ever find out who shot Dan?"

"No, Stephen, we had our suspicions, but no one was ever brought to trial. With Tom being sick at Castaic and since I had so much to handle at the time, we sort of let it go. Thank you for coming. It's been a pleasure to visit." Mary watched as they pulled out of the yard. Then she went back inside.

Joe was not only was the best story teller, he was also ready for a good time, always raring to go. "Why don't we go to the beach," he said to his friend, Tomás Sanchez, while he was visiting at the ranch one day. Tomás was twenty years to the day older than Joe, a good-looking man, very handsome, had black shining hair, lots of it and big black eyes, and a trim figure. Tomás' father, Juan Matias Sanchez, came to the valley in 1842 from New Mexico. Before that the family had emigrated from Spain. His father lost all three of his great ranchos, Rancho Potrero, Rancho Merced and Rancho Chico, in the Workman Temple bank failure. They now lived a short distance away on land their father had bought that had not been included in the bank transaction.

"I'm game," said Tomás who was as happy-go-lucky as Joe. Tomás loved the high-spirited Irish family who was always out for a good time, and spent lots of his time on the ranch. One would never know he was the son of a great ranchero who owned so much land and lived in a beautiful adobe on the bluff. Sometimes the older ones would get together to make plans for an outing.

Tomás, Joe, and Dan put extra planks on the wagon; fixed everything up for the girls to sit on, then, Dan, Nell, Joe, Annie, young Tom, Tomás Sanchez, and some of the Ramirezes all piled into the wagon and started out. When they got to the ocean, they walked along the beach all dressed in their Sunday best. They had their noonday meal on the rocks and on this one particular day, they took a photographer along to take their picture.

Whenever the boys needed money, their mother let them have just about whatever they wanted. If she gave them money for a good time, Joe and his little brother, Edward, now eight years old, were sure to spend theirs, but not Dan or Tom. One day while the boys were in Los Angeles shopping, Joe said, "What are you going to do with the money you brought, Dan?"

"Take it home. Just because I brought it doesn't mean I have to spend it."

Then Joe turned to Edward and said, "If only he would spend his money just once, it wouldn't make us look so bad." When they arrived back at the San Gabriel River, the boys saw their mother waiting for them at the farther bank, whip in her outstretched hand, shaking it in their direction with full intentions of using it.

"I told you, Joe," said Dan, "when Ma says something, she means it, and we're late in getting home. At least Tom and I will be able to give her some money back."

One day Fecundo Ramirez walked in the back door, wearing a brand new pair of shoes. "Good looking shoes, Fecundo. Where did you get them?" asked Joe.

"Bought them at Hamburg's for only six bits. I think they were a real good buy. What do you think, Joe?"

"Looks like it to me. Usually I'm not too keen on bargains, but those look good. I think I'll get myself a pair." Joe not only liked fancy clothes, but expensive clothes as well. In fact, their mother spoiled all four of her boys, but times were hard and she tried cutting down on them and Joe was going to do his part.

He made a special trip to Los Angeles to Hamburg's department store, found just the same kind of shoes, at the same price, and bought them. He decided to put them on and wear them home. He had other errands to do and at one place he got off his horse and accidentally stepped into a puddle.

A little later the shoes got a little snug on his feet. He didn't think too much about it, but by the time he got home, the shoes were so snug he couldn't get them off. He didn't want anyone to know what a bad bargain he'd made, so he wore them to bed that night. The next morning after breakfast he was able to make it to the barn, his feet feeling like dead stumps of wood. Then with a knife in hand he cut them off—and that put an end to his bargain hunting.

Mary's brother passed away and she was raising his two girls, Maryanne and Agnes, two beautiful young ladies. Maryanne, the older one, was nearing sixteen and Agnes had just turned fourteen. Joe and the others had to mind their manners more around them. The girls were both very helpful around the house. They helped Nell in the kitchen and the girls all got along beautifully.

Then one morning without an inkling of what was about to happen, their mother said, "Joe, you're to take Maryanne and Agnes to the train. They're going to live with your father's family in San Francisco." Joe looked up with a surprised look on his face. Maryanne, too, was caught unaware, and quickly left the room, not even glancing back. Her younger sister, Agnes, hung her head and whimpered. Nell walked over to her, put her hand on her shoulder in a vain attempt to comfort her. Joe knew it was useless to try to talk his mother out of it. He walked out of the house and hitched Dick to the buggy. The girls rushed from the house carrying their own satchels, got into the buggy and they rode off, not even looking back.

All the way to Fulton Wells Joe had trouble holding back the tears. He loved his cousins and thought they would always be there. "Don't be upset, Joe." It was Maryanne who spoke up, Agnes still whimpering at her side. "Your mother has too much responsibility running the place by herself with only you children to help her. We'll get by. Your father's relatives in San Francisco are going to take us in. They're wonderful people, and they will look after us and it won't be long before we'll be on our own." They continued riding along in silence to the station.

Joe placed their satchels on the platform and waited for the train. When the girls got on board, Agnes disappeared, but Maryanne called back, "Good-bye Joe. We love you all and we'll write. Remember us in your prayers."

As Joe waved good-bye, he knew in his heart it would be the last time he saw them. He got back in the buggy and drove back to the ranch.

Joe just loved to dance. The others weren't as interested or as good, so often he would have to go by himself. Joe's bedroom was upstairs. He was always the "last dog hung," always got home late.

One night when he got home after the door was locked, he climbed up the lattice work. It was easy enough. He grabbed hold, pulled himself up onto the roof of the front porch, and having prepared himself for this likelihood, had the window cracked. He simply lifted the window and climbed inside.

Next morning his mother trotted up the stairs bright and early, in fact even earlier than usual, walked into his room and threw back the covers.

"Joe, get up. If you have enough energy to dance all night then you have enough to work in the fields all day. Up with you!" And down the stairs she went, with the same old sound, clump, clump, clump.

"Yes, ma. I'm on my way."

Joe got up and dressed and went downstairs, for he had learned long before that his mother wouldn't leave him alone. He ate a hearty breakfast, all the milk he could drink, a big plate of pink beans, some freshly baked bread, several pieces of bacon and a couple of eggs. After he had dallied as long as possible, he looked up at his mother. "Now, Joe, I want you to go out and spend the morning clearing the weeds from under the trees."

Then, without saying a word, Joe walked outside, looked for a nice quiet resting spot under a tree away from his mother's watchful eye and continued his sleep.

One night the Meyers family was attending a dance in Frank Sanchez's barn. As usual Victoria's dueña was trailing along behind to chaperone. Joe thought Victoria the prettiest girl he had ever set eyes on, her shiny, long, black hair, her white skin and rosy cheeks. She always dressed in the latest fashion.

Joe asked his mother if he could keep company with her. This pleased Mary because a better family could not be found, and they owned lots of land.

They danced the night away, Joe wishing he hadn't the reputation of getting around to all the ladies. "Joe, you go dance with Victoria. She'd like that," said Mrs. Guirado.

"Oh, thank you, Mrs. Guirado," for this pleased him very much. "I'll be back," and off he went.

After the musicians had played the whole night through, the polkas, mazurkas, and the waltz quadrilles, Angel put away his violin and said, "The dance is over," and the people would make plans to go home.

One night after a dance, Victoria said, "Joe, if you wish you can take me home."

"I'd like that very much," said Joe, thrilled at the thought of it. He tied his horse on the back of her buggy, helped Victoria in, got in himself and picked up the reins. Just as he was ready to say "giddy-up," the dueña hopped on the back and off they went.

Joe was more than willing to let the romance blossom, but one night when the family attended a dance in the Poyorena adobe, Victoria walked in on the arm of her cousin. Joe didn't think too much about it. After all, he was her cousin. But as they danced, Joe could feel a heavy lump in his throat, for it was obvious that Victoria's thoughts were not on him.

Joe danced with her a time or two, but her eyes were for her cousin, Camille, so Joe made his usual rounds of the ladies at the party and had a dance with each. After it was over, Joe went home with his mother and the rest of the family, not bothering Victoria, for she had other plans.

The Weinshank home on Second Street was a happy one, always bustling with activity. With Jenny about to be married, to Felix Devlin. The Devlins had been close friends with the Weinshanks for years. Felix was very quiet, not exactly the type to sweep a girl off her feet, but he and Jenny had grown up together and it was just taken for granted that some day they would get married. The atmosphere was even livelier than usual. Regina spent more time in the kitchen helping Martha. Frank was busy working around the house, finding many things to fix. Lizzie and James were staying there with their children. Edna was busy looking after their baby, Andrew, changing his diapers, and the other children were old enough to look after themselves.

Jenny was a stickler for getting things done. She was thirty-six years old, settled in her ways. She wanted to make provisions for her nieces in the event something unforeseen should happened to her, so before the wedding she went to Stephen White's office and gave his secretary instructions that if anything happened to her, one lot in Whittier was to go to Emma, one to Edna and one to her husband-to-be, Felix Devlin.

The Devlins had arrived from Sacramento and the house was full of people. Edna had a new dress for the wedding, brown with a beautiful bodice of pink lace and ruffles at her shoulders and a full flowing skirt to the floor. She was very excited, for such events were few and far between. The night before the grand affair she went up to her room. She held her new dress up in front of her. She wanted to see how the gold chain would look with her dress for the wedding, so she went to the dresser to get it.

The cups were there and she carefully took each one off in turn, then lifted the little lid down inside the cups, but the chain was gone. She turned white. The last time she had worn it was when the Breyers had been to supper a few nights before. She hadn't worn it out; she seldom did. She was always careful to put it back in the cups. It had to be there in her room. She looked in all her drawers. The children couldn't have taken it because they weren't allowed in her room. It wasn't likely that someone would have broken in, because nothing else was gone. Martha wouldn't have taken it; she knew how much it meant to her. She was still shaking when she was called down to supper.

When she entered the dining room, everyone looked in her direction. She walked over to the table, sat down and hung her head. Her grandmother was blunt.

"Edna, what's troubling you?"

"My gold chain, it's gone! And if it isn't returned by the time we're ready to leave for the church tomorrow, I'm going to the jail house and bring back the sheriff."

"You wouldn't do that to your Aunt Jenny, not on her wedding day!"

"Leave her be Mother," said Jenny. "I'm on her side. Someone in this house has taken it, and that someone has no appreciation of her only link to her past, that's all she has left. Emma has always had her family here. Edna barely knew her mother and remembers little about her father."

"I didn't take it. I wouldn't do a thing like that," said Emma.

"I know you didn't, Emma," said Edna. "Please, let's eat our food. Martha has gone to a lot of trouble."

After supper the family and friends went to the parlor, which they did on rare occasions. Jenny and Felix opened presents. Edna tried to be gay and took notes about the gifts, who they were from, and everyone had a chance to inspect everything.

"Where are you going to keep them all, Jenny?" asked Felix.

"It'll take a warehouse to store them all, but there's still some room in the adobe until we get a place of our own and settle down."

After the last box was opened, Edna excused herself and went upstairs. Emma wanted to follow her, but Jenny's eyes told her not to. She undressed, got into bed and lay there thinking. Anyone could have slipped in while they were downstairs. She got out of bed, walked over to the dresser and picked up the elk horn cups. Slowly she pulled them off, one at a time, first the large one on the outside, then the next and another until she came to the smallest cup of all, the one on the very inside. She lifted the lid, and there it was, the gold chain. Edna sat there looking at it, tears of joy streaming down her face, knowing full well the mystery would never be untangled.

Jenny and Felix were married the next day. They had a lovely church wedding at St. Vibianas, then went back to the house on Second Street for the reception. Many of the Devlins were there, as were the Childs, the Breyers, the Howards. It was a lovely affair. After the wedding the bride and groom went to Yosemite for their honeymoon.

At Yosemite Jenny and Felix stayed at the lodge. They took long walks and enjoyed the beautiful valley. Then Jenny became ill. At first she thought she had problems with her stomach because of the excitement of the wedding. She had always been in robust health. But even the beautiful surroundings of the lush green canyons and breathtaking waterfalls couldn't quiet her fears. She didn't improve, so they decided to take the stage to San Francisco so Jenny could be checked by a doctor. The tossing and turning as they traveled over the winding dirt roads made the journey a dreadful ordeal and seemed endless. When they arrived in San Francisco Jenny was immediately taken to the hospital.

"I must operate, Mrs. Devlin," said the doctor. "There is no other way to know what's wrong."

"First let me get my mother here, doctor. All her property is in my name, and I want to sign it back."

A wire was sent to Regina in Los Angeles. She took the first train to San Francisco to be at her daughter's side. After signing all the property back, Jenny consented to having the surgery.

It left no doubt as to her condition. Jenny Devlin had cancer throughout her body, so they sewed her back up again. She had been married but such a short time.

Regina made plans to return to Los Angeles. She was a sad little woman, for she and Jenny had always been so close. She wanted Jenny and Felix to have what little time they had left together.

When Regina got home, she said to Edna, "Los Angeles is growing, and the Roman Catholic Cemetery on Broadway is too near the center of town to be very permanent. At the church before I went to San Francisco I learned there is to be a new Calvary cemetery in the country along El Camino Real. It's located on the mesa near the Rio Hondo River, but far enough away to be safe."

A few days later she and Edna went down to Gollers, hired a horse and buggy and went in search of the larger cemetery plot. They traveled over the old dirt road, El Camino Real, to Calvary cemetery grounds. It was marked with a high iron fence and a little stone office building. They drove in, talked to the man in charge, selected a plot of land large enough to accommodate all the family, eighteen plots in all.

As her grandmother was talking to the man, Edna overheard her say, "I want my husband's body and our family monument brought out here. He was buried at the Catholic Cemetery on Fort Street. Of course, its called Broadway now. Every time it rains, the cemetery is under water and it just breaks my heart. If you will take care of that, you can include it in my bill."

"I'll do that, Mrs. Weinshank." She joined Edna who was looking at another monument on the other side of the little narrow pathway. It had the name Phelan on it. There were a few other stones scattered around.

"Is ours like this?"

"Yes, very similar. Just a marker with the family name. It's getting dark, Edna. We'd best go home."

On the way Regina said, "I've always dreaded the thought of ever burying one of my own children. First it was your mother, a terrible blow, and I hate to think of her being buried so far away. We came here today to have a place ready for Jenny. I fear it won't be long."

And it wasn't. Jenny Devlin was buried in the new Calvary Cemetery in the family plot, the one her mother had just bought.

Tootsie Weinshank had spent so much of her time with the Sisters of Charity under their persuasion and guidance, she decided to become a nun. When she told her father and grandmother, they were dismayed at first, but her grandmother said, "If you're determined to do it, I'll make it possible."

Tootsie's grandmother sold a house and lot on Hope Street to pay her way into the convent, and the little angel made plans to go to work in the house of the Lord. It was a day of bittersweet sadness, the day she said good-bye to all the family.

It was Edna who spoke up. "Tootsie, may I have a lock of your hair to remember you by?"

"Of course, Edna, I won't be needing it."

Grandma wept, Martha became busier than usual in the kitchen, and her father went off to the saloon.

St. Mary's Church

Chapter 33

By the turn of the century, the economy was back to normal. With all the building going on in Whittier, the kiln on the Phelan ranch was fired up night and day. Load after wagonload of bricks was sent to town, many being delivered to Greenleaf and Philadelphia streets where a store was under construction.

A frail man by the name of John Croke was hired on as Nell's new piano teacher. He wasn't much to Mary's liking because he made his living by playing the violin, and she didn't think too much of that. But he had come from a wealthy and highly respected family in Ireland, and a park had been named in their honor.

He kept coming around, spending more time on Nell's lesson than he was being paid for. It was some time before Mary caught on that he was there for more than just teaching Nell how to play.

Then, one day, he asked Nell to marry him.

Mary overheard him ask, so she she went storming into the room. But this time it was to no avail.

"I've always done what you wanted me to do, Ma. This time I'm doing what I want to do," answered Nell as she bristled, holding her own against her headstrong mother, and for once in her life her mother had to back down.

Annie was upstairs in bed. She had a cough that was sapping her strength with each passing week. Because of this, they had a simple wedding ceremony at Saint Mary's church. After the wedding Nell and John went to live in a small house on a piece of property Nell's mother owned.

John went off to play his violin in some nearby town, and Nell was left alone. She spent a lot of time back home. After her little Annie was born, Mary started working on Nell.

"Send him packing, Nell, this is no life for you, and I need you here at home, to help me with your sister."

"I love him, Mother."

"Nell, you can't spend your whole life this way. He's a vagabond, always on the move, off playing somewhere while you're left at home by yourself."

"I want to give him more time."

"Suit yourself, Nell, but if you had any sense, you'd consider yourself well rid of him."

One time, while Nell was at the Judson house, caring for Annie, her mother hitched Dick to the buggy and headed for their house. She took everything belonging to John, put it outside, then locked the door and went on home.

After a few days, Nell could stand it no longer and went home. When she got there, she found that John had removed all his belongings and had gone away. She stayed on a few days, waiting for him to return. When she was convinced he wasn't coming back, she moved back in with her mother and took up where she left off: caring for her baby and her sister, cooking for the family and the hired help and picking up after her brothers.

Upstairs in bed, Annie's cough lingered on. One day Nell was told to put a few of Annie's things in a bag for her to take with her to the infirmary in Los Angeles. She was going to be cared for by the Sisters of Charity. Joe was told to hitch Dick to the buggy. He carried his sister out, his mother nowhere to be found. They headed off in the direction of Los Angeles.

Annie said, "Joe, I don't think I'll ever see this place again."

"Oh, Annie! Don't say that," he answered as they traveled along El Camino Real.

After a while Annie weakly asked, "Joe, are you going to come see me?"

"As often as you want me to."

"Come by yourself. I don't want Ma to come."

"Is it because she didn't say 'good-bye'?"

"That's part of it."

"She couldn't, Annie. You know Ma can't show her feelings."

"Let's go fast, Joe. Ma's not here to stop us," and Joe gave Dick the nod.

The house on Second Street held too many sad reminders of Jenny, so when Regina's son, George, got a job at the Whittier State School in their horticulture program, she sold the house and bought one in Whittier on Gregory Street and set up housekeeping for him. Edna and her Uncle Frank went there to live as well.

One day, George hitched the horse to the buggy, walked back into the house for a quick cup of coffee. Noticing Edna sitting at the table he said, "Edna, I'm going out in the country to get a black walnut sapling. Would you like to come along."

"Yes, Uncle George, I'd love to. Wait a minute. I'll get my hat and join you."

They drove along El Camino Real skirting the Whittier Hills to Carbon Canyon, taking several hours to get there. George found a sturdy sapling on a hillside, just what he had in mind. George got out his shovel, dug up the sapling, wrapped a sack around it, poured on enough water to keep it damp and put it in the buggy to take back to Whittier. When they got back to the State School Property, Edna watched her Uncle while he planted it alongside the County Road. "This road used to be called El Camino Real, Edna. It goes back to the rancho days."

"Yes, Grandmother used to love to talk about it, Uncle George. Do you like working here?"

"Yes, I do. I feel fortunate to be here and be part of it. It's wonderful, the things they're doing for both the boys and girls. Most of them leave with a good education in farming and the trades and are making it on the outside. Well, Edna, a little more water for the tree and the job will be done."

"Do you think this tree will grow and provide shade so people can stop and rest a bit?"

"I hope it'll stay here a hundred years or more and grow up to be a beautiful landmark. It'll take some doing, I'll have to water it frequently for a while, and if you wish you can come along."

"I'd like that, Uncle George."

"Let me get that water and we'll head for home."

Edna Lee was sitting in the choir loft at St. Mary's, a few blocks from home, the first time she saw Joe Phelan. She gazed down on his bright red hair, and wanting to get a better look, she wadded up a piece of paper, made it into a spit ball and threw it down, hitting its mark, right on the top of his head. He looked up at her with those flashing blue eyes, and she giggled and looked away.

A few days later John Lynch invited Joe to his house for a social to meet Edna Lee on a Sunday afternoon after church. Edna looked lovely. Her curly light brown hair fell softly around her face and down her back, complimenting her rosy cheeks and fair complexion. She was beautifully dressed making the simple country clothes seem drab by comparison. She wore two pairs of glasses. The people in the country were not accustomed to them but they were impressed because only the wealthy could afford them.

Joe was introduced to Edna by Katie Lynch, his father's best friends when he first arrived in the valley in 1869. The guest of honor, Edna Lee, sat with Katie waiting for the others to arrive.

"Joe's parents had their wedding supper here, Edna, in this very room in fact. All the neighbors were here, the Pallettes, the Sorensons, the Richlings and the Isbells. We were able to get Tom and Mary to dance the 'jig.' It was a grand affair. My, what a long time ago that was, but that's enough talk from me."

The Lynches had the food arranged nicely on the table, making it a lovely affair. After the social, they stood around in the yard talking. Joe walked up to Edna and said, "Edna, If you'd like, I can take you home."

"That's very nice of you, Joe. I'd like that very much."

Just then he was distracted, and when he turned around to look for her, he found her already in the buggy waiting to go home.

A few days later Edna and her grandmother went to the Ott's place where Joe was working. "We're on our way to Los Angeles to see a parade. Would you like to go, Joe?"

"Sounds good. Yes, I would. I'll be through here in a short time, and I'll join you."

"Uncle Frank wants to come too, so will you bring him? Just pick him up at our house." Then she cracked the whip and they were on their way. Joe wasn't nearly as interested in the parade as being with Edna; so he shrugged his shoulders. Well, at any rate, he'd see her later on.

Edna and her grandma continued on. As they rode along El Camino Real, now called the County Road, they passed many Chinamen on their way to market traveling over the mesa and on to the City of the Angels.

One day the Whites visited the Phelans on the ranch and Mary took the opportunity to get some information.

"Stephen, in all your business dealings, have you ever heard of the name of Weinshank?"

"Why yes, we've known them for years. I handled Andrew Weinshank's estate when he died, a fine German family. He came from Alabama. They made foodstuffs for the miners of the territory, did it for years, accumulated quite a lot of money."

"Alabama? Wouldn't they be southern sympathizers?" asked Mary.

"Regina never mentioned it, but if she felt that way, she kept it to herself."

"Our son, Joe, has been courting their granddaughter, Edna Lee, and I wanted to be sure it was all right before letting it go on."

"Her father was an Englishman, a circus performer, traveled all over the world and was very famous in his day. You don't have anything to worry about there."

"It's good to hear this. Tom, go look for Joe. Tell him the Whites are here."

At first Joe took the streetcar when he courted Edna, and one time as he boarded, he stepped into some manure. He didn't see it at the time, didn't even smell it, but when he got aboard, the dirty looks he got made him think something was wrong. Yes, sure enough, the smell was coming from him. Because he had so far to go and it was useless to scrape it off, he just put down the window and suffered it out. After that bad experience, when Joe went to Santa Monica, he hitched Dick to the buggy and off he went to their summer cottage.

He and Edna walked along the beach hand-in-hand, the warm gentle breezes hitting their faces. Joe didn't care for the water. He didn't swim well and wouldn't swim in the ocean. What Joe really wanted was Edna to himself, away from peering eyes, but he knew it was useless to look for cover for fear it would bring either her Uncle Frank or Uncle George from the porch.

Joe was getting sunburned because of his delicate Irish skin, and after a while Edna took pity on him, "My skin can take it out here, Joe, but yours can't. We'd best go back. Your mother will never forgive me if you aren't able to do your chores."

"Yes, you're right. I'm beginning to feel that burn already."

"You look so funny, Joe. Your face is about the color of your hair," and she started running. Joe caught up with her, and she collapsed in his arms, and he kissed her for the first time.

Later in the evening Joe hitched Dick up to his buggy and started for home. On the homeward trip, sunburnt and tired, but knowing Edna was sweet on him, made him tingle. The trip was long and Joe was tired, so he wrapped the reins around the bar, curled up on the seat and went to sleep. When he woke up, he was home, and Dick was outside the barn waiting for something to eat.

It was an exciting day when the pews arrived at St. Mary's church. Joe was on hand to help move them in. Others were there with hammers to secure them to the floor. When the job was done, the Phelans got their assigned pew.

"What about singing in the choir, Joe?" asked Father Lilly.

"Not me, Father. I can't sing. Our mother would love to have our little brother, Edward, sing though. He has a beautiful voice. But I'm not too sure he will. He doesn't like singing before people."

The next time Mary had a barbecue on the ranch, Father Lilly was there. He was having a good time but always had the church in mind. When he saw Mary, he approached her.

"Joe tells me Edward has a beautiful singing voice. Why doesn't he sing in the choir?" asked the good Father.

"If you can talk him into it, more power to you," replied Mary. As Edward was coming toward them, Father Lilly tried to head him off.

"Edward, how would you like to sing in the choir? I understand you have a beautiful voice." Edward with a startled look on his face, turned brick red and ran off without saying a word. "Well, I guess that takes care of that. I'll just have to settle for Nell playing the organ, being the only Phelan participating," he muttered to himself. Father Lilly then went in search of others to take part.

He found Joe and Edna holding hands talking to Tomas Sanchez.

"Well Edna, how about you, do you sing?"

"No father I can't carry a tune in a bucket. Joe can sing better than I can," and Joe gave her hand a squeeze.

Annie never did return home. She blamed her mother for all her troubles, though she had no cause to, and didn't want to see her. But Joe made those weekly trips to Los Angeles over the many months she lay there under the care of the Sisters.

Little by little she wasted away, that little maverick girl who once had been so much like her pa and so hard to tame, so full of life. Then on April 10, 1901, she died of consumption, just twenty-one days shy of her twenty-first birthday.

Joe wanted to ask Edna Lee to be his wife. He was still wearing his mourning band, so he spoke to the priest about it.

"Our sister Annie hasn't been gone a year yet, father, but I want to marry Edna Lee as soon as possible if our mother's willing."

"I think that can be arranged, Joe. I'll prepare the dispensation and let you know as soon as I get word."

When word arrived for their permission to marry, they set the day for October 31st.

Edna's grandmother purchased brown material from Robinsons in Los Angeles for Edna's dress. Edna wrote to her sister Polly, at Columbus, Ohio, where she was stationed for the winter quarters for the circus, to tell her of her plans to marry Joe Phelan and that her grandmother had selected brown material for her wedding dress. Polly wrote back that brown was not appropriate for a young girl getting married and that she was sending blue broadcloth.

When the material arrived, Edna was delighted with it. She took it to the French lady in uptown Whittier, Angie Gordon, who had a store on the southeast corner of Philadelphia and Greenleaf. She made Edna a lovely dress. It had a high lace collar and yoke and was gathered down the front with a long train behind and bustles on either side. She also made Edna's going-away hat with appliques made from left over fabric from the dress.

Joe and Edna made the trip to Los Angeles on Main Street near St. Vibianas to have their wedding picture taken. Edna took both dresses to keep peace in the family.

Then the day of the wedding arrived. The young couple stood at the altar before the priest at St. Mary's Church. Mary sitting in the first row of pews couldn't help but think back to the day when she and her Tom were married by Father Mora at the Lady Queen of the Angels in Los Angeles, a wedding far different from this, for she was dressed in her modest peasant gown. Edna, as lovely as a bride could be, was standing there in the height of fashion in her beautiful light blue gown, billowing to the floor. Around her neck she wore the gold chain.

Joe, standing at her side, straight and handsome with his bright red hair and ruddy complexion was looking down at Edna, no more listening to the priest than he did on communion or any other day in church.

Mary hid her doubts about the marriage, and she tried to keep them to herself, but the Weinshanks being from the South, being southern sympathizers was sticking in her craw. She hated all southerners, and didn't Edna have a Robert E. Lee in her family, and wasn't he a general in that war? That war had taken her Tom from her as surely as if he'd been shot, a war he needed no part of. He left her with six young ones to raise. Dan, hard working, steadfast, but no businessman, was by her side; Nell married to that vagabond off somewhere, sat holding her baby on her lap; her son Tom was off working for the railroad, only God knows where; little Annie, the wild one, already in her grave, gone but such a short time. Sitting beside her was little Edward, a boy of ten. She looked down at him and thought to herself, "Maybe in time he'll be the one to help me run the ranch."

After the wedding the young couple went to the Weinshank home on Gregory for a lovely reception. The table was heaped with all sorts of good German food and everyone had a chance to see the wedding gifts.

The young couple was lavished with a host of things; kitchen furniture; a beautiful oak table and chairs with a sideboard to match; for the living room, a long leather couch; for the dining room a round oak table with chairs; and a bedroom set of bird's-eye maple.

Mary gave them Dick and the buggy as her wedding gift, which pleased them very much because they both were so fond of him. So, they began their marriage in fine style.

They went to live in a little frame house on the Guirado property and started raising their family. Joe named their firstborn Thomas after his own dear sweet father. Their second son, Francis, was named after Edna's side of the house.

When the boys were small they spent a lot of time on the ranch. Francis was too small, but Tom played with his cousins, Annie, Mervyn and Lucille, in the barn where they were surrounded by the delicious smell of newly mown hay. They went to the other barn, but they had an eerie feeling because of the stories they had heard about the Chinamen who made brooms and stayed in that dark and dingy place from morning till night. They loved to hear their dad speak of the time when the Chinamen took the pole to him. They peeked inside and found it full of cobwebs, so they didn't venture in.

After about three years, Joe got the hankering to go to El Centro. A canal had been built by the Chaffee family not too far from the

Mexican border, bringing water to the area, and though the surrounding land was desert, it showed great promise. There were hundreds of acres of tillable soil which up to then had been only wasteland.

Joe planned to produce milk. He got some good cows, the best he could find, and decided to make the trip by train. He loaded them up at the siding, took a good dog along to discourage hobos who might happen to tag along. Edna and the two little boys had good seats in the front part of the train.

When they got to El Centro, they found just the place along the Dogwood Canal, plenty of water, lots of fine pasture land, and the property had a small house on it.

Because Joe was painfully thin, the doctor suggested that if he drank beer he might gain weight. This sounded like a great idea to him, so he talked it over with Edna, and they decided to brew their own.

They had a cellar, cool and dark, a perfect place to age and store the beer. They assembled everything and got to work, and after the last bottle had been delivered down into that dark and dingy place, they were quite pleased with themselves.

A few nights later after the children were sound asleep and they too had crawled into bed, about midnight they heard a popping sound, then another and another. Edna became alarmed, thinking it was someone shooting at them from outside.

"Joe, get up. Someone's out there!" Joe wasn't an easy one to rouse, but finally he woke up and heard the noise, too.

"Edna, that noise isn't coming from the outside—it's coming from the cellar!"

So they got out of bed. Edna put on a robe, Joe still in his long underwear, and the two went down to investigate. Sure enough many of the bottles had burst and beer was everywhere. Edna buried her face in her hands, sat down on the cellar steps, "Oh Joe, all our hard work and all the money we spent has gone up in one big explosion. But, even so, it's hilarious, something I'll never forget." Just then another one exploded and sprayed all over Joe, and they laughed till their sides ached.

Edna helped Joe with milking cows and transporting the milk into town tied onto the back of the buggy.

One day, Joe hitched up old Dick, helped the two little boys in, and lifted Edna in. She was all dressed in white because of the heat. Joe then sent them on their way.

Edna had put her gold chain in a little brown sack because after delivering the milk she was going to town to see a friend and show the chain to her.

They traveled along on a narrow dirt road, and after a while, the boys began to scuffle. The little bag on the seat beside them fell out, and they continued on down the line. Following them some distance back was a man on horseback. He saw something fall from the buggy. He quickened his pace, and when he came to the place where he thought he saw it fall he stopped, and sure enough he found it and picked it up. He could see the buggy in the distance and thought to himself, "I wonder if that's Edna Phelan and her boys." He remounted his horse, picked up his pace, caught up with her and pulled her over to the side of the road.

"Oh, hello Bert," said Edna. "Sure hot out here, isn't it?"

"It certainly is. I think those two boys of yours must have been rough housing, because this little bag fell out of your buggy."

"Oh! And you saw it drop! It is mine. How nice of you to bring it back to me. I don't think I could have ever found it on my own."

He handed her the bag. She looked inside, and all rolled in the bottom of the sack was her prize possession—the gold chain.

When she got home that night, Edna told Joe the story.

"Edna, for pity sakes, let that be a lesson to you, and thank God for Bert while you're at it."

Their third child, Marie, was born while they were living at El Centro. When she was a baby, they decided to sell their dairy stock and go back to Whittier. Edna had agreed before they left for El Centro that if she were to work alongside Joe milking cows and delivering milk, it was going to mean a new home for the family if and when they moved back to Whittier.

When they set out, they had a large wagon loaded with hay and the family furniture. Tom was seven now, and he was given the job of driving the buggy and watching his baby sister. Joe and Edna were on the big wagon, and their son, Francis, two years younger than Tom, was with them.

They traveled over flat country on the way to San Diego, met a Mexican deserter who needed food, which they gladly shared, and continued on, traveling farther south than Kearny when he brought the Army of the West to California. The Phelans were going to visit friends south of San Diego.

They climbed fairly steep hills, Joe put blocks under the wheels, Edna took over the ribbons hoping it would do the trick, but to no avail. "Edna, we're going to have to take off the sides of this wagon, or we'll never make it through the pass. And besides that, we're going to have to lighten the load."

"You mean we're going to have to leave the hay?"

"No, Edna, we can't do that. The animals have to eat."

"Then you mean my furniture? "

"Only the sewing machine, Edna. Then maybe we can make it."

"All right, Joe, if that's the way it has to be," and together they took the sewing machine off the wagon and left it along the roadside.

When they arrived in San Diego, they visited their friends for a few days, then headed north, following El Camino Real.

It was a week of traveling and stopping along the seashore. Edna was happy, for the weather was beautiful and the trip was a continuous holiday.

When they got to Whittier, they moved into a house on the ranch and stayed there several years. It was just a little white frame house with an outhouse out back.

They had a mother cat that had seven kittens. The little one, Marie, just toddling around, wanted to play with them, but her brother, Francis, wouldn't share.

She had to go to the bathroom, so she went into the outhouse and the kittens followed her in. Marie was so angry at her brother she dropped them down the hole.

When Francis discovered what happened, he went crying to the house.

"Ma, sister threw the kittens down the hole."

"Oh, mercy me! What'll we do now?"

No sooner had Joe walked in the door after spending the day hauling oil for the roads, than he was faced by Edna, still in a dither. "Joe, am I glad to see you! Marie threw the kittens down the hole."

"Calm down, Edna. It may take some doing, but one way or another I'll get them out."

He walked out the back door, looked the situation over. He could see the kittens way down in the hole moving around, mewing helplessly, trying to get out. He decided he had no other choice than to push the outhouse over and pull the kittens out, one by one. After he got the last one out, Francis dried his tears, Edna gave all the kittens a bath and little Marie was sent to bed without any supper.

The circus had come to town. They were performing at Santa

Ana. Edna's sister, Rosa, was on the bill. She got in touch with Joe and Edna, and they made plans to spend the day with her at the circus grounds.

They were thrilled to watch Rosa as she juggled eight flaming torches while riding bareback around the ring. Then later on in the program she juggled while balancing on a large ball. This was quite remarkable because Rosa was about forty years old.

"It was wonderful watching you perform, Rosa. You're looking fit as a fiddle with no apparent plans for retirement," remarked Edna.

"The training father gave me made it possible for me to make a good living."

"I've often wondered whatever happened to our father's money. Do you know?" asked Edna.

"No, I don't. Polly was in charge. She did get daddy's horse Mazeppa, traveled all over the world putting him through his paces. Our father did such a wonderful job of training Mazeppa and he could do such wonderful feats, he made Polly wealthy."

"How long can you keep this up?" asked Joe.

"As long as I'm able and God is willing. I hope that will be a long time," she answered. "I have no reason to quit. I'm healthy, and I have many more good years ahead of me. Of course if I fall and am injured like Polly, that would be a different matter.

"Oh, no!" said Edna. "I didn't know Polly was injured."

"Didn't you know, Edna? Polly died. She fell while riding bareback and had to give it up. She worked quite a while as a wardrobe mistress, at least four or five years."

"I didn't know that. I thought she was still riding."

"Then a few years ago she got cancer. The doctor thought it was due to the fall."

"That's so sad. I really loved her. She had always been so kind. She must have been very ill at the time we were getting married. Grandma picked out brown material for my wedding dress. When I wrote to Polly and told her about it, she sent me a beautiful piece of light blue material and sent a sweet note with it. She must have died right after that."

"Yes, I'm sure she was very ill."

"And what about Harry and Lavater? asked Edna.

"They're dead, too, Edna. Lavater is buried in Southhampton, England, where our father was born."

"Oh! He died young, too. How old was he?"

"Thirty-six. He worked for Barnum and Bailey. He was the only bareback rider in America who was able to do a pirouette from knee to knee and backward in a back somersault."

"That's unbelievable" said Joe.

"And Harry?" asked Edna.

"He didn't come back to the United States with the others. He married a lady in Penang and lived there for a while. Later he came back to California. He died in Sacramento in August of '93. Now you, Emma, Robert and I are the only ones left."

"What about Robert?"

"Oh! He's still in the business. You know, our father always thought his parents were circus people because he was so easy to train. He's back east somewhere."

"I used to hear from him from time to time."

"Yes, he was very fond of you," said Rosa. Then continued on to say, "Bud Gorman, our sister Polly's husband, is still at the top. He's the equestrian director for Ringling, and he has his own railroad car. He is a champion hurdler. When he and Polly were married, he was one of the greatest performers of all time. He could do a backward somersault over a banner as he rode around the ring. Now he drives a string of thirty-five Kentucky thoroughbreds at a full gallop circling the hippodrome track."

"That's hard to believe!" said Joe. "I can't imagine anyone being able to do that."

"What about Emma?" asked Rosa.

"She went to England to live on Frank's family estate. Frank was a descendant of Sir Francis Bacon, the great writer. Their children, Francis and Winnie, were born there. Frank's asthma again became troublesome, so they came back to California. They live in Glendale.

"Then she did marry well. What about the others?" asked Edna.

"Francis and Eugene could still be living. We lost track of them sometime back. Just think, our father had seventeen children."

"What about the rest of them?" asked Edna.

"All I know is they all died young. Our folks never talked about them, and we never had the heart to ask."

"My grandmother could name them all. Let's see. There was Eugene, Francis, Theodore, Polly, Ellena, John, James, Lavater, Harry, you, the baby that went down on the Brother Jonathan with your mother, Charles, Emma, Robert, Frank, Augusta and me."

"That's a feat in itself!" said Rosa.

"I wonder how he took care of us all," said Edna.

"Children can be an asset, especially when you're in the circus," and they all laughed.

"Then you didn't know I was a star for Ringling Brothers?"

"No, I didn't," said Edna.

"You didn't hear of the terrible train accident?"

"No."

"I thought everyone in the United States knew about that. I was working for Walter L. Main in '94. Our circus train, loaded with performers, equipment and animals, was creeping up the summit of the mountain near Altoona, Pennsylvania, two miles from Horseshoe Bend, when suddenly, without a word of warning, the train lurched forward, then toppled down the side of the mountain. It was pandemonium. People were lying all around, lots of dead animals, many out of their cages walking around in a daze. By the time they got all the animals rounded up and counted the dead, it amounted to eighty performers and one hundred animals. I'm surprised you didn't know this, for days the papers across the country covered the story."

"We don't get the Los Angeles paper here, and so I didn't know."

"Did your grandmother ever tell you about our father's pavilion?"

"Oh, yes! She talked a lot about it. It burned down a few years ago. It was Sacramento's best opera house for years."

"A lot of important people performed there. Mark Twain gave speeches there, Buffalo Bill and Lotta Crabtree performed on his stage. Lotta captivated the audience of miners with 'Whisky in the Jug' and 'Annie Laurie' and her imitation of Lola Montez in her 'Spider Dance'."

"I wish I could have seen his pavilion."

"I wish you had, too—it was beautiful. Did she ever mention a man by the name of Maguire?"

"Yes, she said he took it over and re-named it the Metropolitan."

"He made over a million dollars in his lifetime. Of course he owned or managed other theatres, but our father's was the best. He lost it all and died a poor man. That happens so much in our business."

"Grandmother talked a lot about it and about our family too. That's why I know as much as I do."

The men were tearing down the tent and putting all the properties away. Little petite Rosa was saying "Goodbye-bye" to her little sister.

"I'm so glad your grandmother was able to bring you back to this great land, Edna and that you were able to meet this fine young man, and I do hope you'll be very happy. I'm sure you wouldn't remember this, but as our father always said, the optimist that he was, 'Another town, another place, another fortune to be made, we must not give up hope.' So when things get you down, try to remember what he stood for."

Joe and Edna Phelan

Whittier Public Library

Chapter 34

St. Mary's Church in Whittier was being torn down. A new, larger Catholic church was being built on the same site. Our folks were offered the chance to buy the lumber from the old church, which was a great savings for them. Our mother was pleased, because she was going to have a new home for the family, one up on a hill on North Newlin. It was in this house where Annie, Rosemary, Vivian and I were born.

In 1920 a French Basque by the name of Gracian Arranbide suggested our father give up the lovely home in Whittier and move further out in the country. "Get a couple of acres, he said. "Land with fruit trees and raise some animals. This way you'll always be able to put food on your table. In order to get you started, I'll buy you a cow." He was as good as his word. He gave us a beautiful little Jersey cow and we named her "Betsy."

Our father had a lot of respect for his Basque friend. Gracian never married, but raised thirteen children, those of his relatives. His two favorites, Mary and Pete had been abandoned. They were told their father and mother had died, but Gracian learned from the Pellisiers their father was living in Paris. Then another member of the family wanted to take over some of the children and took Gracian to court to get custody. Gracian spoke very little English, so he asked our father to go to court with him to interpret. One of the witnesses got up and said, "Joe Phelan isn't interpreting right."

This infuriated the judge. He pounded his gavel and said in a firm voice, "I speak Spanish myself, and he's doing a great job." Then the witness sat down and kept quiet. Gracian was given custody of the children.

Our mother and father both felt Gracian was right. With seven children, they needed to think in terms of a larger place. They found a two acre piece outside of town on King's Lane. On it were fruit trees and a large chicken house. Our father moved us into the large old frame house with high ceilings and long narrow windows, all the family furniture, the big oak sideboard, table and chairs, the leather couch, dining room table and the birds-eye maple bedroom set they had received as wedding gifts.

The railroad ran along our property and every year the circus came to town. While Dad was doing his early morning chores he could hear it in the distance as it came lumbering into town. By the time it passed our property, those of us who were lucky enough to be there, found it was something to be remembered for the remainder of our days.

We didn't attend the circus often because there were so many of us. Money was too tight for that, but every year the circus came rolling into town. Our dog, Lassie, couldn't resist the sound of the Calliope, and with no one to join her, she went by herself. The constable, Bob Way, would call our father up, "Joe, come get your dog. She's here again. Seems as though I have to make this call every time the circus comes to town."

"Yes, Bob, " our father answered, "I'll be right up, but it really isn't our fault. One day Lassie just walked into our yard, and we've had her ever since. I wouldn't be surprised if she traveled with the circus before she came to us. There is no doubt about it, she has circus in her blood."

Our father's brother, Tom, died of a lung condition in 1925, that sensitive, brilliant boy who so wanted to be like his pa, to get up in court and plead cases.

I remember being at the funeral standing under a tree, during the graveside service. My mother was holding my hand. I looked up at her with a child's curiosity, not knowing nor comprehending the gravity of the situation. The mourners stood by, heads bowed in prayer, the men around the casket let out the ropes little by little, until it reached its final resting place. Dirt was thrown, in and we solemnly walked away. One month to the day after the funeral, word was received that our Uncle Tom had passed the bar.

When we were growing up, it was sheer joy sitting around the kitchen table at supper time hearing the stories of the "old days."

Our father loved to tell us about the time he and Jack Lane ran off during afternoon recess to swim, how he got a switching the next day from Mrs. Bower, knowing full well he would get another to match it when he got home.

He also told us about the time he made funny faces at the Chinamen looking down at them from the tree top, how they kept poking him, till he thought they'd never quit, and about going to El Ranchito and going out to the corral to watch the Don and Pete Serrano brand the calves. Then he would go back to the patio, and if he was lucky and waited long enough, one of the Indian servants would offer him a bunelo.

For us it was always fun going to the dances sponsored by "Ye Olden Time Club," a club our folks belonged to, made up of couples who enjoyed dancing. They hired a band, rented a hall, tucked us children, Annie, Vivian and me, into bed in a room adjacent to the dance hall. They allowed Marie to stay and dance, and then danced the whole night through. The boys never attended. They found other things to do.

Our father had been crippled in an accident just before World War I, but that didn't keep him from dancing. While our mother sat and watched and talked with the other women, dad got around to all the ladies. He didn't care if they were fat or thin; he had a dance with each and was a favorite for it.

Life wasn't made up entirely of gaiety and fun. There were always chores to be done, animals to feed, eggs to be gathered, and if the cow dropped a calf or the pig had piglets, we were all there to watch it happen, but mostly life was uneventful and not very exciting but for this one exception, the day our father brought home a brand new Model-T Ford. To start it, the boys took turns at the crank, and our father got behind the wheel and goosed it up.

The following day, we were invited to "Ye Olden Time Club" picnic at the Orange County Park. Marie sat with the folks in front. Vivian and I dressed in brand new matching jump suits sat on our brothers' laps, while Annie sat between us. We were so excited we kept bouncing up and down as we traveled along the Country Road.

Vivian spoke up, "I'll bet I see the park first."

"I'll bet I see it first," I answered.

But it was our father who spoke up. "You both lost, girls. Your mother and I saw it first."

"How fast are we going, Dad?" shouted Tom.

"Fifteen miles an hour, Tom. Listen, boys, we're coming to a little grade up ahead, so get ready to get out and push when I stop. Maybe we can make the grade, and maybe we can't, but I don't want to take that chance." At that command, the boys jumped out, one on either side and pushed. Then on the downhill side they jumped back in, and we were again on our way.

We arrived at the park in time for lunch. Our mother and our sister, Marie, helped set the food on the table. While they were doing that, we went on the giant slide, some went for a ride on the lake and the boys played ball nearby.

After a wonderful day at the park, we piled back into the car, and dad drove us home. I sat curled up on Francis' lap and went to sleep.

On the sheep ranch, our friend Marius Meyers, the Basque, Victoria's father, drilled a water well. Steaming water spurted forth indicating the presence of oil and soon after that, the "oil boom was on." The Standlee family also came to California early. They owned a small chicken ranch in Santa Fe Springs. They sold it, but the man they sold it to couldn't make a go of it, so they had to take it back. Then, along came a chance for them to drill for oil, and a good producing well came in on their property. One day while Mert Standlee was in town walking down the street he stopped to talk to our father.

"Well, Mert, I hear you struck it rich," our father said enthusiastically.

"Sure did, Joe, and every cent is up there in Washington Hadley's bank."

The next time our father talked to Mert's wife, Gertie, he said to her, "I was talking to Mert the other day, and he said all your oil money is up in Washington Hadley's bank."

"That's right, Joe. When we were poor, once in a while I'd get a new dress. I haven't had a new one since we struck it rich."

"Just be patient Gertie, I'm sure he'll loosen up."

"You may be right, Joe. From what I've heard, the oil under the ground in Santa Fe Springs is unlimited."

"Paul Getty and Alfonso Bell are certainly doing well," added Joe. "I'd like to have that kind of luck."

One of our brother Tom's classmate friends was Eddie Guirado, Bernardino Guiardo's grandson. Bernardino had the lovely Victorian home in Fulton Wells where the Phelans spent many a night dancing while Nell played the piano and Angel the violin.

Guiardo's grandson, Eddie, had aspirations to become a boxer and had a few bouts in his time. When he was in high school, Eddie, now called "Babe," Joe Stringfield and our brother, Tom, went off to the Ozarks in Tom's Ford fliver. It had a windshield and a canvas top, otherwise it was open, all held together by a frame.

By the time they got to the Ozarks, they ran out of money. So, our brother went to work unloading cement sacks from the railroad cars at night. Otherwise they wouldn't make it back to California.

When the boys got back to Whittier they stopped at "Rosies" newstand at the corner of Comstock and Philadelphia Streets. It was only a matter of minutes before word reached our house that the boys were back and "Why don't you come take a look at the car?"

"That we did, and what a sight it was." Tom's fliver was decorated all over with dirty clothes, especially their "stinky" socks. Years later, Babe became a Superior Court judge and we were all very proud of him.

We attended the old Bailey Street School, then the new Bailey Street School was built facing Hadley. Mr. E. K. Bishop was principal.

After school, my sister Vivian and I went to the town library, which was elevated above street level facing Greenleaf. There were several steps to climb and more after reaching the library itself. This imposing building was ornamented with several columns in front. As we walked through the big front door, we faced the large check-out desk. It was such an imposing place we seldom went up there, but, Vivian had a book to return for our sister, Annie, the bookworm of the family. Even after she went to bed at night, she read by flashlight under the covers.

We went downstairs to the children's section, around to the side by the grape arbor to the stairs going down to the basement. The first few were easy enough to maneuver, but as I got nearer to the door, as usual I got excited, stumbled, ending up by falling into the library. Each week as regularly as not, I was challenged to maneuver the steps at the library basement.

Five of us attended Whittier High School and Whittier College, all majoring in physical education. In those years teaching jobs were hard to come by and harder still to keep. Tom taught at Whittier High. Marie married "Pop" Halliday, the quarterback on the football team. "Pop" taught in Los Angeles. They had two children, John and Maryanne. John is the father of Michelle; Maryanne is the mother of Karina, Jason and Brian. Annie and Vivian both moved to other places to find work; Vivian near Fresno, married Jack Walton and they had two girls, Kathleen and Mary Lee. Kathleen is the mother of Meghen. Annie went to teach the high school at Tehachapi and married Bill Wills. I, the unmarried one, taught at Hudson Elementary School in Puente.

One night the telephone rang. The voice on the other end of the line asked, "Are you the Phelans who live on land that is planted to walnut trees?"

"We did at one time. We've planted orange trees here now, why do you ask?"

"I'm Lil Callahan. Does the name Callahan mean anything to you?"

"No, I'm afraid not." Then my brother, Francis, sitting nearby spoke up, "Ask her if its Mushy Callahan? He's the boxing referee, known all over the world."

"You mean Mushy Callahan?"

"Yes, you do know him then?"

"My brother sitting here certainly does."

"Rosa Lee used to be my mother-in-law. She's now living with us, and she is looking for her sister, Edna. Does she live there?'

"Yes, she's my mother," I said, getting excited about the call, so together, Lil and I made plans for a meeting. I took down her address. We agreed on an early date and made plans to pay little Rosa, now ninety-two years old, a visit.

After we got settled in comfortable chairs in their lovely living room, Rosa and our mother began talking about their family, of their tour of New Zealand, Australia, India, of living on the palace grounds in Calcutta, of British Burma and of the tragedy there. She spoke of how she and the others went on to the Philippines, Java, Siam, Japan and the northernmost coast of China and of all the wonderful places they had been, a truly fairyland adventure.

She showed us one of her costumes that her father made. They talked and talked about their family; how her father had each performer pack up his own properties, sending them on their way, making it easier to take the tent down. Then as quickly as it began, we said our last good-bye to our little Rosa Lee, the Empress of the Arena.

One night we were having "open house" at Hudson School in Puente. The grandmother of one of my pupils attended.

After the session was over, she walked up to where I was standing talking to a parent. When I finished, she asked me, "By any chance are you related to Thomas Hackett Phelan?"

"Yes, he was my grandfather," I said, wondering why she asked. Then she told me a story. . . "This is a story about my father, a half-breed, Jap Reynolds. He was in a saloon at Fulton Wells one evening about dusk, drinking at the bar minding his own business. One of the patrons flew at him in a rage. He had a gun in his hand and pointed it at my father. He shouted that my father had no right to be there, being a half-breed and all. My father struggled with the man, the gun went off and the man fell to the floor. A quick trial was held, they took him outside, put him in a wagon and put a noose around his neck. Just as they were ready to send the wagon on its way, a big, husky Irishman with a heavy black beard mounted on his beautiful sorrel horse came charging up. He demanded they release my father. The angry crowd protested loudly, but Phelan held his ground. Then slowly the men dispersed and the last ones cut him down. My father jumped on the back of Phelan's horse and they sped out the yard. So, had it not been for your grandfather, I wouldn't be here tonight"

"I've heard wonderful things about my grandfather, and thank you for this story. I'll include it in my book."

Our brother, Francis, was never a student, didn't do well in school, so he went to work. He was the one who kept in touch with all the families the folks had been acquainted with over the years. He was especially close to Derb Hartnell. Derb came from one of the first families to come to California, a descendent of William Hartnell, an Englishman, married to a Mexican woman. It was William Hartnell who was asked to listen to the complaints about the missions after the Desecularization Act of 1833.

If our father wanted to visit the Lopez family nearby our home place on King's Lane, now called Washington Boulevard, Francis was always ready to go. Dad spoke fluent Spanish, allowing him to spend countless hours talking to Tranquilino and other members of his family, a family that dated back to the Gabrielino Indians from the San Gabriel Mission. It was after the desecularization act that the Indians were herded down to the San Juan Capistrano mission.

Tranquilino's sons, Frank and Robert, were especially close to Francis. Frank's daughter, Adeline, later worked at the First

Interstate Bank in the escrow department, and her daughter became a doctor. Robert's wife was a descendent of one of the first eleven families who came to Los Angeles with governor Felipe de Neve in 1771.

When I started working on this book, I asked Francis to go with me to pay a visit to the Sanchez family in Montebello, the descendants of Juan Matis Sanchez, to get information about their family. He always kept in touch with them and always knew just where to find them.

It proved to be very interesting, because we had no sooner settled down for a pleasant afternoon than members of the Palomares and Verdugo families dropped in to visit a while, giving us the chance to reminisce about the "old days," about the great ranchos and all the land they owned; how the vaqueros went looking for the cattle in the high mustard and of the wonderful fiestas they had when all the work was done.

Years later, the house we had been living in on King's Lane burned down.

We were getting ready to move into a new house, and so we were not there at the time. The year was 1954. It was November 25th, the day after Thanksgiving. I was hanging draperies in the living room of my new home in La Habra Heights, when our neighbor ran over to tell us that our old family residence was in flames.

Of course, my mother's first thought was, "That means the gold chain is gone," for she kept it in the secretary at home. We got in the car, drove as fast as possible, traveling west along Whittier Boulevard, the old El Camino Real. As we rode along, mother started muttering to herself. "I'm sure it has melted from the heat."

"Oh, mother!" I said, "Don't give up hope. That's what you always told us."

"If I lose it, and I'm sure I have, the only things I'll have left are my little brown diary and my mother's beautiful black silk fan."

As we turned the corner at Washington Boulevard, we could see the old black walnut tree on down the street, the one her Uncle George had planted, barren of all its leaves. When we approached the house, we knew immediately it had been entirely gutted.

A large crowd had gathered. A chair was brought for mother, and our sister, Marie, put wet compresses on her head. She sat there quietly in the yard waiting for a verdict.

As I walked into the house, the front door was gone. All the furniture that was given to our folks as wedding presents had gone up in smoke. Mother had always kept a lot of money in books because she had needed lots of cash in her business. I saw the money everywhere lying in the watered down debris. People were picking it up, and I went from one to another grabbing it from them. My brother, Tom, was standing there with the elk horn cups in his hand.

"I hate to tell you this, Regina, but the gold chain is gone."

"Oh! Let me have that," I said and I took the cups in my hand, for the money was no longer important. I peeled off the outer cup. It was so badly burned, I dropped it to the floor. I pulled off the second, and dropped it to the floor as well. Then the third, and it seemed all right. Tom took the cups back.

"See, I told you, the gold chain is gone."

"Oh, no! That can't be, not the gold chain! This is not the bottom of the cups. This last one has a lid." I again took it from his hands. I slowly took off the lid, and nestled inside the little elk horn cup was the gold chain.

After the house burned down, our folks moved to live with me in La Habra Heights. In 1956 our folks leased that little two acre piece of land to Dr. Christman and George Gillette, a Whittier attorney. George Gillette appeared at the hearing for the Hill-Burton funds needed to build the Presbyterian hospital, speaking about the need for a new, larger hospital for our area. Later a group of leaders of Whittier, two of whom were Dee Essley and Hubert Perry went to San Francisco for the final hearing. When the funds were made available, they called other interested parties in Whittier. George Gillette called me and said, "The Hill-Burton money has been awarded so we're now in business. We're going to have a medical center on your land."

In the years that followed, the descendents of the Weinshanks, the Lees and the Phelans were leaders in political and ecclesiastical life, in education as teachers, many of whom were in physical education, librarians and athletic coaches, in medicine as doctors and nurses, in finance, in industry, in the trades, real estate development, in sales and law. One member stands out, Thomas Patrick Phelan, the son of Irish Dan, whose idol was Thomas Hackett Phelan, the immigrant Irish boy. Our cousin, Tom, went to work for the stock exchange in Los Angeles and worked his way to the top, to the presidency of the Pacific Stock Exchange.

Many of the family possessions are still in the hands of various members of the family. The picture of George Washington made by our grandmother, the clay jugs from Mexico, the horse hair furniture that was brought around the horn, the bedroom set are all in the home of our grandmother's sister, Lizzie's daughter, Elizabeth Fostler. She has the chouncer too, just a log with a stick attached that Arturo used to press down the cabbage when he helped our great-grandmother make sauerkraut. The feather tick our great-grandfather put on the back of the donkey for their Panama crossing was broken up and made into pillows for us and are still in use. Our cousin, Jere Stefani, has the Phelan piano and our grandfather's breech loader from the Civil War, her prized possessions. The horseless carriage Willie Breyer built wore out eventually, but his brother, Carl, sold the patents on his parts to Chrysler Corporation. Don Pio Pico's remains are now in the Workman-Rowland family cemetery, a fitting tribute to the last Mexican governor.

Our folks are gone now, mother died in 1970 and dad in 1971. They both lived long and useful lives raising six children. Our sister, Rosemary, died young and our brother, Francis, has since passed away. Our folks lived through a depression, the most devastating the world has ever known, an earthquake causing unbelievable damage, and through four wars causing untold hardship and heartache.

As the reader of this family saga, I'm sure you'll want to know, if the family still has the gold chain.

Yes, I'm proud to say we do. On June 16, 1984, Mary Lee Walton, the great-grand-daughter of Henry Charles Lee and Thomas Hackett Phelan, was married. Mary Lee favors the Irish side of the family.

She married a fine young man, Kenneth Otto, of medium height, dark eyes and hair. Several members of our family attended the wedding in Fresno. Kenneth stood waiting at the alter, dressed in a light gray tuxedo, form-fitting shirt with ruffles at his neck. Mary Lee was radiant, walking down the aisle on her father's arm, her sparkling blue eyes, her sensitive Irish skin, her reddish cast hair was arranged in soft ringlets about her face. She wore a garland of white flowers attached to her waist length veil. She looked lovely in her old-fashioned, high-collared dress of soft white tule net with a delicate lace collar, falling softly over her shoulders. As they stood at the altar, exchanging vows, I couldn't help but think what a fitting tribute this was to Henry Charles Lee, the Englishman, the circus man, for around her neck she wore the gold chain.

And now the story has been told, and you, too, have read this book. As you travel to another town, another place, I hope you, too, share the belief that you cannot give up hope.

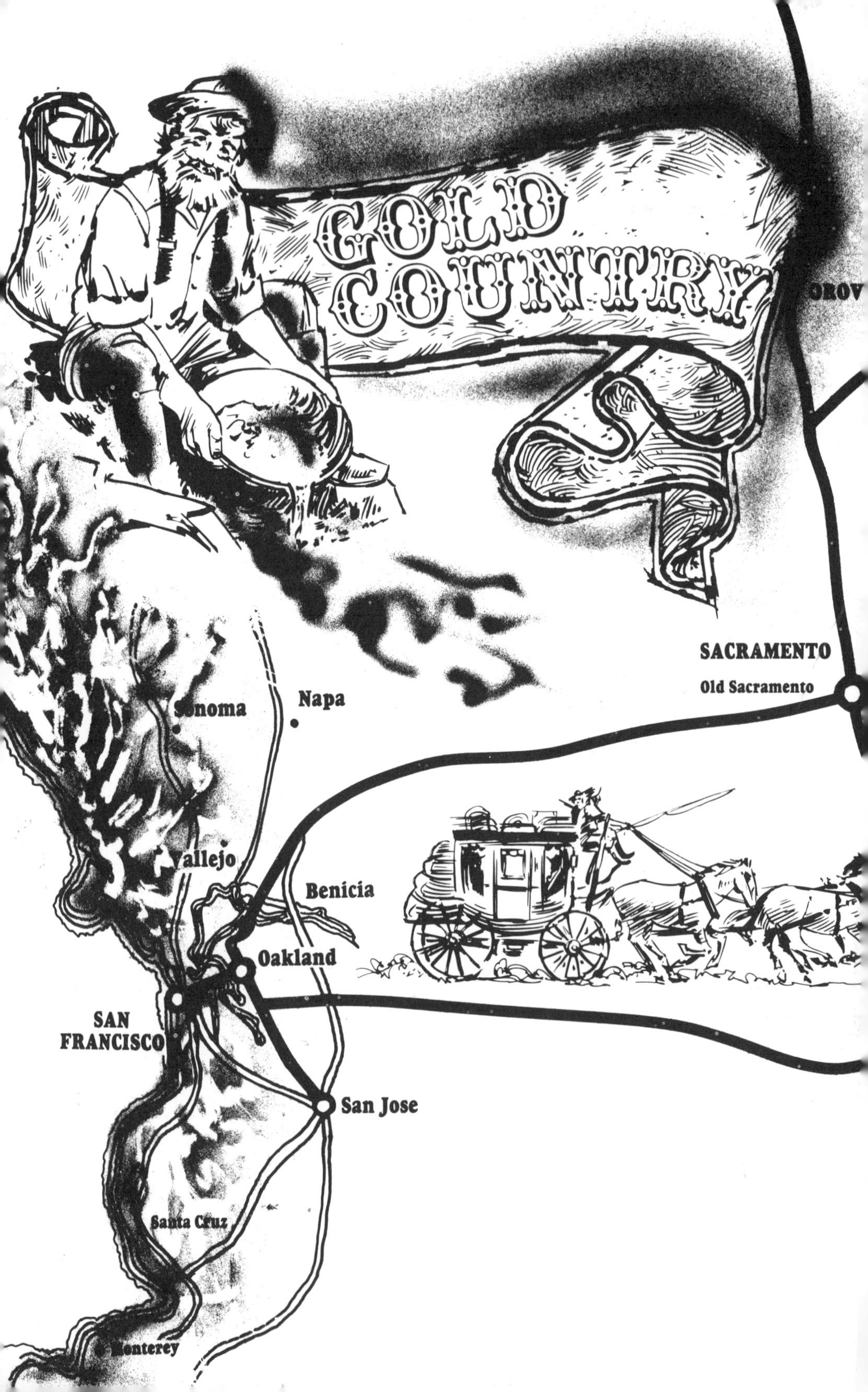
GOLD COUNTRY
OROV
SACRAMENTO
Old Sacramento
Sonoma
Napa
Vallejo
Benicia
Oakland
SAN FRANCISCO
San Jose
Santa Cruz
Monterey